NEW
TESTAMENT
TIMES

OTHER BOOKS BY MERRILL C. TENNEY

The Genius of the Gospels
John: The Gospel of Belief
Galatians: The Charter of Christian Liberty
Philippians: The Gospel at Work
Interpreting Revelation
New Testament Survey

Book design and layout
and picture editing by Cornelius Lambregtse
Maps by Francis K. Lake

NEW TESTAMENT TIMES

BY

Merrill C. Tenney

Dean of the Graduate School, Wheaton College
Wheaton, Illinois

WILLIAM B. EERDMANS PUBLISHING COMPANY
GRAND RAPIDS, MICHIGAN

Library of Congress Catalog Card Number: 65-18099.
ISBN 0-8028-0418-7

Paperback edition first published 1988

Preface

The revelation of God in the New Testament was imparted through men who lived in a definite locale of time and space, and who spoke in the imagery and circumstances of their own era. While the truth and application of the message are unquestionably eternal and unchanging, the correct interpretation depends largely upon a proper comprehension of its historical setting.

Because the authors lived within the milieu they described, they took for granted that their contemporaries would understand it, too, and consequently did not attempt to explain many details which would be quite patent to their readers. To us of the twentieth century the facts which they assumed to be obvious and hence unnecessary to explain are obscure. We can comprehend the historical context of these writings only by careful research and reconstruction of the environment from which they emanated.

Such a reconstruction can never be fully satisfying since it is impossible to project ourselves mentally into the world of two millenniums ago and since the available sources of information are at best desultory and incomplete. On the other hand, some sort of attempt is essential if the characters and events of the New Testament are to be viewed in their proper historical perspective.

The following treatise does not purport to provide a full account of all events that took place from the opening of the Hellenistic period in which the Jewish antecedents of Christianity were shaped until the established Christian movement of the time of Hadrian. At best the presentation must perforce be compressed and skeletal. It does endeavor to show the social forces and cultural trends that affected the world into which Christ came and to identify the successive political regimes within which the action of the New Testament took place. This book is not intended primarily to deal with the literary or theological content of the New Testament (for which see the author's *New Testament Survey*), but to provide a better background for correlating its historical allusions, and thus facilitating its interpretation.

The numerous sources to which the author is indebted for information are listed in the bibliography. Acknowledgments of timely assistance are due to the Wm. B. Eerdmans Publishing Company and its editors, at whose request the work has been undertaken; to the author's secretary, Miss Margaret Heindl, who diligently copied the original manuscript; and most of all to his wife, Helen J. Tenney, whose editorial acumen and counsel aided incalculably in its production.

—MERRILL C. TENNEY

Wheaton, Illinois

Contents

List of Illustrations

xi

List of Maps

List of Charts

NEW
TESTAMENT
TIMES

The Sources
of New Testament History

The Nature of History

H ISTORY IS THE AUTOBIOGRAPHY OF MANKIND. WRITTEN BY learned and ignorant alike, it is contained in inscriptions carved on monuments, in the clay tablets of Babylonia, in the fragile papyrus sheets exhumed from the sands of Egypt, in broken potsherds from the ruins of Palestine, and in the scrolls and manuscripts that caves and monasteries have yielded to the patient research of the antiquarian. The task of collecting, interpreting, and evaluating these records belongs to the historian who seeks to construct from their fragmentary and often conflicting testimony an orderly and coherent account of "what really happened." The problem of being completely accurate is in itself colossal, for the evidence is often scant and may have been expressed in an unfamiliar idiom. Broken sequences of chronology and of cause and effect are frequent. The undertaking is further complicated by the bias, unconscious or purposeful, inherent in the available sources. Was the original writer truthful, or was he merely a propagandist for some forgotten cause? Did he have full knowledge of the events he described, or was he dependent upon some other source which may have been falsified or mistaken? An aspiring historian must be able to discriminate between truth and error and between objective fact and tendentious propaganda.

Objectivity, however, does not require that a historian abandon moral distinctions or discard positive convictions. If there is a God in history, His intervention must appear at times in the direction of human affairs. Since the reality of a personal sovereign God cannot be excluded from the origin of man, one may reasonably suppose that He would not be indifferent to the fate of His creation.

The New Testament states that God intervened in history with a redemptive purpose. "When the fulness of the time came, God sent forth his Son, born of a woman, born under the law, that he might redeem them that were under the law, that we might receive the adoption of sons" (Gal. 4:4, 5). The advent of Christ among men is not only the revelation of a new basis for theology, but is also as much a part of the total story of humanity as the founding of Rome or the defeat of Napoleon at Waterloo. The event belongs to history; the meaning of the event belongs to theology.

A history of the New Testament must inevitably partake of both aspects, but the purpose of this work will be chiefly to orient its factual content with the world events of its time, and to interpret its content by its background. In consonance with the principles which it declares concerning itself, there will be a frank recognition of the irruption of supernatural revelation into the course of natural events without minimizing the reality of either. If "the Word became flesh and dwelt among us" (John 1:14), one cannot logically deny the reality of the divine visitation, nor neglect the human scene which He visited. The New Testament, like the Christ of whom it speaks, is inextricably involved in human history, yet it cannot be limited by humanity; for while the process of history may aid in its interpretation, it is itself the final key to the understanding of the process.

Scope of History

The events chronicled in the New Testament cover a period beginning shortly before the death of Herod the Great in 4 B.C. and ending with the writing of the book of Revelation about A.D. 95. A longer span of time must be considered, however, to afford adequate understanding of the causes and effects of the New Testament revelation. Jesus did not enter the world with the abruptness of lightning, nor was the conclusion of the canon marked by a sharp change in the nature and work of the first-century church. His advent was the climax of the divine purpose which began with the first promise of Eden, and which was developed through the selection, formation, and education of the Jewish nation from which He sprang. That purpose was continued in His influence on the world through the ministration of the Holy Spirit in the church which is still a continuing historical institution. In order to provide a broader setting for the events of the first Christian century, this history will commence with the rise of the Second Jewish Commonwealth in the Maccabean Revolt of 168 B.C., and will terminate with the close of the subapostolic age in or shortly after the reign of Hadrian (A.D. 117-138). The rise of the Maccabees constituted the renewal of the semi-independence of Judaism and the growth of the culture which formed the seedbed of the early church; the reign of Hadrian marked the emergence of the church as a group publicly recognized by the leaders of the Roman empire and the beginning of the conflict between Christianity and paganism on all fronts — religious, cultural, and political.

Josephus and His Sources

The leading historian, from whom the greatest amount of information has been derived, is Flavius Josephus. He was born in Jerusalem in the first year of the emperor Caligula (A.D. 37-38). His parents were well-to-do and belonged to a priestly family. Josephus was thoroughly educated in rabbinic learning and proved so apt a scholar that at the age of fourteen he was frequently consulted by the learned men of the city on the interpretation of the Jewish law. In his sixteenth year he visited the schools of the three main religious parties of Judaism, the Sadducees, the Pharisees, and the Essenes, to examine the principles of each, and completed his study by spending three years in the desert with the hermit Banias.

Upon his return to Jerusalem, Josephus joined the party of the Pharisees. Seven years later he went to Rome on a diplomatic mission to obtain the release of some priests who had become prisoners of the state. His mission was successful, and he returned to Jerualem high in the favor of the Roman officials.

The war with Rome began in A.D. 66, shortly after Josephus' arrival in Palestine. Like many others of the Jewish aristocracy, he attempted to remain neutral, for he feared the armed might of Rome. The rank and file of his contemporaries, however, had no such qualms. They organized a revolt and persuaded Josephus to become one of its leaders in Galilee. He commanded the defense of Jotapata, a northern fortress, which fell to the Romans in A.D. 67. Although the survivors of the siege had entered into a compact to kill each other in case of defeat, Josephus and one other person, being the last of the band, agreed to surrender to the Romans. When he was brought before Vespasian he predicted that the Roman general would become emperor. Two years later, when Vespasian was elevated to the throne by his legions, he remembered Josephus' forecast and liberated him. At this time Josephus assumed the Flavian name and accompanied Vespasian to Alexandria. Later he returned to Palestine with Titus, who had succeeded his father in command of the forces then besieging Jerusalem. Josephus assisted in the negotiations with the Jewish defenders at the risk of his life, and when the city fell he obtained the freedom of many of the prisoners, including his own brother.

After the war he retired to Rome, where he enjoyed the favor of Vespasian, who granted him a pension, provided him with a residence, and bestowed upon him Roman citizenship. He remained in the good graces of Titus (A.D. 79-81) and Domitian (A.D. 81-96), who exempted him from taxes on his Judean property. The details of his life under Nerva (A.D. 96-98) and Trajan (A.D. 98-117) are not known, but he seems to have lived until after the turn of the century.

During the period of his residence in Rome Josephus wrote the works which have supplied the bulk of information concerning the intertestamental period.

The Wars of the Jews comprises seven books narrating the history of the Jews from the accession of Antiochus Epiphanes IV (175 B.C.) to the capture of Jerusalem in A.D. 70. The first book contains the period from Antiochus to the death of Herod the Great in 4 B.C.; the second explains the origins of the Jewish Revolt in A.D. 66 and recounts the first year of the war; the third deals with the first year of the war in Galilee; the fourth carries the history down to the beginning of the siege of Jerusalem; the fifth and sixth complete the siege and capture of the city; the seventh concludes the story and describes the results of the war.

Josephus wrote first in Aramaic, his mother tongue, and later reissued the work in Greek.[1] The content was based on his own experience, for he was an active participant in the entire conflict and took notes even during the active campaign. He completed the account during the reign of Vespasian, for it was presented to the emperor before his death.[2]

Josephus' large historical work, *The Antiquities of the Jews,* dealt with the history of the Jewish people from their earliest origins down to the outbreak of the war with Rome in A.D. 66. He completed it in the thirteenth year of Domitian (A.D. 93/94).[3] It was designed to be a defense of the Jewish race. The ignominy of defeat, ending in exile and slavery, had demeaned the Jews in the eyes of the world.

---

[1] *Wars of the Jews* i. 1.
[2] *Against Apion* i. 9.
[3] *Antiquities of the Jews* xx. 11.

Josephus, who had achieved a degree of acceptance with the ruling class at Rome, wished to convince them that he sprang from a people who possessed an elevated culture and moral virtues of their own.   To defend himself, he wrote an autobiographical account of his part in the Jewish war in A.D. 66/67, when he deserted to Rome after a futile resistance to the attack on Jotapata.   The Jews regarded him as a traitor to their cause, and the Romans were suspicious of his origin.   Both his *Antiquities* and *Life* were an attempt to establish himself and his nation in the good graces of his associates.

Josephus' works, therefore, create a dilemma for any historiographer, for they are obviously a reaction against contemporary anti-Semitism, and are therefore biased.   In some instances he glosses over unfavorable episodes in Jewish history, or exaggerates the culture and capabilities of the people.   On the other hand, he quotes many other historical writers whose works are no longer extant, and his firsthand testimony concerning the events of his lifetime, particularly the Jewish war of A.D. 66 - 70, cannot be duplicated elsewhere. If due allowance be made for his avowed prejudice, he remains the best authority for this general period.

Josephus himself, however, was dependent on others for much of his information.   Schürer, in his monumental work on *The Jewish People in the Time of Christ*,[4] lists no less than eighteen different authors of the post-Maccabean period to whom Josephus may have been indebted.   The writings of many of these authors have been lost completely, or else only small fragments of them exist.   The more important of these are listed here.

Strabo, a Greek geographer and traveler, was born about 63 B.C. and died after A.D. 21.   He wrote a series of historical works in forty-seven books which are now lost, and a geography in seventeen books, almost all of which have been preserved.   The information contained in the *Geography* is of uneven value, since he attributed equal credence to all his sources.   Josephus utilized his work frequently.

Timagenes of Alexandria, probably a Syrian, was carried captive to Rome in A.D. 55 by Gabinius, the Roman proconsul of Syria.   He resided in Rome for the rest of his life and gained a high reputation as a historian.   Josephus usually quotes him indirectly, using the references of other historians.

The *Commentaries of Herod,* or his personal memoirs, seem to have been known to Josephus, although they may not have been directly accessible to him.   In similar fashion he may have used the *Commentaries of Vespasian.*[5]

---

[4] Emil Schürer, *A History of the Jewish People in the Time of Jesus Christ*, I, i, 47-75.
[5] *Life* 65.

Justus of Tiberias was, like Josephus, a Jew who received a Greek education and who participated in the revolt of A.D. 66 - 67. Before the final capture of Galilee by the Romans he took refuge with Herod Agrippa II. Vespasian condemned him to death, but his sentence was commuted to imprisonment on the petition of Berenice, Agrippa's sister. Agrippa appointed him to a secretarial office, but he was finally discharged for altering the royal letters. Like Josephus, he wrote a *History of the Jewish War,* and a *Chronicle of the Jewish Kings from Moses to Agrippa.*[6] Justus and Josephus were contemporaries whose careers were much alike. Both were Jews, both were engaged in the wars of rebellion against Rome, and both capitulated to the Roman power when they realized that resistance was futile. No love was lost between them, for Josephus narrates in his *Life* that Justus had falsely characterized him as a rebel and had justified himself as friendly to Rome. It is doubtful whether Josephus used much of Justus' material, since he regarded it as distorted.

The Greek Historians

Among the Greek historians were Polybius, Diodorus, Strabo (who has already been mentioned), Plutarch, and Dio Cassius.

Polybius (203? - c. 120 B.C.) was a Greek who departed to Rome in 167 B.C., where he became so enamored of the Roman character and culture that he wrote a forty-volume history extolling Rome's development and destiny. He is a useful authority for a part of the intertestamental period.

Diodorus of Sicily (died c. 21 B.C.) was contemporaneous with Julius Caesar and Augustus. He composed a historical survey of mankind beginning with Egypt and Assyria and continuing to the conquest of Gaul by Caesar. He also dealt with the career of Antiochus Epiphanes.

Strabo was utilized by Josephus, and has already been discussed.[7] In his *Geography* he described Palestine and alluded to events which antedated Pompey's conquest of Palestine in 63 B.C.

Plutarch was born about A.D. 50 and lived to be approximately seventy years of age. He lectured and wrote voluminously. His most important work was *Lives* in which are sketches of Roman statesmen who were actively involved in the rise of the early empire. *Lives* shows a high degree of research which must have occupied a long period of time. The basic facts are accurate, though Plutarch was inclined to indulge in moralizing.

---

[6] *Life* 65.
[7] *Vide supra,* p. 7.

Dio Cassius was a native of Bithynia, born about A.D. 155. He lived most of his life in Rome where he entered politics and finally became proconsul of Africa. In A.D. 229 he retired. His work on Roman history, which occupied the last eighteen years of his known life, contained the entire course of Roman affairs in eighty books, only eighteen of which remain complete.

The Roman Historians

Among the Roman writers Cicero (106 - 43 B.C.) provided considerable information on the history of Syria. Livy (59 B.C - A.D. 17), like Dio Cassius, wrote a complete history of Rome, of which thirty-five books are now extant. His work is valuable chiefly for the period of the early Maccabees.

Later historians dealt with the development of the empire and alluded occasionally to the Christian church. Tacitus (A.D. 55 - 120?), in his *Annals,* sketched the reigns of the Caesars from Tiberius to Nero, and his *History* continued the narrative from Nero to Domitian. Tacitus was somewhat biased by his dislike of the imperial regime and consequently exaggerated its faults. Nevertheless he had a sense of what was historically important, and his allusions to Jews and Christians afford at least some understanding of their place in the empire.

Suetonius (A.D. 69? - 121?) was a friend of Pliny and a beneficiary of the emperor Trajan. He held the position of secretary to Hadrian, who later discharged him, and thus had access to the court. He was scholarly in his habits and able to write acceptably both in Greek and in Latin. He was sufficiently versatile to discuss intelligently numerous subjects, including history, customs, chronology, natural history, and grammar. His most important historical work was *The Lives of the Caesars,* published in A.D. 120, which included the biographies of the rulers from Julius Caesar to Domitian.

Suetonius was a painstaking antiquarian but not always a discriminating biographer. He employed sources of varying bias and value with little effort to evaluate them. He was perhaps less prejudiced than Tacitus, although the scandalous reports he gives of the private lives of the emperors may have been motivated somewhat by his dislike of their autocracy. His occasional references to events mentioned in the New Testament make his accounts valuable to the student of Biblical history.

The Jewish Sources

The fullest direct accounts concerning the period from 175 B.C. to A.D. 135, aside from Josephus, are found in the writings of Judaism.

In these bluffs northeast of the Dead Sea, the caves containing the Dead Sea Scrolls were discovered by wandering Bedouin tribesmen and later by excavating archaeologists. (Matson Photo Service.)

The semi-canonical books of I and II Maccabees begin with the revolt of the Jews against Antiochus IV of Syria, and narrate the history of the guerrilla struggle waged by the loyal Jews under the leadership of the sons of Mattathias, the priest of Modin. I Maccabees traces the growth of Jewish independence from the first successful battle under Judas Maccabaeus to the reign of John Hyrcanus, closing about 103 B.C. II Maccabees covers a briefer portion of the same period, ending with the death of Nicanor in 161 B.C.

I Maccabees was one of Josephus' sources. Originally written in Hebrew, it exists now only in Greek. Since it alludes to the "chronicles of his [Hyrcanus'] priesthood,"[8] it must have been composed after his death, probably not later than 100 B.C. The author of the chronicle was a Jewish patriot who observed the law conscien-

[8] I Maccabees 16:24.

tiously.[9]   His history was translated quite literally into Greek, so that the wording of the original text can be reconstructed almost exactly.   Apart from a few mistranslations, I Maccabees is one of the most reliable authorities for the intertestamental period.

II Maccabees is a digest of an older work by Jason of Cyrene.[10] Of Jason himself nothing is known, except that he was probably a Jew of the Dispersion who lived at the end of the second century

[9] I Maccabees 2:50.
[10] II Maccabees 2:23.

The Dead Sea Scroll of the Manual of Discipline of the Qumran Community. This scroll is in the possession of the Hebrew University of Jerusalem. (Courtesy Israel Information Services.)

B.C.[11] Whether the author of II Maccabees attempted to epitomize
Jason's five volumes or whether he reproduced only that part which
concerned the early Maccabean period is debatable. Pfeiffer concludes that Jason intended to write a book of religious instruction
rather than a full historical treatise. His motive was to confirm
the faith of the Jews by demonstrating that God would defend His
nation and Temple against impending danger. In contrast with the
writer of I Maccabees, Jason wrote in Greek, and stressed most
strongly the supernatural aspects of the deliverance of his people.
Pfeiffer characterizes Jason's writing as "a typical example of
rhetorical Hellenistic historiography."[12]

The epitome did not improve the history, but omitted some connections so that contradictions appear occasionally. Nevertheless
II Maccabees supplements I Maccabees at a few points where the
latter is deficient and corroborates it at others.

The Dead Sea Scrolls

A new contemporary witness to the culture of the pre-Christian
period came to light in 1947. A Bedouin boy herding goats in the
wilderness at the northwest end of the Dead Sea threw a stone after
one of his flock that had taken refuge in a cave. Hearing the sound
of breaking pottery, he clambered into the cave and found several
jars containing manuscripts wrapped in cloth. According to the
current report, he took the scrolls to a sheikh in Bethlehem. The
sheikh saw that the writing was unfamiliar and sent them to a merchant who could read Syriac. He, in turn, sent them to another
friend who recommended them to the archbishop of Jerusalem.

When the archbishop examined the manuscripts he realized that
they were not Syriac but Hebrew and offered to buy the scrolls.
After some delay through misunderstanding, the archbishop purchased five scrolls; a third Bedouin, who claimed some of them, sold
his elsewhere. Burrows conjectures that these were the scrolls that
later were purchased from a dealer by Dr. E. L. Sukenik.[13]

The manuscripts so discovered were in varying states of preserva-
tion. The largest and finest, which was unrolled with a minimum
of difficulty, proved to be a copy of Isaiah almost a thousand years
older than any previously known. There was also a commentary
on Habakkuk, two sections of the *Manual of Discipline,* a handbook
of conduct for the sect to which the writings belonged, and another

[11] See Robert H. Pfeiffer, *History of New Testament Times with an Introduction to Apocrypha,* pp. 514-518.
[12] *Ibid.,* p. 518.
[13] Millar Burrows, *The Dead Sea Scrolls,* pp. 3-6.

Qumran Cave 1 (indicated by man pointing), where the Ta'amireh tribesman searching for a lost goat discovered the first Dead Sea Scrolls. Among the scrolls found here were the Isaiah scroll, the Habakkuk Commentary, the Thanksgiving Psalms, and The War of the Sons of Light with the Sons of Darkness. The cave was excavated by Père de Vaux and Harding in 1949. (Courtesy Prof. B. Van Elderen.)

in such poor condition that its identity could not be determined immediately. It proved later to be a commentary on Genesis.

The scrolls purchased by Dr. Sukenik contained an allegorical work entitled *The War of the Sons of Light with the Sons of Darkness,* and four sections of Thanksgiving Psalms.

An examination of the handwriting in these manuscripts showed that it was unlike any in existing collections, and that it most closely approximated the Nash papyrus, a fragment dating from the second or third century A.D. Further comparison with the styles of Hebrew letters in inscriptions indicated that the writing was of a very early period, probably from the second and first centuries before Christ.

In addition to the palaeographical evidence, the type of text appearing in these manuscripts tends toward the conclusion that the documents in their present form belong to the Maccabean period. According to Burrows, Kahle points out that the use of *scriptio plena,* the creation of a vowel letter from consonants to fill the gap left without them, must have originated after Hebrew became a dead language, i.e., after the Exile, when many Jews who spoke Aramaic were attempting to renew their study of Hebrew.[14] Various opinions have been proffered concerning the age of *scriptio plena.* Some have suggested that it belongs to the time of Origen, before vowel-pointing was invented; on the other hand, vowel letters were used in inscriptions as early as 700 B.C. No sure criterion is supplied by the textual variants, but the cumulative evidence confirms the pre-Christian origin of these manuscripts.

The linen in which these scrolls were wrapped was tested by the carbon 14 method for their date. The result gave a median of A.D. 33, plus or minus two hundred years.[15] The imprecise nature of the evidence does not enable one to fix the date of writing but tends to confirm the conclusion that they are of ancient origin.

The interest aroused by the multiplied discoveries of manuscripts in the caves at Wadi Qumran stimulated further investigation of an adjacent ruin which had been generally regarded as an early Roman fortress. In 1951 Lankester Harding, Curator of Antiquities for Jordan, and Père de Vaux, with a crew of men, undertook to excavate part of the ruin. They discovered that it was not a Roman fortification, but that it had been the site of an older community. The ruins contained aqueducts and cisterns used for collecting rainwater from the nearby wadi, a dining hall equipped with dishes where the former inhabitants ate common meals, and a scriptorium, complete with desks and benches, in which manuscripts were copied.

---

[14] *Ibid.,* pp. 110-114.
[15] G. Lankester Harding, *The Antiquities of Jordan,* p. 173.

There seemed to be a clear connection between the scrolls secreted in the neighboring caves and the inhabitants of the Qumran ruins.

In the spring of 1953 the excavation was resumed. Coins found on the site indicated that there had been three main periods of occupancy.[16] The first period, marked by coins belonging to the reign of John Hyrcanus (135-104 B.C.), extended almost to the end of the Hasmonean period in 39 B.C. Josephus says that a severe earthquake shook Palestine in the seventh year of Herod, just prior to the battle of Actium.[17] The buildings show a definite rift, which can be attributed to such a cause. It may be that since the cisterns were damaged, the community was forced to move and that the site was abandoned.

Beginning with the reign of Archelaus (4 B.C - A.D. 6) the coins indicate a new occupation which terminated with the close of the first Jewish revolt and the capture of Jerusalem by the Romans (A.D. 70). Burrows concludes that it may have been restored by the same group that had originally occupied it, since no radical changes were made in its arrangement and use. It seems probable that the Romans who occupied Jericho may have captured the site and may have used it for an outpost during their subsequent possession of the territory. A few Roman coins belonging to the period from A.D. 70 to 86 were found in the ruins, and may have been dropped by the garrison.[18]

After the Romans left, the buildings were desolate, but a few coins of the Second Revolt under Hadrian (A.D. 132 - 135) show that the premises may have been used again by Jewish guerrillas.

Later excavations confirmed the previous impressions concerning the nature of the Qumran community and the periods of occupation. Evidently between the days of the Maccabees and the final extinction of Jewish political independence a thriving religious group had been settled there. The presence of the scriptorium and the great number of scrolls found in the caves indicate that they had utilized the Old Testament books as the basis for their teaching, and that they had created a fairly extensive literature of their own. The identity of these people and the nature of their teaching will be considered later. The remains of their works, however, constitute an important firsthand source of New Testament history.

The Canonical Text

The most direct and valuable source for knowledge of New Testament times is the canonical text of the New Testament itself,

---

[16] Burrows, *op. cit.*, p. 65.
[17] *Wars of the Jews* i. 19. 3.
[18] Burrows, *op. cit.*, p. 66.

the collection of twenty-seven books that constitute the second half of the sacred Scriptures. Of these assorted documents, thirteen were written by Paul, a preacher and theologian whose active ministry extended from A.D. 45 to 65; five have been attributed to John, one of the early disciples of Jesus, whose writing career closed not later than A.D. 95; two were composed by Peter, another disciple; Luke-Acts, a brief history of the Christian movement from the birth of Christ to the end of Paul's first Roman imprisonment, was composed by a companion of Paul about A.D. 60 or 62; two other Gospels were ascribed to Matthew and Mark, contemporaries of Jesus and John; and three single epistles, James, Jude, and the anonymous Epistle to the Hebrews can also be traced back to the church of the first century.

The writings of Luke, the Gospel and Acts, provide the largest amount of consecutive historical data by any one writer, for together they comprise almost a quarter of the New Testament. Luke was a contemporary of the growth of the early church. According to the use of the first person in his account, he became active in the Gentile mission not later than A.D. 50, and was engaged in missionary service until A.D. 60. Although his name does not appear in his writings, he can be identified by his association with Paul, who alludes in his epistles to "Luke, the beloved physician" (Col. 4:14) as one of the companions of his Roman imprisonment. The Pauline epistles indicate that he was with Paul at the end of his career (II Tim. 4:11). He possessed the dual advantage of acquaintance with the leaders of the Christian movement and of personal knowledge of its theology and mission.

Although the Lukan narratives do not profess to be complete accounts of all that transpired in the development of the church, they are reliable primary sources. Despite recent skepticism and a tendency to exalt the historical value of the Pauline Epistles at the expense of Luke,[19] the Gospel and Acts remain unshaken. Not every allusion is easily comprehensible, and not every statement can be corroborated from some external source, but history and archaeology have confirmed the Lukan record whenever correspondence can be established. Sir William Ramsay, an eminent archaeologist and expert on Asia Minor, said:

> The question among scholars now [1913] is with regard to Luke's credibility as an historian; it is generally conceded that he wrote at a comparatively early date, and had authorities of high character, even when he himself was not an eyewitness. How far can we believe his narrative?
>
> The present writer takes the view that Luke's narrative is un-

[19] John Knox, *Chapters in a Life of Paul,* pp. 30, 31.

surpassed in respect of its trustworthiness. . . . You may press the words of Luke in a degree beyond any other historian, and they stand the keenest scrutiny and the hardest treatment, provided always that the critic knows the subject and does not go beyond the limits of science and justice.[20]

Henshaw, a more recent writer, who is by no means committed to any presuppositions of Biblical inerrancy, accords with Ramsay's opinion:

> The value of Acts is enormous. It is the only history of the growth of Christianity which we possess until Eusebius almost three hundred years later, and without it Eusebius would be almost impossible. . . . The contrast between Luke and the writers of the second century apocryphal "Acts" of various apostles is the difference between the historian and the romancer. . . . The writer has a clear purpose, which he accomplishes: each act in the drama fits into its place in the whole; the decisive events and speeches combine to produce the desired impression; its persuasive power is obtained not by distorting history, but by presenting it.[21]

Luke himself acknowledged directly or indirectly his indebtedness to others: to the "many" who had undertaken to draw up a narrative of Christ preceding his (Luke 1:1), to the "eyewitnesses and ministers of the word" whom he knew (v. 2), to the disciples of Jesus whom he met in Palestine, to the various Roman officials with whom he made contact in his travels, and to Paul and his associates with whom he worked. Much of the latter part of Acts is based upon Luke's own observation. Though there are gaps in his narrative which cannot be filled with the limited information available, Luke is still the chief authority for the history of the early church in the first century. To the extent that his narrative can be compared with external witnesses in other historical writers and in archaeology, it has proved accurate and truthful.

The Pauline Epistles are firsthand reflections of one of the prominent leaders. Paul, or Saul, as he was called before his conversion, was a Jew of Tarsus, born about the year 1 of the Christian era. His earliest extant letter was probably Galatians,[22] which was written about A.D. 48 at the height of the controversy over circumcision, and his last surviving work was II Timothy, which can

[20] William M. Ramsay, *The Bearing of Recent Discovery on the Trustworthiness of the New Testament*, pp. 81ff.

[21] T. Henshaw, *New Testament Literature*, pp. 199, 200.

[22] See D. B. Knox, "The Date of the Epistle to the Galatians," *Evangelical Quarterly*, XII (1941), 262-268.

be dated in the middle sixties.[23]   The genuineness of Galatians, Romans, I and II Corinthians is conceded by all schools of thought; I Thessalonians, Philippians, and Philemon are seldom challenged; II Thessalonians and Colossians have sometimes been regarded as dubious; Ephesians has been variously explained as an editor's cento of Pauline sentiments, a circular letter of Paul, and downright forgery. A large number of scholars deny the Pauline authorship of the Pastoral Epistles, but in recent years there has been a distinct trend toward accepting their genuineness.[24]   The total Pauline corpus is an invaluable index to the expansion and doctrinal temper of the first-century church, even though it relates to only one segment of the whole.

The Johannine writings, the Gospel, Epistles, and Revelation, contain less historical information than do the Pauline Epistles, but they reflect the theological and ecclesiastical mood of the period in which they were composed.   They were not written primarily for the purpose of providing a continuous narrative of the life of Christ nor of the progress of the church.   They were intended to be didactic and doctrinal, although there is no reason to assume that they misrepresented the facts of which they spoke.

All of the Gospels, including Matthew and Mark, which are not parts of a larger literary complex, emanate from the evangelistic and didactic ministry of the church.   They were written for the express purpose of presenting the facts concerning Christ in such a way that men might believe on Him and, having taken the initial step, might continue in an intelligent faith.   Although it is impossible to present these facts without some interpretation, the interpretation does not necessarily pervert the facts.   They may not be narrated solely for their own sake, else the Gospels would be only dry chronicles; but neither have they been so warped by prejudice that they are unreliable.   To say that the Gospels are the product of the church does not mean that they were created by the church for its amusement or to please its fancy. Matthew professes by its name to have been derived from a disciple of Jesus, a tax collector whose occupation required him to take notes and to keep accounts.   The unadorned simplicity and directness of Mark bespeak a witness who told plainly what he knew without attempting to embellish it with fanciful additions.   His knowledge may have been derived from the testimony of the apostles with whom he associated, or it may have been drawn partially from his own observation.   In any case, it

[23] For a thorough discussion of the problem of the Pastoral Epistles, see Donald Guthrie, *New Testament Introduction: The Pauline Epistles,* pp. 198-238.
[24] J. B. Lightfoot, *The Apostolic Fathers,* pp. 97-104. See also J. N. D. Kelly, *The Pastoral Epistles.*

reproduced the earliest stratum of Christian teaching and preaching concerning Jesus.

The remaining books of the New Testament represent varying times and viewpoints. James is probably a product of the first half of the century, reflecting the Jewish-Christian reaction to the extremists who made salvation by faith an excuse for ethical indifference. I and II Peter characterize the provincial church of the seventh decade, subsequent to the first wave of missionary evangelism and prior to the open conflict with the Roman state. Hebrews illustrates the transition from Judaic Christianity to the full independence of the new faith, and possibly presages the impending fall of the Jewish commonwealth. Jude shows the theological unrest which agitated the church after the middle of the century and imperiled its peace.

Although the traditional authorship of the Petrine Epistles has been questioned, especially that of II Peter, the sober quality of the canonical texts makes them superior witnesses to the historical situation that prevailed at the end of the first century.

The Apostolic Fathers

The Apostolic Fathers are those writers of the early church who presumably had personal contact with the apostles though they did not belong to the immediate followers of Jesus. The term is inexact, for there is no clear proof that all of them were so connected with the apostles, and in some cases the real authors of these early works are unknown. The term is a convenient means of classifying those writings which can be ascribed to the end of the first century and the first half of the second.

The period extending from the close of the book of Acts (A.D. 62) and from the fall of Jerusalem (A.D. 70) to the rise of the great apologists, Irenaeus, Tertullian, and Clement of Alexandria in the late second century, is quite obscure. Few records have survived if, indeed, many were written, and those that are available contribute comparatively little to historical knowledge. Nevertheless the period is tremendously important as the bridge between the rise of the primitive church in which the New Testament originated and the world organization that braved the persecutions of Marcus Aurelius and his successors.

The Apostolic Fathers are the clue to the development of the church in the hundred years between A.D. 70 and 170, except for archaeological remains and a few scattered references in secular works. The sequence of history can be partially reconstructed from these books and occasionally from the allusions in the New Testament Apocrypha.

The earliest of the Fathers, Clement of Rome, was contemporary with the last writings of the New Testament. He has been identified with the Clement of Paul's acquaintance (Phil. 4:3) and with a Clement mentioned in the *Shepherd of Hermas* (Vis. 11.4.3), who was charged with the duty of sending books to other churches. Probably he would have been too young during Paul's lifetime to be an associate of the apostle, and too old at the time of the writing of the *Shepherd*. Clement, however, was an active member of the church at Rome and was well acquainted with Paul's Corinthian correspondence. His letter resembles the canonical literature in form and contains fewer doctrinal vagaries and legendary embellishments than the Apocrypha. *II Clement* is not the product of the same author, but belongs to a later period.

The writings of Ignatius are a valuable link in the ecclesiastical history of the early second century. Ignatius was bishop of Syrian Antioch up to the time of his martyrdom under Trajan in A.D. 108. Having been arrested by the authorities, he was condemned to fight with wild beasts in the amphitheater at Rome. While being taken under guard from Antioch to Rome, he wrote seven epistles to the Ephesians, the Magnesians, the Trallians, the Romans, the Philadelphians, the Smyrnaeans, and to Polycarp, the bishop of Smyrna. Three collections exist: a long recension, which includes the seven letters mentioned above, plus six others, which are generally considered spurious; a shorter recension of the seven, lacking numerous interpolations, which Lightfoot has shown to be probably genuine; and a Syrian abridgment, discovered by Dr. Cureton in 1845, containing three epistles to Ephesus, Rome, and to Polycarp. Lightfoot[25] and Lake[26] both adopt these seven as the standard Ignatian corpus for translation and for historical study.

Ignatius' writings illustrate the transition from the pioneer underground church of the first century to the settled ecclesiastical organization of the second and following centuries. They combine the doctrinal tenor of I John with the atmosphere of harassment and persecution.

The Epistle of Polycarp to the Philippians may be dated somewhat later than the correspondence of Ignatius. Polycarp was bishop of Smyrna in the early part of the second century, and was martyred in A.D. 155 at the age of eighty-six. Ignatius must have known him when he was in the prime of life. According to tradition, Polycarp was a pupil of John, presumably the son of Zebedee, and transmitted to the later church some of the Johannine teaching.[27] His epistle

---

[25] *Ibid.*
[26] Kirsopp Lake, *The Apostolic Fathers*, pp. 166-170.
[27] Irenaeus *Against Heresies* iii. 3. 4.

must have been written about the same time as the Letters of Ignatius, unless, as P. N. Harrison has suggested, it is really a conflation of two epistles, one written about A.D. 108, and the other in the reign of Hadrian, possibly between A.D. 135 and 137.[28] Neither Harrison nor any other modern scholar has challenged the authorship of this epistle (or epistles). It is still an acceptable source for early Christian history.

The *Didache,* or *Teaching of the Twelve Apostles,* was discovered by Bishop Bryennios, Greek Metropolitan of Nicomedia, in a manuscript written in 1056, in the library of the Greek patriarch of Jerusalem at Constantinople. The manuscript, part of a collection of other works including the *Epistle of Barnabas* and the *Epistle of Clement to the Corinthians,* consists of less than ten pages, written in an abbreviated minuscule hand. It was intended to be a handbook on church discipline. The first section deals with the "Two Ways" of death and life, the second with a discussion of the ritual of the church, and the third with the leaders and officers of the church. Much of this work seems primitive; some of it implies an institutionalized church, with fasts, fixed periods for prayer, and an itinerant ministry which was giving way to regular settled pastors. The dating of the document is uncertain. It cannot be much later than the middle of the second century, and Père Audet, a Catholic writer, places it as early as A.D. 60.[29]

Related to the *Didache* by similarity of phraseology is the Epistle of Barnabas, the closing chapters of which are almost identical with the opening section of the *Didache.* Both may have drawn on an ancient Jewish handbook which they adapted to Christian usage. The Epistle of Barnabas was probably not written by the friend and companion of Paul mentioned in the Acts, for it contains a clear reference to the destruction of the Temple in Jerusalem in 16:3. Since the Temple was burned in A.D. 70, the book must have been written after the death of most of the apostolic group. Furthermore, the allusions to the Epistle to the Hebrews that occur in Barnabas indicate that it must have been published after Hebrews attained circulation in the church, which could hardly have been before the eighth decade of the first century. It may have been published at any time between A.D. 80 and 150, although its plain anti-Jewish prejudice seemingly belongs to a time when Judaism was still strong enough to be a serious rival to the church. Barnabas

---

[28] P. N. Harrison, *Polycarp's Two Epistles to the Philippians,* pp. 15-19. Harrison contends that chapters 13 and 14 of Polycarp's Epistle to Philippi were a covering letter for sending Ignatius' Epistles to Philippi while Ignatius was on his way to Rome. The first twelve chapters were another epistle, written many years later.

[29] Père J. P. Audet, *La Didache.*

is a treatise on the errors of Judaism in thinking that the Mosaic law was a final revelation. The law, according to this epistle, was intended to be a prologue for the gospel and a preparation for Christ.

The *Shepherd of Hermas* was produced about A.D. 140 by Hermas, a brother of Pius, the bishop of Rome, who ruled from A.D. 140 to 150. The work may have been written over a long period of years so that the earliest statements, which were the simplest, may well have been composed shortly after the turn of the century, while the sections following were written much later. The book is a protracted allegory of the church, dealing with the problem of post-baptismal sin. While its subject matter is chiefly doctrinal and ethical, it affords indirectly some understanding of contemporary historical conditions. The church had already become a powerful influence in society, and its members had begun to create a community of their own.

The Apologists

With the expansion of Christianity came increasing conflict with the surrounding pagan culture and the consequent necessity of defending Christian beliefs and practices. The leaders who assumed this task were called apologists, from the Greek *apologia,* or "defense." The earliest of the group was Justin Martyr, a Syrian Greek philosopher, who became a Christian before A.D. 135,[30] and whose *Apologies* probably followed soon afterwards. Justin is one of the earliest witnesses to the beliefs and practices of the church and to the conditions that affected the Christian community in and after the reign of Hadrian. The apologists as a group are dated late in the second century and are consequently outside the scope of this history.

The last of the Fathers whose works contain extensive historical material pertinent to the New Testament period was Irenaeus. Cross calls him "the most considerable theologian of the second century."[31] He was probably born in Smyrna during the first third of that century, and in his early youth was a pupil of Polycarp. Irenaeus' chief work, *Against Heresies,* was a counterblast against the teachings of Gnosticism advocated by several contemporary teachers. His occasional allusions to the apostles and their preaching afford early witness to the history of the first century. Even though they may be only tradition, they provide some clues to the development of Christianity in that era of silence.

[30] *Dialogue with Trypho* 1 and 9.
[31] Frank L. Cross, *The Early Christian Fathers*, p. 110.

The Church Historians

Except for Luke, the church produced no historians in the first three centuries of its existence. Its greatest chronicler was Eusebius of Caesarea (c. A.D. 260-340), whose *Historia Ecclesiae* is the sole account of the early church that has survived. Eusebius was acquainted with a vast store of documents, many of which are preserved only in his narrative. Unfortunately he did not supply the context for many of these extracts, and consequently their meaning is obscure. He did, however, quote accurately, and so transmitted a body of material from which modern historians can draw their own conclusions. To Eusebius they are indebted for the bulk of their knowledge concerning the activities and theology of the primitive church.

Apocrypha and Pseudepigrapha

During the second and third centuries a large number of legendary works ascribed to apostolic authors circulated among Christians. Published under the names of apostolic writers, these documents purported to convey information missing from the canonical text. Much of their content is worthless, except as it illustrates the mental outlook of the period in which they were written. Occasionally, however, a fragment of historical verity may be embedded in a mass of superstitious fiction. Ramsay argued that a genuine story of Paul's sojourn in Phrygian Galatia was incorporated in the fictional *Acts of Paul and Thekla,* a second-century work known to Tertullian.[32] The tale contains a description of Paul that is probably authentic because it is unflattering, and may preserve some trustworthy details of his career. The ratio of fact to legend in these writings is so small that they are generally worthless as historical sources. Their testimony to episodes in the life of Christ was borrowed mainly from the canonical Gospels, which they resemble in organization and phraseology.

Evaluation

These scattered writings are often enigmatic because their authors did not intend to narrate the total history of the movement in which they were involved. Generally they took for granted that the setting of events was familiar to their readers. In some cases they misunderstood the sources upon which they depended, or else

[32] Ramsay, *The Church in the Roman Empire Before A.D. 170,* pp. 409-414.

embellished the narratives with imaginative detail. The writers of the New Testament did not tell all that one would like to know for a complete understanding of this period but confined themselves to the facts which illustrated their teaching.

To sift positive facts from doubtful tradition and to organize them into an integral whole with definite meaning is the task of the historian. In this case, the task is doubly difficult, for the purpose of God is involved in the cosmic process, and theology must be combined with history.

2

The Political Scene

T HE DEATH OF ALEXANDER THE GREAT AT BABYLON IN 323 B.C.
effected a profound change in the political organization of the
Western world. In campaigns of almost lightning speed and
with astounding success the young Macedonian king in eleven years
had marched his armies from the Hellespont to the Indus River and
had attempted to disseminate the culture, ideology, and political
organization of Greece. He pacified the small warring states in the
conquered territories and shattered the power of the Persian empire. _Eur._
Upon its ruins he began to build a new structure, half Occidental
and half Oriental, which he evidently hoped to make an enduring
dominion, but he failed. His army rebelled against the long
marches, incessant fighting, and increasing distance from their
homeland. Within the upper echelon of command there were
jealousies and dissensions, while Alexander himself assumed more
and more the mien of an Oriental despot. In a drunken debauch he
killed one of his best friends. He finally succumbed to a fever,
leaving no single successor powerful enough to consolidate the
empire which he had conquered.

Alexander's realm was partitioned among four of his generals.
Ptolemy took Egypt; Antipater, Macedonia and Greece; Lysimachus,
Thrace; and Seleucus, Babylonia. Antigonus, king of Phrygia, endeavored to carve an empire for himself in Asia Minor out of the
remains of Alexander's domain but was opposed by the other suc-

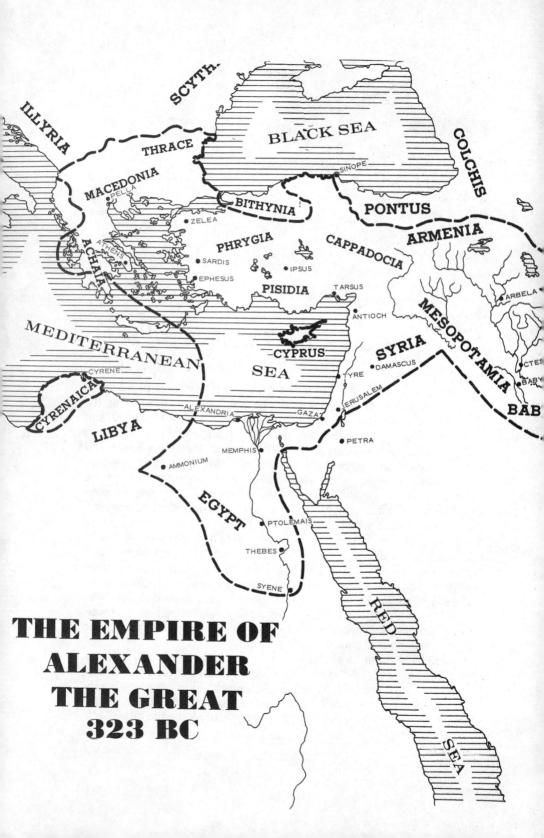

THE EMPIRE OF
ALEXANDER
THE GREAT
323 BC

A mosaic representation of Alexander the Great on his horse Bucephalus in Casa del Fauno, Naples. (The Bettmann Archive.)

cessors and was ultimately defeated at the battle of Ipsus in 301 B.C. The final division of the territories followed this battle. Lysimachus retained Thrace; Cassander, son of Antipater, became ruler of his father's kingdom; Ptolemy, who assumed the title of Ptolemy I, and Seleucus claimed the sovereignty of Egypt and of Syria respectively.

Egypt

The dynasty of the Ptolemies began auspiciously with Ptolemy I. He established Egypt as the leading power in the eastern Mediterranean region, and under his mild and beneficent rule the country prospered. He established the first extensive library of antiquity, the great Museum of Alexandria, which became the leading depository for the literary wealth of the ancient world and the home of scholars who wished to engaged in intellectual pursuits. It was the prototype of the modern university.

For approximately a century Egypt dominated the south Mediterranean littoral. Ptolemy gathered a mercenary army, and appointed

his government officials from his personal friends. To insure protection he built a large navy and fortified Egypt on the south and
east. He gained control of Cyrene, Cyprus, and Palestine and
established suzerainty over some of the free cities of Asia Minor, the
Aegean Islands, and Greece. In 312 B.C. he invaded Palestine and
overcame Demetrius, son of Antigonus, the ruler of Syria, in a
pitched battle near Gaza, though he was forced to evacuate a few
months later when Demetrius and Antigonus defeated his army. The
conflict with Demetrius was waged with varying fortunes. Ptolemy
was finally compelled to relinquish his claims on Greece and Asia
Minor. He did succeed in gaining permanent control of Cyprus in
295 B.C., and reduced Cyrene to a province which was assigned to
his stepson, Magus. He abdicated the throne in 285 B.C. in favor
of his son, Ptolemy II Philadelphus, and died in 283 B.C.

Ptolemy I, in his initial invasion of Palestine, captured Jerusalem
after a determined resistance on the part of the Jews by attacking
on the Sabbath while they were resting. He did not treat the population with severity but did deport a number of captives to new
homes in Egypt. Some were settled in Cyprus, a few were used to
garrison his frontiers, but the majority were kept in Alexandria.
They proved to be sober and industrious colonists and were
granted a charter which made them semi-independent in their own
quarter of the city. They enjoyed their privileges, and the colony
grew rapidly. Morally superior to the Egyptians and Greeks, they
obtained important government posts and prospered in business.
They learned the Greek language and absorbed Greek culture.

The three succeeding Ptolemies, Ptolemy II Philadelphus (285-
246 B.C.), Ptolemy III Euergetes (246-221 B.C.), and Ptolemy IV
Philopator (221-204 B.C.), maintained the tradition begun by
Ptolemy I. Under their reigns the Alexandrian court maintained
a brilliant though brittle culture. Ptolemy Philadelphus enlarged
the library of Alexandria and fostered the critical study of the Greek
classics. Many of the manuscripts from which modern texts are
derived were edited and preserved in Egypt. Perhaps the most
important heritage of his reign is the Septuagint, the Greek version
of the Old Testament, which probably made its appearance between 275 and 250 B.C. Tradition ascribes the translation to the
work of seventy-two scholars, sent by the Jewish commonwealth
of Palestine to translate the books of the law and the prophets at
Ptolemy's request. According to the legend, the scholars were confined by pairs in separate houses and ordered to translate from
Hebrew into Greek. When the results were compared, the manuscripts proved to be identical and were consequently adjudged to be
correct since they could have agreed only by miracle. The legend is

doubtlessly incorrect, for it is far more likely that the translation was made for the use of the Jewish colonists in Egypt rather than simply as a collector's item for the library.

By the first century A.D. the Septuagint had become the Bible of the Jews of the Dispersion and was widely circulated through the Roman world. It became also the Bible of the early Christians who preached from it and quoted it in their writings. A large proportion of the allusions to the Old Testament contained in the Gospels and in the Epistles are taken from the Septuagint.

The decline of Egypt began with the opening of the second century before Christ. Ptolemy IV Philopator (221-204 B.C.) succeeded to a strong empire which enjoyed peace both at home and abroad. His chief adviser, Sosibius, planned the murder of his brother, Magus, and his mother, Berenice. When Sosibius died, Ptolemy was strongly influenced by his mistress, Agathokleia, sister of Agathocles, his companion in debauchery. He neglected public business and consequently alienated the loyalty of his supporters who were endeavoring to administer the kingdom efficiently.

Syria

The weakness of Egypt allowed for the rise of Syria under the Seleucid king Antiochus the Great. The Seleucid dynasty had commenced with Seleucus I (312-280 B.C.), another of Alexander's generals. He shared in the division of the empire in 323 B.C., and in 321 B.C. took the Babylonian satrapy for his domain. In 316 B.C. he was forced to flee to Egypt, where he lived under the protection of Ptolemy I, but in 312 B.C. returned to Babylon. He conquered the eastern half of the empire, and by defeating Antigonus in Asia Minor in 301 B.C. made himself master of Syria.

Under his new regime the city of Antioch was founded in 300 B.C. Built on the plain by the Orontes River, it quickly acquired political and commercial importance. The location at the crossroads of the caravan routes from the Far East and the seaways to Egypt, Greece, and Italy was strategic. Antioch became the capital of the Seleucid kings and the foremost city of Syria.

Seleucus I Nicator undertook to extend his kingdom westward but was killed in 280 B.C. while attempting to conquer Macedonia. His son, Antiochus I Soter, relinquished Macedonia and Thrace to Ptolemy. He earned his title Soter (Saviour) by a victory over the Gauls in Asia Minor in 278 B.C., which successfully checked their invasion and secured the Syrian frontier. He fought with Ptolemy II Philadelphus in 275 B.C. for the control of Syria, but was unable to cope with Ptolemy's naval power. He was defeated and killed in a war with Pergamum in 262 B.C.

Antiochus II Theos succeeded to his father's throne in 261 B.C.
A protracted war with Ptolemy II dragged on for eleven years, until
peace was declared in 250 B.C. Antiochus confirmed the pact by
divorcing his wife Laodice, and by marrying Berenice, Ptolemy's
daughter. Four years later he abandoned Berenice and returned to
Laodice, who poisoned him and then murdered her rival and her
son.

Seleucus II Callinicus, the son of Laodice, was acknowledged as
king but found himself embroiled in a second war with Egypt.
Ptolemy III, Berenice's brother, incensed by the murder of his
sister, invaded the eastern provinces of the Seleucid territory and
captured the seacoast of Asia Minor. Forced by Ptolemy's attack
to retire to the hinterland of his realm, Seleucus fought back and
recovered northern Syria and the Persian provinces. He lost control
of northern and western Asia Minor and died in 227 B.C.

Seleucus III Soter, the son of Callinicus, reigned for a brief period
of four years. He attempted to recover the territory in Asia Minor
which his father had lost, but was assassinated by conspirators. His
younger brother, Antiochus III, surnamed the Great, took his place.
The kingdom was badly disorganized. Asia Minor was lost and
the eastern provinces had revolted. Antiochus failed to recover the
western provinces of Asia Minor, but he subdued the rebellious
leaders in the east and attempted to invade Palestine. Ptolemy IV
defeated his forces at the battle of Raphia in 217 B.C. and drove
him out of the territory of the Lebanons. A second attempt was
more successful. Ptolemy's general, Scopas, lost the battle of
Panium in 198 B.C., and Antiochus became master of Palestine.

The protracted war had placed Egypt under serious financial
strain. It is probable that the Jews in Palestine, weary of the increasingly heavy taxation, transferred their allegiance to the Seleucids. For a century or more they had enjoyed comparative peace
under the rule of the Ptolemies, who seem to have demanded little
of them and to have extended to them the privilege of maintaining
an almost autonomous government. As the strife between the
Ptolemies and the Seleucids increased, the Jews found themselves
in the unenviable position of being the buffer between two rival
powers. For approximately two centuries following the victory of
Antiochus the Great they were under the domination of Gentile
kings who made and unmade high priests at will, and who at times
persecuted them severely. From the conquest of Palestine by the
Seleucids to the Roman capture of Jerusalem in A.D. 70 the Jewish
people were the political football of alien rulers. Their heroic
struggles to gain independence from foreign domination were only
partially successful, and their tenacious attempt to keep their faith

in spite of persecution and martyrdom ended in tragedy. That struggle, however, formed the matrix in which Christianity originated and gained its initial growth.

Antiochus, having allied himself with Hannibal of Carthage, extended his domain westward and in 192 B.C. invaded Greece. His advances were resisted by Rome, which regarded unfavorably his growing dominion. Antiochus was defeated by the Roman army under Acilius Glabrio at Thermopylae. The Romans followed him across the Aegean Sea to Asia Minor where they attacked him again and wrested from him the control of all the territory north of the Taurus Mountains. Antiochus died in 187 B.C. while engaged in a military venture in the East.

Antiochus' successor, Seleucus IV Philopator, inherited a realm comprising Syria, Mesopotamia, Babylonia, Media, and Persia. After a short reign of eleven years he was assassinated by his prime minister Heliodorus. Since his son was at that time a hostage in Rome and unable to take over the kingdom, his younger brother, Antiochus IV Epiphanes, succeeded him in 175 B.C., and eliminated Heliodorus who had tried to usurp the throne.

Antiochus IV Epiphanes

The reign of Antiochus Epiphanes was a turning point in Jewish fortunes. The death of Ptolemy V Epiphanes of Egypt in 181 B.C. left his kingdom to an infant son, Ptolemy VI Philometor. While his mother Cleopatra, daughter of Antiochus the Great, lived, peace prevailed between Egypt and Syria. At her death war broke out again over the claims to Palestine. Antiochus IV Epiphanes invaded Egypt (170 B.C.) and captured the young king. He made Ptolemy VI regent. A few years later (168 B.C.) Ptolemy rebelled against Antiochus, who promptly invaded Egypt a second time and threatened to take over the kingdom.

His plans were balked by a new power that had begun to take an active interest in the politics of the Middle East. In Egypt Antiochus was confronted by the envoy of Rome, C. Popilius Laenus, whom he had formerly known while residing in Italy. Antiochus greeted Laenus warmly, but was coolly received. Laenus informed him that there would be no negotiations until he relinquished all claims to Egypt. When Antiochus replied that he would consider the matter, Laenus drew a circle around him with his sword and told him to make up his mind before he stepped out of the circle. Unwilling to risk a major war with the rising power of Rome, which had already defeated Carthage and which was fast obtaining control of the Mediterranean, Antiochus sullenly withdrew, leaving Egypt to Ptolemy.

Seething with frustration, Antiochus retreated northward to Palestine, where he vented his spite on the Jews. He was an ardent Hellenist, having been educated in Graeco-Roman culture in both Rome and Athens. He determined to unify his realm by compelling his subjects to adopt Greek ideals and customs. To the rank and file of the Jews the Greek culture was odious, since it involved the worship of foreign deities and partaking of food which they deemed unclean and participation in games which they regarded as indecent. Among some of the younger and more sophisticated priests Antiochus found willing collaborators, however. They were enamored of the physical culture which the Greeks promoted, and they requested permission to build a gymnasium in Jerusalem.[1]

Upon his withdrawal from Egypt Antiochus seized Jerusalem without fighting, plundering it of as much wealth as he could find, and returned to Antioch. Two years later he invaded Judea a second time and seized the city by treachery. He stripped the Temple of its furnishings and confiscated its treasures. Having ravaged the city, he massacred many of the inhabitants and carried away a large group of captives, estimated by Josephus to be about ten thousand.[2] He demolished the walls so that the city was defenseless, and having built a tower of his own overlooking the temple site, he garrisoned it with Macedonian mercenaries. His worst offense was the desecration of the Temple, which he devoted to heathen worship by sacrificing a sow upon the great altar. He compelled the Jews to erect shrines to the Greek deities in their villages and to sacrifice swine on the altars. His officers seized and burned all copies of the books of the law and executed their possessors. Circumcision was forbidden and women whose infants had been circumcised were strangled together with their children. Many complied with the king's regulations, but a large number resisted them and paid for their convictions with their lives.

The ancient tension between Jews and Samaritans became more acute during this period because the Samaritans were willing to comply wholly with Antiochus' regulations. They even denied their Jewish antecedents by claiming to be Sidonians. They declared that their temple should be called "The Temple of Jupiter Hellenios" — the god of the Greeks. Naturally this wholesale capitulation to heathenism aroused the enmity of the Jews who had risked martyrdom rather than abandon their loyalty to the law and so widened the breach between the two peoples.

1 Josephus *Antiquities* xii. 5. 1.
2 *Ibid.*, xii. 5. 4ff.

The Maccabean Revolt

Although a group of Jewish officials either advocated the adoption of Hellenism or were secret admirers of it, the rank and file of the people opposed it bitterly. The smoldering resentment against the highhanded tactics of Antiochus IV burst out into a flame of revolt when some of his agents visited the small village of Modin about eighteen or twenty miles northwest of Jerusalem. Approaching Mattathias, a priest of the order of Joiarib (a priest who had returned from Babylon with Zerubbabel, Neh. 12:6, 7) and one of the leading citizens of the town, they asked him to offer sacrifice. Mattathias refused to participate in any worship alien to that of the true God. Another Jew of Modin completed the sacrifice. Enraged by this betrayal of faith, Mattathias and his sons drew their swords and attacked the king's messengers, killing both the man that made the offering and Apelles, the king's general, with a few of his soldiers. Tearing down the idolatrous altar which had been erected for the sacrifice, Mattathias called out to the bystanders, "If anyone be zealous for the laws of his country and for the worship of God, let him follow me!"

Mattathias with his sons, John, Simon, Judas called Maccabaeus, Eleazar, and Jonathan, fled to the wilderness, accompanied by a great many others who took their families with them, pursued by the military force of Antiochus. Many who took refuge in caves were trapped by the Syrians, who built fires at the mouth of the caves and smoked them out or burned them alive. Mattathias organized many of the refugees into an army. At the outset they refused to fight on the Sabbath, but after the first disastrous massacres Mattathias assured them that they had the right to defend themselves on the sacred day. He recruited a strong force and maintained a guerrilla warfare against pagans and recreant Jews who had supported Antiochus' program. His forces had been considerably augmented by loyal Jews and he was able to hold at bay the power of the Syrian king even though he did not dare to risk a pitched battle.

At the end of the first year, realizing that his health was failing, Mattathias called his sons together and committed to them the completion of his mission. He urged them to maintain unity in the cause of freedom and to restore the commonwealth which the Hellenizing efforts of Antiochus had disrupted. He appointed Simon as administrator and Judas as the general of the army. Shortly afterwards he died and was buried in Modin by his sons.

Judas' command was challenged first by Apollonius, the commander of the Samaritan army. In the ensuing battle Judas dispersed the Samaritans with heavy losses, including Apollonius himself.

PALESTINE IN THE TIME OF THE MACCABEES

Saron, the general in charge of Coele-Syria, hearing that Judas had acquired a large army, decided that the time had come for action. He marched into Judea and camped at the pass of Bethhoron. Judas attacked him with a group of poorly equipped but desperate men and drove him down across the pass into the coastal plain. Saron was killed and the Syrians were scattered.

Antiochus, chagrined by the defeat, mustered another army and prepared to institute a second attack. A financial shortage caused by delinquent taxes compelled him to march into Persia to collect the funds due to him. He left Lysias, the governor of Syria, in charge of the kingdom, with orders to educate his son Antiochus and to proceed as rapidly as possible with the conquest of Judea.

Lysias organized an army of forty thousand infantry and six thousand cavalry under the command of three generals, Ptolemy, son of Dorymanes, Nicanor, and Gorgias. These marched as far south as Emmaus and camped on the plains. They were joined by Syrian auxiliaries and by renegade Jews. So confident were they of victory that they brought with them slave traders prepared to purchase the prospective captives for sale in foreign markets.

Gorgias set out with five thousand infantry and a thousand horsemen in pursuit of Judas. Judas, aware of his intentions, abandoned his camp, leaving the fires burning, and marched toward Emmaus. Gorgias, finding the empty camp, concluded that Judas had withdrawn into the mountains and advanced further in pursuit of him. The latter, however, with a small but valiant force of about three thousand men, reached the Syrian camp at daybreak. Their sudden appearance was wholly unexpected and the Syrian force disintegrated into a precipitate rout. With great prudence Judas forbade his men to plunder the camp, for he knew that Gorgias with a fresh detachment of men might appear at any time. When Gorgias' expedition returned, they saw the smoke of the burning camp and fled in terror. Judas and his men captured a large quantity of money which filled their depleted war chest.

In the following year Lysias appeared with another army of sixty thousand picked men and advanced upon the village of Beth-sur in Judea. Judas had in the meantime augmented his forces and was able to muster about ten thousand men. Although still outnumbered by the Syrians, he gave battle and repulsed Lysias, who suffered about five thousand casualties. Discouraged by his repeated failures, and fearful of further contact with such desperate fighters as the Jews, Lysias withdrew to Antioch.

Since the war had reached a stalemate, Judas seized the opportunity to restore the Temple in Jerusalem. During the hostilities it had been deserted. Grass was growing in its courtyards, its gates had been burned in the siege, and its contents had been plundered. New vessels and furniture were provided, the heathen altar was removed and replaced by another not constructed with iron tools, and the divine worship was restored on the twenty-fifth day of Kislev, 165 B.C., exactly three years from the time of the Temple's desecration.

The joyous celebration lasted for eight days, accompanied by sacrifices, feasting, and singing. The people declared that it should be observed as the annual festival of "lights" (*Hanukkah*). Judas rebuilt the city walls and stationed guards in the towers. He fortified Beth-sura (also called Beth-zur, II Chron. 11:7, and Beth-sur) on the southern boundary as an outpost against attack from that direction.

The rapid rise of Maccabean power aroused the suspicion and hostility of the surrounding nations. Intrigues multiplied and Judas found himself ringed with enemies who were conspiring against him. In two vigorous campaigns he fought and disarmed the Edomites to the south, and captured the Ammonite city of Jazer east of the Jordan. Upon his return to Jerusalem, Timotheus, the Ammonite commander, collected an army in Gilead, while another coalition threatened Judea from Galilee.

Judas divided his forces, sending three thousand men into Galilee under the command of his brother Simon, while another brother, Jonathan, invaded Gilead with eight thousand men. Judea was placed under the command of two trusted lieutenants, Joseph and Azarias, whom he instructed to hold the territory and to fight with no person whatsoever until he returned.

Simon's campaign was successful. He routed the enemy in Galilee, recovered the captives whom they had taken, and returned to Judea in good order. Judas himself with his brother Jonathan crossed the Jordan and marched three days into the desert. From the friendly Nabateans they learned that the Jews in Gilead had been imprisoned in large fortified cities. He captured Bosorra and slaughtered the male population. Surprising the army of Timotheus while engaged in the siege of a city, he attacked it from the rear and drove it into headlong flight. By a series of rapid movements he took the other fortified town of Gilead and freed his countrymen who had been incarcerated in the fortresses.

Timotheus recruited another army with Arab mercenaries and encamped near Raphia on the opposite side of a mountain stream from Judas. Without halting to pitch camp, Judas crossed the river and assailed the Syrians who fled to Carnaim. Judas took the city and burned its temple. Collecting the Jews in Gilead, he returned them and their families to Judea. Halted at Ephron, which was located in a narrow valley, he petitioned the inhabitants for permission to pass through the city peacefully. When they refused, he camped before the city and captured it within twenty-four hours. Having thus opened the road, he returned to Judea with the Jews whom he had rescued.

During Judas' campaign in Gilead, Joseph and Azariah undertook to clear Gorgias' forces out of Jamnia. Ignoring the instructions issued by Judas, they marched down to the coastal plain where they encountered heavy resistance. They were driven back to the hills with a loss of two thousand men. Judas continued the war with Edom by leveling Hebron and by capturing Ashdod on the Philistine coast.

The early successes of Judas and the defeat of Lysias were reported to Antiochus in Persia, where he had suffered a sharp defeat in his attempt to plunder the city of Elymas. Forced to return to Babylon, he learned there of the disaster that had befallen his armies in Judea. According to the writer of I Maccabees,[3] the shock unnerved him. He was taken seriously ill and realized that his end was approaching. Summoning one of his associates, Philip, he invested him with the royal authority, including a commission to rear his son Antiochus and to establish him on the throne. Lysias, however, announced the king's death and elevated his own son to the throne, giving him the title of Antiochus V Eupator.

The citadel in Jerusalem was held by a garrison of Jews who were friendly to the Syrians and who were a constant threat to the peace of the city. They frequently assaulted the visitors to the Temple and supported the heathen population. Judas decided to eliminate them and laid siege to the citadel. A few escaped and petitioned Antiochus to come to their relief. He responded with an army of 100,000 infantry, 20,000 cavalry, and thirty-two elephants trained for war.[4] Judas left the siege of the citadel and encamped at Beth Zachariah, a town southwest of Jerusalem, opposite Beth-sura. Antiochus attacked in force, interspersing the elephants among his troops in such a way that they would force an entry for his infantry. Five hundred cavalry were assigned to each elephant to protect it from mass attack and to follow up its advance.

In the course of the battle, Eleazar, noting that one of the elephants was carrying the royal arms, thought that the king was on it. Slipping through the ranks, he stabbed the elephant from beneath and was crushed by its fall. The Syrians took Beth-sura, which was evacuated by the Jews, and advanced on Jerusalem. Lysias was

---

[3] I Maccabees 6:5-14.
[4] These figures follow the statement of I Maccabees 6:30. They are probably exaggerated.

preparing to besiege the city when he learned that Philip, whom Antiochus had commissioned to rear his son, had returned from Persia with the main army and was preparing to seize the government. Lysias proposed that the king should conclude a truce with the Judeans, allowing them to maintain their own worship without interference. The plan was acceptable and the treaty was signed.

The withdrawal of Lysias and his troops left Judas once again in command of the city. Apparently he purged it of all Hellenizing Jews, for subsequent events indicate that a number of them fled for refuge to Antioch, where they put themselves under the protection of the Syrian king.

Antiochus V Eupator had a short and calamitous reign. His uncle Demetrius, the brother of Antiochus IV, who had been a hostage in Rome, escaped and made his way back to Syria. A revolt of the army overthrew the government of Antiochus and Lysias, who were promptly executed. When Demetrius became king, the Hellenizing refugees from Judea petitioned him to take action against Judas and his brothers, asserting that they had killed the king's friends, expelled the Hellenists from the land, and damaged the king's interests. Demetrius responded to the petition by deputing Bacchides, one of his associates, to recover Judea for the Syrian empire. Since the former high priest Menelaus had been executed by Antiochus V, Demetrius confirmed Alcimus, whom Antiochus had elevated to the high priest's office. Alcimus was a Hellenist who sympathized with the cause of Demetrius and who proved to be a valuable ally.

The policy of conquest differed from that of Lysias, for they preferred stealth to violence. Sixty of a group of scribes who had trusted Alcimus because of his priesthood were seized and executed. Bacchides, after butchering many of the deserters who seemed to have no permanent allegiance to either side, left Alcimus in charge and returned to Antioch. Judas Maccabaeus, however, realizing that Alcimus was a menace to him and to his party, resumed hostilities.

Demetrius promptly dispatched Nicanor, one of his ablest officers, to Judea with orders to dispose of Judas. He tried to kidnap him by treachery, suggesting that he should visit Judas peacefully with only a few men. When the plot failed, Judas realized that Nicanor could not be trusted and refused a second interview. Nicanor, seeing that his plot had been discovered, attacked Judas in force, but he was beaten and driven back to the fortress in Jerusalem. When he was greeted peacefully by the priests, he threatened them, saying that unless Judas and his army were delivered to him he would burn down the Temple.

Nicanor joined his army at Bethhoron; Judas camped at Adasa, a village about three miles from Bethhoron on the road to Jerusalem. In the following battle Judas won a notable victory. The Syrians took flight to the coast but were intercepted by the Jewish guerrillas. Nicanor was killed and his army annihilated.

Evidently Judas realized that he would need a powerful ally to support him, for the infiltration of the Hellenists was increasing and the power of the Seleucid kings was a continual threat to the peace of Judea. The fame of the Romans was spreading through the Middle East because of their conquest of western Asia Minor from Antiochus the Great and because of their qualities of statesmanship. Judas sent an embassy to the Roman Senate to establish a treaty of friendship. The Romans replied by sending back a treaty inscribed on brass tablets which required the Jews to fight for Rome in case of war, to withhold economic support from the enemy as Rome should decide, and to keep the agreement without expectation of payment. In return, Rome promised to aid the Jews as allies in case of war and agreed to warn Demetrius that if he did not abstain from oppressing the Jewish nation, war would follow.

Just how seriously Rome or Demetrius took this treaty is difficult to ascertain. For nearly a century Rome paid little attention to the fortunes of Judea, and the subsequent actions of Demetrius seem to indicate that he did not regard Rome as a major threat. Although Roman arms had defeated Antiochus the Great in Asia, and had compelled Antiochus IV to evacuate Egypt, Demetrius disregarded the Roman-Jewish treaty. Between the accession of Demetrius in 162 B.C. and the invasion of Palestine by Pompey in 63 B.C., Rome was engaged in subduing Spain, Carthage, Greece, and western Asia. The Roman government was sufficiently occupied with pacifying the lands near at hand without embroiling itself in the tangled quarrels of the Seleucids and the Jews. The treaty may have given Judas Maccabaeus a greater feeling of security, but it is doubtful whether it afforded him any solid protection.

Bacchides and Alcimus attempted a second conquest of the Maccabean forces. Although the Greek text of I Maccabees seems somewhat confused,[5] they probably marched southward through Galilee. In the early spring of 161 B.C. they camped near Jerusalem with a force of twenty thousand men. Judas had only three thousand in his army, but desertions soon reduced it to eight hundred. With this pitifully small number Judas attacked and drove back the right wing of Bacchides' army, only to be enveloped from the rear by the left wing. Judas himself was killed, and his army was

[5] See I Maccabees 9:1-8 in the edition of Tedesche and Zeitlin, pp. 153, 154. The text reads Gilgal, but Josephus says Galilee.

overwhelmed by sheer numbers.   His brothers Jonathan and Simon
recovered his body and buried it in the family tomb at Modin.

The loss of Judas' leadership produced a period of retrogression
and anarchy.   Bacchides followed a policy of extermination of
Judas' friends and followers.   The survivors made Jonathan, Judas'
brother, their leader, and reverted to the guerrilla tactics that had
first won success for them.   They retired to the wilderness of Tekoa.
Bacchides, learning of their place of refuge, crossed the Jordan to
give battle.   Jonathan had sent his brother John, with their baggage,
to the Nabateans, who had agreed to guard it for them.   A group
of Amorites from Medeba intercepted John, killed him, and stole
the baggage.   Jonathan and Simon learned soon afterward that the
same Amorites were celebrating a wedding nearby.   They set an
ambush, attacked the wedding party, and captured the spoils, returning to their hiding place in the marshes of the Jordan.

Bacchides undertook reprisal and pursued Jonathan to his lair. In
the ensuing battle Bacchides lost a thousand men, while Jonathan
and his guerrillas escaped.   Alcimus, after demolishing the wall of
the inner Temple court which separated the Court of the Gentiles
from the inner court, died of a stroke.   Bacchides returned to
Antioch, and for a brief span of time the land had peace.

A conspiracy to bring back Bacchides and to arrest Jonathan
failed.   When Jonathan was informed of it, he arrested fifty of the
ringleaders and executed them.   He withdrew to Bethbasi, which
he fortified.   While Simon defended the city, Jonathan maintained
a skirmish warfare against Bacchides.   Baffled by Simon's hit-and-
run tactics, Bacchides was persuaded to make a treaty with Jonathan by which he agreed to release all prisoners and to establish
peace.

Jonathan's stubborn resistance to the overwhelming might of the
Syrian army proved that the Jews were a potent factor in the affairs
of Palestine.   They were not simply a pawn on the chessboard of
Middle Eastern politics but were capable of wielding a decisive
influence in the struggle for power between the Ptolemies of Egypt
and the Seleucids of Syria.   In spite of frequent invasions and
reverses, they had finally driven their enemies back within their own
borders and had achieved a degree of independence.   The retreat of
Bacchides to Antioch ended the first stage of the Maccabean struggle which freed the Jews from Hellenistic domination and gave to
them the opportunity of developing their own culture.

In 150 B.C. a fresh conflict broke out in Syria.   Alexander Balas,
who claimed to be a son of Antiochus IV Epiphanes, took possession
of Ptolemais.   The garrison was dissatisfied with Demetrius' harsh
and negligent government and welcomed a change of rulers.   Both

Alexander and Demetrius recognized that the Jewish rulers held the balance of power, and both courted their favor. Demetrius promised to give Jonathan the right to rearm and to restore to him the hostages that Bacchides had incarcerated in Jerusalem. The Hellenizing party, frightened by the possibility that Jonathan might soon be in a position to wreak vengeance on them, took refuge in Antioch. Jonathan rebuilt the walls of Jerusalem and prepared for war. Alexander, hearing that Demetrius had made overtures to Jonathan, ordained him a high priest of the Jews and sent him a resplendent purple robe and crown.

Jonathan accepted these insignia of office and began military preparations. Demetrius, alarmed by Alexander's diplomatic success, attempted to outbid him by freeing Judea from tribute and from the salt tax, and by relinquishing claims to the tax on crops and the poll tax. He assigned the city of Jerusalem to Jonathan, who had assumed the role of high priest, and declared complete religious tolerance for all Jews. He donated 150,000 drachmae for repairing the Temple and offered to pay for restoring the walls of the city.

His lavish promises, however, availed him little. Alexander, supported by a large army of mercenaries augmented by deserters from Demetrius, gave battle to the king. Demetrius' left wing overcame the right wing of Balas' army, but the right wing of Demetrius' host was driven back into a swamp. Demetrius fought bravely but was mired in a slough and was killed.

Alexander took the kingdom of Syria and immediately attempted to consolidate his position by an alliance with Ptolemy Philometor of Egypt, whose daughter he married. He treated Jonathan with great deference and commended him publicly as a friend. Alexander's reign, however, was interrupted by a revolt under Demetrius II Nicator, the son of Alexander's predecessor, who invaded Cilicia from Crete. Alexander left Ptolemais and went to Antioch to prepare for the coming struggle. In his absence his lieutenant Apollonius, the governor of Syria, challenged Jonathan to battle. Jonathan defeated him completely. Alexander, however, maintained his friendly attitude.

Ptolemy VI Philometor, Alexander's father-in-law, came to his aid against Demetrius. Alexander treacherously plotted Ptolemy's assassination. Ptolemy, thinking that the conspiracy emanated from one of Alexander's lieutenants, complained, only to discover that Alexander himself was responsible. Angered by Alexander's perfidy, Ptolemy transferred his support to Demetrius II and, taking his daughter from Alexander, gave her to Demetrius. Alexander fled to Cilicia and Ptolemy was crowned king by the inhabitants of Antioch. He refused to retain the title and transferred it to

Demetrius. Alexander invaded Syria in an attempt to recover his kingdom, but was beaten, and was murdered after the battle. Ptolemy did not long survive him.

Jonathan was besieging the citadel at Jerusalem which had been garrisoned by Macedonian mercenaries and refugee Hellenists of Judea. The latter requested assistance from Demetrius, who summoned Jonathan to Palestine. Without interrupting the siege of the citadel, Jonathan visited Demetrius, taking with him costly gifts. Having successfully bribed Demetrius, he secured from him gifts of additional territory and exemption from taxation.

Trypho, one of Demetrius' officers, having become aware that a number of soldiers were disaffected because their pay was delayed, arranged with Antiochus, the son of Alexander Balas, to restore the kingdom to him. Demetrius, engaged in civil strife, asked assistance from Jonathan, who sent him three thousand soldiers. These joined Demetrius and defended him against the rioting inhabitants of Antioch. The city was burned and the populace subdued. Demetrius, although he rewarded the soldiers well at the time, later threatened to make war on Jonathan; he was deterred from his purpose only by the revolt of Trypho. Demetrius' mercenaries, whom he had not paid, joined Trypho, and expelled Demetrius from Antioch.

Antiochus VI Dionysius (145-143 B.C.) was placed upon the throne by Trypho. He confirmed Jonathan in the priesthood and appointed Simon the general in charge of the troops in Palestine. Jonathan agreed as his ally to make war on Demetrius. He promoted Antiochus' cause in Palestine and after a hard battle in Galilee defeated the army of Demetrius. Demetrius was subsequently killed while engaged in a campaign against the Parthians.

Trypho, aware that the death of Demetrius had removed Antiochus' rival for the kingdom, conspired to seize it for himself. Since Jonathan had allied himself with Antiochus, Trypho resolved to remove him first. When Jonathan met him at Beth-shan with forty thousand men, Trypho determined to use stealth rather than force, for Jonathan was a determined fighter and could easily oust him from Palestine. He persuaded Jonathan to disband his army and to visit him at Ptolemais under a pretense of peace. Jonathan, with a thousand men, marched to Ptolemais. When he entered the city, the gates were shut. Trypho captured Jonathan alive and butchered his soldiers.

Taking Jonathan in chains, Trypho invaded Judea with a large army. Simon, Jonathan's brother, had succeeded to the command. Trypho offered to release Jonathan for a ransom of a hundred talents of silver and the surrender of his two sons as hostages. Simon knew that Trypho would not keep his word, but complied with the terms lest he should be accused of having failed to release his brother. Trypho attempted an invasion of Judea but was prevented by a heavy snowfall. He removed to Gilead, where he executed Jonathan. Simon recovered his body and buried it in the family tomb at Modin.

Simon succeeded in conquering the surrounding territory of Gazara, Joppa, and Jamnia. He captured the citadel at Jerusalem, which had been held by the rebellious Hellenists, and levelled it to the ground.

Trypho murdered Antiochus and secured the support of the army by promising them wealth if they would make him king. When he failed to fulfill his promise, the army revolted and deserted to Cleopatra, the wife of Demetrius II. She appealed to his brother, Antiochus VII Sidetes (138-129 B.C.), to take the kingdom, and offered to marry him. He drove Trypho out of Syria into Phoenicia and with the aid of Simon finally overcame him and executed him.

Having disposed of Trypho, Antiochus turned upon Simon, who succeeded in keeping him at bay. Simon was treacherously murdered by his son-in-law, Ptolemy, who imprisoned his wife and his two eldest sons. The third son, John Hyrcanus, escaped to Jerusalem, where he was protected by the multitude.

The tide of war soon turned. Hyrcanus besieged Ptolemy in the fortress of Dagon near Jericho. Ptolemy tortured Hyrcanus' mother and brothers to compel him to raise the siege, but to no avail. He finally killed them and fled to Philadelphia (now 'Amman) on the east of the Jordan.

Antiochus, in the meantime, attacked Jerusalem and ringed the northern wall of the city with towers. Hyrcanus was unable to break the siege and finally capitulated. He agreed to an indemnity of four hundred talents of silver and to give hostages if Antiochus would withdraw his forces. Antiochus accepted the terms and raised the siege after breaking down the fortifications of the city.

Antiochus was killed in a fruitless campaign against the Parthians. Demetrius II, his brother, succeeded him, but reigned only a short time. The Syrian people and the mercenary army despised him because he was a sick man, and invited Ptolemy Physcon of Egypt to send them another scion of the Seleucidae to take the kingdom. Ptolemy sent Alexander Zabinas, who defeated Demetrius. When the latter took refuge with his wife, she abandoned him to his enemies, who tortured and killed him.

The death of Antiochus and the rise of John Hyrcanus marked a new era in the affairs of Palestine. The dynasty of the Seleucids perished in confusion, while the Hasmoneans, as the descendants of the Maccabees were known, flourished independently until the invasion of Palestine by Pompey in 63 B.C. Syria had eleven kings in sixty-two years, no one of whom was strong enough to salvage the kingdom nor sufficiently eminent to deserve special mention.

The Hasmoneans

The name "Hasmonean" (143-37 B.C.), derived from Hasmon, the great-great-grandfather of Mattathias of Modin, the progenitor of the Maccabees, was applied to the dynasty founded by Simon and continued through his son, John Hyrcanus. Simon was the first of the family to assume the prerogatives of a king. His brothers had been warriors and liberators, but they had been too busily engaged in throwing off the yoke of Syria to pay much attention to the internal organization of the country. With the decline of the Seleucids, and under the friendly patronage of Egypt, which was already strongly influenced by its Jewish population, Simon and his descendants were able to maintain an independent rule for a century.

Simon began the consolidation of the kingdom of Judea and issued a separate coinage. His son, John Hyrcanus I, reigned for thirty-one years (135-105 B.C.) in relative peace. Josephus states that he held both the power of civil government and the office of the high priesthood.[6] He seems to have exercised a temperate but firm sovereignty over the nation. Defeated in battle by Antiochus VII Sidetes, he became a vassal of Syria, but the death of Antiochus in 129 B.C. released him. The civil wars in Syria so occupied the attention of Hyrcanus' northern neighbors that they let him alone, and he, in turn, paid no regard to them.

Hyrcanus' death passed the kingdom to his son Aristobulus. He promptly imprisoned his mother, to whom Hyrcanus had entrusted the government, and let her starve to death in a dungeon. He had favored his brother Antigonus, but when the latter was misrepresented to him by enemies, he killed him. Aristobulus died within a year and was succeeded by his widow, Salome Alexandra.

Salome freed Aristobulus' brothers from prison where he had incarcerated them, and married the oldest of them, Alexander Jannaeus, who became king (104-78 B.C.). He put out of the way one of his brothers, who was a possible rival, and allowed the other to live in retirement. He undertook to conquer Ptolemais and beseiged the city. The citizens appealed to Ptolemy Lathyrus of Cyprus who had been driven from Egypt by Cleopatra, his mother. Ptolemy landed in Palestine with an army of thirty thousand men, only to

[6] *Antiquities of the Jews* xiii. 10. 7.

find that Ptolemais would not welcome him because they feared to precipitate a war with Egypt.

Alexander Jannaeus attempted double dealing by promising Ptolemy his friendship if he would conquer the coastal plain for him, and by simultaneously confirming a private alliance with Cleopatra against him. When Ptolemy discovered Alexander's duplicity, he prepared for war. Failing to take Sepphoris, a city in Galilee, Alexander fought a bitter battle at the Jordan and lost. Ptolemy overran the entire country and captured Ptolemais.

Cleopatra of Egypt, alarmed by Ptolemy's successes, lifted the siege of Ptolemais and made an alliance with Alexander. Ptolemy retired to Cyprus and Cleopatra to Egypt, leaving Alexander once more in possession of Palestine. He recovered his throne but was singularly unpopular. At the Feast of Tabernacles the populace pelted him with citrons and on a later occasion, when he asked them what they wanted him to do, they recommended that he commit suicide. He remained in power by the Pisidian and Cilician mercenaries in his army. For six years the nation was virtually in revolt against him. They appealed to Demetrius Eucerus of Syria for aid. Demetrius promptly attacked Alexander and in the ensuing battles destroyed Alexander's army and drove him into the mountains. In pity for his plight, six thousand Jews deserted Demetrius and joined him. Demetrius, having lost his mercenaries, withdrew. Alexander subdued the rebels and indulged in murderous reprisal. After the capture of one city he ordered that eight hundred of its citizens should be crucified, and while they were still living he slaughtered their wives and children before their eyes. Josephus attributes this deed to exasperation with the traitorousness of those Jews who had betrayed him to the Syrians and who had introduced foreign troops to fight against him. There can be scarcely any excuse for the frightful brutalities he perpetrated upon his countrymen. They exceeded even the miseries that Antiochus IV had inflicted on Alexander's ancestors.

The remainder of Alexander's rule was afflicted by a series of wars in which he was generally successful, but which drained his financial and physical resources. He died after a reign of twenty-seven years, leaving the kingdom to his widow, Alexandra.

Alexandra, contrary to her husband's tendencies, was a fair, though firm, ruler. Wisely she appointed her rather phlegmatic older son Hyrcanus as high priest; the younger son, Aristobulus, who was aggressive and erratic, she left in private life. She made the Pharisees her counselors, who took over the affairs of state, leaving the responsibilities to Alexandra while they arrogated to themselves the privileges of rulership. They urged her to execute

the advisors of Alexander who had incited him to the wholesale
crucifixion of his opponents, and succeeded in disposing of many
of their personal enemies. A few took refuge with Aristobulus, who
persuaded his mother to spare these men and to substitute exile for
execution. Alexandra built the army to new efficiency and strengthened the position of the nation by diplomatic negotiations with
Armenia.

When Alexandra became ill, Aristobulus seized the fortresses
and proclaimed himself king. She promptly retaliated by imprisoning
his wife and children, but before she could take further action, she
died. Hyrcanus was the rightful heir to the throne, but Aristobulus,
being the more aggressive, seized the kingdom. Hostilities were
averted by the reconciliation of the brothers. Aristobulus retained
the title of king; Hyrcanus relinquished the throne but retained the
other honors.

Antipater

At this juncture a new and important person appeared — Antipater. An Idumean by birth, he was gifted with wealth, craftiness,
and power. He persuaded Hyrcanus to ally himself with Aretas, the
king of the Nabateans, in an attempt to regain his kingdom. Antipater put Hyrcanus under the protection of Aretas in Petra, who
furnished him with an army of fifty thousand men. Aristobulus
was unable to cope with Aretas' power and soon found himself
besieged in Jerusalem.

In all probability Hyrcanus and Aretas would have won the day
had not Rome intervened. Scaurus, a Roman general who was the
lieutenant of Pompey, had been sent into Syria while Pompey was
campaigning in Armenia. He took over Damascus and then, hearing of the civil strife in Judea, threatened Hyrcanus with an invasion
by Pompey's forces if the siege were not lifted. Aretas immediately withdrew from the contest and Aristobulus pursued Hyrcanus'
army, killing six thousand or more.

Hyrcanus and Antipater made overtures to Pompey. He immediately set out in pursuit of Aristobulus, who had secluded himself in
a mountain fortress, and ordered him to surrender. After some
hesitant negotiations, he finally abandoned the fortress to Pompey
and returned to Jerusalem to prepare for conflict.

Pompey pursued him to the gates of Jerusalem and besieged the
city. When Aristobulus went out to him as a suppliant, Pompey
seized him as a prisoner and attacked the city. Approaching from
the north, the only side from which the city was accessible, the Romans battered down the towers and entered the precincts of the

Temple. Twelve thousand of the defenders were killed, but Pompey refrained from plundering the sanctuary. He reconstituted Hyrcanus as high priest, executed those responsible for the war, and took Aristobulus and his family prisoners to Rome.

Alexander, one of Aristobulus' sons, escaped while on the journey to Rome and returned to Judea. By his guerrilla tactics he threatened Hyrcanus' security and might have taken over the kingdom had not Gabinius, the successor of Scaurus, opposed him. Gabinius' troops, in conjunction with those of Antipater, Hyrcanus' supporter, defeated Alexander and drove him out of Jerusalem. Gabinius quelled the rebellion and resettled many of the cities that had been devastated or abandoned in the civil strife. He pursued Alexander to the fortress of Alexandrion and compelled him to capitulate. He divided Palestine into five sections, which were placed under the rule of an aristocracy.

For a short time the land was peaceful, but the escape of Aristobulus from Rome renewed hostilities. With a large following of Jews he recaptured Alexandrion and attempted to fortify it. The Romans moved against him swiftly, captured him, and sent him and his son Antigonus back to Rome in chains.

The arrival of Pompey in Palestine ended the real rule of the Hasmoneans. Later attempts to recover the throne failed completely, and although the titular priesthood remained with Hyrcanus, his power steadily diminished before the rising strength of Herod the Great.

The Shadow of Rome

With the defeat of Antiochus III by Acilius Glabrio in 191 B.C. the influence of Rome began to overshadow the Middle East. Although the Roman Senate for almost fifty years after Glabrio's victory was involved in a struggle with Carthage that prevented any extensive action in the eastern Mediterranean, it succeeded in checking the ambitions of the Seleucids for westward expansion. Antiochus was expelled from Greece, and a subsequent Roman campaign in Asia Minor compelled him to relinquish the territory north of the Taurus mountains and west of Pamphylia; to surrender his navy and his elephants, the equivalent of a modern tank corps; and to pay a crushing indemnity which crippled him financially. Although Antiochus himself was not taken as a hostage and although his kingdom was not invaded, the power of Syria was sharply curbed.

No direct hostility ensued between Rome and Syria, but fifteen years later, when Antiochus IV Epiphanes invaded Egypt, he was confronted by the Roman envoy who ordered him to desist from making war on the Ptolemies. Having removed the threat of Carthage in Africa and of Macedonia in Greece, the Roman Senate was determined not to allow any Eastern rival to acquire equal power. Egypt was an important source of Rome's grain supply, and Seleucid control might mean economic strangulation for Rome if war should occur. Antiochus retreated to Antioch, leaving Egypt under the protection of Rome.[7]

During the period of the Maccabean wars Rome interfered little in the affairs of Palestine, although Judas Maccabaeus sought an alliance with the Romans. He endeavored to negotiate a treaty with them, but while they listened to his ambassadors and agreed to peace, they lent no military aid whatsoever. Judas was killed in battle with the Syrians, and the negotiations produced no result.

From the collapse of Carthage and the capture of Achaia in 146 B.C. to the victory of Sulla in the civil contest with Marius in 83 B.C., Rome was preoccupied with internal affairs in the war of the dictators. During that period Tigranes of Armenia had endeavored to build an empire for himself by annexing Cappadocia and Syria (83 B.C.). Mithradates VI of Pontus, the ally of Tigranes, had gradually been gaining power and had taken control of a large section of Asia Minor. In 74 B.C. he invaded Bithynia and Asia. Two years later the Romans defeated him and drove him back to Armenia. In 69 B.C. Lucullus, the Roman general in charge of the campaign, took the capital of Armenia but was unable to hold it because of enmity at home and mutiny in his own army. Pompey, Sulla's lieutenant who had succeeded him as the strong man of Rome, had concluded a campaign in Spain and was given authority to take military command of the Mediterranean in order to eliminate the pirates who had become increasingly bold during the political confusion of the wars. Not only did Pompey crush the pirates, but by the passage of the Manilian law in 66 B.C. his authority was extended to command of the provinces of Bithynia and Cilicia and the war against Mithradates. Pompey acted immediately by invading Pontus. He compelled Mithradates to withdraw into Armenia and dispersed his forces. Tigranes yielded to Pompey and became an ally of Rome. Pompey subdued the entire region of Pontus and reduced it to a Roman province.

The way was then clear for a further advance to the East. In 64 B.C. Pompey ended the Seleucid dominion in Syria and annexed the territory as another province. Judea also was taken by the Romans and added to the general domain.

From the time of Pompey Palestine was under Roman domination. Julius Caesar, Mark Antony, and Octavian, who became

---

[7] *Vide supra,* p. 32.

Caesar Augustus, successively took an indirect interest in the province of Judea. The rivalry between Julius Caesar and Pompey ended in exile and death for the latter in 47 b.c., shortly before Caesar reached Egypt in pursuit of him. Antipater, who was the *de facto* ruler of Judea, quickly attached himself to Caesar's cause, and by his aid Pompey's supporters were speedily crushed. As a recompense, Caesar supported Antipater against the Hasmoneans by making him procurator of Judea.

The assassination of Caesar in 44 b.c. enabled Cassius to take over Syria and Palestine. He demanded heavy tribute from Judea and Galilee. Herod, the son of Antipater, quickly responded and obtained the favor of the Romans, while Malichus, an influential Jew who supported Hyrcanus the high priest, delayed. As a result, Herod rose in the estimation of the Roman authority. Malichus, prompted by jealousy, succeeded in poisoning Antipater, Herod's father, and was himself assassinated a few months later with Herod's connivance. The rule of Herod was firmly established by Roman consent.

In 42 b.c. Cassius and his partner Brutus were defeated at Philippi by Antony and Octavian, the grandnephew of Julius Caesar. Antony assumed command of the eastern provinces. Remembering previous contacts with Antipater, Antony made Herod and his brother tetrarchs of Judea, despite loud protests from the Jews. Antony's friendship with Herod remained unbroken until the rise of Octavian. His position was confirmed again when, in 40 b.c., he fled to Rome after a revolt in Judea aided by the Parthians. Antony and Octavian declared him king of Judea and formally deposited the decree in the archives of Rome. Aided by Roman troops, Herod regained possession of Galilee and Judea.

Antony's defeat at the battle of Actium in 31 b.c. convinced Herod that another change of allegiance was expedient. Deserting Antony, he visited Octavian at Rhodes and informed him that whereas he had been the friend of Antony, he would henceforth serve Octavian with the same loyalty he had shown to his rival. He expressed dissatisfaction with Antony's reaction to his advice and assured Octavian of his hearty co-operation. When Octavian invaded Egypt, Herod provided him with funds and supplies, receiving in return the cities of Jericho, Gadara, and Samaria, with the territories of Gaza, Joppa, and Strato's Tower, which later became Caesarea.

Through the co-operation of Herod, Rome's gradual encroachment on the East finally crystallized into complete control. Although Palestine remained nominally independent until his death, its real sovereignty lay in the hands of the Roman legate of Syria, and later in the command of the procurators. Throughout the period of the New Testament the shadow of Rome fell over the land, and under its oppression and protection Christianity was born and flourished.

The Herods

The active rule of the Hasmoneans came to an end with Alexandra and her sons. Upon her death, Antipater retired to Edom, where he busied himself with fomenting intrigue among the Jewish rulers. He persuaded Hyrcanus that Aristobulus was plotting to kill him, and bargained with Aretas, the Nabatean king, to replace Hyrcanus upon the throne. Aristobulus was besieged in Jerusalem, but Scaurus, the Roman quaestor, came to his aid and compelled Aretas to withdraw. Aristobulus, thus relieved, in turn attacked Aretas' troops near Jericho and inflicted upon them a resounding defeat. Antipater's plans were upset completely, and once again he retired to Edom to await another opportunity.

Antipater soon had occasion to improve his fortune. Pompey, having concluded his eastern campaign by conquering Armenia, approached Damascus with the intention of pacifying Syria and Palestine. Antipater journeyed northward to bring official greetings, and so did Nicodemus, who was Aristobulus' spokesman. Antipater was shrewd enough to let Nicodemus present his case first. He accused Scaurus and Gabinius, two of Pompey's lieutenants, of having attempted to extract bribes from Aristobulus. The accusation may have been true, but it did not ingratiate Nicodemus with the Romans. Antipater withheld comment until a later occasion, when he accused Aristobulus of robbing the Greek cities. Pompey, evidently more impressed by Antipater than by Aristobulus, deferred action and said that he would investigate the affairs of Palestine after he had settled accounts with the Nabateans.

Pompey, Antipater, and Aristobulus began the journey to Jerusalem, attended by their respective retinues. At the Sea of Galilee Aristobulus left the others and withdrew into the fortress of Alexandrium. Pompey, instead of proceeding south toward Petra, digressed to Alexandrium and demanded that Aristobulus abandon the fortress and surrender it with his other strongholds. Under duress he acceded, but quickly retreated to Jerusalem. Unwilling to leave Aristobulus in command of the city, Pompey demanded that he surrender. Aristobulus refused to open the gates, whereupon Pompey besieged the city and cut the aqueduct, depriving the city of water. After two months Jerusalem was captured, its walls were leveled, and thousands of its captives were sold into slavery. Hyrcanus was proclaimed high priest of the nation; Aristobulus, his two sons, Alexander and Antigonus, his daughters, and his uncle were carried off to Rome. Antipater remained the dominant figure in Judea.

Antipater found himself in a precarious situation. His opposition to Aristobulus had made him unpopular with the Jewish nationalists who had lost their independence, and he had brought the Romans into Palestine, who were quite as likely to appropriate his territory as that of anyone else. He had to maintain a difficult equilibrium between the Jews who hated him because he was an Idumean and the Romans who distrusted his loyalty.

During the hostilities that prevailed in Palestine from 63 to 48 B.C. Antipater constantly adhered to the Roman side. By devious diplomatic manipulations he succeeded in averting crises within his domains, and he curried the favor of the Roman governors and military leaders, among whom were Mark Antony and Gabinius, the general under whom Mark Antony served. In an invasion of Egypt Antipater provided rations and water for Mark Antony's squadrons, and Antony remembered the favor. He and Antipater's son, then about sixteen years old, became close friends and remained so until Antony's death in Egypt.

During the years of this period the Hasmoneans made numerous but futile attempts at independence. On each occasion they lost some strength, while the vassal kings, like Antipater, became more powerful. In the war between Caesar and Pompey for the sovereignty of the Roman world, Antipater supported Pompey, but when the latter was killed in 48 B.C., and when Caesar invaded Egypt, Antipater transferred his allegiance to the conqueror. He helped Caesar in his Egyptian campaigns, and succeeded in enlisting the aid of the Jewish settlements near Alexandria. Caesar conquered Egypt and, after a pleasant vacation in the company of Egypt's Queen Cleopatra, set out on a new campaign. He conquered Pontus, and upon returning to Antioch he established Antipater's hegemony in Palestine by making him procurator. Hyrcanus he confirmed in the office of high priest.

Antipater thus became the virtual king of Palestine. To satisfy the rate of Roman taxation he exacted one quarter of the total annual wheat crop in addition to the tithe that was paid to the priesthood. He reconstructed the walls of Jerusalem, for the city had been defenseless since Pompey's siege. Because Hyrcanus was becoming old and feeble, Antipater proposed that his son Phasael be made prefect of Jerusalem, and his next son, Herod, governor of Galilee. Hyrcanus gave his consent, and the rulership of Palestine passed officially into the hands of an Idumean.

Herod the Great

Herod at this time was twenty-six years old, full of vigor and ambition, a skilled athlete and soldier, charming in manners and capable in statecraft. He was a subtle diplomat, a passionate lover, and a ruthless enemy. He could be both intensely loyal and insanely jealous. The conflicts of his character were numerous and his actions were often inexplicably impulsive. At the outset of his career Herod had to combat the jealousy of the Sanhedrin, the highest council of the Jewish nation. On the ground that he had executed some Jews without official consent, the court summoned Herod to trial. They were about to demand the death penalty when Hyrcanus called for adjournment and secretly urged Herod to leave the country. He took refuge with the Roman procurator, Sextus Caesar, who gave him the governorship of Coele-Syria and Samaria, and sent him back to Galilee. Sextus' action cemented Herod's connection with Rome and made him lean more heavily than ever on the imperial authority.

The civil strife in the Roman world between the factions of Julius Caesar and Pompey produced violent repercussions in the East. Sextus Caesar was assassinated by one of Pompey's followers, Caecilius Bassus, who seized command and allied himself with native Arab princes and with the Parthians. Julius Caesar, fearing the Parthian intervention, promptly dispatched troops to check Bassus' threat. Antipater sent reinforcements to aid the Caesarean party. A few months later Julius Caesar was murdered in the Roman Forum, and one of his assassins, Cassius, became ruler of the East. He effected a compromise with Bassus and imposed heavy taxes on Palestine to pay for his campaign.

Herod co-operated with Cassius and quickly raised the amount apportioned to him. Hyrcanus, in Jerusalem, temporized and delayed. Cassius retaliated for the delay by selling four Judean towns into slavery. Antipater, by providing the money he desired, dissuaded him from further violence, only to fall a victim to poisoning by one of Hyrcanus' friends. Hyrcanus evidently feared Herod's growing power and desired alliances that would hold him in check. Herod, realizing that the Hasmoneans would always be a threat to him, resolved to end the danger by marriage. He took for his second wife Mariamne, the granddaughter of Aristobulus, who had been executed by Pompey at Antioch, and on her mother's side the granddaughter of Hyrcanus himself. By this politic stroke Herod hoped that he would become acceptable to the Jewish public, who doted on the Hasmoneans, and that he would win the full support of Hyrcanus.

The Nabatean rock-cut temple el-Khazne in Petra. Notice size of human figure in the doorway in relation to the temple. (Matson Photo Service.)

When Cassius and Brutus were defeated by Antony and Octavian at the battle of Philippi, Antony assumed control of Asia. The Jewish leaders waited for Antony to denounce Herod as a usurping tyrant who had seized their country by deceit, using Hyrcanus as a tool. Herod's bribes and Antony's previous friendship with him won the day. Antony confirmed Herod and Phasael as tetrarchs, giving to them the jurisdiction of Judea.

The deep ravine of Petra, showing the temple el-Khazne at the right.
(Matson Photo Service.)

Antigonus, the rival of Hyrcanus, summoned aid from the Parthians. By a ruse, Pacorus, the Parthian commander, persuaded Phasael to accompany him to the Parthian king in order to perfect negotiations between them. Phasael learned of a plot against him but refused to desert Hyrcanus. The two were placed under arrest, while the Parthians attempted to capture Herod in the same way. Herod escaped to Idumea with Mariamne, his fiancée, and her mother. He left them with a garrison in the fortress of Masada while he removed to Petra.

Hyrcanus and Phasael were handed over to Antigonus, who became king. Hyrcanus was mutilated so that he could no longer be priest; Phasael, according to one account, committed suicide.

Herod was refused aid by the Nabatean king of Petra. Having learned of his brother's death, he proceeded to Alexandria. Cleopatra, hoping to use Herod as a tool, offered him the generalship of an expedition, but he refused and sailed for Rome. He begged Antony for aid against Antigonus. Octavian took his part and convened the Senate, to whom he presented Herod. The Senate appointed him king and sent him back to his kingdom with official approval.

In the meantime Antigonus had besieged Herod's family in the fortress of Masada, but the Roman general Ventidius, attacking Antigonus, had distracted him sufficiently so that the siege was unsuccessful. Herod, returning from Rome, landed at Ptolemais. In co-operation with the Roman forces he captured Joppa, rescued his friends and family at Masada, and marched on Jerusalem. Throughout the winter and without the aid of the Romans, who

The remains of a Roman-style amphitheater which has been excavated at Petra. The theater, like the other buildings in Petra, was carved out of the red sandstone, and has eroded considerably through the years. (Courtesy Prof. B. Van Elderen.)

The upper portion of the temple ed Deir. The human figure standing in front of the cupola at the highest part of the temple indicates its size. (Courtesy Prof. B. Van Elderen.)

had given themselves to pillaging and idleness, Herod recovered Idumea, Samaria, and Galilee. He cleared the bandits from Galilee and went to join Antony, who was conducting a campaign on the Euphrates. By assisting Antony in the capture of Samosata he ensured his friendship with the Romans.

Herod had instructed his brother Joseph to refrain from offensive warfare while he was away. Disregarding Herod's instructions, Joseph attacked Antigonus, and was defeated with heavy losses while he himself lost his life. Herod learned of this calamity while he was in Antioch. He marched into Galilee, drove back Antigonus' army, and decapitated Pappus, the general who had killed his brother. He besieged Jerusalem, which he took in five months. Antigonus was captured and Sossius, the Roman general collaborating with Herod, took him away in chains.

The mounting tension between Antony and Octavian posed a diplomatic dilemma for Herod. If he remained loyal to Antony, he would be championing a lost cause and would probably forfeit

A view from the Shechem Road of the Arab village of Sabastiyeh, the site of ancient Sebaste, a town built by Herod the Great on the ruins of Samaria, the capital of the Northern Kingdom, to honor Augustus. (Matson Photo Service.)

both his head and his kingdom. If he deserted to Octavian, he would break a friendship of many years. The decision was made for him by Cleopatra, Antony's consort, who desired to gain control of Herod's realm. She embroiled him in a war with the Arabs who routed his army and captured his camp. His officers had been too rash and had laid themselves open to attack. Herod succeeded in

The Herodium, six miles south of Bethlehem. Herod the Great built an artificial top on this hill and built a castle there, the remains of which can be seen in this picture. (Courtesy Prof. B. Van Elderen.)

restoring order and finally broke the Arab resistance. When he returned from his expedition, he found that Antony and Cleopatra had been beaten at the battle of Actium. Acting swiftly but shrewdly, Herod instantly surrendered himself and his kingdom to Octavian, acknowledging his defeat and stating that he had tried to dissuade Antony from his infatuation with Cleopatra. Octavian, won over by Herod's frankness, confirmed his status as king of Judea. Herod entertained him when he visited Egypt and furnished him with troops and supplies for his campaign. Octavian added to Herod's realm the region of Trachonitis and the adjacent district of Batanea and Auranitis. Ten years later he made Herod procurator of Syria and gave him also the territory between Trachonitis and Galilee.

Having thus achieved a measure of peace, Herod undertook a vast building program. In the eighteenth year of his reign (20 B.C.) he began the reconstruction of the Temple. He enlarged the site by building a new retaining wall of huge trimmed stones, some of which constitute the "wailing wall" of the Jews in Jerusalem. He rebuilt the fortress adjacent to the Temple and named it Antonia in

Ruins of a temple built by Herod the Great in Sebaste. (Courtesy Prof. B. Van Elderen.)

Remains of Roman columns in Caesarea on the Mediterranean, a town built by Herod at the site of Strato's Tower, which he was given by Octavian in gratitude for his assistance during Octavian's campaign in Egypt. (Courtesy Israel Information Services.)

Antony's honor. In addition, he constructed a palace for himself consisting of two buildings more beautiful than the Temple. The latter was unfinished even in Jesus' day (John 2:20). He enlarged the city of Samaria and built in it a temple to Augustus Caesar, to whom he also dedicated a white marble shrine at Panium, near the source of the Jordan. He constructed a summer palace at Jericho. At a town on the coast called Strato's Tower he founded the city of Caesarea, and formed an artificial harbor by breakwaters surmounted by towers. The city itself contained an amphitheater, a hippodrome, a theater, temples, public squares, and colonnades covering acres of ground that still await the spade of the archaeologist. He fortified his borders with castles and strongholds and gave

The podium of a Roman temple at Caesarea. This temple has been tentatively identified as the temple of Augustus, built by Herod. Notice the large stone blocks with the marginal draft characteristic of Herodian masonry. (Courtesy Prof. B. Van Elderen.)

public works to many cities outside of his own realm, including Antioch, Rhodes, and Pergamum.

The last years of Herod's life were plagued with frustration and suspicion. He had sent Antipater, his eldest son by his first wife Doris, out of the capital, retaining with him the two sons by Mariamne, Alexander and Aristobulus, who were educated at Rome. His love for Mariamne was passionate, but she hated him because he had been responsible for the death of her grandfather Hyrcanus and of her brother Jonathan. Herod was so intensely jealous of his throne that the right of succession which had belonged to Hyrcanus and Jonathan as members of the Hasmonean house was equivalent to a death warrant.

On his departure to Rome to interview Antony he had consigned Mariamne to the care of his brother-in-law Joseph, instructing him to kill Mariamne if he should not return. Joseph disclosed the secret to Mariamne, who chided Herod with it when he returned. His mother Cypros and his sister Salome hated Mariamne and accused her of adultery. Upon learning that Joseph had betrayed his secret, Herod was sure that he had seduced Mariamne. Incensed beyond reason, he gave orders that she should be executed. After a considerable delay because of public protest, he put her to death.

From that time Herod was not the same man. Remorse drove him to the edge of insanity and ultimately brought on disease that hastened his end. Mariamne's two sons were naturally resentful of the injustice to their mother and were at times indiscreet enough to give voice to their sentiments. Herod recalled Antipater, who lost no time in taking full advantage of the situation. He flattered his father and repeatedly slandered his half brothers so that they steadily declined in Herod's estimation.

Herod finally took Alexander to court in Rome and accused him before Caesar of attempting to poison him. Alexander defended himself so ably that Caesar acquitted him and effected a reconciliation. Upon reaching home Herod confirmed Antipater's first right to the throne but declared all three sons kings and commended them to the populace.

The reconciliation was more apparent than real. The rift between Antipater and his brothers had not been closed. Although Antipater

Caesarea on the Mediterranean, one of the many cities built by Herod the Great. The large stone blocks and marginal draft around them are characteristic of Herodian masonry. (Courtesy Prof. B. Van Elderen.)

did not dare to make direct accusations, he constantly twisted the remarks of Alexander in reporting them to his father. Alexander and Aristobulus, goaded by the constant insinuations of Antipater, were not always as cautious as they might have been. Alarmed by the reports of treachery which informers brought to him and scarcely knowing what to believe, Herod instituted a spy system that only complicated an already confused situation. In desperation he finally arrested and tortured Alexander and a number of his friends. Some of the latter professed that Alexander had plotted to assassinate his father and to flee to Rome — a story which Josephus characterized as "improbable."[8]

Alexander was rescued from his perilous position by his father-in-law Archelaus, who visited Herod and persuaded him that Alexander's advisers, not he, were guilty of a plot. Once again the tension was eased, but not cured. Shortly afterwards a Greek, Eurycles, visited the court. After discovering the quarrels that were latent, he lost no time in fomenting them to further his own interests. In exchange for pay from Antipater, he pretended friendship with Alexander and Aristobulus and betrayed their grievances to Antipater. Finally he accused them directly to Herod. Frightened by the mounting intrigues of the court and believing only the worst reports, Herod put both his sons in chains and petitioned Caesar for the right to execute them.

The emperor recommended trial before a court of provincial governors and relatives, which convened at Berytus (Beirut). The council was divided and did not render a clear verdict. Herod withheld action until an impetuous friend of Alexander threatened Herod with a potential revolt of the army if the young princes were executed. The officers charged with disloyalty were beaten to death, and Alexander and Aristobulus were strangled at Caesarea.

The death of Alexander and Aristobulus left the way clear for Antipater to succeed his father, but his intrigues finally recoiled upon him. The death of Pheroras, Herod's brother, was open to suspicion, since some of his freedmen complained to the king that he had been poisoned. Investigation revealed that Antipater's mother, together with Antipater, Pheroras, and others had feared that they would be Herod's next victims. By a circuitous inquiry Herod learned that Antipater had secured a deadly poison from Egypt which he had planned to administer to his father, and that he had forged letters intended to incriminate his brothers Archelaus and Philip. When Antipater returned to Caesarea from Rome his father gave him a cool reception and instructed him to prepare

---

[8] *Wars of the Jews* i. 24. 8.

for trial. He made an emotional appeal, but the accusations against him were strong and he was remanded to prison.

The emotional tension and frustration of these dismal years reacted disastrously upon Herod. Mad with suspicion and grief, he rapidly deteriorated physically and mentally. He was almost seventy years of age, broken in spirit, racked by disease, and tortured with doubts and remorse. A low fever, accompanied by dropsy, inflammation of the abdomen, and asthma afflicted him; death was not far distant. He attempted suicide but was restrained by his cousin. Believing that he had died, the retainers of the palace began to wail. Antipater, hearing the sound in his prison and thinking that Herod was dead, endeavored to bribe the jailer to free him. The jailer reported Antipater's action, and Herod in a final fit of rage ordered his execution. He amended his will by appointing as his successor Archelaus, his eldest son, and by making Antipas tetrarch.

Five days later he died. Few men of his era had greater potential for good, or a darker record for evil. Herod was an outstanding athlete, soldier, and builder. He was passionately devoted to his family, yet unspeakably depraved and cruel. He was responsible for the death of his favorite wife Mariamne, of her grandfather, and for the execution of three of his sons, to say nothing of the large number of lesser persons who fell victims to his suspicion or anger. He changed loyalties with the wheel of political fortunes and succeeded in making himself thoroughly mistrusted and hated by the general populace. The Temple which he built, the cities which he founded, and the political system which he organized under the aegis of Rome became the cradle of Christianity; for Jesus of Nazareth, its founder, "was born in Bethlehem of Judea in the days of Herod the king" (Matt. 2:1). Matthew's account of Herod's reaction to the visit of the Magi is quite in keeping with his known temperament, and the butchery of a few infants in Bethlehem by Herod's guards would, in comparison with his greater crimes, have passed almost unnoticed.

With the death of Herod a new era was born. The semi-independence of Judea was virtually ended, for Herod had made the assignation of his realm subject to the will of Caesar Augustus, who partitioned the domain as he saw fit. Although Rome had been the real ruler of Palestine since Pompey's invasion in 63 B.C., it now asserted its sovereignty more directly and, as the Gospels declare, the Jewish people were compelled to admit that they had no king but Caesar.

Seleucids, Ptolemies, Hasmoneans, Herods, and Caesars — all made their contributions to the prologue of history that introduced the coming of Christ. Greek culture and language had permeated the Jewish and Aramaic world, bringing a new familiarity and linkage with the Western life and thought. The Hasmoneans, descendants of the valiant and patriotic Maccabees, had revived dreams of Jewish independence, had infused a warrior spirit into the nation that had been in subjection since the Exile, and had promoted zeal for the Law. The Idumean Herods, alien by blood but Jewish by religion, had re-established the Temple with its ritual and sacrifies, and under Roman suzerainty had given Palestine comparative peace after the bitter strife under the Hasmoneans. Greek culture, Jewish nationalism, and Roman justice prepared the way for the New Testament revelation.

3

The Cultural Tensions

T HE WORLD OF THE FIRST CENTURY WAS A WELTER OF CON-
flicting cultures. Like the rivers which ran into the Mediterranean Sea from all sides, pouring into it their sediment and
feeding its waters, so the many peoples comprised within the constantly expanding domain of Rome brought into it all their cultural
contributions. Africans, Teutons, Greeks, Jews, Parthians, and
Phrygians mingled in the provinces and cities and shared their
national heritages with the Latin people.

The combination of social and religious forces under one political
rule produced a unique setting for the birth of Christianity. Although the gospel is essentially independent of any human origin, the
media through which it was expressed and the influences that affected
its interpretation can be traced back to the philosophies and theolo-
gies of the contemporary period. These in turn were the products
of the peoples from whom they sprang and can be understood best in
terms of the cumulative historical processes and conflicts that cul-
minated during the first century of the Christian era.

Three great types of culture prevailed in the empire: Judaism,
Hellenism, and Roman imperialism. Judaism provided the roots of
Christianity; Hellenism, the intellectual soil in which it grew; and
imperialism, the protection that opened the field of its growth.
Paradoxically, these three cultures became Christianity's bitterest ene-
mies, for Judaism regarded it as a pernicious heresy, Hellenism as

67

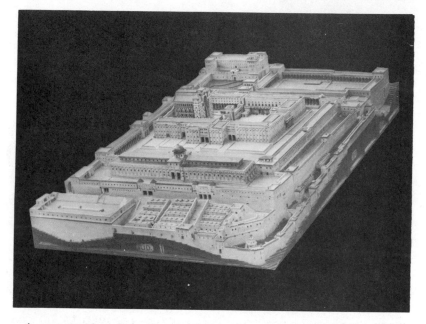

A reconstruction of the Temple of Herod the Great, which took more than forty years to build (John 2:20). (Matson Photo Service.)

philosophical nonsense, and Roman imperialism as impractical weakness. Each of these three conflicted with the other two, differing both by ancestry and by viewpoint; yet together they formed the matrix in which the Christian church was formed.

Judaism

Until the destruction of the Temple in A.D. 70 the focus of Judaism remained in Jerusalem, although the Dispersion had carried Jews into almost every city of the empire. The Temple, with its organized priesthood and regular ritual, provided the center to which all devout Jews gave their allegiance and to which they made their pilgrimages at Passover and Pentecost. Josephus states that at a Passover in the time of Nero about 2,700,000 Jews were present in Jerusalem.[1] His estimate, based on the number of sacrifices, may have been high, but even with a drastic reduction the figures attest a large Jewish population in the other cities and a continuing interest in the religious life of Jerusalem. Both within and without Palestine Jewish faith and Jewish customs flourished.

[1] *Wars of the Jews* vi. 20. 3.

The Jewish people, despite severance from their ancestral land, retained a solidarity of religion and culture that preserved their distinctive quality. Although they possessed neither an independent government nor, after A.D. 70, a common center of worship, they preserved in their Law and tradition a stabilizing body of teaching that fixed their theology and their customs. While they adapted themselves to their environment by conformity in language and in dress, they perpetuated their worship through the synagogues and their racial identity through the careful education of their children. They were never completely absorbed by the Roman world. In every sizable city a colony of Jews existed. Some of their groups were large, as in Alexandria or Antioch; others were small, as in Philippi, where there were too few to support a synagogue (Acts 16:13, 16). Wherever they gathered, they constituted a block of resistance to polytheism and a center from which Jewish lore and ethics were disseminated among the population.

Aerial view of Jerusalem and environs, taken from the southeast corner of the city. The large area in the center foreground is the "Temple area"; the site where the Temple stood is now covered by Haram esh-Sherif, the Dome of the Rock, located in the center. (Matson Photo Service.)

In Palestine the Jewish population was fiercely loyal to the traditions of the fathers. The catastrophe of the Babylonian captivity uprooted the Jews from their native soil and compelled them to substitute the study of the Law for the ritual which had been destroyed. The families that returned in the Restoration under Ezra and Nehemiah were the loyal remnant who valued their homeland above their own ease and comfort, and who consequently were staunch defenders of the Law. The tensions of the Maccabean rebellion strengthened their resolution to preserve their own worship and customs rather than to accept the paganism which the Seleucids tried to force upon them. The Hasidim, the pietistic element in Judaism, remained suspicious of any attempt to introduce alien philosophies into their society, and they obstinately resisted all tendencies toward Hellenization.

There were, however, segments of Judaism that were not strictly devoted to the Temple. Cullmann has observed that the Qumran scrolls seemingly indicate that the members of that desert community maintained a strict worship and obedience to the Law quite separate from the rest of Judaism, and that they paid little attention to the official national religion. He even suggests that "Hellenist" did not refer exclusively to a Jew who spoke Greek rather than Aramaic, but rather to a Jew who lived like a Greek.[2]

Josephus states that as early as the beginning of the second century before Christ there were Jews who adopted the ideals and practices of paganism, and whose observance of the Law was very broad. Some went so far as to repudiate the outward signs of Judaism and to identify themselves completely with Gentiles. The divergences within Judaism were numerous, and it is possible that some of those who were only loosely attached to the Temple were at the outset attracted to faith in Christ. Stephen and his colleagues, among whom were some of the strongest early evangelists, may have belonged to this group (Acts 6:1-6). Stephen's speech indicates that he did not conceive of God's presence as restricted to a building, and that he laid greater emphasis on obedience to God than on ritual (7:44-53).

Whether, then, Judaism be interpreted in terms of strict adherence to the Temple ritual or by the Hellenists and Samaritans who were independent of the Temple, it was a preparation for the gospel of Christ both directly and indirectly. The God of the Old Testament is the God of the New Testament — holy, just, merciful, self-revealing, and loving. The great doctrines of the Old Testament such as creation, the fall of man, holiness, and the coming of a Messiah

---

[2] Oscar Cullmann, "Beginnings of Christianity" in *The Scrolls and the New Testament*, pp. 26, 27.

were incorporated into Christianity and were more fully developed. The synagogue was the platform for early evangelistic preaching, and many of the first converts came from the Jewish attendants and from the proselytes who had abandoned their original paganism in search of a purer and more satisfying faith. On many of these proselytes the legal system of Judaism had only a slight hold, for they demurred at circumcision and full commitment to all the ceremonial requirements that accompanied the observance of the Law. The sentiments of these people were probably reflected in the controversy over circumcision that arose in the Christian church late in the first half of the first century, and that precipitated the council of Jerusalem in A.D. 48/49. While the majority of Christians who reacted against legalism may have been direct converts from paganism, it is equally probable that some of them had first become acquainted with the gospel through the medium of a Judaism which extended to them a positive revelation that was lacking in the vague and irrelevant legends of their gods.

Judaism, however, was in certain respects irreconcilable with the predominant cultures of the early empire. Fiercely intolerant of polytheism, it seemed ridiculous to men who believed that a multiplicity of gods insured safety; for if one god could protect a devotee, two gods would be even more potent. The Jewish adherence to the Ten Commandments stamped them as morally different from the rest of the world who regarded them as intransigent fanatics. To the Gentiles a pinch of incense offered on the altar of some god was insignificant; to a Jew it would be blasphemy, since only God is worthy of worship. The rigid loyalty of the Jews to God and to the Law impressed their contemporaries as foolish intolerance, and their peculiar habits of life separated them from the general current of civilization.

The Jew differed sharply from the Greek in mental attitude as well as in religion. His thinking was channeled by the Law and was largely confined to a development of the Torah's implications. The Greek maintained a spirit of free inquiry stimulated by an insatiable intellectual curiosity which impelled him to probe all aspects of the world and to offer new hypotheses concerning its nature and laws. The Jews were religious, the Greeks, scientific in their outlook; and despite mutual tolerance, they never found a lasting union of faith.

Hellenism

As a result of the conquests of Alexander the Great in the fourth century B.C., Hellenism prevailed east of Greece. The *lingua franca* of the eastern Mediterranean world was Greek, the cities were built according to Greek plans, and the rulers descended from Alexander's generals and officers were also Greek. Hellenistic thought and learning had penetrated the West also. The better educated Romans used Greek as a second language and sent their sons to Greek universities, such as Athens and Rhodes. Greek literature, drama, and art became the models for their own production. In the field of philosophy the Greek tradition prevailed, for the Romans did not possess the speculative type of mind that produced abstract systems of thought.

The Greeks, being individualists, never built a cohesive commonwealth. The city-states of the Peloponnesus and of Asia Minor were incapable of federating in permanent alliances or of combining into a single enduring empire. Insofar as the domain of Alexander seems to be an exception to this principle, one must concede that he, though Greek by education and ideals, was a Macedonian by temperament. His dominion might have crystallized into another Rome had he lived to administer it, and had his successors been as able as he. Although the Ptolemies and the Seleucids created kingdoms that lasted for several centuries, they did so because they possessed the military power to dominate their subjects rather than because they evoked from them a co-operation based on patriotism. Hellenism was not endowed with Rome's organizing power. The Greek democracy was brittle and, even in the heyday of Athens, it could not build a structure that would outlast two generations. The reason for this lack of cohesiveness was the essential independence of the Hellenistic mind, which lacked both the religious unity of the Jew and the military discipline of the Roman. Whereas every Jew, insofar as he was a loyal adherent to the Law of Moses, held the same essential view of God that his neighbors did, the Greek might worship one deity in his home city and another elsewhere if he changed his residence. Even if the same god were worshiped in both cities, its characterization might be different in the two places. Conflict in religion did not trouble him; he overcame it by syncretism, which allowed for a maximum of variety within the general concept of religion. The result was that each city-state was a little island, both religiously and politically. Interested chiefly in pursuing the welfare and concerns of their immediate group, the Greeks never bound themselves together either by a common religion or by a common enterprise.

Although the Romans differed little from the Greeks in their religious diversity, they developed a consciousness of empire that served to unite the varied peoples of their realm. The civil wars of the two centuries before Christ had exhausted the resources and the nerve of the republic, and the inhabitants longed for peace. The emergence of the principate under Augustus, with the accompanying deification of the emperor by many of the provincials, created a sense of oneness in a common cause organized around one central leader. Despite the dissatisfaction with subsequent emperors and the turbulent centuries in which the throne was sold to the highest bidder, the sense that Rome was one was never abandoned. The contending factions strove for control of the one state rather than seceding to form a new organization. Hellenism thus differed from both Hebrew and Roman culture in its insistent individualism.

The influence of Hellenism, however, did not depend on political sovereignty but upon the penetrativeness of its ideas and the lure of its culture. The Greek conquest of the Near East left an ineffaceable imprint upon the nations from the Aegean Sea to the Indus River, even though the Macedonian empire did not long survive the death of its founder. The influence of Hellenistic art affected the contemporary Brahman and Buddhist sculpture and painting of India and can be traced in some of the early Buddhist art of Japan. Greek words were incorporated into the vocabularies of the Indian and Persian people; Alexander's name is disguised in the syllables of cities like Secunderabad and Kandahar, and the legends of his conquest are still common tales in Oriental lore. In Palestine the Greek language obtained a firm foothold, and under the rule of the Seleucids Greek customs, Greek buildings, and Greek habits of thought became common.

The spirit of Hellenism underlies much of the New Testament. In spite of Jewish origin, the earliest members of the church were deeply imbued with Greek culture. Eleven of Jesus' twelve disciples had spent most of their lives in settlements near the Sea of Galilee, around which lay the Greek cities of the Decapolis. They had constant contact with Gentiles who had immigrated from the West, and they must have been familiar with the language and customs of these residents. The construction which Herod the Great began at Caesarea and Tiberias incorporated much of Greek art and architecture. The inquisitive Hellenic mind was reflected in the request, "We would see Jesus" (John 12:20, 21), reported by John and spoken by Greeks who had come to Jerusalem to participate in the Feast of the Passover. The record does not stipulate whether these were proselytes who had adopted the religion of Israel or whether they were merely casual visitors. In any case, they were distinctly Hellenic in viewpoint.

The wide dispersion of the Jewish people had led to a partial Hellenization of their thinking. Living in the midst of a Greek-speaking populace who scorned to learn their language, they were compelled to become adjusted to the surrounding world if they expected to pursue their business acceptably. Many of them dropped their Jewish names and customs and became thoroughly Hellenized except for their religious faith.

The cities to which the Epistles of Paul, Peter, and John were addressed owed their culture more to a Hellenistic than to a Roman background. For that reason the teaching of the Epistles bears traces of conflict with the general trend of contemporary thought. The materialism of Corinth, the speculative intellectualism of Athens, the superstitious idolatry and demonism of Ephesús, the mysticism of Colosse, the smug indifference of Laodicea are all expressive of some aspect of the Hellenistic attitude. Investigative in disposition, broad in interests, intellectual in its approach, it nevertheless lacked the depth and stamina to create an enduring civilization. Hellenism could not maintain its independence against the hard practical force of an armed state and was consequently absorbed by the military civilization of Rome.

Absorption, however, was not extinction. Within the framework of Rome's superior organization Hellenism persisted and contributed to its hardheaded conquerors the larger part of their aesthetic heritage. Their music, painting, history, literature, poetry, oratory, and sculpture were borrowed from or based on Greek models. The vigorous cadences of Vergil's *Aeneid* were a Latin copy of Homer's flowing hexameters; the numerous temples that filled the Roman cities were built on the models of Athens and Ephesus; and the modes and manners of the patricians were softened by the Greek influence much as the rugged and sometimes crude American manners of the colonial period were affected by the Gallic influence that crept in from the writings and diplomatic contacts following the French Revolution.

Roman Culture

The Roman culture, though inferior to the Greek and largely dependent upon it, was not entirely imitative. In literature the Roman writers developed a terseness and a factual precision that was less ornate than Greek rhetoric but more concise. The poetry of Vergil was not so graceful as Homer's fluid epics, but it was often more arresting in thought and pungent in expression. Latin became the language of barristers and theologians because of its clarity and definiteness; Greek was the tongue of philosophers, historians, artists, and merchants.

Roman sculpture lacked the symmetrical and idealized beauty of Greek carving but was far more realistic and rugged. The Apollo Belvedere was a beautiful ornament representing masculine beauty in general and nobody in particular; the grimacing bust of Vespasian

The Thermae (baths) of Caracalla, on the Appian Way. This magnificent center for recreation and culture, one of hundreds in Rome, was begun in A.D. *206 by Septimius Severus, and finished some thirty years later by Severus Alexander.* (Courtesy Ente Provinciale per il Turismo di Roma.)

Section of the Roman aqueduct in Segovia, Spain, built under Trajan (A.D. *53-117*) *and still in working order until recently.* (H. Armstrong Roberts.)

with the wry humor of its wrinkled eyes and the stubborn vitality of its bull neck doubtlessly portrays with unflattering accuracy the individuality of the blunt and shrewd general who became emperor.

The Romans excelled in engineering. If the baths of Caracalla lacked the studied grace of the Parthenon, they possessed a massiveness that is almost equally impressive. The roads that traversed mountain and plain in every direction from Rome to the utmost frontiers of the empire were so well drained and paved that the remains of many of them are still visible, and some are still in use. The aqueduct in Segovia, Spain, functioned for eighteen centuries and only recently was retired from active service. Rome's practical genius was memorialized in her buildings.

Roman efficiency and resourcefulness became a part of the missionary procedure of the church, and its policy of extension was patterned on the Roman strategy of conquest. As time went on, the church absorbed the organizational pattern of the empire until its papal hierarchy became the logical successor of the absolutism of the Caesars.

To each of these three cultures the Christian church owes some of its characteristics, though its genius is not the product of any one of them. Judaism provided the revelation in the Scriptures, through which God made Himself known, and gave the initial training to men like Saul of Tarsus, who, after their conversion, interpreted the Law and the Prophets in terms of Jesus, the Messiah. The morality of Judaism was perpetuated in the standards of conduct upheld by the church. The assiduous study of the Law which Judaism main-

Another view of the Thermae of Caracalla. Caracalla, emperor from 211-217, was the first emperor to use these baths, although he neither began their construction nor finished it. (Courtesy Ente Provinciale per il Turismo di Roma.)

tained was by the church turned into the study of their own Scriptures. The Greek ability to build a philosophic system from an
axiom by means of deduction supplied the means of constructing a
theology out of the doctrinal teachings of Jesus and the propositional
declarations of Scripture. The order and system of Rome permeated
the atmosphere of the church, making it aware of its need for
organization and direction. The warring cultures found a common
ground in Christ. No outward change was visible in the faces,
practices, or dress of the Christians, yet there was a perceptible
alteration in their behavior, for they began to build a culture of
their own almost as soon as they professed conversion. Hebrew
theology, Greek speculative thinking, and Roman jurisprudence
united in the new society which the gospel created.

4

The Jewish Heritage

THE FOUR CENTURIES WHICH ELAPSED BETWEEN THE TIME OF
the Exile (606-586 B.C.) and the rise of the Maccabees
(168 B.C.) brought a radical change in the religious life of the
Jewish people. Prior to the Exile the fundamental monotheism
taught by Moses (Deut. 6:4ff.) and the essential ethic of the Ten
Commandments had been obscured by the infiltration of foreign
cults. The introduction of foreign shrines into Jerusalem by the
alien wives of Solomon (I Kings 11:4-8), the establishment of bull
worship in the northern kingdom under the revolt of Jeroboam
(I Kings 12:28-33), and the later corruption from the propagation
of Baalism by Jezebel of Tyre (I Kings 16:31-34) and by Manasseh
of Judah (II Kings 21:1-8) had perverted the uniqueness and purity
of the revelation of Jehovah. Although the reformation under Josiah
just preceding the Captivity had checked the declension and had
renewed to some degree the knowledge of the Law, it came too late
to arrest the downward trend of the national life, or to reverse the
current of doom (II Kings 22:14-20). The invasion of Palestine
by Nebuchadnezzar, king of Babylon, in 605 B.C. and the final destruction of the city twenty years later swept away the old culture
with its evils and compelled the people to seek a reaffirmation of
their national faith. They were confronted with the choice of revival or extinction.

79

The conquest of Palestine began at the battle of Carchemish early in 605 B.C., when the Babylonian army under Nebuchadnezzar, the crown prince, defeated the Egyptians and their northern allies. Nebuchadnezzar's campaign was interrupted by his father's death, which recalled him to Babylonia, so that his subjugation of the land was probably hasty and incomplete. Shortly afterward in September of 605 B.C. he was appointed king and received tribute from the rulers of Palestine, including Jehoiakim of Judah. The Babylonians occupied Judah briefly and deported a few of the well-educated scions of the royal house whom they intended to make into liaison officers (II Kings 24:1; Dan. 1:1-7).

The Babylonian Chronicle records that in 601 B.C. the Egyptians inflicted severe defeat on the Babylonians, which encouraged Judah to rebel against Nebuchadnezzar and to ally itself with Egypt. In 598-597 B.C. Nebuchadnezzar again invaded Palestine because of Jehoiakim's revolt, captured the city, plundered the Temple,[1] and removed ten thousand captives, including the aristocracy and all of the skilled craftsmen in the land (II Kings 24:10-17). He deposed Jehoiachin, the reigning ruler, and took him captive to Babylon, placing the rule of the country under Mattaniah, Jehoiachin's uncle, whose name he changed to Zedekiah. Nine years later Zedekiah rebelled against Nebuchadnezzar, who took swift vengeance. He besieged Jerusalem again and after a year and a half overcame its resistance. He burned the Temple, broke down the fortified walls, and deported the citizens, leaving only the poorest of the rural population to cultivate the land (II Kings 25:8-12). The nation ceased to exist politically.

The termination of the independent commonwealth did not mean the extinction of the people. Sobered by the calamity that had overtaken them, and stimulated to new zeal by the competition of surrounding paganism, the exiles resisted assimilation into the culture of Babylon. They had been given freedom to settle in communities where they could maintain a social and religious life of their own, so that they were able to perpetuate their own customs and faith. Although some probably abandoned their separatism and were absorbed into the Babylonian population, the majority persisted in the worship of Jehovah and renounced completely the perversions which had prevailed in the latter days of the divided kingdom. When permission was given by Cyrus of Persia for the captives to return to Judea, not all of them availed themselves of the privilege, but those who removed to Palestine perpetuated their national traditions and contributed in large measure to the creation

---

[1] See D. A. Wiseman, *Illustrations from Biblical Archaeology*, pp. 69, 70.

of the theological literature found in the Palestinian and Babylonian Talmuds.

The Return to Palestine

The main body of Judaism that affected the rise of the Christian church descended from the exiles who returned to Judea in 536 B.C. under the leadership of Zerubbabel, a lineal descendant of the kings of Judah. Sheshbazzar, possibly Zerubbabel's uncle, was appointed governor of the colony (Ezra 1:8, 11; 5:14); Joshua, the high priest, conducted the ritual worship; the prophets Haggai and Zechariah became the popular preachers. The rebuilding of the Temple was begun in the second year after the return from Babylon but was not completed until the twentieth year. Its reconstruction gave back to the nation a center of religious life which persisted until the final destruction of Jerusalem in A.D. 70. This group that repossessed Judea together with their descendants constituted the stable core of Judaism for almost six hundred years. Ezra, the scribe who in the reign of Artaxerxes of Persia (c. 458 B.C.) led another expedition back to Judea (Ezra 7:1-10), helped to consolidate the work which had been begun by those who first returned. He was probably the author of the book which bears his name and also of I and II Chronicles. He interpreted and applied the Law publicly for the people (Neh. 8:1-8). Ezra's teaching and the reforms of Nehemiah which renewed the tithes, checked the abuse of the Sabbath, and prohibited mixed marriages (Neh. 13:10-30) renewed the strict observance of the Law which characterized the Pharisees of Jesus' day.

The Babylonian Exiles

Severed from the Temple and from the environment of their own culture, the exiles in Babylonia were compelled either to conform to the ways of the peoples around them and so to be absorbed into their life, or else steadfastly to reject the Gentiles' standards and to shape a community of their own. For the most part they chose the latter alternative and stubbornly adhered to the Law and to the traditions of their fathers, making only such adjustments as were necessitated by the circumstances. Instead of the Temple they developed the synagogue; instead of sacrifices they substituted observance of the Law; in the place of the priest, the scholar, scribe, and teacher became prominent. Even at the time of the Restoration under Zerubbabel there were already many who had settled into the new mold and who refused to leave it. Judaism survived not only among those who returned to Judea and reconstituted the ancient

The Elephantine Island, Aswan, Egypt, where archaeologists have found a large number of Aramaic papyrus documents left by the Jewish military colony there. (Matson Photo Service.)

commonwealth, but also among those who chose rather to become part of the permanent Dispersion.

Elephantine

Two minor groups retained something of the older ritual, although they had little influence upon later Judaism. One was the Jewish colony at Elephantine, an island in the Nile opposite Aswan.

Excavations carried on at this site in 1907 and 1908 unearthed a
large collection of Aramaic papyri which had been written by Jews
belonging to a military colony. The origin of the settlement is
obscure; it may be that it began with a group of Jewish mercenary
soldiers in the service of Egypt whose ancestors had been refugees
from the Assyrian conquest of the northern kingdom of Israel in
722 B.C. The fact that the documents were written in Aramaic
militates against the idea that these soldiers came from Judea at the
time of the deportations under Nebuchadnezzar, for their presence
would have been needed in the Judean army, and they would more
likely have spoken Hebrew than Aramaic. There may have been a

*The tombs and ceremonial stairways of the princes of the sixth dynasty of
Egypt on the west bank of the Nile above Elephantine Island.* (Courtesy
Unesco/Rex Keating.)

steady though small migration of Jews from the troubled conditions of Palestine to the more settled land of Egypt, extending over the period of a century or more. Jeremiah refers to Jews who were dwelling in Egypt in his day (Jer. 44:1-8) and reproaches them for worshiping other gods.

The Elephantine papyri were written during the fifth century between 494 and 400 B.C. Most of them were business documents, but among them were a few letters. One of the most important was addressed to Bigvai or Bagoas, the governor of Judea. It reported that Egyptian priests with the assistance of a local military garrison had demolished and burned the Jews' temple, and had taken away its treasures and furnishings. Because of this loss the Jewish inhabitants of Elephantine had appealed to Jerusalem for help, but since they had no reply, they were renewing their petition. They asked that funds be sent to them to rebuild their temple in order that they might worship Yaho (Jehovah) again.

The erection of a temple to Jehovah in any place outside of Jerusalem seems to be wholly out of keeping with the Law, which stipulated that there should be only one center of worship (Deut. 12:5-14). The Elephantine Jews maintained a regular priesthood, offered sacrifices regularly, and observed the Passover and the Feast of Unleavened Bread. In their letter, however, they mentioned other

Two Aramaic papyrus documents discovered at Elephantine. The upper photo shows a sealed contract with the Aramiac words spr bî zî ktb, "*letter concerning a house, written by. . . ." The lower papyrus is a folded contract.* (Courtesy The Brooklyn Museum.)

gods — Ishumbethel, 'Anathbethel, Herembethel, and 'Anathyahu. 'Anath was the feminine counterpart of Baal, mentioned in the Ugaritic literature. Since the names are Semitic, they do not represent deities which these settlers had adopted in Egypt; the syncretistic worship must have been brought from the land of their origin. The usage parallels the conditions in Palestine in the last years before the collapse of the northern and southern kingdoms, when the worship of Jehovah was combined in popular usage with elements of the Canaanite religions (II Kings 23:4ff.; Ezek. 8:7ff.).

The appeal of the Elephantine colony to Jerusalem seems to have brought no response, possibly because the leaders there were reluctant to subsidize a rival temple. A second letter to the sons of Sanballat in Samaria requested their intervention with the Persian rulers for permission to rebuild the temple. The Samaritans seemed more sympathetic, for they also had established an independent worship at Mt. Gerizim and were effective in obtaining the desired consent.

The Samaritans

The Samaritans were the descendants of the northern Israelites who had been left after the Assyrian deportations of 722 B.C. and of the new settlers whom the conquerors had imported to populate the devastated territory. The neglect of the farms had emboldened the wild animals so that the inhabitants were threatened by lions. Thinking that the ravages of these beasts were promoted by the wrath of the local god, they petitioned the king of Assyria for someone who could instruct them in the religion of Israel.

The king of Assyria dispatched one of the exiled priests to Bethel, where he set up a center for the instruction of the immigrants in the worship of Jehovah. The result was a syncretism in which the worship of the pagan deities was maintained simultaneously with that of Jehovah. "They feared Jehovah, and served their own gods," says the narrative in II Kings 17:24-33.

During the century and a quarter that elapsed between the Assyrian conquest of the northern kingdom and the first Babylonian invasion of Judah, Samaria was comparatively at peace. Technically a province of the Assyrian empire, it took no active part in the constant warfare between Assyria and Egypt. Judah, on the contrary, was continually embroiled in border disputes and tried to make common cause with the victor in order to preserve its independence. When Judah finally succumbed to Nebuchadnezzar of Babylon, Samaria continued to prosper, for it possessed a more fertile territory and enjoyed relative tranquillity.

There had always been friction between the northern and southern kingdoms ever since the division under Jeroboam and Rehoboam following the death of Solomon, but during the period of the Exile it was aggravated by a number of causes. The poverty-stricken inhabitants of Judea, imperilled by Egypt on the south and by Assyria or Babylon on the north, were undoubtedly jealous of the superior prosperity of their northern neighbors who were exempt from political tension and who were able to make a good living from their richer territory. When Nehemiah undertook to rebuild the walls of Jerusalem, the Samaritans offered vigorous opposition (Neh. 4:7, 8), and Sanballat the governor invited Nehemiah to a conference, evidently with the intention of assassinating him (6:1-9). A complete breach between Jews and Samaritans was reached when the grandson of Eliashib, the high priest, married Sanballat's daughter contrary to the statute prohibiting mixed marriages (13:23-28). Since he refused to annul the marriage, he was promptly expelled from the priesthood and exiled. He retired to Samaria, where Sanballat built a temple for him on Mt. Gerizim, and where independent worship was maintained until the building was destroyed in 128 B.C. by John Hyrcanus.

This secession from the worship of Jehovah at Jerusalem, coupled with the known heathen ancestry of the Samaritans, caused the Judeans to repudiate the Samaritans completely. They, on the other hand, contended that Mt. Gerizim and Mt. Ebal were the original sites

Mt. Gerizim, one of the twin mountains forming the pass of Shechem near the modern city of Nablus in Jordan. The tents shown here are being occupied by present-day Samaritans preparing to celebrate the passover. Mt. Gerizim is the mountain of blessing mentioned in the ceremony prescribed for the Israelites' entrance into Canaan (Deut. 11:26-32). (Courtesy Prof. B. Van Elderen.)

of worship designated by Jehovah after the conquest under Joshua, and that the erection of the shrines and temples in Jerusalem was a perversion of His command (cf. John 4:20). Although the Samaritans compromised with paganism under Antiochus IV Epiphanes by dedicating their temple to Zeus Hellenios, they returned later to the worship of Jehovah and in the first century maintained a form

An Arab village thought by some to be identical with Sychar, where Jesus spoke with the woman at the well (John 4). In the background is Mt. Gerizim. (Matson Photo Service.)

of the Old Testament ritual that paralleled that of Jerusalem. To this day the small remnant that inhabit Nablus (Shechem) preserve an ancient roll of the Pentateuch and observe sacrificial rites of the annual Passover on the summit of Mt. Gerizim. They are a living witness to the religion of the dissident group who diverged from the main stream of Judaism after the Exile.

The message of Christ found an early acceptance among the Samaritans. During His lifetime He had ministered occasionally in their territory, although He had not allowed His disciples to work there (Matt. 10:5). On one of His first journeys northward from Jerusalem to Galilee He had passed by Sychar and had interviewed a Samaritan woman at Jacob's well. Her response to His message brought Him into contact with her fellow villagers, who listened to Him readily and "believed" (John 4:1-43). Although on a subsequent trip some of the Samaritans refused to welcome Him because He was a Jew and obviously traveling to Jerusalem (Luke 9:52-56), there were other occasions when they treated Him graciously (Luke 17:16). When the persecution of the early church in Jerusalem drove many of the believers out of the city, Philip, the Hellenistic evangelist, found a responsive audience in Samaria (Acts 8:1b-25), possibly because the Samaritans were less rigid in their interpretation of the Pentateuch and less attached to the Temple worship than the ruling priesthood of Judea.

The Diaspora

The majority of Jews in the Roman world of Jesus' day belonged to the *Diaspora,* or Dispersion, living outside of Palestine. Uprooted from their land by the Assyrian and Babylonian captivities, they had made their permanent home in the countries to which they had been exiled. Because of the many wars that ravaged Palestine during the intertestamental period, others had migrated to settlements where they were ensured peace in return for their services as colonists. Some had settled in cities for the sake of the business opportunities which commerce afforded them; others became small farmers in rural districts. Although a few were absorbed into the surrounding Gentile population and so lost their identity as Jews, there were many others who adhered in some fashion to the faith and practices of their ancestors.

Because of their sobriety, industry, and astuteness, the Jews were favored as colonists and were used both by the Greek kings of Syria and Egypt and by the Romans in settling new territory. Alexandria, which was founded in 332 B.C. by Alexander the Great, contained a large colony of Jews. The collapse of the Persian empire had rendered their position in the East insecure and many moved westward to the Greek cities where they were assured of religious liberty and of commercial opportunity. In Alexandria they were almost autonomous, for they occupied a separate quarter of the city and governed themselves. Strabo, the Greek geographer, quoted by Josephus, stated that "it is hard to find a place in the habitable earth that hath not admitted this tribe of men and is not possessed by it: and it hath come to pass that Egypt and Cyrene . . . and a great number of other nations imitate their way of living, and maintain great bodies of these Jews in a peculiar manner, and grow up to greater prosperity with them, and make use of the same laws with that nation also."[2]

In Rome itself the Jewish immigrants had constituted an independent group since the first century before Christ. Cicero, in his defense of Flaccus in 63 B.C., remarked that the Roman Senate had forbidden the Jews of Asia and of Italy to send gold to Jerusalem, both in his time and previously. Furthermore, he declared that it was necessary to speak in a low tone because the Jews had gathered in large numbers outside of the courtroom to hear what was said, and that they threatened to demonstrate against any speech or action unfavorable to them.[3] If there were enough Jews in Rome so that their contributions to the Temple in Jerusalem would make a significant outflow of gold from the capital, and so that a demonstration on their part would exert pressure on a court of law, there must have been a large and wealthy group in the city. "Sojourners from Rome" were present in Jerusalem on the day of Pentecost (Acts 2:10), and in spite of their expulsion from Rome in the reign of Claudius (18:2), a sizable community was still living in the city when Paul arrived there a few years later (28:17-22). Probably the ban was lifted after the death of Claudius in A. D. 54, for Paul's letter to the Romans indicates that Aquila and Priscilla who had left Rome in the time of stress had returned to the city by A.D. 57.[4]

The wide distribution of Jews through the lands bordering the Mediterranean is confirmed by the entire New Testament. On the day of Pentecost pilgrims were present from every quarter of the compass: "Parthians and Medes and Elamites, and the dwellers in Mesopotamia, in Judea and Cappadocia, in Pontus and in Asia, in Phrygia and Pamphylia, in Egypt and the parts of Libya about Cyrene, and sojourners from Rome, both Jews and proselytes, Cretans and Arabians, we hear them speaking in our tongues the mighty works of God" (Acts 2:9-11).

---

2 *Antiquities* xiv. 7. 2.
3 Cicero *Pro Flacco* 28.
4 This argument assumes that Romans 16 is an integral part of the Epistle.

The Jews of the *Diaspora* proved to be a fertile field for the sowing of the gospel. Severed from the Temple by distance, many of them had given their primary allegiance to the local synagogue which provided a center of worship, instruction in the Law, and a social atmosphere enabling them to maintain their distinctive identity. Their firm belief in God gave a theistic basis for the message of the gospel which the Gentiles did not have, and the prophetic Scriptures of the Old Testament which had been translated into the Koiné Greek, the *lingua franca* of the Roman world, were as familiar to them as to the Christian preachers. Wherever the missionaries of the first century proclaimed their message, they were able, with few exceptions, to begin in the local synagogue, and they usually obtained a hearing from the proselytes if they did not from the Jews themselves. The book of James was addressed to "the twelve tribes which are of the Dispersion," and I Peter was directed to "the elect who are sojourners of the Dispersion in Pontus, Galatia, Cappadocia, Asia, and Bithynia" (Jas. 1:1; I Pet. 1:1). The Epistle to the Hebrews, although containing no definite salutation, was evidently written for men of Jewish background who were uncertain whether to cling to the older tenets of Judaism or to advance into a full faith in Christ (Heb. 6:1-12; 8:13).

A strong element of the *Diaspora,* however, was inimical to Christians. Throughout his travels Paul constantly encountered bitter opposition from Jews in the cities where he preached. In Damascus his life was threatened and he was forced to escape at night over the wall in a basket let down by his disciples (Acts 9:23-25). In Cyprus a Jew who had become a sorcerer attacked him before the proconsul (13:6, 8). In Antioch of Pisidia the adherents of the synagogue openly contradicted and slandered him in an attempt to counteract his influence (13:44, 45, 50) and secured his expulsion from the city. In Iconium and in Lystra the same action was repeated (14:2, 5, 6, 19). Opposition was not so strong in Europe, due probably to the fact that there were fewer Jews in the Western cities, but in Thessalonica they precipitated a riot and followed it by invading Berea while Paul was there (17:5-13). At Corinth they attempted to accuse him before Gallio, the Roman governor, who dismissed their case because religious disputes were not amenable to Roman law (18:14-16). Paul's final visit to Jerusalem was interrupted by a riot incited by Hellenistic Jews of the Dispersion, who were visiting Jerusalem at the Feast of the Passover. Seeing Paul in the Temple, they falsely deduced that he had brought with him Trophimus, an Ephesian Gentile, who had accompanied him to the city. In the ensuing mob scene he was rescued by the Roman soldiery, who took him into protective custody and rescued him from violent death. The Jewish ardor for the Law manifested by the *Diaspora* and exemplified by Paul himself prior to his conversion produced a sharp antagonism against the followers of Jesus of Nazareth and was one of the chief obstacles which Christianity encountered (I Thess. 2:14-16). As the century progressed, the rift between Jewish Christians became wider, until the church denied that the synagogue represented true Judaism (Rev. 2:9; 3:9). Despite this breach, however, the Judaism of the *Diaspora* was the seedbed in which the gospel found lodgment and grew into the far-flung missionary church.

Judaism, however, was not theologically homogeneous. Within the one broad category of adherents to the Law were numerous sects and splinter divisions. As already observed, the Jews stationed at Elephantine preserved a worship of Jehovah with a separate temple; they observed some of the standard feasts, but they also worshiped other deities of heathen origin. They did not have the attitude of exclusiveness that characterized the Jews of Jerusalem in Jesus' time, nor the puritanical zeal of their contemporary, Nehemiah. There were those who were quite willing to compromise with the Gentile culture and religion that surrounded them; there were also those who resisted violently any infraction of the Law and were fanatical nationalists.

The Pharisees

The three chief religious groups within Palestinian Judaism were the Pharisees, the Sadducees, and the Essenes. The Pharisees were the strictest sect of Judaism, whose name, derived from the Hebrew verb *parash,* "to separate," characterized their strict exclusiveness. Josephus said that they were to be considered the most accurate interpreters of the Law.[5] Although they believed in the sovereignty of God, they thought that the choice of right or wrong lies open to the human will, and that God (or Fate, as Josephus phrased it for his Gentile readers) co-operates with men. According to their theology, the individual soul exists eternally, but only the virtuous will be resurrected; the wicked are doomed to eternal punishment.

The Pharisees were the direct ecclesiastical descendants and heirs of those who tenaciously refused to compromise their faith during the Exile and who, like Daniel and his companions, maintained the purity of their worship in the midst of a degrading paganism. Their habits of resistance to the religious currents around them tended to make them aggressive and intolerant of others' opinions. The return of the exiles under Zerubbabel and the reorganization of community life by Ezra established a wider contact with the Law and an increas-

[5] *Wars of the Jews* ii. 8. 14.

ing sense of personal responsibility for obedience to its precepts. Finkelstein has pointed out that the village shrines or "high places" which had been centers of worship during the period of the Davidic kingdom gave way to synagogues where the Law was read publicly and where preaching and prayer were observed regularly. In the absence of easy transportation to the Temple in Jerusalem the synagogue quickly took a central place in the life of the people. It never supplanted the Temple, to which great crowds of villagers made pilgrimages at the time of the sacred feasts, but it became the rallying point for those who craved instruction and a less perfunctory faith than the national cult.[6]

No specific mention of the synagogue worship appears in Ezra's writing, but there can be little doubt that both in the Dispersion, where access to the Temple was impossible, and in Palestine, where local worship was desirable, the gathering of the devout built up a class of worshipers who reverenced the Law and sought to observe it. The reforms of Nehemiah accentuated Ezra's emphasis on separation from the people of the land. Opposition from without, particularly from the Samaritans, fostered religious patriots who were militant in defending the Sabbath against the encroachment of secular activities, who were scrupulous in paying tithes, and who repudiated mixed marriages (Neh. 13:12-30). The stern righteousness of Nehemiah was imitated by his followers and perpetuated by their descendants.

Within the populace of Judah there was in the late fifth and early fourth centuries B.C. a nucleus of Jewish puritans. Their convictions were both challenged and strengthened when, after the collapse of Alexander's empire, they found themselves under the Hellenistic rule of the Ptolemies and the Seleucids. The priestly aristocracy was enchanted by the new ideas which Hellenism introduced, and was ready to accept them, even to the point of repudiating its Jewish heritage. The rural populace who had been schooled in the Torah by their local teachers were less willing to accept cultural innovations. In the process of the struggle which was consummated in the Maccabean wars, the Hasidim, or pietists, emerged victorious. While they did not succeed in dominating all of Jewish life subsequent to the restoration of the Temple, they did become a powerful factor in the social and political life of the second commonwealth.

The sect of the Pharisees, first named in the reign of John Hyrcanus (135-104 B.C.), must have developed from the Hasidim.[7] Belonging to the middle class of Judaism that was scattered through Jerusalem and the villages of Judea, it became the backbone of Jewish

---

[6] Louis Finkelstein, *The Pharisees*, II, 568.
[7] I Maccabees 2:42.

national life. It was opposed to the priestly aristocracy, which was more interested in economic and political opportunism than in religious fervor.

The zeal of the Pharisees for the Law appears in the allusions of the New Testament. They were meticulous about paying tithes, even of the small seeds and spices that grew in their gardens (Matt. 23:23). They studied the Law assiduously to determine the duties that they owed to God and often drew unnecessarily fine distinctions in their interpretation (vv. 16-21). They were excessively conscious of their virtues and paraded them before God when they prayed (Luke 18:11-12). Because their ideals exceeded their performance, Jesus branded them hypocrites and blind guides (Matt. 23:13, 16). Nevertheless He recognized their loyalty to the Law, and agreed with the current concept that they "sit on Moses' seat" (v. 2) as the successors of the great lawgiver. Jesus took exception to the practice of the Pharisees rather than to their basic teaching. He was more nearly in accord with them theologically than with any other religious sect in Judaism. Nicodemus (John 3:1) and Paul (Acts 23:6) were both Pharisees by birth and by training.

Doctrinally the Pharisees represented the orthodox core of Judaism. They were supernaturalists who held firmly to the belief in one personal God who had revealed Himself primarily through the Law given to Moses and through the prophets who had compiled their history and had from time to time been the spiritual mentors of the nation. They accepted as canonical not only the Torah, the five books of Moses, but also the prophets and the writings, which included Ruth, Psalms, Job, Proverbs, Ecclesiastes, Song of Solomon, Lamentations, Daniel, Esther, Ezra, Nehemiah, and Chronicles. Their method of interpretation of the Law was detailed and exact. Every statement was scrutinized carefully, lest any command, whether expressed or implied, should be overlooked. Allegorical interpretation was often employed to adapt the statements of the Law to new situations. All requirements were observed strictly and even overemphasized lest accidental neglect should violate any one of them. Prayer, fasting, and tithing were observed meticulously (Matt. 23:23; Luke 11:42), and sometimes ostentatiously (Matt. 6:1-5). Their Sabbath observance circumscribed the activities of the day with so many prohibitions that it became burdensome and often ludicrous.

The extremes of Pharisaism are attributed to its rigid adherence to tradition. Schürer quotes the Talmud as saying, "It is more culpable to teach contrary to the precepts of the scribes, than contrary to the Torah itself."[8] In their zeal to protect the Law, they exceeded its commands, and at times made their doctrine ridiculous by its unreasonable minutiae.

The main tenets of Pharisaism included a firm belief in an invisible God, who was historically involved with Israel's destiny and who was personally concerned for His people. He had revealed Himself through the Law given to Moses, in which His will for man's behavior was plainly stated. Obedience to the Law was meritorious; disobedience to the Law could entail excommunication from the synagogue and from membership in the covenant people. The Pharisees acknowledged the existence of angels and spirits, who acted as God's messengers to man, and they believed in the resurrection of the individual after death.

The Sadducees

The Sadducees were a smaller party than the Pharisees numerically, but they were influential because of their position, for they were composed chiefly of the upper echelon of the priesthood. The name of the group was probably derived from Zadok, the progenitor of the high-priestly line under Solomon (I Kings 1:32, 34, 38, 45). Ezekiel, prophesying at the time of the Exile, alluded to the chief priests as "sons of Zadok" (Ezek. 40:46; 44:15ff.). Because of their learning and hereditary position they became the leaders of the dispersed people. With the Restoration they regained their position in the Temple and constituted the dominant aristocracy of Judaism. From the beginning of the Restoration in the Persian period they were the real rulers of the nation, although they did not claim for themselves the title of king.

Josephus states explicitly that the high-priestly families belonged to the Sadducean party.[9] Not all priests were Sadducees, nor were all the Pharisees plebeians, for Nicodemus, a Pharisee, was "a ruler of the Jews" (John 3:1). They did, however, represent the more sophisticated element who adhered to a literal formalism in ritual and exercised considerable latitude in the application of the Law.

Their attitude toward the Law was quite different from that of the Pharisees, for they acknowledged only the written code as binding and rejected the traditional interpretation to which the Pharisees adhered rigidly. Probably they gave greater weight to the Torah than to the prophets, although there is no evidence that they rejected the latter. Josephus implies that in judicial cases they

---

[8] Sanhedrin XI. 3, in Schürer, *The Jewish People in the Time of Christ,* II, ii, 12.

[9] *Antiquities* xviii. 1. 4.

applied the letter of the Law more rigorously than the Pharisees.[10]
In ritual matters they differed also, though generally their disagree-
ments were so small that they had little practical consequence.

The theological differences between them were wider. Basically
the Sadducees were anti-supernaturalists. Because of their extremely
literal interpretation of the Law, they denied the existence of angels
and spirits and repudiated any idea of a resurrection (Acts 23:8).
Their worship was formal rather than personal and their general
attitude was materialistic. For this reason they were more susceptible
to policies dictated by the expediency of the moment and yielded
more quickly to the religious and cultural pressure of Hellenism in
the Greek period under the Seleucids. Their involvement with politics induced the Sadducean priesthood to compromise more easily
with the Seleucid kings like Antiochus IV Epiphanes, and they
readily introduced into Jerusalem the activities of a heathen culture,
even though they may not have accepted the worship of foreign
deities.

Their willingness to make these concessions contributed to the
Maccabean revolt and evoked the enmity of the devout nationalists.
Though the priesthood was too strongly entrenched in tradition and
political prestige to be expelled from its position, it did not enjoy
popular favor. The Pharisees outnumbered the Sadducees and had
a greater influence on the populace. Perhaps the Sadducean priesthood had a lurking sense of insecurity which appears in Caiaphas'
decision concerning Jesus: "If we let him thus alone, all men will
believe on him: and the Romans will come and take away both our
place and our nation" (John 11:48). Undoubtedly the Pharisees
concurred in this sentiment; but it is evident that both feared an
uprising which might evoke Roman intervention and consequently
unseat them from their position of leadership.

The Sadducees continued to be a factor in Judaism until the destruction of Jerusalem in A.D. 70, for they participated in the council
before which Paul had appeared in A.D. 58/60 (Acts 23:6). Their
doctrine, however, did not prevail in Judaism, and after the fall of
Jerusalem their party disappeared. The slaughter of the aristocracy
and the disbanding of the priesthood destroyed them.

The Essenes

Josephus mentions the Essenes in his catalog of Jewish religious
groups. Nowhere does the New Testament take cognizance of them,
and until recent times their identity was known only from the rather
sparse references in Josephus, in Philo of Alexandria, a casual allu-

----

[10] *Ibid.,* xx 9. 1; xiii. 10. 6.

Excavations of the monastery of the Qumran Community, with the Judean hills in the background. (Matson Photo Service.)

sion in the letters of Pliny, and a somewhat extensive discussion in Hippolytus. Unlike the Pharisees and the Sadducees, they were not a part of the normal community life but were withdrawn from the sphere of public activity. Instead of being a party they were more nearly comparable to a monastic order, for they settled in restricted rural communities or in the desert, where they maintained an isolated existence. Both Philo and Josephus agree in estimating the number of Essenes at approximately four thousand.

The meaning of their name is uncertain. Josephus calls them both *Essenoi* and *Essaioi*.[11] Various explanations of the origin of this

---

[11] *Essenoi: Wars of the Jews* ii. 8. 11, 13; v. 4. 2, *Essaioi: ibid.* i. 3. 5; ii. 7. 3; ii. 20. 4; iii. 2. 1.

name have been offered. Philo suggested that it may have been derived from the Greek *hosioi,* meaning "holy," though "not according to any accurate form of the Greek Dialect."[12] Though the derivation may be uncertain, the character of the Essene community is quite clearly outlined by Josephus and the others who refer to it.

The Essenes were more closely akin to the Pharisees in their theology than to the Sadducees; in fact, if the Pharisees were Puritans, the Essenes exceeded them and became ascetics. They formed a community of their own, to which candidates were admitted only by adoption or by initiation. They were sober in temperament, shunning all levity and indulgence in pleasure for its own sake. Emotional display of any kind they avoided. They were usually voluntarily celibate, although some groups allowed marriage, but only for the propagation of children. All persons upon admission to the sect surrendered their property to the common funds which were equally available to all. Any personal needs for clothing, food, or shelter were readily supplied from the general stock. Traveling members of the group could always depend upon the hospitality of fellow members in whatever city or town they visited. Among themselves

---

12 Philo *Quod Omnis Probus* xii.

In these bluffs in the wilderness northeast of the Dead Sea, Qumran Caves 4, 5, and 10 were discovered. Cave 4 provided fragmentary manuscripts of all the Hebrew Old Testament books except Esther. (Courtesy Prof. B. Van Elderen.)

they neither bought nor sold but freely gave or received in accordance with their possessions or their needs.

In personal habits they were scrupulously clean. They ordinarily bathed before meals and dressed in white except while working at the ordinary tasks of the day. Food was served in a common dining hall, with thanksgiving before and after each meal.

The communities of the Essenes were normally located in small villages rather than in large cities. They preferred the isolation of the country where they could engage in agriculture and withdraw from the distractions and evils of the crowded city life. They refrained from all activities of war and commerce and devoted themselves wholly to peaceful occupations. Their educational program was built on the use of the Scriptures, which were read publicly and expounded in their synagogues on the Sabbath day.

Both Josephus[13] and Pliny the Younger[14] stated that their largest single settlement was located on the west side of the Dead Sea, north of Engedi. Josephus added that they had not colonized any one city but appeared in large numbers in every town.

Candidates seeking admission to the Essene society were required to live outside the community for a year under conditions prescribed by the group. Each was given a small mattock, a loincloth, and white clothing. If during this period he conformed to all rules and gave evidence of a temperate and disciplined life, he was put on probation for two years more. Before final acceptance he was required to swear that he would be devoted to God, that he would treat all men justly, that he would never commit any act of violence toward another, and that he would keep faith with all men. He was forbidden to exalt himself or to assert personal superiority, to tell a lie, to steal, to conceal any information from members of his order, or to divulge any of their secrets. If he violated his pledge, he was expelled from the order. Since he was forbidden to eat food from any source other than the community, expulsion meant starvation, for he could neither eat what others offered him nor obtain aid from his former associates.

The recent excavation of the Qumran monastery on the bluffs overlooking the eastern shore of the Dead Sea has cast new light on the Essenes. The ruins which were formerly regarded as the remains of a Roman military post proved to be the relics of a communal settlement occupied both by men and women, though the former predominated. The ruins comprised a large dining hall where common meals were served, a scriptorium equipped with benches and ink pots, and aqueducts and cisterns for conserving the

---

[13] *Wars of the Jews* ii. 8. 4.
[14] *Natural History* xv.

infrequent rains that fell on the valley of the Dead Sea. According to the dating of the pottery and coins, the Qumran site must have been occupied from the second century B.C. to the close of the Jewish War and the destruction of the third Temple in A.D. 70. No traces of their occupancy can be dated later, though the remains indicate that probably a Roman garrison was stationed there until the war with Hadrian in the first third of the second century.

The best reason for identifying the Qumran community with the Essenes is the geographical location. Josephus and Pliny agree that the Essenes had an independent settlement in the general neighborhood of the spring Ain Feshkha and the present hill of Qumran. Since there is no trace of a second community in this locality, one is almost compelled to conclude that the Essenes and the inhabitants of Qumran were one and the same.[15]

The identification is supported by other evidence than geographic proximity. According to Josephus and the *Manual of Discipline,* both the Essenes and the Qumran group required two years' apprenticeship before admitting women to their order.[16] The oath which Josephus says was exacted from the Essenes is duplicated by the initiation described in the *Manual.* Both groups observed similar regulations for seating and for speaking in the assembly; both ate meals in common; both decided judicial questions by vote of the assembly.

The members of the Qumran community were constantly subject to critical scrutiny by their associates, and their qualifications and behavior were reviewed annually. They were divided into four classes: the priests, the Levites, the children of Israel, and the proselytes. Promotion from one class to another seems to have been possible, so that they comprised a fluid society rather than a group divided into fixed castes, which agrees with Josephus' description of the Essene organization.[17]

The theology of the Essenes and that of the Qumran group were strikingly similar in some respects and dissimilar in others. Both acknowledged one God, sovereign over the world and the origin of all good. To Him were ascribed the creation of material things animate and inanimate, the regulation of the historical forces of human development, the division of peoples, and the establishment of times and seasons.

[15] See Millar Burrows' excellent but cautious discussion in *The Dead Sea Scrolls,* pp. 279-298.

[16] See Theodore H. Gaster, Ed., *The Dead Sea Scriptures in English Translation,* pp. 51, 56.

[17] *Wars of the Jews* ii. 8. 10.

Both the Essenes and the Qumran brotherhood were devoted to the study of the Law, and both employed an allegorical method of interpretation.   Strict Sabbath observance was enjoined.   Josephus noted particularly the interest of the Essenes in angelology, which seems to have occupied the thinking of the Qumran community also.[18]

The Essenes' belief in a future life is reported differently by Josephus and Hippolytus.   Josephus said:

> For it is a fixed belief of theirs that the body is corruptible, and its constituent matter impermanent, but that the soul is immortal and imperishable . . . .   Sharing the belief of the sons of Greece, they maintain that for virtuous souls there is reserved an abode beyond the ocean, a place which is not oppressed by rain or snow or heat, but is refreshed by the ever gentle breath of the west wind. . . .[19]

Hippolytus, on the other hand, represented their beliefs as more nearly akin to the later Christian teaching:

[18] See William S. LaSor, *The Amazing Dead Sea Scrolls and the Christian Faith*, pp. 178-189.
[19] *Wars of the Jews* ii. 8. 11.

Two cisterns from the ruins of Khirbet Qumran, to the left a rectangular one, and to the right a circular one. These may have been used for water storage or ceremonial washings by the community living here. About forty such pools and reservoirs have been discovered around Khirbet Qumran. (Courtesy Prof. B. Van Elderen.)

Professor B. Van Elderen in front of Qumran Cave 11. Manuscripts found in this cave included the famous Psalms scroll which preserves the so-called "Psalm 151." (Courtesy Prof. B. Van Elderen.)

> They acknowledge both that the flesh will rise again, and that it will be immortal, in the same manner as the soul is already imperishable . . . that the soul, when separated in the present life, departs into one place, which is well ventilated and lightsome, where, they say, it rests until judgment.[20]

Which of these quotations more accurately describes the Essene eschatology is uncertain. It is possible that within the group there were divergent opinions, and that the Qumran community represented only one of these. The teaching preserved in the Dead Sea Scrolls accords better with the report of Hippolytus than with that of Josephus. Since, however, there were numerous companies of the Essenes scattered among the various cities of Palestine, and possibly elsewhere, it would not be surprising if some theological differences developed between them.

The essential oneness of these two groups seems reasonably certain, despite the differences mentioned above. It is scarcely possible

[20] *Refutation of All Heresies* ix. 22.

that there should have been two separate cults who settled on the west side of the Dead Sea in a barren wilderness which would barely support one colony. No remains of any settlement other than Qumran have been discovered. It is much more likely that "Essene" was a general title for the ultra-separationist wing of the Pharisees who in times of religious and political stress retired from society in order to shield and preserve their peculiar beliefs and ways of life. Some of them, like the Damascus community, remained in the cities; others, such as the Qumran ascetics, betook themselves to the wilderness. Some may have become political agitators, akin to the Zealots; others were monks who spent their time in agricultural pursuits and in the study of the Law.

The absence from the New Testament of any direct allusion to these people may mean that they had little influence on the main current of Jewish life. Jesus' ministry was exercised in the more populous districts and generally in the larger cities and villages. When He did return to the desert He preferred to be alone for prayer and meditation. The hypothesis that John the Baptist was an Essene, and that Jesus had been trained in their company, is not supported by facts. It is true that John's appearance and practices resembled somewhat those of the Essenes, but his membership in their ranks cannot be proved. Jesus Himself was not popularly classed with them, for He quoted His enemies as calling Him "gluttonous and a winebibber, a friend of publicans and sinners" (Luke 7:33, 34). Such an accusation would never have been leveled against Him had He followed the practices of the Essenes. Their doctrines may have been known to the populace and have been reflected in the popular religious sentiments of the time. The doctrines of Christianity, however similar in some respects, cannot be traced directly to those of Essenism.

The chief documents of the Qumran sect are *The Manual of Discipline, The Damascus* [or *Zadokite*] *Document, The Commentary on Habakkuk, The War of the Sons of Light and the Sons of Darkness,* and *The Thanksgiving Psalms.*

The Manual of Discipline is the handbook of rules for the life of the community. It prescribed a rigidly righteous conduct, requiring all adherents to abstain from association with outsiders, to abide by the rulings of the priests, to bear no hatred or ill will toward a neighbor, never to speak in anger or bitterness, to maintain modesty in speech and action, and to be loyal to the community as a whole. The organization of the community was subject to a board of twelve laymen and three priests who interpreted the standards of the *Manual* and applied them. The priests alone possessed authority to pass judgment on legal and economic matters and to determine the social status of members.

The Damascus [or *Zadokite*] *Document* is the counterpart of an ancient writing discovered in the Genizah (repository for outworn manuscripts) of the Cairo synagogue in 1910. This fragment found at Qumran defines the covenant which bound the members of the community together. The document indicates that it was written by pious Jews who attributed their origin to those who remained faithful to God during the Captivity. Three classes are mentioned: the priests, the Levites, and the sons of Zadok. The "priests" were those in Israel that repented and departed from the land of Judah, and the "Levites" were their associates. The "sons of Zadok" were the elect of Israel that were designated by name and that were destined for ministry in the last days. The *Zadokite Document* reiterates many of the principal stipulations of the *Manual of Discipline,* and formulates rules for the government of urban and rural societies. Evidently both existed and were parts of the one broad association.

The Commentary on Habakkuk accords in general with the allegorical rabbinic style, which attempts to translate the strictures of the prophet into terms of the contemporary conflict between the faithful remnant and the unbelieving world. It contains mysterious references to the "Kittim," who may be either the Hellenistic kings of Syria or the Romans. Unfortunately the *Commentary* has been damaged by the ravages of time and is consequently incomplete. The frequent gaps in its text cannot be restored with certainty. Positive identification of the characters and historical situations described seems unattainable at present. A number of scholars relate the document to the reign of Alexander Jannaeus, who crucified eight hundred of the Pharisees who had opposed his assumption of political sovereignty, and who drove several thousand others into exile. He is identified with the wicked priest of the *Commentary,*[21] "who, when he came to rule in Israel, grew arrogant and abandoned God, betraying His statutes for the sake of wealth. . . ."

The War of the Sons of Light and the Sons of Darkness is a figurative description of the hostility between Israel and her enemies in Palestine. While the "Sons of Light" are represented in conflict with Edom, Moab, and Ammon, and the "Kittians of Assyria," it is plain that the Old Testament names describe contemporary foes. The precise identification of these titles seems uncertain. Edom, Moab, and Ammon could represent the inhabitants of these respective territories regardless of nationality, but the Kittians of Assyria could be either the Seleucids of Syria who invaded from the north, or possibly the Romans. Yigael Yadin argues that they are the Romans because the description of military equipment in the *War* manuscript fits the Roman arms better than any other. Burrows

[21] *Commentary on Habakkuk* II.5.6.

A page from the Thanksgiving Psalms of the Dead Sea Scrolls, discovered in Cave 1. (Courtesy Israel Information Services.)

avers that the fragmentary *Nahum Commentary* defines a time extending "from Antiochus to the rise of the rulers of the Kittim."[22] Since Antiochus was Seleucid, the Kittim cannot be identified with the Greek kings of Syria, and therefore must be the Romans who followed them. If so, the *War of the Sons of Light and the Sons of Darkness* must commemorate the struggle between the Hasmonean rulers of the first century and the gradual growth of Roman domination between 50 B.C. and A.D. 50. The book contains certain apocalyptic elements, for it predicts a great battle between the Sons of Light and the Sons of Darkness. The order of battle is described in detail, and victory is promised to the Sons of Light whom God will aid by angelic visitation.

The fragmentary state of this manuscript increases the difficulty of interpretation, for many of the gaps must be completed by conjecture. However skilled a linguist an editor may be, he cannot be absolutely certain that his emendation or addition is correct. Were the manuscript complete, the identification of the persons and nations mentioned might be more positive. According to the present situation, one can say little more than that the *War* scroll represents the conflict of the Jews with some foreign power that threatened their existence.

The Thanksgiving Psalms is a collection of religious lyrics quite similar in form to the Psalms of the Old Testament. They convey in the first person the faith, fears, and aspirations of the adherents of the sect, and express lamentation over evil, suffering under persecution, and expectancy of God's final vindication of His servants. Although the language of the Psalms is inherently personal, they may have been used in the united worship of the community. They contain a strong note of mourning for sin, of consciousness of weakness, and of the conviction of the goodness and mercy of God.

In some of these Psalms may be found phrases which seem to anticipate the language of the New Testament. "Covenant," "saints," "wellspring of life," "the holy spirit," "the Word" are terms that appear in the Gospels and Epistles with substantially the same meaning. There is not enough coincidence in language to warrant the inference that the writers of the New Testament were dependent on the Qumran Psalms, but it would be fair to conclude that both employed the common religious vocabulary of the pious Jews of Jesus' generation. The Qumran Psalms are a link between the classical Psalms of the Old Testament and the theological expressions of the New Testament. They provide a picture of the devout Jew between 200 B.C. and A.D. 100 who, conscious of his own shortcom-

---

[22] For a full discussion of the identity of the Kittim, see Miller Burrows, *More Light on the Dead Sea Scrolls*, pp. 194-203.

ings and confident in the forgiving love of God, sought comfort in His mercy and direction. They illustrate the fact that piety and hope did not perish in the turbulence and decadence of the inter-testamental period, but that among a remnant of the Jewish people these aspirations still persisted.

Millar Burrows, in his extensive treatment of the Dead Sea Scrolls, has shown that although there are similarities of thought and language between the scrolls and the early Christian Scriptures, the differences are so great that they preclude direct derivation of Christianity from the Qumran sect.[23] There is no trace in their teaching of a pre-existent Messiah. The atoning character of Christ's death and His fulfillment of the typical sacrifices of the Old Testament have no parallel in these writings. The "Teacher of Righteousness," whom Allegro identifies with Jesus because of his sudden death, may not have been crucified at all, for the language of the *Nahum Commentary* is ambiguous because the text is fragmentary. No unique resurrection was predicted for the "Teacher," but Jesus' resurrection was the central theme of apostolic preaching and the definitive basis of the message. The Qumran sect associated the gift of the Holy Spirit with the ultimate realization of the Messianic hope, but for the church the prophecy was already fulfilled (Acts 2:16ff.).

No accord exists between the Gospels and the Qumran writings on the nature of the Messianic hope. The Gospels centered their expectation on the historic person of Christ, on whom the prophecies of the Old Testament converged. The Qumran sect expected that the Messiah would be the conquering leader of the sons of light, and that upon his arrival he would establish sovereignty over the nations. Jesus informed Pilate that His Kingdom was not of this world, and that He did not expect His servants to fight (John 18:36).

Pharisees, Sadducees, and Essenes (the last category probably including the Qumran community) contributed to the religious atmosphere of Judaism in which Christianity was born and grew into a separate faith. The influence of these religious parties can be traced directly or indirectly in the concepts and language of the New Testament, yet the dynamic of the gospel is not attributable to any one of them, nor can it be explained as an outgrowth of their beliefs. Christianity is original with Christ.

[23] *Ibid.,* pp. 65ff.

5

The Pressure of Paganism

T HE CHRISTIAN CHURCH WAS BORN INTO A WORLD FILLED WITH competing religions which may have differed widely among themselves but all of which possessed one common characteristic — the struggle to reach a god or gods who remained essentially inaccessible. Apart from Judaism, which taught that God had voluntarily disclosed Himself to the patriarchs, to Moses, and to the prophets, there was no faith that could speak with certainty of divine revelation nor of any true concept of sin and salvation. The current ethical standards were superficial, despite the ideals and insights possessed by some philosophers, and when they discoursed on evil and on virtue, they had neither the remedy for the one nor the dynamic to produce the other.

Even in Judaism revealed truth had been obscured either by the encrustation of traditions or by neglect. Paul's arraignment of the Jew in the second chapter of Romans charged him with the inconsistency of disobedience to the Law in which he professed to rest his hope (Rom. 2:17-29). In the same section of Romans (1:18-32) Paul depicted the degeneration of paganism which began with alienation from God and ended in the complete dismissal of the knowledge of God and the inversion of all ethical values. Paganism is the human attempt to satisfy an inner longing for God by the worship of a deity which will not obstruct one's desire for self-

107

satisfaction. The gods that men worship are of their own making, whether visible or invisible.

Paganism is a parody and a perversion of God's original revelation to man. It retains many basic elements of truth but twists them into practical falsehood. Divine sovereignty becomes fatalism; grace becomes indulgence; righteousness becomes conformity to arbitrary rules; worship becomes empty ritual; prayer becomes selfish begging; the supernatural degenerates into superstition. The light of God is clouded by fanciful legend and by downright falsehood. The consequent confusion of beliefs and of values left men wandering in a maze of uncertainties. To some, expediency became the dominating philosophy of life; for if there can be no ultimate certainty, there can be no permanent principles by which to guide conduct; and if there are no permanent principles, one must live as well as he can by the advantage of the moment. Skepticism prevailed, for the old gods had lost their power and no new gods had appeared. Numerous novel cults invaded the empire from every quarter and became the fads of the dilettante rich or the refuge of the desperate poor. Men had largely lost the sense of joy and of destiny that made human life worthwhile.

The Ethnic Religions

During the civil wars that plagued Rome in the first century before Christ the older state religion fell into decline. The shift of population from the country to the city and the replacement of the free native citizens by foreign slaves diminished the number of the worshipers of local and village deities. Among the educated classes a growing skepticism decreased religious leadership, though many maintained an outward allegiance to the ancestral gods for the sake of public relations.

When Octavian became sole ruler in 27 B.C. he began a campaign to rehabilitate the old Roman religion as a means of promoting the solidarity and integrity of the state. In the *Monumentum Ancyranum* he stated that he rebuilt eighty-two temples of the gods in obedience to a decree of the Senate[1] and that in addition he subsidized them with costly gifts. He purged the current religious literature by burning more than two thousand books written by anonymous or unimportant authors, and by retaining only the oldest and best of the Sibylline prophecies, which he enshrined in the temple of the Palatine Apollo. He recruited new candidates for the priesthood and for the Vestal Virgins and increased their stipends and privileges. Some of the ancient rites and festivals were restored, such as the

---

[1] Lawrence Waddy, *Pax Romana and World Peace*, pp. 53ff.

Lupercalia and the Compitalia, annual games which celebrated respectively fertility rites and the honor of the spirits that guarded the homes of the people.[2] It would be inaccurate to say that the old religion of Rome was dead when the temples of the gods still maintained their ascendancy in civic life and commanded the allegiance of a considerable part of the population.

Lawrence Waddy observes, however, that "Roman religion in the days of the Republic was already losing its integrity. But under the Empire we find a steady crumbling of nerve and will, which was a great factor in the Romans' inability to survive."[3] Even Augustus, despite his organizing genius and vast authority, could not check the transition which had already begun from the unemotional obeisance to the ancestral gods, many of whom were adopted from subjugated nations, to the more vital personal cults that sprang up on every hand. His efforts to revive the ancient worship were in large measure artificial, though among the Roman aristocracy there persisted some nostalgic affection for the glories of the past.

[2] Suetonius, *The Deified Augustus* ii. 30, 31.
[3] *Op. cit.*, p. 216.

Remains of the temple of Zeus in Athens, with the Parthenon and Acropolis in the background. This temple was the largest in Greece, and was built over a period of more than six hundred years. (Philip Gendreau.)

The Parthenon, the peak of Doric architecture, designed by Ictinus and Callicrates on the Acropolis at the commissioning of Pericles. The temple, dedicated to the goddess Athena Parthenos (the virgin), was used in medieval times as both a church and a mosque. (Philip Gendreau.)

Whatever may have been the individual attitudes of the populace toward the ancestral pantheon, ranging from cool skepticism to hysterical devotion, the massive temples and gilded shrines that adorned the heights and highways of every city and town exercised a powerful though silent influence. They may have been the monuments of a moribund faith, but they still marked the highest aesthetic and religious achievement of the past. In Athens, the cultural center

A stone altar discovered at Pergamum. The top line indicates that it was dedicated "ΘΕΟΙΣ ΑΓ[ΝΟΣΤΟΙΣ" — "to unknown gods." This altar is comparable to the one mentioned by Paul in his sermon at Athens (Acts 17:23). (Courtesy Prof. B. Van Elderen.)

The Ara Pacis Augustae, *the altar of the Augustan Peace, founded by the emperor in 13* B.C. *to celebrate the peace throughout the empire. It is likely that the carvings on it were made by Greeks from Pergamum.* (Courtesy Ente Provinciale per il Turismo di Roma.)

of the Hellenic world, Paul, gazing at the magnificent buildings dedicated to the Olympian deities, exclaimed, "I perceive that in every way you are very religious" (Acts 17:22, RSV). The entire religious culture of the past was represented by the buildings and rites of pagan worship; its legends and ethics were ingrained into the people; and as Christianity slowly penetrated the fabric of society, it met the resistance of these antecedents.

Emperor Worship

Because of the decline of the state worship it was a less formidable rival of the new faith than were some others. Among these, emperor worship was perhaps the most prominent. In the Roman regime it

Detail of the Ara Pacis Augustae. *Another detail has been reproduced on the cover of this book.* (Courtesy Ente Provinciale per il Turismo di Roma.)

began in the rule of Augustus, although the divinity of royalty had long been a concept of the Hellenistic world. Both the Ptolemies and the Seleucids had been worshiped by their subjects, and the noun *kyrios,* or "lord," when applied to the ruler, had definite connotations of deity. Deissmann writes: "It may be said with certainty that at the time when Christianity originated 'Lord' was a divine predicate intelligible to the whole Eastern world."[4] He cites a series of inscriptions, papyri, and ostraca that apply this title to the reigning king or emperor.

Augustus refused the title because it contravened the principle that he was simply the first citizen (*princeps*) of the commonwealth, not a divine ruler; in fact, he considered the title to be insulting.[5]

[4] Adolf Deissmann, *Light from the Ancient East,* pp. 354-360.
[5] Suetonius, *op. cit.,* liii.

Ruins of Herod's palace at Sebaste, the site of ancient Samaria. The Greek word σεβαστός is the equivalent of the Latin "Augustus," the emperor to whom the city was dedicated. (Courtesy Prof. B. Van Elderen.)

Nevertheless, the eastern Greek-speaking provinces, where kings had long been regarded as gods, insisted on deifying him even before his death. The plebs in Narbo, a city of Gaul, erected an altar to *numen Augusti,* the genius of Augustus, and in 12 B.C. Drusus built an altar at Lugdunum (Lyons) to Roma and Augustus.[6]

In Palestine Herod the Great named his new city of Samaria *Sebaste,* the Greek equivalent of Augustus, and dedicated the temple, its most imposing structure, likewise to Roma and Augustus.

Augustus' reluctance to claim divine honors was not prompted by theological considerations. He himself had inaugurated the custom of deifying the ruler at death by building a temple to Divus Julius Caesar in the Forum. His unwillingness to be worshiped sprang from political caution, for he did not wish to assume the mien of an Oriental autocrat so soon after the fall of the Republic.

Tiberius, his successor, restrained the popular impulse to worship the imperial statues. He scarcely allowed his birthday to be noticed

[6] *Cambridge Ancient History,* X, 209ff.

and prohibited the voting of temples, flamens, and priests in his honor. He allowed his image to be erected in public only if it were not to be classed with likenesses of the gods, nor would he allow anyone to address him as "Lord."[7] In A.D. 23 he did permit the province of Asia to build a temple at Smyrna to himself, Livia, and the Senate, but two years later forbade the people of the Spanish province of Baetica to do so.[8]

His successor, Caius Caligula, broke with tradition. He had proposed that Tiberius should be deified, but the Senate had refused. In A.D. 40 he began to seek worship for himself. He ordered that a statue of Zeus with his features be placed in the Temple in Jerusalem, and demanded also that he be worshiped at Rome. His obvious insanity and sudden death postponed the crisis that he had almost precipitated, but the concept of emperor worship had been injected into the minds of the Roman people, and it remained there.

Claudius (A.D. 41-54), who followed Caligula, declined to accept a high priest and temple dedicated to him. During his lifetime, however, writers spoke of him as "our god Caesar," and after his

---

[7] Suetonius, *Tiberius* xxvi.
[8] *Cambridge Ancient History*, X, 493.

The ruins at the top of the Herodium, six miles south of Bethlehem. Among the stones remaining from Herod's palace, the outline of a Byzantine basilica later erected on the hill can be traced. In the background is the wilderness of Judaea. (Courtesy Prof. B. Van Elderen.)

decease he was exalted to the company of the gods by vote of the Senate.[9]

Nero followed the example of his predecessors by refusing to allow the dedication of a temple in his honor built at public expense. Later he placed in front of his new palace a colossus of the sun-god with his own features and represented himself with a radiant crown, the emblem of the sun-god, in the coins of the realm.[10]

Vespasian, whose dour practicality kept him from illusions of grandeur, is reported to have said when he was dying, "Alas! I think that I am about to become a god!" His second son, Domitian (A.D. 81-96) was the first emperor to demand public worship while he lived. He insisted that he be hailed as *Dominus et Deus,* "Lord and God."

With the exception of madmen like Caligula, or egotists like Domitian, none of the emperors seems to have taken his putative divinity very seriously. Politically, however, emperor worship was a very effective bond of unity. Whatever gods the several peoples of the empire may have worshiped, they could unite on the adoration of the ruler who was the visible guardian of their peace and prosperity. There were some who refused to participate in such worship. Political opponents of the empire, particularly those who had mourned the demise of the Republic, would not endorse any such claims. The Jews would not elevate any man to the place of God, nor would the Christians. As Paul said, "For us there is one God, the Father . . . and one Lord, Jesus Christ" (I Cor. 8:6).

Emperor worship was a political rather than a religious cult, though it eventuated in the worship of the state. Evidently it was not uniformly enforced; it seems to have been much more prevalent in the provinces than in Rome, particularly in the Middle East. Christians were placed in the irreducible dilemma of being compelled to apostatize by token worship of Caesar if they would save their lives, or of appearing unpatriotic because they would not conform to state requirements. Irregular and perfunctory as emperor worship was, it symbolized the desire for protection by some visible power that was more real than the older gods who had proved ineffectual. The Romans felt that their security was personified in the head of the state, who was responsible for their food, their pleasures, their safety, and their future. The result was a state cult which set the emperor in the place of God and created an atmosphere of man-worship. Such an attitude was hostile to Christianity, which was as rigidly uncompromising toward idolatry as Judaism had ever been. The constant pressure of the state was an unremitting

9 *Ibid.,* p. 498.
10 *Ibid.,* p. 501.

threat to Christianity even under those emperors who did not take it seriously and who consequently did not promote any active persecution of dissidents. On the other hand, the very name "Christian" became synonymous with subversion and in the eyes of the general public Christians came to be classed with criminals (I Pet. 4:15, 16).

The Mystery Religions

The lack of personal involvement with deity in the ritual of the state religion and the obvious humanistic and political character of emperor worship engendered an intense desire on the part of many for some religion that would satisfy the individual quest for peace and immortality. Immediate contact with deity, giving assurance of present protection and of future bliss, was a chief desideratum. Because the traditional ritual of the state religion was largely irrelevant to the immediate personal needs of the average citizen, and because the worship of the emperor was a political tool rather than an intimate faith, neither of these satisfied the spiritual cravings for personal reality. The ancestral gods were distant and unreal, capricious in their attitude and often less ethical than their worshipers. The emperor, for all his power, was only a man, even though a fictional godhead was ascribed to him by the Senate at his death or by popular adulation during his life. Neither of these could intervene supernaturally in the individual life or satisfy the desire for salvation and immortality.

The conquests of Alexander in the fourth century B.C. had established new contacts with the Far East and had facilitated the syncretism of Western organized religions with the Eastern mysticism. When the armies of Alexander returned to Europe, they brought with them a new attitude and new teachings. Religion became increasingly the affair of the individual rather than of the state, and the gods of the Western pantheon were identified with the Eastern deities, who promised direct revelation to their devotees and who might be approached personally through mystic rites. Because of the esoteric character of their worship they were called "mystery religions." Some were attached to particular localities which were visited by pilgrims, similar to the worship of "Our Lady of Lourdes"; others were conducted wherever a shrine could be erected in honor of the gods.

The Eleusinian Mysteries

The oldest of the popular mysteries was the cult of Eleusis, a town not far from Athens. It originated before the time of Alexander and attracted visitors from all parts of the known world. A truce was proclaimed among the Greek states so that travel would not be endangered and so that all might participate in the celebration without distraction.

Early in the fall, usually in September, the pilgrims gathered at Athens. The directors announced that only those who were pure and who spoke an intelligible language could participate. The sacred objects, emblematic of deity, were brought from Eleusis and placed in the Eleusinium at the foot of the Acropolis.

The candidates for initiation went down to the harbor to wash themselves in the sea and then, after a formal sacrifice in the late afternoon, formed a procession on the way to Eleusis, twelve miles from Athens. As they marched toward their destination they sang hymns and choruses to Iacchos, the infant Dionysus, god of wine. They stopped to bathe in the sacred lake outside of Athens, and at midnight arrived at the Telesterion, or Hall of Initiation, at Eleusis.

The initiation was conducted in the darkness, illuminated by the weird flickering of torches. After more sacrifices, a sacred banquet, and a consecrated drink, they witnessed a sacred drama, enacted by the priests of the shrine. The nature of the drama is not known exactly; probably it reproduced the rape of Persephone, daughter of Demeter, whom the god of the underworld snatched away to his cheerless abode beneath the earth and was later compelled to restore to her mother. The legend may have originated in an ancient fertility rite which personified the death of vegetation in the fall and its reappearance from the earth in the spring. For the participants at Eleusis it probably signified an entrance into life after death, or a taste of immortality.

A second act of the drama was probably the union of Zeus and Demeter and the birth of the divine Iacchos or Dionysus, originally a second stage of the fertility worship. The initiates were conducted on a pilgrimage through a dark passageway to represent the cheerless wanderings of the dead in the underworld, and then were brought back to the upper air and light, where they were shown the sacred objects of the cult. The vision of these objects was the culmination of the initiation, for they represented the personal revelation of deity to the individual.

The Worship of Serapis

The cult of Serapis, popular in the first and second centuries, was derived from Egypt. The name was a Hellenization of the Egyptian Asor-hapi, the appearance of the god Osiris in the guise of a bull. A serapeum, or temple, existed in Rome about 80 B.C., and the temple of Isis, the consort of Osiris, was a popular resort in the days of the early empire. Although Augustus on one occasion expelled the priests of the cult for complicity in a case of flagrant immorality, worshipers still persisted in Rome. Under Nero the cult was recognized by the State and ultimately appeared in every province.

Serapis, called "Lord of Totality," was identified with the sun-god. He was the protector of his worshipers, the savior $(\Sigma\omega\tau\acute{\eta}\rho)$ of men, who could be approached through sacred ritual. In essence, the worship of Serapis was monotheistic pantheism. The nature of the god was not clearly defined, but it was opposed to polytheism and asserted the pervasive power of his deity through all nature. Serapis was called a healer, and his temple became a clinic for the ailing and a refuge for the hopelessly ill.[11]

Isis was the sister and wife of Osiris, who was killed and dismembered by his brother Set, the god of darkness and of evil. Isis assiduously searched for the pieces of Osiris, and when she had assembled them, brought them back to life. She became the mother of Horus, the god of culture and of wisdom.[12]

The worship of Isis had long flourished in Egypt, but began to penetrate the Mediterranean world in the third century B.C. Augustus, in 30 B.C., destroyed the temples of Serapis and Isis, and two years later the Senate debarred the cult from building an official temple within the city limits of Rome. Later it obtained a foothold in the city, but in A.D. 19 Tiberius destroyed the shrine and crucified the priests. Caligula, however, introduced the worship of Isis into his palace and took part in celebrating the mysteries. The Flavian emperors also favored the cult.

The mysteries of Isis are dimly known through Apuleius' work, *The Golden Ass*. He described the experience of Lucius who was metamorphosed into an ass by a witch but who was restored to human semblance by the aid of Isis. Her devotees held a ten-day festival of ascetic preparation, sacred lustrations, and public processions to celebrate the grief caused by Osiris' death and the joy of finding his body.

The cult of Isis had a strong attraction for women. The colorful processions, the magnification of her womanly grief over the death and dismemberment of Osiris, her unremitting quest for his body, and her joy in the child Horus glorified the sorrows, sacrifice, and satisfaction of the ideal wife and mother.[13]

Atargatis

As Isis was the gift of Egypt, so the cult of Atargatis was the legacy of Syria. Together with her consort, Baal-hadad, she was worshiped

---

[11] See Francis Legge, *Forerunners and Rivals of Christianity*, pp. 35-43, 53ff.
[12] Walter W. Hyde, *Paganism to Christianity in the Roman Empire*, pp. 49-55.
[13] *Ibid.*, pp. 55-59.

throughout the Middle East as the fish goddess. The first part of her name is related to the names of the goddess Ishtar, Astarte, or Ashtoreth, who was likewise the deity of fertility, love, and life. Her worship was accompanied by ritual prostitution and by human sacrifice until it was outlawed by Hadrian. Her priests were eunuchs who on fast days danced in her honor and scourged each other in orgiastic frenzy. Immortality was not stressed in this cult as in the Eleusinian mysteries and in the worship of Isis, but greater attention was paid to astrology and its concomitant teachings of good fortune guided by the stars and planets.

Mithra

Probably the strongest rival of Christianity in the first and second centuries was the cult of Mithra. Mithra was the sun-god, the apotheosis of light, purity, and righteousness, who gave the mastery over darkness and evil. His followers underwent an elaborate initiation, proceeding step by step from the first rudimentary rites to the final test which presumably prepared them for immortality. It was less tainted by sexual indulgences than the other mystery religions and appealed strongly to the more heroic qualities of human nature.

Mithraism entered Roman civilization in the first century B.C. during the Mithradatic wars in Asia Minor (88-63 B.C.). Again, in the early second century, when the armies of Trajan invaded Mesopotamia, they came in contact with Mithraism in Parthia. Through the returning veterans and the Oriental travelers and businessmen who visited the West it became a popular faith, particularly in the army. Mithraic shrines abounded in the Rhineland of Germany, and the ruins of one were unearthed in London after the bombings of World War II.

Mithraism began to become popular during the reign of the Flavians. The oldest Mithraic inscription found in Italy belongs to the time of Vespasian, and the first Roman writer to mention the worship is Statius, who lived in the same period (A.D. 40-96). It is not mentioned in the New Testament, possibly because the latter reflected generally the life of the church more than contact with other religions, or perhaps because the influence of Mithraism was weak until the end of the century when the canon of the New Testament closed.

No literature of this religion has survived; its ritual is known chiefly from the temples and sculptures it has left. Its chapels were underground caves in which a perpetual flame burned, symbolizing the light of truth. Water for ceremonial purification was supplied by a system of aqueducts. The entrance was usually a small colonnade from which a stairway descended to the vestibule of an oblong assembly hall seating fifty to one hundred persons. · The participants sat on benches around the sides of the room; the center was reserved for the performance of the ritual. Usually at the end of the hall there was a sculptured representation of Mithra slaying the bull. The god was depicted as a youth wearing a Phrygian cap on his head and a cape flung over his shoulders, crouched on the back of the bull while thrusting a sacrificial knife into its throat. Attendants stood beside him holding inverted torches. By slaying the sacred bull Mithra proved his strength. He ascended to heaven with the sun, where he continued the struggle against evil.

Little if anything is known of the ritual, since it was observed secretly. The followers of Mithra were pledged not to reveal the mysteries of their faith. There seems to have been a series of grades or degrees through which initiates passed, corresponding to the seven celestial spheres attained by the soul in its final pilgrimage: the raven, the hidden one, the soldier, the lion, the Persian, the messenger of the sun, and the father. Masks and costumes representative of the various degrees were worn on appropriate occasions.

Trials of strength and endurance accompanied promotion to such degrees. Tertullian (c. A.D. 200) said that the soldiers of Mithra, when presented with a crown at sword's point, were supposed to reject it, saying, "Mithras is my crown."[14] For some degrees, candidates were passed through flames while bound, or plunged in water, symbolic of death.

Mithraism had no sacerdotal class supported by the cult; its ritual was conducted by those who had reached the highest degrees. In contrast to the other mystery religions, women were excluded from Mithraic worship. It seems to have been free from the sensuality and orgiastic excesses of the other cults. Its tremendous popularity in the army can probably be attributed to its emphasis on the virtues of fidelity and courage; it was predominantly a soldier's faith.

The Atmosphere of Paganism

More influential than the specific cults was the atmosphere of paganism which they all shared and utilized. Fear of the supernatural pervaded idolatry in general, however the mythology of any one cult might express it. Astrology professed to find in the physical process of the universe the controlling powers of life. Magic and demonism that offered occult means of ensuring disaster to one's enemies and good fortune for oneself were real though sometimes undefinable forces that determined the background of popular thought. Although these cults can scarcely be called religious, they permeated all religious thought and were connected with the worship

---

14 *De Corona* xv.

of all existing deities. There was a close relationship between the occult practices and the mystery religions and the worship of the ancient pantheon of the state. Behind the colonnaded shrines, the sculptured images, the smoking altars, and the precise ritual was an undefinable something that could only be felt, but was none the less real.

The papyri, the poetry, and the drama of the first century bear insistent witness to this fact. Vergil's great epic, the *Aeneid,* written to glorify the achievements of Augustan Rome and to predict the high destiny of the reconstituted commonwealth, acknowledges the support of the gods and the overshadowing power of divine destiny. Among the papyri recovered from the sands of Egypt were a large number of amulets, charms, and formulas of exorcism revealing that the common people lived in constant dread of malevolent powers that might harm them, and whose malice must be averted or whose power must be restrained by magical charms. Even the Jews were not immune to such superstitions; on the contrary, many Jews were deeply involved in magical practices, in spite of the strictures of the Old Testament which forbade them (Deut. 18:10-12, 20; Micah 5:12). The pagan world took for granted that men were under the influence of invisible forces of evil which continually sought their destruction. Only by obtaining an ascendancy over these powers through magical arts could they retain their freedom.

The writers of the New Testament recognized these numinous powers. Paul spoke of "the rudiments [elements] of the world" under which the Galatians had formerly been held in bondage (Gal. 4:3), and then added, "Ye were in bondage to them that by nature are no gods" (v. 8), the powers that cannot legitimately be called deities, but that were worshiped by the world. After stating that a sacrifice made to an idol is nothing because the idol itself is nothing (I Cor. 10:19), he affirms that "the things which the Gentiles sacrifice, they sacrifice to demons, and not to God" (v. 20). The Apocalypse, which probably reflects the period of the Flavians (A.D. 69-96) says that "the rest of mankind . . . repented not of the works of their hands that they should not worship demons, and the idols of gold and of silver, and of brass, and of stone, and of wood" (Rev. 9:20). The oppressive darkness of idolatry and demonism is amply recognized in the New Testament, yet is counteracted by the positive faith in a living God that has rendered superstition ridiculous and occultism ineffective.

Astrology

Having noted that the seasons accorded with the movement of the heavenly bodies, which were also identified with the gods, or at least assumed to represent them, the ancients concluded that the stars and planets controlled the destinies of the world. Their varying positions in relation to the signs of the Zodiac would therefore establish the fortunes of men, and consequently the future welfare or disaster of any person could be predicted by calculating the motions of the planets and stars in relation to his birth date and biography.

The fallacy of this reasoning is obvious, for several persons having the same birth date will differ widely in character, social station, activities, and experience, whereas if they were all governed by the same influence their personalities and careers would tend to be identical. Nevertheless the concept that fate is determined by the physical powers of the universe was so widespread that astrology became a popular fad. Oriental soothsayers migrated westward into the empire in large numbers and were eagerly welcomed. Tiberius, suspicious and superstitious as he was, had his horoscope cast regularly and leaned heavily on the advice of astrologers for deciding the affairs of state. Nero also consulted astrologers in his major decisions. The effects of the widespread faith in astrology appears even on the money of the empire. Augustus imprinted on one of the coins issued in his name the sign of Capricorn, under which he had been conceived. When Domitian's little son died, a coin struck in his memory depicted him seated on the earth, exalted as a young god among the seven planets. The symbolism indicated that he had been translated to a celestial sphere where he assumed the power of deity to rule over the cosmos.[15]

Although the intelligentsia of Rome rejected the spurious pretensions of astrology and on several occasions expelled the *mathematici,* or professional soothsayers, from the city, they invariably returned and resumed their practices. Their teachings filtered down into the popular consciousness so that the deterministic concept of a fate controlled by the stars was largely taken for granted. There is a possible reflection of this in Paul's declaration that "neither height, nor depth, nor any other creature shall be able to separate us from the love of God, which is in Christ Jesus our Lord" (Rom. 8:39). "Height" and "depth" (*hypsoma* and *bathos*) were terms used technically of the celestial spaces above and below the horizon within which the stars move and from which they rise,[16] or possibly their rising and setting.[17] The belief that human life was

15 Cf. Ethelbert Stauffer, *Christ and the Caesars,* pp. 151-152.
16 Moulton & Milligan, *The Vocabulary of the Greek New Testament,* p. 662. See P. Lond. 110¹⁴ (horoscope A.D. 138); p. 101, *Bathos:* the space below the horizon out of which the stars rise.
17 See Samuel Angus, *The Mystery Religions and Christianity,* p. 252.

controlled by the heavenly bodies led to a dual consequence: the oppression of a fatalism that left no room for human choice, since the destiny of every man was settled by the star that dominated his birth, and superstitious practice of magic that invoked demonic powers to free man from the tyranny of the planets.

The mood of fatalism predominated especially in the first century. Manilius, a poet who flourished in the reigns of Augustus and Tiberius, wrote:

> Fate rules the earth and all things stand firm by a fixed law . . . the moment of our birth also witnesses our death, and our end depends upon our beginning.[18]

Vergil depicted the wanderings of Aeneas as controlled by a formless but irresistible power that led him on to new adventures and that subordinated the individual will to ineluctable destiny. Less articulate than the Stoic philosophy, but equally deterministic, this concept of fate appeared in all the literature of the Augustan age and to a large degree created its emotional climate.

Into such a superstitious and materialistic world Christianity was born. Fate, demons, and gods of every description haunted the atmosphere; spells, incantations, and magic were the means by which the individual could fend off the dangers that encircled him. Security was obtained by bribing the deities, or by ascertaining from horoscopes what course of action to pursue, or by discovering some potent charm to keep the threatening powers of darkness at bay. The uncertainty of the future held the masses of mankind in mental and spiritual bondage. Not until the light of the gospel of Christ penetrated to the Gentiles did men begin to lose their dread of the unseen powers and to achieve a true freedom.

The Social Pressure

Parallel to the hostile religious atmosphere was the social tension which placed Christians at a signal disadvantage. The beginning of the movement was closely connected with Judaism, for Jesus was a Jew, His disciples were mostly Jews, and His teaching was founded on the Jewish Scriptures. In some ways this connection was an advantage, for it gave the new faith soil in which to grow. Doctrinally its heritage was great; but socially it shared in the obloquy which has been the lot of Israel since time immemorial. Because of their rigid monotheism and because of their insistence on moral and ceremonial purity, the Jews stood aloof from the pagan ideals and practices. Christians took substantially the same position, but they

---

[18] Manilius, iv. 14.

did not have a national origin as their defense. Rome was generally tolerant of the peculiarities of a national cult but could not understand why men who were not obligated by racial ties would wish to abstain from the pleasures in which the majority indulged. The Christians were consequently under constant suspicion and were deprived of privileges freely accorded to others. An echo of this conflict appears in the First Epistle of Peter. Warning his friends that a "fiery trial" was impending, he told them not to regard it as exceptional since they could normally expect to suffer rejection and enmity from a pagan community. They were, however, not to suffer as murderers, or as thieves, or as malefactors, but were to keep their moral record clear. If they were charged with being Christians, they should not be ashamed but should glory in the title, since it associated them with Christ (I Pet. 4:13-16). The plain implication of Peter's language is that in the popular mind Chrisians were usually classed with criminals and nuisances. Tacitus, writing of the times of Nero, calls Christians "enemies of the human race."[19] It is hardly possible that Tacitus should have applied to them this epithet because of sadism or sourness on their part. It is more likely that he considered them to be antisocial because they did not conform to the social habits of the time.

The prevailing laxity in sexual behavior, the gluttonous and idolatrous feasts, the incessant holiday-making in honor of the emperor or of the gods, and the interchange of entertainment in pagan homes must have affected many Christians. Particularly are these pressures mirrored in I Corinthians, an epistle written to the church in a prosperous heathen city. The moral degeneration of Corinth had infiltrated the church so that one man had taken his father's wife and had consequently created a public scandal. Others had been so affected by the atmosphere of idolatry that they did not know whether they should eat food that had been offered to idols or not (I Cor. 10:23-31). Living as they did under the constant influence of idolatry, it was easy for the Christian to lose sight of the niceties of distinction in ethical behavior.

The Intellectual Pressure

The intellectual framework of any age is usually set by the mental outlook of the prevailing majority. Harold Mattingly says:

> We have learned today to put a high value on the blessed trio of honesty, candour, care. We see in them the chief guarantees of that disinterested inquiry on which progress seems to depend. These virtues stood at a low ebb under the Empire. The scientific

[19] *Annals* xv. 44.

spirit was only feebly alive. Little fresh work was done on the advancement of knowledge. What was already known in different fields might be carefully recorded, but there was little careful scrutiny, very little that could be called research. The Empire . . . held what it inherited from the past; it did not go on to utilize it for further advance.[20]

The Roman mind did not lend itself to speculative subjects but was materialistic in outlook. The early church in the western half of the Roman empire did not produce any prominent theologians until Tertullian in the late second century, and he lacked the flexibility of thought and the facility of expression that characterized his Greek contemporary, Clement of Alexandria. Furthermore, the early Christians were probably drawn chiefly from the lower classes. While there may have been among them numerous persons of keen intellect, the majority were unschooled and were consequently unable to assume a commanding position in society. Several generations passed before they developed an apologetic that expressed a logical and defensible faith, and still longer before they made an appreciable impression upon the public mind. Nevertheless, the ideas which Christianity produced bore fruit and created a new intellectual atmosphere that challenged the best that paganism could offer. Clement of Alexandria and Augustine of Hippo have been listed among the world's great philosophers because of their contribution to human thought.

Christianity, therefore, had to shape a new intellectual system by applying the principles of the gospel of Christ to Greek idealism and Roman materialism. It was compelled to wrestle with the problems of the age and to produce answers. Because it succeeded in answering many of the riddles of the day, it gained a hearing and, in many instances, general acceptance.

The Economic Pressure

Until the era of the major persecutions, which did not begin until the second half of the second century, Christians were probably not the object of general economic discrimination. Although they may have been distrusted and disliked by those who were acquainted with them, no laws were enacted against them until the time of Trajan, and even then they were persecuted only when they refused publicly to do obeisance to the emperor or to worship the gods. Such persecution was sporadic and local; no broad economic campaign against them is recorded.

---

[20] Harold Mattingly, *Roman Imperial Civilization*, p. 179.

On the other hand, the imagery of Revelation 13, though prophetic, seems to indicate that it was modeled on some type of existing economic pressure:

And he causeth all, the small and the great, and the rich and the poor, and the free and the bond, that there be given them a mark on their right hand, or upon their forehead; and that no man should be able to buy or sell, save he that hath the mark, even the name of the beast or the number of his name (vv. 16, 17).

Deissmann has shown that in imperial times from Augustus to Trajan the seal of the emperor was affixed to bills of sale and similar documents. The seal contained the year of the reigning Caesar, his name, and sometimes the abbreviation for indicating that it must be validated by the proper official.[21] There is no evidence that Christians were compelled to wear this stamp on their persons, as Revelation states. If they did suffer economic discrimination, it was more likely because they had refused to use the seal on their business documents, since it implied worship of the empire. Such tension, however, could easily have arisen.

The extension of the principle that only supporters of state policy may possess economic rights has been put into effect in recent years, and could easily be made a potent means of religious and social control. R. H. Charles observes:

> The necessaries of life are to be withheld from such as have not the mark of the beast in order to bring them under the notice of the imperial authorities, and that thus none should escape. A ruthless economic warfare is here proclaimed with a view to the absolute supremacy of the State. This is not represented as a part of the present but as the future in store for the inhabitants of the earth.[22]

Whether Christians of the first and second centuries experienced a general boycott is doubtful, but they must have been aware that such action was a constant threat. The warnings of Revelation would have had little weight if they had not already endured some of the hardships which a hostile society can inflict by economic repression.

Christianity, therefore, originated among enemies. Its doctrines were either distasteful to its hearers or else directly inimical to the tenets of the populace at large, and its ethic was opposed to the prevailing moral practices. There were, of course, some resemblances between the tenets of Christians and the current religious concepts, and undoubtedly there were individuals who cherished lofty ideals of conduct which they desired to attain. For these the gospel of

---

21 Adolf Deissmann, *Bible Studies*, pp. 240-247.
22 R. H. Charles, *The Revelation of St. John*, I, 360-364.

redemption had a strong appeal; had it not been so, the church would not have grown in the Gentile world as indeed it did. In the main, however, the church had to fight for survival, and although there were periods of comparative peace in which advance was unobstructed by official interference, the atmosphere was unfriendly. As Paul stated it: *Our wrestling is not against flesh and blood, but against the principalities, against the powers, against the world-rulers of this darkness, against the spiritual hosts of wickedness in the heavenly places* (Eph. 6:12).

6

The Augustan Age:
The Youth of Christ

L UKE, THE FIRST HISTORIAN OF THE CHRISTIAN CHURCH, COMMEN-
ces his two-volume work with three references to contemporary
history. The first, which introduces the preparatory steps for the
advent of Christ, is dated "in the days of Herod, king of Judea"
(Luke 1:5), who was the last titular king of Palestine, although in reality he was a vassal of Rome. The second places the birth of Jesus
in the reign of Caesar Augustus, the first Roman to wear the imperial
purple as the sole ruler of the empire (2:1). The third correlates
the opening of Jesus' ministry with "the fifteenth year of Tiberius
Caesar" (3:1), and mentions also the lesser officials who presided
over Palestine at that time: Pontius Pilate, the Roman procurator;
Herod Antipas, son of Herod the Great, who was tetrarch of Galilee;
his brother Philip, who was tetrarch of the northern territory of Iturea and Trachonitis, northeast of the Sea of Galilee; and Lysanias,
tetrarch of Abilene, which lay between the Lebanon and Anti-Lebanon mountains. The borders of their kingdoms were not sharply defined but their general location is known.

The ecclesiastical authority of the Jewish people was vested in the
Sadducean house of Annas, high priest *emeritus,* who had first been
appointed to office in A.D. 6 by Quirinius, the imperial legate of
Syria, and who held his position until he was deposed by Valerius
Gratus, the procurator of Judea, about A.D. 15. Annas' son-in-law,
Caiaphas, became high priest in A.D. 18, and Annas continued to be

the "power behind the throne" until both were deposed in A.D. 36. Probably because of his continuing influence he is mentioned in conjunction with Caiaphas both in Luke's chronology (Luke 3:1) and in the narrative of the trial of Jesus (John 18:24).

The Roman World

The accession of Augustus marked a new era in world history. Under the Republic the domain of Rome had been rapidly expanding through military conquest and peaceful annexation. By the time of the battle of Actium, which closed the period of civil war and left Octavian the undisputed master of the world, the generals of Rome had already conquered Gaul and most of Spain, had destroyed Carthage and had made North Africa a Roman farm, had subdued Macedonia and Achaia and had razed Corinth to the ground. Rome had acquired later the rich province of Asia through the bequest of the last king of Pergamum and had gained control of Egypt and the Mediterranean coast. This vast country, populated by races of different colors, cultures, temperaments, and religions, was now for the first time brought under the sovereignty of one state and of one man.

The cessation of the bitter civil wars that had distressed Rome for nearly a century inaugurated a welcome peace. The moderation and sagacity of Augustus fostered confidence in his rule, and his wise refusal of a titular dictatorship allayed the fears of those who had been apprehensive of a return to monarchy. He spared the lives of all his opponents who asked for pardon and refrained from the wholesale slaughter of enemies in which his predecessors had indulged. Augustus demilitarized the empire by discharging more than 300,000 soldiers from the army and by settling them in colonies or in their own towns. In times of economic stress he paid for free grain out of his own purse and erected numerous public buildings at his own expense. He reformed the laws concerning adultery and usury, enforced a just assessment of taxes, and improved the organization of the government. The catalog of his numerous achievements, carved on the wall of a temple at Ancyra in Asia Minor (now Ankara, the capital of Turkey), credits him with the erection of fourteen temples and the restoration of eighty-two public buildings, together with extensive construction of aqueducts and roads.[1] Piracy and brigandage, which had flourished in the last disorganized days of the Republic, were firmly repressed. A salutary *esprit de corps* sprang up in the empire so that people began to pride themselves upon being Romans and to become con-

[1] *Res Gestae Divi Augusti Monumentum Ancyranum,* translated by Shipley, pp. 344ff.

A statue of Caesar Augustus sacrificing, clad in a toga. (The Bettmann Archive.)

scious of a new unity in the state. Although the cultures varied widely from the cringing fellahin of Egypt to the independent mountaineers of the Alps, and from the miners of Spain to the merchants of Syria, they shared alike in the protection and privileges of the Roman government. Stability created prosperity, and while poverty was always present, the subjects of the empire enjoyed a greater sense of security than ever before.

Augustus obtained control of the empire slowly but insistently through the personal appropriation of governmental authority. He had the right to purge the rolls of the Senate, to initiate legislation, to superintend the public treasury, to hold the supreme military command, and to act as *pontifex maximus,* or religious head of the state. He was, in effect, dictator of Rome, though he seemed to be singularly discreet in his exercise of these tremendous powers. He desired "to make life secure and tolerable for every class in the empire."[2] In order to do so, he had to reorganize the machinery of the state and to make sure that every part of his domain was well governed. To the limit of his ability he endeavored to do so, for during his reign he visited almost every province and evinced keen interest in the welfare of his subjects. He succeeded in establishing a system that survived the shocks of external attack and the blight of internal decay for more than four centuries after his death — an achievement that has probably been equaled by no other political administrator.

Unlike the preceding empires of Assyria, Babylonia, Persia, and Greece, Rome was a national unit. It absorbed into one commonwealth the varied and sometimes discordant cultures of the subject peoples, and made them Roman. By government, by training in the legions through which so many of her men passed, and by the silent pervasive influence of the imperial culture, Gauls, Spaniards, Germans, Syrians, Greeks, and others became Romanized. To this day Roman law, Roman literature, and the court languages of Latin and Greek still prevail among the nations of the Mediterranean basin.

The Birth of Christ: The Family

The greatest event of the Augustan age was the birth of Jesus in an obscure village a few miles south of Jerusalem. His mother, Mary, was probably young, and was at the time of His birth affianced to Joseph, an artisan of Nazareth, a town located in the hills about twenty miles west of the Sea of Galilee. Both Mark and Matthew affirm that Joseph and Jesus were engaged in a building trade (Matt. 13:55; Mark 6:3). The word *tekton,* usually translated "carpenter," is somewhat broader in meaning than the English term which implies only woodworking. It may mean either carpenter or mason and by one author is applied to a man who manufactured plows. Build-

---

[2] John Buchan, *Augustus,* pp. 166, 167.

The grotto of the nativity, traditional site of the birth of Christ, located in the basement of the Church of the Nativity in Bethlehem. According to this tradition, the "manger" of Christ's birth (Luke 2:7) was located in a cave-like stable. (Matson Photo Service.)

ing in the Near East involved stone and brick much more than wood, for lumber was scarce. "Builder" might be a better rendering of this term. Probably Joseph was an ordinary craftsman, able to make a fair living, but not wealthy. The fact that he had to return to Bethlehem to register for the imperial census may indicate that he or his family owned property there for which he had to give account.

The Census

The historicity of this census has been disputed by theological scholars more than by the classicists and historians. Schürer argued that (1) there is no historical record of a general imperial census in the time of Augustus; (2) under Roman procedure neither Joseph nor Mary would have been obliged to register at Bethlehem; (3) a Roman census could not have been conducted in the territory of an associate king like Herod; (4) Josephus states explicitly that the first Roman census took place under Quirinius after Judea became a Roman province in A.D. 7; (5) such a census held under Quirinius could not have occurred under Herod, since Quirinius was not governor of Palestine until ten years or more after Herod's death.[3]

Schürer's objections which were fairly representative of the historical difficulties involved have been largely dissipated by recent discoveries. Although a categorical affirmation of an early census under Quirinius is still lacking, the statement of Luke is corroborated by current evidence. The argument from silence does not prove the impossibility of an early census, since many historical events have escaped the notice of the ancient chroniclers who either overlooked them or deemed them unimportant. During the twenty-five years preceding the birth of Christ Augustus was endeavoring to reorganize the finances of the empire and to put them on a sound basis. Certainly it is not beyond probability that he would make an official review of the alien kingdoms under his sovereignty. The *Monumentum Ancyranum* evidently refers to such an occasion: "A second time, in the consulship of Gaius Censorius and Gaius Asinius, I again performed the *lustrum* alone with the consular imperium. In this *lustrum* 4,233,000 Roman citizens were entered on the census roll."[4]

The existence of regular enrollments every fourteen years has been conclusively established by the discovery of receipts and decrees among the papyri of Egypt. Deissmann cites an edict of G. Vibius Maximus,·governor of Egypt in A.D. 104, stating that the customary household enrollment was due, and that persons who were for any cause outside of their home territories should return to complete their registrations.[5] Joseph's presence in Bethlehem may have been imperative. While a second-century procedure in Egypt may not necessarily determine the first-century procedure in Judea, the edict

---

[3] Emil Schürer, *A History of the Jewish People in the Time of Jesus Christ,* Div. I, Vol. II, 107-143.
[4] *Res Gestae Divi Augusti,* II. 8. Probably the census in Judea was considerably delayed because of local conditions.
[5] Adolf Deissmann, *Light from the Ancient East,* pp. 268, 269.

does indicate plainly that the practice of registration for tax at the family home was not exceptional. Mary may not have needed to return to Bethlehem, but doubtlessly she accompanied Joseph because she did not wish to be left alone. Only Joseph would understand the secret of her condition, and the birth of the child in Bethlehem would probably evoke less gossip than in Nazareth. By the time they returned to Nazareth some years later few questions would be asked.

The relation of Herod to Augustus at the time of this census was precarious. Augustus, according to Josephus,[6] was angry with him because he had declared war on the Arabians without Roman permission and had thereby endangered Rome's frontiers. He wrote Herod that whereas he had previously treated him as a friend, he would thereafter treat him as a subject. Whether this irate note was merely a threat or a definite declaration of policy may be debatable, but in either case Herod was warned that it would be unsafe for him to ignore Roman preferences. Augustus had begun to exert political pressure on Herod which he would not dare to resist. If Augustus contemplated an empire-wide survey, Herod would have been in no position to refuse co-operation. The succession to his kingdom was subject to the approval of Augustus, and Herod must have known that his remaining span of life was short. If he had any preferences concerning his successor, he could not afford to offend the power that could confirm or deny his appointment.

Augustus therefore could have demanded a census of Herod's domain, but it may be that the process of the census was delayed. According to the fourteen-year cycle, it should have begun in the year 9/8 B.C. The Jews, however, were restive and rebellious, and would have resented deeply any apparent invasion of their rights by a foreign power. If the enrollment could be conducted under the guise of a family or tribal census, it would be less likely to offend the populace, since it would be more nearly Jewish in character. The account of Luke seems to indicate that it was organized by tribal and clan lines, since the ancestral ties of Joseph were emphasized. It may even be possible that the census was delayed longer, if Herod's family problems and the troubled state of the country precluded prompt action. Augustus might also be tolerant of some delay if he realized that a more gradual procedure would avert rebellion.

Schürer's objection that the first Roman census took place under Quirinius after Judea became a Roman province in A.D. 7 is based on his interpretation of two authorities. Luke says, "This was

6 *Antiquities* xvi. 9. 3.

the first enrollment made when Quirinius was governor of Syria" (Luke 2:2). Josephus states also that "Cyrenius, a Roman senator, and one who had gone through other magistracies, and who passed through them until he had been consul, and one who, on other accounts, was of great dignity, came out at this time into Syria, with a few others, being sent by Caesar to be a judge of that nation and to take account of their substance. . . ."[7]   Josephus specified that this taxation took place in A.D. 7: "When Cyrenius had now disposed of Archelaus' money, and when the taxings were come to a conclusion, which were made in the thirty-seventh [year] of Caesar's victory over Antony at Actium. . . ."[8]

Cyrenius or Quirinius seems to have been the financial officer associated with the procurator Coponius. His command was independent of the regular provincial governor, though there was a close affiliation between the two. Nowhere in Josephus' account, however, does he state that Cyrenius' collection of money in A.D. 6 was the first taxation. To assume that Luke's statement refers to the same action of Quirinius is consequently unwarranted; it is much more likely that the collection of A.D. 6 is the one mentioned by Gamaliel in the speech recorded in Acts 5:37, for he couples it with the revolt of one Judas, to whom Josephus alludes in the same context. The very fact that Luke specifies the first enrollment under Quirinius may indicate that two were conducted under his supervision.

There is some evidence that Quirinius was twice in charge of affairs in Syria. On January 1, 12 B.C., P. Sulpicius Quirinius was made a consul. In that same year Marcus Vipsanius Agrippa, Augustus' trusted friend and viceroy, whom he had placed in charge of Eastern affairs, died, and Augustus sent Quirinius to the East to act as overseer, probably in Agrippa's place. He seems to have served as general military commander in conjunction with the civil provincial governors. From 9 to 6 B.C. the governor of Syria was C. Sentius Saturninus, under whom Tertullian said the first enrollment took place;[9] from 6 to 4 B.C., P. Quintilius Varus. In 2 B.C. the two sons of Agrippa, Gaius, and Lucius Caesar, were recognized as potential heirs of Augustus, and Gaius Caesar was sent to the East, where he was placed under the tutelage of Quirinius. He died in A.D. 4, and Quirinius remained in command until replaced by Germanicus, the appointee of Tiberius in A.D. 17.[10]

Luke's language does not imply that Quirinius was the procurator of Syria, but only that he was "ruling" or "in command" (*hege-*

---

[7] *Ibid.,* xviii. 1. 1.
[8] *Ibid.*
[9] *Adversus Marcionem* iv. 19. See also *Adversus Judaeos* vii.
[10] Ethelbert Stauffer, *Jesus and His Story,* pp. 29, 30.

moneuontos). Perhaps his language could be paraphrased as "The initial enrollment took place during Cyrenius' command over Syria" (Luke 2:2). That Quirinius had two periods of active administration in Syria seems clear from the *Lapis Tiburtinus,* a fragmentary marble inscription found near Tivoli in 1764. The inscription memorialized the deeds of a Roman official who served during the reign of Augustus. He was honored with two official thanksgivings (supplications) and the *Ornamenta Triumphalia,* or the honorary dress of a triumphing general; he was proconsul of Asia and twice was the *legatus* of Augustus in charge of Syria. The only likely candidate whose qualifications fit this description is Quirinius, and a large number of prominent historians agree that he had two Syrian governorships.

The dates of his administration are uncertain, except for his consulship in 12 B.C. and his second government of Syria in A.D. 6. Ramsay calculates that the years during which Quirinius was administering Syria were 5 to 3 B.C., or may have been still earlier.[11] While this figure does not coincide exactly with the fourteen-year cycle mentioned above, it is quite possible that Augustus' decree was obeyed only with reluctance by Herod, and that it took the pressure of the Eastern commander-in-chief to make him act. Sentius Saturninus governed Syria from 9 to 7 B.C., and Quintilius Varus from 7 to 4 B.C. If the relation between Quirinius and either or both of these men was analogous to his later relationship to Coponius as previously stated, there is no reason why Luke cannot be right when he says that a census was inaugurated under Quirinius. It may have been proclaimed during the procuratorship of Saturninus, and have been actively enforced during the rule of Varus. Luke may have referred to Quirinius rather than to the procurators because at that time Quirinius, the imperial legate, was the real head of the government. Probably he did not reside in Syria during all of this time but made his headquarters wherever he was needed most. Ramsay concludes that "the enrollment of Palestine was delayed by the causes described until the late summer or autumn of 6 B.C. At that time Varus was controlling the internal affairs of Syria, while Quirinius was commanding its armies and directing its foreign policy."[12]

One more comment seems pertinent concerning Luke's historical allusion. Luke deserves no less credit for historical accuracy than would be assigned to Josephus or to any other contemporary writer. His notation of Quirinius' enrollment is clear, though brief, and is more definite than many statements in Josephus which are accepted

---

11 Sir William Ramsay, *Was Christ Born at Bethlehem?*, pp. 227-248.
12 *Ibid.,* p. 244.

Terraced Judean hills near Abu Ghosh, Israel. (Courtesy Israel Information Services.)

at face value. Not all details are yet corroborated by external evidence, but the essential trustworthiness of the Lukan account has not yet been disproved.[13]   In fact, Stauffer has shown that quite probably the taxation of A.D. 7 that provoked the revolt of Judas of Galilee may have been only the collection of dues that were established by the survey which began in 7 B.C.[14]

[13] Norval Geldenhuys, "Special Note: The Enrolment Under Augustus" in *The Gospel of Luke,* in "New International Commentary on the New Testament," pp. 104-106.
[14] *Op. cit.,* pp. 19-32.

The Birth and Ministry of John the Baptist

All four Gospels record with greater or less fulness the prophetic ministry of John the Baptist, whose preaching prepared the way for the public appearances of Jesus. John's parentage came from priestly stock; his father Zacharias was a member of the Temple priesthood, and his mother Elizabeth was a descendant of Aaron. According to the description given by Luke, both were singularly devout, but probably not eminent in the hierarchy at Jerusalem. They resided in a village in the hill country of Judah, near enough to Jerusalem so that Zacharias could participate in his duties in the Temple.

Zacharias was a member of the course of Abijah, one of the twenty-four clans or ranks of priests who maintained the Temple ritual (I Chron. 24:10). The "courses" took turns in conducting the ceremonies of worship and each member usually had the privilege of presiding once in his lifetime. The opportunity of offering incense was the high point of Zacharias' career, for he was delegated to enter into the Holy Place of the Temple, where the altar of incense stood before the mysterious veil that concealed the Holy of Holies.

The wilderness of Judea, where John preached, and the northern end of the Dead Sea. In the background are the mountains of Moab. (Matson Photo Service.)

On this particular occasion, as he offered the incense and repeated the customary prayers, he was astounded to find another person present in the chamber where he supposed that he was alone. "An angel of the Lord" appeared, standing on the right side of the altar of incense. Zacharias was frightened by the unexpected apparition, but the angel calmed him with the assurance that his prayers had been heard. Geldenhuys suggests that the angel referred to Zacharias' prayers for the redemption of Israel rather than to prayers for a child, since Zacharias and Elizabeth were so far advanced in age that they had probably abandoned hope.[15]

If this interpretation be accepted, the words of the angel made a connection between the fulfillment of Israel's hope which Zacharias had uttered in his ritual prayer and the gift of the child for whom he had longed. The promised heir would, like Samson, be dedicated to God from birth and, like Elijah, he would become an agent of revival in the nation. The assurance was guaranteed by the speechlessness which overcame Zacharias, and he remained dumb until the promise was fulfilled.

In due time John was born, and Luke says that "the child grew, and waxed strong in spirit, and was in the deserts until the day of his showing unto Israel" (Luke 1:80). The silent years in John's biography, no less than in the life of Jesus, raise numerous questions. Where was he "in the deserts"? What was he doing? What was his preparation for his active and influential ministry? Since Zacharias and Elizabeth were already old when John was born, it is improbable that they survived until he opened his ministry, for he was only six months older than Jesus and did not begin to preach until a short time before Jesus Himself was baptized. John may have obtained some of his education from his priestly father, but it seems likely that other influences affected him also. His words show that he was conversant with the Old Testament Scriptures, and that he even applied some of them to his own ministry (John 1:23, quoting Isaiah 40:3). He evinced definite ascetic tendencies, for he wore the rough clothing of the desert dweller and ate locusts and wild honey (Mark 1:6).

Because of his separatist and iconoclastic tendencies, John has been classed by some scholars as an Essene. He was uncompromising in devotion to the ethic of the Law and dared to reprove Herod Antipas publicly for his adulterous marriage with Herodias, his brother's wife. He emerged from the same desert where the Qumran community had been established, which flourished during the time of his preaching.

[15] *Op. cit.,* pp. 62-64.

His favorite text was Isaiah 40:3: "The voice of one crying in the wilderness, Prepare ye the way of the Lord; make his paths straight." According to the *Manual of Discipline,* the Qumran community made the same text the reason for their mission:

> When these men [twelve laymen and three priests, the leaders of the congregation] exist in Israel, these are the provisions where- by they are to be kept apart from any consort with froward men, to the end that they may indeed "go into the wilderness to prepare the way," i.e., do what Scripture enjoins when it says, "Prepare in the wilderness the way . . . make straight in the desert a high- way for our God . . . ."[16]

Both John and the Essenes practiced lustrations or washings for purification, with the difference that the Essenes stressed baptism only for initiates within their ranks, while the baptism of John seems to have been administered to any who expressed a desire for repentance (Mark 1:4).

Duncan Howlett suggests that John was an Essene who had taken a broad view of the mission of the sect:

> John the Baptist became a missionary, and perhaps tried to make the Essenes into a missionary movement. In this he reversed the Essene concept, which had originally been developed by men who felt they had no other course but to withdraw into the wilderness and prepare there the way of the Lord.[17]

Interesting and plausible as this thesis may be, it is by no means a certain conclusion that John the Baptist had been a member of the Qumran community, or even an Essene. No exact parallel can be established between his preaching and the content of the Scrolls, though there are some likenesses. Probably there were many small independent sects in first-century Palestine, founded by would-be reformers and messiahs. Within his own generation he would be classed with them; from the long perspective of history one can now discern his superior message and function.

Although he was avowedly the forerunner of Jesus (Mark 1:7, 8), not all of his disciples transferred to Jesus, for he had a sizable following after the Lord began His preaching (Matt. 11:2; John 3:22, 23; 4:1). Long after the founding of the church there still existed groups that adhered to his teaching, and that finally adopted the fuller view of Christianity preached by the apostles (Acts 19:3).

16 *Manual of Discipline* viii. 14.
17 Duncan Howlett, *The Essenes and Christianity,* pp. 134, 135, 137, 142ff.

The Retirement to Egypt

The flight into Egypt of Joseph and Mary with the infant Jesus reflected the social and political uncertainty of the times. Herod was nearing the end of his career; Roman intervention under the expanding power of Augustus was increasing, as the imperial order for the census demonstrated, and popular unrest was growing. Joseph and Mary, now charged with the care of the child who had been miraculously entrusted to them, must have felt these pressures keenly. The Wise Men may have informed them of Herod's sudden and malicious interest in the baby, and the divine warning corroborated whatever apprehensions they might have had. Silently and suddenly they withdrew from Bethlehem, but instead of returning to Galilee, they went southward to Egypt (Matt. 2:13-15).

Egypt differed from all the other provinces of the Roman empire because it was directly subject to the administration of the emperor. Since it was the source of grain for the teeming populace of Rome, and was consequently essential to the control of the empire, Augustus was careful to keep it in his own hands. No senator or general could even set foot in Egypt without special permission. The governor was an appointed prefect of equestrian order, responsible to the emperor himself, and the armed forces stationed there were not commanded by senators or by professional soldiers but by equestrians who were members of the wealthy upper middle class.

The population of Egypt was cosmopolitan. The peasants were Egyptian; Alexandria, the chief port city, second in size in the empire, contained a large community of Jews; and many of the aristocracy were Greek by ancestry.[18] An exile from any part of the Roman world could more easily lose himself in Egypt than anywhere else, for he could find compatriots speaking his own language, and he would no longer be subject to the ordinary surveillance of a Roman governor, nor would he be at the mercy of some petty king.

The Gospel of Matthew tells nothing of Joseph's employment in Egypt, nor does it state exactly how long he remained there. Possibly he obtained work in Alexandria, or he and Mary may have faded into the anonymous multitudes of the city while they lived on the bounty of the Wise Men, which they could have sold easily in the open market without incurring any suspicion. It is not unlikely that the family may have spent as much as two years in Egypt, for if Jesus was born during the close of the census period in 5/4 B.C., they could have returned to their homeland in 4/3 B.C. after Herod's death (2:14, 15).

[18] Edward T. Salmon, *A History of the Roman World from 30 B.C. to A.D. 138,* pp. 93, 94.

The Massacre of the Infants

Herod's massacre of the infants in Bethlehem, though not chronicled in any other source, is not incompatible with historical facts. Herod was already a sick man, suffering the last stages of hardening of the arteries, which affected both his body and his mind. His insane jealousy of his sovereignty prompted the execution of his sons, one only four days before his death. The slaughter of a few peasant infants in an obscure town would never have been noticed by the ordinary historian of his time because it would have been negligible in comparison with Herod's other crimes.

Archelaus, the son who succeeded Herod, inherited his father's cruelty without his father's ability. His reign was marked by armed rebellion that could be quelled only through the intervention of Varus, the Roman governor of Syria. In A.D. 6, ten years after his succession to the throne, Archelaus was deposed by Augustus and was banished to Gaul. Coponius, a Roman knight, was appointed procurator of Judea, and under his rule the property tax was imposed that provoked the revolt of Judas of Galilee.[19]

The Return from Egypt

One may fairly deduce from Matthew's language that the original intent of Joseph and Mary was to settle in Bethlehem, but such was the reputation of Archelaus that they did not wish to be subject to his rule (2:21, 22). Instead, after a divine warning, Joseph continued northward and resumed his residence in Nazareth, which was in the realm of Herod Antipas. There Jesus grew to manhood. Luke informs his reader that "the child grew, and waxed strong, filled with wisdom, and the grace of God was upon him" (Luke 2:40). The impression conveyed by these words is that Jesus was in no way abnormal, except that his development was marked by an unusual perfection. He increased in size as children do; He gained in physical strength; but He possessed the keenness of mind and the spiritual grace that was not marred by erratic impulses and moral imperfections.

The Youth of Jesus: The Silent Years

All of the Gospels maintain a complete silence concerning this period of Jesus' life, with one exception. Luke, who evidently had access to some source of family information, records the visit of Jesus to the Passover Feast at Jerusalem when He was twelve years

---

[19] Josephus, *Wars of the Jews* ii. 8. See also Acts 5:37.

of age (Luke 2:41-51). Joseph and Mary must have been devout Israelites, for Luke states that the pilgrimage to Jerusalem was their annual custom. The visit of Jesus, however, had a special significance, since the age of twelve marked His becoming *bar-mitzvah*, "a son of the law." At that point the Jewish boy reached the age of accountability and was formally inducted into the privileges and responsibilities of the community.

The Lukan account seems to imply that Jesus had not previously accompanied Joseph and Mary to Jerusalem. If this occasion was His first visit, it must have been singularly impressive. Jerusalem was the largest and most populous Jewish city of Palestine, for Caesarea and Samaria, which were built by Herod, were more Roman in style and atmosphere. For centuries the stone and stucco walls of Jerusalem had crowned the hills on which it stood, gleaming like a jewel in the barrenness of the surrounding country. As the family joined the other Passover pilgrims in their journey to the city, they shared in the festal spirit and undoubtedly were thrilled at the first sight of Jerusalem's towers while they climbed the road that led to its gates.

The Mt. of Olives, showing the Church of All Nations, the Garden of Gethsemane, the Russian Church of Mary Magdalene, and (right) the Chapel Dominus Flevit, the traditional site where Jesus wept over the city on Palm Sunday. (Courtesy KLM — Royal Dutch Airlines.)

The Damascus Gate in Jerusalem, Jordan, leading into the suq *or market place. The gate and the wall at this point were built by the Ottoman Turk Suleiman the Magnificent in the sixteenth century.* (Courtesy KLM — Royal Dutch Airlines.)

The response of Jesus to the visit was twofold: He evinced an interest in the learning of His nation and He revealed a consciousness of His unique relationship with God. When the Passover had ended, the pilgrims dispersed to their homes. Joseph and Mary, with their neighbors, left for Nazareth, but Jesus remained in the Temple where He was listening to the discussion of the rabbis and engaging in dialogue with them. Because they supposed that He had traveled with some other segment of the caravans, Joseph and Mary did not miss Him until the close of the first day's journey. When He failed to appear among the travelers bound for Nazareth, they retraced their steps to Jerusalem to search for Him. They found Him in the Temple and reproved Him gently for causing them undue concern. His reply reveals the development of His consciousness: "How is it that ye sought me? Know ye not that I must be in my Father's house?" (2:49).

Looking north from Herod's Gate in Jerusalem, one can see the rocky hillock behind the bus station which the British general Charles G. Gordon identified as Golgotha, "the place of the skull." "Gordon's Calvary," as the rock has been called since 1883, is an alternative to the Church of the Holy Sepulchre as the site of the crucifixion. (Courtesy Prof. B. Van Elderen.)

Luke comments that they did not understand the significance of His words. Undoubtedly such interest in the Temple and its teachers would have been exceptional for a twelve-year-old boy. The anomaly, however, was not wholly psychological; Jesus' attitude shows that He had already a strong consciousness of His unique relation with the heavenly Father which demanded more of Him than His obligation to Joseph and Mary. There is no evidence that He reacted against them; on the contrary, Luke affirms that He returned to Nazareth with them "and was subject to them" (2:50).

This brief glimpse of Jesus in His adolescent years indicates that He had the normal home life and training of a Jewish boy. The careful observance of the Passover by Joseph and Mary marks them as devout observers of the Law, and His participation in the discussion of the teachers shows that He must have studied the Law himself and have had some interest in its interpretation even in His earliest years. At the same time He had a practical training, for Joseph was an artisan and his sons probably followed his trade according to custom.

Little if anything is said in the Gospels concerning the cultural contacts that Jesus may have had with the Graeco-Roman influences in Palestine. Nazareth itself was not a prominent city of Galilee, for it is neither mentioned in the Old Testament nor in the Apocrypha nor in the histories of Josephus. Nathanael's contemptuous query, "Can any good thing come out of Nazareth?" (John 1:46), indicates that it was not held in high esteem by Jesus' contemporaries. It was not completely isolated, for the caravan routes from the East passed just to the south, and the main road to the cities of the Decapolis from Caesarea and from Ptolemais, one of the chief ports on the Phoenician coast, crossed the hills a little north of Nazareth. In all probability its inhabitants were constantly in contact with the bustling life of the lake cities and were well aware of contemporary political and social movements. Jesus was not brought up in primitive isolation but was acquainted with the cosmopolitan culture of Gentile Galilee, as well as with the more restricted Jewish community of which He was a member.

Through trade and through the contacts with the ebb and flow of pilgrims, military personnel, and the general influence of the

The Old City of Jerusalem, seen from the Damascus Gate. The two large domes in the center mark the Church of the Holy Sepulchre. (Courtesy KLM — Royal Dutch Airlines.)

Graeco-Roman civilization in Palestine, Jesus must have become acquainted with the Greek language and mode of life. The legions that tramped the highways and city streets moving toward or from posts of duty, the peddlers and agents who traveled for business, and the government officials who occupied the positions of power would have been known to Him as a boy. Curiously enough, Sepphoris and Tiberias, two of the largest and most populous cities of Galilee, are never mentioned in the Gospels, possibly because their predominantly Gentile character was distasteful to Jews. Nevertheless their influence must have been felt in the surrounding countryside so that the character of Roman culture would have been known even among the conservative peasantry.

While Jesus was undoubtedly familiar with Greek culture and Roman militarism, He was probably not affected seriously by either. His later teaching reveals His awareness of both, but insofar as it can be traced to influences external to Himself, its chief source was Judaism. The Old Testament Scriptures, from which He quoted extensively, and the total theistic basis of His teaching were distinctly Jewish. He utilized the ethic and imagery of the Law in His discourses, and He conformed to Jewish custom in His daily life. He was circumcised on the eighth day of His infancy (Luke 2:21) and, as stated above, shared the Passover pilgrimage to Jerusalem when He came to the age of religious responsibility.

To say that Jesus was nurtured in Judaism is not to say that He was the product of Judaism. The originality of His teaching and the miraculous paradox of His person transcended mere tradition. Yet it is impossible to understand His career if He is divorced from the setting in which He lived. His teaching was gauged for the contemporary audience and the events of His life are inextricably involved with the current of the times.

7

The Age of Tiberius:
The Ministry of Christ

T HE DEATH OF AUGUSTUS IN A.D. 14 ENDED THE "BRAVE NEW
world" which had been born with the principate. Augustus'
policies had been firmly established; peace and prosperity prevailed; but he had bequeathed one unsolved problem to the empire
— the problem of succession. He had no direct heirs to whom he
could assign the seat of power, nor had he created any adequate
machinery for selecting others. When he announced the adoption
of his stepson Tiberius as his successor, the appointment was
founded on personal choice rather than on constitutional principle.
The failure to establish a regular procedure for such an emergency
brought disaster to the empire in later years.

The Historical Introduction

Luke dates the beginning of his narrative of the active ministries
of John the Baptist and Jesus in the reign of Tiberius Caesar. He
is mentioned once directly by his name (Luke 3:1) and indirectly
on two occasions as the reigning emperor (20:22; 23:1, 2).
Matthew (22:17-21) and Mark (12:14-17) duplicate Luke's general allusion to his image in the current coinage, and the more
specific reference in John (19:12-15) to Pilate's relation to Caesar
presupposes the irritable character of Tiberius as revealed through
the accounts of the Roman historians. Although Tiberius had no

149

immediate relation to Jesus, his personality is discernible in the background of the New Testament.

Tiberius was a strange and tragic figure. Born in 42 B.C., he became the stepson of Augustus four years later when his mother, Livia, divorced his father to marry Octavian. He grew up in the stormy years of the final wars between Antony and Octavian and did not receive the favorable attention that was given to his younger and more personable brother, Drusus. Augustus' first choice for a successor was his nephew, Marcus Marcellus, to whom he gave his daughter Julia, but Marcellus died in 23 B.C. Augustus promptly married Julia to his assistant Agrippa, but he died in 12 B.C. Augustus then compelled Tiberius to divorce Agrippa's daughter, Vipsania, whom he loved, and to marry Julia, twice a widow, with two sons whom Augustus now regarded as heirs apparent. Although Tiberius was invested with civil and military power and accorded a prominent place in the state, he was disgusted with the slights heaped upon him and by the scandals and immoralities of Julia. He quit the public scene and retired to Rhodes, where he lived as a private citizen.

Gaius and Lucius, the sons of Julia, whom Tiberius had virtually made his own, did not live long. Lucius died of illness in A.D. 2, and Gaius was killed in Armenia two years later during a military campaign. Julia, in the meantime, had been banished by her father as a punishment for her licentious conduct. Once again Augustus turned to Tiberius, recalled him from private life, and in A.D. 4 formally adopted him as his son and successor. In A.D. 13 he became Augustus' colleague, and in A.D. 14, at the age of 55, assumed the full rulership at Augustus' death.[1]

The rule of Tiberius showed that he was a wise and able administrator. He followed closely the pattern set by Augustus. He was popular with the provincials, for he insisted on honest financial policies and appointed experienced governors who worked for the welfare of the people. He treated the Senate with respect and sought to avoid the irresponsible use of power. Tiberius was not popular with the masses because he refused to permit extravagant expenditures for "bread and the circus," nor was he liked by some of the aristocracy because of his stern and withdrawn manner. The latter years of his life were clouded by tragedy that made him morose and suspicious.

Tiberius' son Drusus died in A.D. 23 under questionable circumstances. Later discovery revealed that he had been poisoned by his wife Livilla and by Sejanus, the prefect of the Pretorian Guard,

---

[1] A. E. R. Boak, *A History of Rome to 565 A.D.*, pp. 285-287.

who was stealthily laying plans for seizing the throne, possibly as regent for Livilla's children, Nero (not the later emperor) and Drusus II. At Drusus' death, Tiberius, shattered and disillusioned, retired to his villa at Capri, leaving Sejanus as the virtual ruler of Rome. The tension in the state grew worse and finally Tiberius became aware of Sejanus' treachery. In a sudden coup he denounced Sejanus' villainy to the Senate, which quickly decreed and executed a death sentence. The cumulative bitterness of his many disillusionments soured Tiberius' temper. A number of Sejanus' associates were also executed and an atmosphere of terror pervaded Rome. In all fairness to Tiberius it should be said that there were no mass proscriptions, and that relatively few people lost their lives. It is true that informers were employed who made irresponsible accusations, so that the senators were in terror lest they should be denounced publicly and sentenced to death. On the other hand, Tiberius could not know who were his friends or his foes and so was compelled to use the best facilities available for detecting the danger spots. He died, an embittered and disappointed man, in A.D. 37.

The character of Tiberius, molded by the misfortunes that befell him, helps to explain the attitude shown toward him in the Gospels. He was stern, withdrawn, unpredictable of temper, and, toward the end of his career, irascible and suspicious. In consideration of his misfortunes his gloomy disposition can be explained, if not pardoned. It was said that after his compulsory divorce from Vipsania he could never glimpse his former wife without gazing longingly after her, and the disgusting adulteries of Julia shamed and repelled him. The untimely death of Drusus, the treachery of his trusted lieutenant Sejanus, and the constant friction of court intrigues made him loathe the position which he could not relinquish. Thanks to the good foundation laid by Augustus and to his own administrative skill, the government of the provinces did not suffer greatly and the empire was not immediately jeopardized. Sejanus' plot was detected in time to avert assassination or revolution. Even to the end Tiberius retained the full use of his faculties, though the threat of the unexpected preyed on his emotions.

The public career of Jesus probably occurred between A.D. 28 and 30. Unfortunately the fifth and a large part of the sixth book of the *Annals* of Tacitus covering this segment of Tiberius' life have been lost, so that knowledge of historical events in this period is severely limited. Tiberius had withdrawn to Capri in A.D. 26. During this period Sejanus was still the favorite and had embroiled Tiberius in a feud with Agrippina and Nero, whom he banished, while Drusus II was imprisoned. These complicated intrigues may

Enlargement of a silver denarius of Tiberius. This was the coin brought to Jesus when the Pharisees and Herodians tried to trap Him in a question about paying taxes to Caesar (Matt. 22:15-22).

not have affected the provinces directly, but wild rumors and an atmosphere of unrest may have prevailed. During this time, when Tiberius was in seclusion and Sejanus was at the peak of his power, the Pharisees and Herodians posed the question to Jesus whether they should pay tribute to Caesar or not.

The tax money (*phoron,* Luke 20:22; *kenson,* Mark 12:14) refers to the direct poll tax individuals had to pay rather than to the indirect tax on goods or farm products. The poll tax was not heavy, but it was an annoyance to the Jews, who felt that by paying it they were acknowledging the authority of a foreign ruler.[2] The emperor's image on the coin was contrary to the second commandment, "Thou shalt not make unto thee a graven image, nor any likeness of anything that is in heaven above or that is on the earth beneath or that is in the water under the earth" (Exod. 20:4). Furthermore, the inscription on Tiberius' coin read "TI[berius] CAESAR DIVI AUG[usti] F[ilius] AUGUSTUS," or, in translation, "Tiberius Caesar Augustus, son of the deified Augustus." The inscription was virtually an ascription of deity to the reigning emperor, which would insult the religious conviction of any Jew that no man could claim to be God. The irritating presence of the coin was a constant reminder to the Jews of their subservient condition. They longed to throw off the yoke of Rome, and each new Messianic pretender made capital of their desires. In this instance Jesus took full charge of what might have become an embarrassing or dangerous situation, and averted it.

The tribute money itself was the *denarius,* a silver coin about the size of a dime, and worth approximately seventeen cents. Curiously enough, Jesus Himself did not possess a specimen of the disputed

---

[2] See E. Stauffer, *Christ and the Caesars,* pp. 112-137.

money, but His enemies did. His question reveals His purpose: "Whose image and superscription hath it?" Obviously it carried the features of Tiberius with his titles. Jesus was not in doubt concerning the identity of the image; He wanted His questioners to admit that the coin belonged to Caesar. When they did so, He gave His classic rejoinder: "Then render unto Caesar the things that are Caesar's, and unto God the things that are God's" (Luke 20:25). As long as they were using Tiberius' coinage for their medium of exchange they could not consistently refuse to pay the tribute that supported the government guaranteeing their economic welfare.

The coin which Jesus held in His hand represented the power of the Roman imperium that overshadowed the whole of the Mediterranean world. It had to bear the image of the reigning sovereign, for it was the sole means whereby the average man could become familiar with his ruler's face. Only by the likeness stamped on the *denarius* could Tiberius make himself known to the subjects who had heard his name but who had never met him personally.

The use of the coin was a tacit acknowledgment of the emperor's lordship. Jesus stated the view of ancient times that taxes were paid only by subject nations (Matt. 17:25, 26). If the Jews rendered the poll tax to Caesar, they were admitting that he was their rightful ruler — admission which they made articulate when they cried out in Pilate's court, "We have no king but Caesar" (John 19:15).

The temper of Tiberius probably explains Pilate's hesitation to act at the trial of Jesus. Convinced by the outcome of the examination that Jesus was not a dangerous revolutionary, Pilate would gladly have released Him, if only to rid himself of an embarrassing prisoner. The insinuation of the priests, "If thou let this man go, thou art not Caesar's friend: every man that maketh himself a king speaketh against Caesar" (John 19:12), was a veiled threat. Pilate was an appointee of Sejanus, who at that very time was deeply involved in the intrigue to secure the succession for the children of Livilla, Drusus' widow. Tiberius, apprehensive of conspiracy, was in no mood to tolerate any kind of disloyalty. If the Jews complained to the emperor, who was partial to the welfare of the provinces, that Pilate had endorsed or condoned an armed rebellion against the government, his political doom would be certain. Pilate had to make a quick decision between Roman justice toward Jesus, which he was sworn to support as an officer of the government, and offending the hierarchy who could by a well-placed word with Tiberius effect his ruin. The outcome of his decision is too well known to need elaboration.

Luke's chronological introduction to the life of Jesus names six other personages beside Tiberius. First in the list is Pontius Pilate,

An inscription discovered in 1961 in the ruins of the Roman theater at Caesarea mentioning the names of the emperor Tiberius and the prefect Pontius Pilate. Pilate served as prefect from A.D. 26-36. (Courtesy Prof. B. Van Elderen.)

Close-up of the Pilate inscription showing detail of the lettering:
"TIBERIEVM . . . TIVSPILATVS. . . ." (Courtesy Prof. B. Van Elderen.)

procurator of Judea, mentioned in the preceding paragraph. He was appointed to office in A.D. 26 and remained until A.D. 36, one year before Tiberius' death. When Pilate moved the Roman troops from Caesarea to winter quarters in Jerusalem, he brought with them the military standards on which Caesar's image was prominently displayed. As soon as they were discovered, the people petitioned for their removal, but Pilate refused. When the multitude presented their petition on the sixth day of his court session, he surrounded them with a cordon of soldiers and threatened to massacre them if they would not withdraw. They flung themselves on the ground and unitedly said that they were ready to die rather than to tolerate a violation of their laws. Pilate was compelled to acknowledge defeat and to recall the standards to Caesarea.

Pilate's administration of Judea was conducted in arbitrary and reckless fashion. In order to obtain funds for the construction of a needed aqueduct, he made use of "sacred money," according to Josephus.[3] When the populace protested this desecration of the Temple treasury, he sent among them soldiers in plain clothes who beat rioters and bystanders indiscriminately, killing some and wound-

---

[3] *Antiquities* xviii. 3. 2.

ing others. The mob was dispersed, but the hostility between Pilate and the crowd increased.

Just how he succeeded in obtaining the money from the Temple Josephus does not explain. There is no hint that he seized it forcibly, for had he done so, the protest would have been even more violent. There may have been some sort of political transaction with the priesthood, who "lent" money for his project in return for political favors or as a strategic move to gain influence. Pilate would have acquired prestige for having added to the resources of the province; the priesthood would have gained a certain amount of power over him, for they needed only to report to Tiberius that Pilate had attempted to plunder their province to have him recalled in disgrace. Possibly some such situation as this lay behind the sentence of Jesus. Pilate did not dare to refuse the request of the Sanhedrin lest they should send an adverse account of his administration to the imperial office.

Pilate's contemporary, Philo of Alexandria, characterized him as "naturally inflexible and implacable in his conceit,"[4] and charged him with corruption, violence, and extortion. Jesus alluded to the slaughter of some Galileans who had been killed while offering sacrifice, possibly because Pilate suspected that they were insurrectionists. The inner hardness of his character appears in the narrative of the crucifixion where, having yielded to the pressure of the chief priests, he refused to alter the sarcastic inscription on the cross: "Jesus of Nazareth, the King of the Jews." To the objection of the priests he gave the haughty and laconic reply, "What I have written, I have written" (John 19:19-22).

Pilate was finally removed from office in A.D. 36 after an incident in Samaria. A "prophet" had told the Samaritans that if they would meet him at Mt. Gerizim, he would disclose to them the sacred vessels of the Temple that had been buried there. A large crowd assembled. Since they were armed, Pilate probably feared a revolt and intervened promptly by sending a detachment of cavalry and infantry who quickly dispelled the crowd, killing some and capturing others, and by ordering the execution of the leaders.

The Samaritans protested to Vitellius, the military governor of Syria, that the intent of the multitude was peaceful and accused Pilate of murder. Vitellius replaced Pilate and sent him to Rome to plead his case before the emperor. By the time he reached Rome, Tiberius had died.[5]

Pilate's ultimate fate is unknown. The sources vary. Some state that he was executed by Nero, others, that he committed suicide in

4 Philo, *De Legatione ad Caium* 38.
5 Josephus, *Antiquities* xviii. 3. 1, 2.

exile.[6]   Numerous legends concerning him were extant in the Middle Ages; some of them related that before his death he had become a Christian. These are, however, devoid of any historical basis. His association with Tiberius has been amply corroborated by the recent (1961) discovery at Caesarea of an inscribed stone bearing both their names, evidently from some building erected during his administration.[7]

The Herod mentioned in Luke's dating was Herod Antipas, son of Herod the Great, to whom Augustus assigned Galilee and Perea at the death of his father in 4 B.C. He was sly and treacherous, for which reason Jesus alluded to him as "that fox" (Luke 13:31f.). His illegal marriage with his niece, Herodias, who had been the wife of his half-brother Philip, outraged the Jews and evoked the public protest of John the Baptist, whom Herod imprisoned and finally beheaded (Mark 6:14-28). Herod was the reigning vassal king of the Jews at the time of Jesus' death. He was curious concerning Jesus' person (Luke 9:7, 9) and sought an interview with Him. His desire was gratified when Pilate sent Jesus to him, but Jesus would not deign to waste words on such a trifler (23:7-15). Herod treated Him scornfully and returned Him to Pilate's jurisdiction.

Like his father, Herod Antipas was a builder. He rebuilt Sepphoris, a city four miles north of Nazareth, and Tiberias, a port on the Sea of Galilee, which he named in honor of his patron, the emperor. It is not impossible that Joseph and Jesus may have worked at both of these sites during the process of construction.

Philip, the half-brother of Antipas, tetrarch of Iturea and Trachonitis, was probably the best of the sons of Herod the Great. Little is known of him beyond what is recorded in the Gospels. According to Josephus, his mother was Cleopatra of Jerusalem. He was brought up at Rome, and received his domain by Augustus' settlement of his father's will. He ruled quietly and peaceably over his own territory until his death in A.D. 33/34, and administered the affairs of his realm diligently.[8] Since he left no heirs, Tiberius added his territory to the province of Syria. During his reign he rebuilt the town of Panias, located at the springs of the Jordan, into Caesarea Philippi, which he named for Tiberius, and Bethsaida Julias, named for Tiberius' granddaughter. He married Salome, the daughter of his niece Herodias, who survived him.[9]

---

[6] Eusebius (*Historia Ecclesiae* ii. 7) stated that the record of his suicide was chronicled by Greek historians.

[7] Jerry Vardaman, "A New Inscription Which Mentions Pilate as 'Prefect,'" *JBL* (March, 1962), pp. 70, 71.

[8] *Antiquities* xvii. 1. 3; xviii. 4. 6.

[9] *Ibid.,* xviii. 5. 4.

Of the seven persons mentioned in Luke's account, Lysanias of Abilene is the most difficult to identify. The country of Abilene lay to the north of Galilee and Iturea, between the Lebanon and Anti-Lebanon range of mountains, and west of Damascus. His reign must have ended before A.D. 53, in which year the tetrarchy of Abilene was assigned to Herod Agrippa II by Claudius.[10] His name appears in a dedicatory inscription of a temple in Abila "for the salvation of the Lords Imperial, by a freedman of Lysanias, the tetrarch."[11] "The Lords Imperial" was a technical title given jointly to Tiberius and his mother Livia, the widow of Augustus, so that the inscription must have been written between A.D. 14, the date of Tiberius' accession, and A.D. 29, when Livia died. Since Jesus' ministry began not later than A.D. 29, the archaeological evidence and the testimony of Luke coincide.[12]

Annas and Caiaphas, respectively high priest emeritus and the high priest of the Jewish state, were the dominant ecclesiastical authorities of Palestine. Annas had been appointed to office by Quirinius about A.D. 6 and continued in office until A.D. 18. He was succeeded by Caiaphas who served until A.D. 36 when he was removed by Vitellius, the Roman governor of Syria. Both men were involved in the trial and death of Jesus (John 11:49, 18:13) and appear later in Acts in relation to the arrest and trial of Peter and John (Acts 4:6).

Two facts are noteworthy in regard to the chronology: it sets the opening of Jesus' ministry between the accession of Pilate in A.D. 26 and the death of Livia, Tiberius' mother, in A.D. 29, and it reflects in each case the influence of Rome on the political life of Palestine. Luke was an accurate and discerning historian. Although he did not gauge his chronology by the modern device of referring to a fixed calendar, he located events correctly by the standard of his time, and he had a sense of political and cultural overtones which enabled him to recapture the atmosphere of a historical event. Rome provided the background for the events of Jesus' life. It was "the kingdom of the world" which was to become ultimately "the kingdom of our Lord and of His Christ" (Rev. 11:15).

The Ministry of John the Baptist

The preaching of John probably began about A.D. 28/29, "the fifteenth year of Tiberius Caesar," unless Tiberius' reign might be reckoned from his first assumption of tribunician power which made

---

[10] *Ibid.*, xx. 7. 1.
[11] *Corpus Inscriptionum Graecarum*, 4521.
[12] J. A. Thompson, *The Bible and Archaeology*, pp. 377, 378.

him co-ruler of the provinces with Augustus in 11/12 A.D. The latter seems unlikely, since the historical sources for his reign do not so calculate their dates. A more plausible explanation is that in Syria the reigns of monarchs were measured by the royal year, which, according to the tradition, began in September or October. Since Tiberius became emperor in August, he had begun his second year in September of A.D. 14, and would, therefore, by September of A.D. 27, be already in the fifteenth year of his accession. This method of calculation produces results that agree better with the other chronological facts of Jesus' life. If Jesus was born in 5 B.C., He would be about 32 years of age at the opening of His ministry.

The period was chaotic and confusing. Tiberius had withdrawn from active participation in public affairs, leaving them largely in the hands of Sejanus. Pontius Pilate, Sejanus' appointee, operated by expediency rather than by principle and took delight in provoking the Jews to exasperation. The Sadducean priesthood under Annas and Caiaphas was more concerned with the niceties of ritual and theology than with high ethics and personal faith. Unrest prevailed among the populace, and Messianic leaders who promised independence and prosperity gained a ready hearing.

The initial ministry of John the Baptist attracted considerable attention. Josephus attributed the defeat of Herod's army in warfare against Aretas of Arabia, whose daughter he had divorced to marry Herodias, to his violation of divine law,[13] and remarked that John was a good man who summoned the people to righteousness toward one another and virtue toward God.

The ministry of John was moral rather than political and could not be called revolutionary in any ordinary sense. He did not initiate the concept of the Kingdom of Heaven, a concept which parallels to some extent the kingdom of the sons of light mentioned in the Dead Sea Scrolls. In John's preaching, however, there was no military note. He emphatically disclaimed Messianic status, saying that he was only the forerunner of the kingdom depicted in the prophecy of Isaiah 40:4-5 (Matt. 3:1-6; Mark 1:2-6; Luke 3:3-6). John maintained an appearance of the utmost simplicity, eating the food and dressing in the clothing the desert supplied. He was ascetic in his tendencies, though apparently he did not demand that his followers should imitate him in every particular.

Luke shows how John adapted his preaching to the social conditions of the time. The supercilious religiosity of the Pharisees and Sadducees evoked his comment that "even now the axe also lieth at the root of the trees: every tree therefore that bringeth not forth

[13] *Antiquities* xviii. 5. 1, 2.

good fruit is hewn down and cast into the fire" (Luke 3:9). Neither ancestry nor ecclesiastical prestige could avert divine judgment; repentance alone could save the nation.

Against the prevailing class selfishness that separated the affluent from the poor he said: "He that hath two coats, let him impart to him that hath none; and he that hath food, let him do likewise" (v. 11). The prosperity of Palestine had not been evenly shared by all the inhabitants, and he proposed that a voluntary solicitude for the oppressed would relieve their miseries.

The financial dishonesty of government agents was reflected in his charge to the tax-gatherers (publicans): "Extort no more than is appointed you" (3:13). Contrary to the policy of Tiberius, many of the revenue officers had abused their authority by demanding more from the people than their rightful taxes. By such illegal means many had enriched themselves, as Zacchaeus did (19:2, 8).[14] Their extortion had created deep dissatisfaction in the provinces, particularly in Palestine.

The question of the soldiers elicited a reply from John which revealed another center of friction in the social structure. Palestine, as a subject province under the emperor, was governed by a procurator with military powers. The technical independence of the nation had ended when Archelaus was deposed in A.D. 6 and Judea was placed under provincial government. The military occupation was irritating to the Jews, and the soldiers, who were mostly foreign legionaries, were arrogant and brutal. They indulged frequently in extortion, intimidation, and blackmail in an attempt to supplement the army pay, which was already more than unskilled labor would receive. A literal translation of John's word to them according to Luke would be, "Don't 'shake down' anyone, nor extort money by threats, and be satisfied with your wages" (3:14).

The social unrest implied in their questions addressed to John and in his answers had a definite bearing upon the content of his preaching. The announcement of a Messiah who would baptize with the Holy Spirit and who would execute judgment against the current abuses and inequalities was welcomed by the populace. The pedantry of the scribes, the tension between the affluence of the rich and the wretchedness of the poor, the greed of the tax collectors who plundered the peasants of the little surplus that might be left to them after they had paid the legitimate dues, and the careless cruelty of the foreign soldiery, together with the prevailing immorality

---

[14] The Greek condition in Luke 19:8, "If I have wrongfully exacted aught of any man. . . ," implies that such was the fact, and that Zacchaeus was admitting it.

of the populace, called for a new manifestation of divine power. John's ministry was preparatory to the work of Christ, but was gauged perfectly for the social and spiritual needs of the close of Tiberius' reign.

The optimistic expectation of a new era which had pervaded the Roman world during the reign of Augustus had been chilled perceptibly by the conflicts that arose under Tiberius. The struggle for primacy within the royal house between the Julian line of Germanicus' sons and the Claudian line of Tiberius' grandchildren gradually transferred the interest of the ruling group from a desire to promote national welfare into a contest for power. A new generation had risen which took for granted the peace and prosperity of the empire and consequently sought to exploit it rather than to promote it. Once again the cycle was beginning to turn from the sacrifice that envisions achievement to the consciousness of success that ends in political rivalry and social disintegration. Rome's decline was not immediately perceptible; in fact, the tide of political fortune did not ebb for more than a century and a quarter after the death of Christ. On the other hand, the first advent of Christ introduced to the world a new regenerative power which outdated the civilization in which it first appeared, and which accomplished far more for the world than the organization of Rome could have done.

Perhaps Jesus had these contrasting principles in mind when He gave His disciples their final instructions before His death: *And he said unto them, The kings of the Gentiles have lordship over them; and they that have authority over them are called Benefactors. But ye shall not be so: but he that is the greater among you, let him become as the younger; and he that is chief, as he that doth serve. For which is greater, he that sitteth at meat, or he that serveth? is not he that sitteth at meat? but I am in the midst of you as he that serveth* (Luke 22:25-27). His language was drawn from the current usage of His day. "Kings" (Greek, *basileis*) may apply either to vassal rulers of client kingdoms or to the emperor himself; "lordship" (Greek, *kyrieuousin*) is derived from *kyrios,* which in the Middle East ascribed to the ruler a type of deity; "Benefactors" (Greek, *euergetai*) was applied to the Ptolemies in particular in order to indicate that they were the nourishers of the nation through the grain supply, which was the peculiar possession of Egypt. Jesus reminded His disciples that their power would be drawn from love, not from fear; from humility, not from haughtiness; and from service, not from authority. In these respects His principles were diametrically opposed to those of Rome or of any other Gentile power, yet His approach was not negative. He outlined the constitution for a new type of dominion which the Father had appointed for Him, a kingdom in which the disciples would be given judicial authority over the tribes of Israel and would reign in an eternal setting.

The Life of Jesus

The ministry of Jesus was begun within the framework of the Roman philosophy and practice of government, but it contrasted sharply with these. By accepting baptism at the hands of John, Jesus avowed His agreement with the spiritual principles that John proclaimed and His acceptance of the destiny that John had predicted for Him. He became the embodiment of all that Rome was not: humility, love, absolute righteousness, and self-sacrifice.

The Temptation

Immediately after His baptism Jesus was led by the Holy Spirit into the wilderness of Judea to be tested by Satan. All three Synoptic Gospels mention the temptation; only Matthew and Luke give a full summary. The wilderness of Judea was a barren stretch of mountainous country extending from the western side of Jerusalem to the Jordan valley. Cut off by the central ridge of mountains from the moist westerly winds which deposit most of their rain on the plain of Sharon and on the western side of the plateau, the wilderness of Judea is totally devoid of rain during most of the year. In summer one can hardly see a blade of grass anywhere along the road that leads from Jerusalem to Jericho. Rugged crags of rock jutting out of an absolutely dry ground make as inhospitable a country as one could find anywhere.

Into this uninhabited region Jesus retired for a period of forty days. During that time He was confronted with the three major temptations that face every human being: the temptation to gratify bodily appetites, the temptation to seize power, and the temptation to seek for prestige by unlawful means. Each of these had a definite relationship to the imperial culture in which He was about to begin His ministry. The dominant motive of the populace was "bread and the circus." If they had enough to eat and to amuse them, they were content. Jesus' reply to the temptation was that man's deepest nature cannot be satisfied with material things. His kingdom must be sustained by dealing with the deeper need for God.

The second temptation concerned the acquisition of power. Power was the keynote of Roman authority, but it involved the worship of the state in the person of its ruler. When Satan demanded that Jesus worship him as the price of world-empire, He refused. There

Since Crusader times the traditional site of the temptation of Christ has been Jebel Qarantal, this mountain west of Jericho. Qarantal is an Arabic corruption of the Latin quarantana — *forty days* — *in commemoration of Christ's fasting for that period of time during his temptation. On the side of the hill is a Greek Orthodox monastery.* (Matson Photo Service.)

could be no compromise between the kingdom of this world and the Kingdom of God, of which He alone can be sovereign.

The third temptation, which offered Jesus the prestige and following that a spectacular manifestation of power would insure, paralleled the policy of advertising the emperor's accomplishments by inscriptions and monuments and by the military triumphs that were accorded to him after victorious campaigns. Jesus repudiated such ostentation as presumptuous and chose rather the way of humility.

The ministry of Jesus was thus a reaction against the authoritarian and materialistic atmosphere which the policies of Rome created. The peace which Rome enforced and the facilities which it provided aided the establishment of the kingdom which Christ founded, but between the dominant pagan state and the invisible empire of Christ there was an inherent antagonism. Although there was no immediate conflict in the sense of official persecution, the disparity of spiritual ideals became increasingly evident and ultimately terminated in the open strife of the second and third centuries.

The Chronology of the Life of Jesus

Few fixed points of chronology can be established for the life of Jesus, and those that do exist are susceptible to varying interpretations. As a result, the events of His career cannot be settled with final precision. The Gospel writers were more interested in presenting Jesus' person than they were in dating His activities. While they may not justly be accused of carelessness or of ignorance, they assumed a knowledge of contemporary events on the part of their readers that could not be expected of subsequent generations. Undoubtedly their witness was truthful and accurate, but it was too fragmentary to provide adequate data for the modern reader who was not living when the Gospels were written. Of the four evangelists, Luke is the most explicit, but he does not synchronize the acts of Christ so completely with the external history that he removes all ambiguities.

The birth date of Jesus was probably between 6 and 5 B.C., according to Luke's notation of the census under Quirinius. The opening of the ministry may be placed either in A.D. 28, or in A.D. 26, depending on the method used in reckoning the fifteenth year of Tiberius. If it represents the fifteenth year of Tiberius' full accession to the imperial power after the death of Augustus, it cannot be earlier than A.D. 28. It is possible that Luke, as a provincial, counted the years from the time of Tiberius' co-regency with Augustus in A.D. 12 when he assumed control of the Eastern provinces. If so, the date agrees rather closely with two other clues afforded by allusions in the Gospels.

The former of these is Luke's remark that when Jesus commenced His ministry He was "about thirty years of age" (Luke 3:23). The language of the text is peculiar: "And Jesus himself was beginning about thirty years of age. . . ." The participle, "beginning," does not seem to connect logically with the rest of the sentence. The King James Version renders it, "And Jesus himself began to be about thirty years of age . . .," which conveys the impression that He was less than thirty when He began preaching. If the participle refers to the beginning of His preaching, as seems more likely, it accords with the Lukan introduction to Acts: "The former treatise I made, O Theophilus, concerning all that Jesus began both to do and to teach . . ." (Acts 1:1). Luke seems to indicate that at the outset of His ministry Jesus was approximately thirty years old, the age at which teachers generally entered upon professional life. If He was born in 5 B.C., and if the fifteenth year of Tiberius Caesar was about A.D. 26, the figure coincides fairly well with the stated dates.

A second clue is the protest of Jesus' antagonists against the misunderstood prediction of His resurrection: "Forty and six years was this temple in building, and wilt thou raise it up in three days?" (John 2:20). The imperfect tense of the verb (was) implies that the construction was still in process; nor was it completed until after Jesus' death. According to Josephus, Herod commenced the building in the eighteenth year of his reign, which would have been about 20/19 B.C.[15] The forty-sixth year of construction would thus fall in A.D. 26/27, which synchronizes with the calculation of the Lukan figures.

Absolute precision may be impossible, but the most likely date for the initial appearance of Jesus during the ministry of John the Baptist seems to be between the years A.D. 26 and 27, or possibly 28. If the fifteenth year of Tiberius, which may imply the lapse of only fourteen calendar years between his accession and the appearance of Jesus, be reckoned from Augustus' death in A.D. 14, then Jesus probably began His ministry in the fall of A.D. 28.

The Ministry of Jesus

The length of Jesus' ministry has been variously calculated at one year or a little more, two years, and three and a half years — the last of which is the traditional span. Although the events enumerated in the Synoptic accounts could possibly be compressed into little more than a year, there are indications that they must have extended over a longer period. From the feeding of the five thousand, which occurred in the spring, since two of the Gospels mention grass (Matt. 14:19; Mark 6:39), to the close of Jesus' life must have been a full year because a protracted ministry of teaching and preaching intervened between the two. To this John agrees, for he says that the miracle of the feeding of the five thousand occurred at a Passover (John 6:4), while the crucifixion followed at another Passover (11:55). Between the two was the Feast of Tabernacles (7:2) in early fall, and the Feast of Lights or Dedication (10:22), which occurred at the winter solstice in the last of December.

According to Matthew, the last years of Jesus' life began shortly after the execution of John the Baptist, who had been imprisoned by Herod Antipas for publicly denouncing his marriage with Herodias, his brother's wife (Matt. 14:1-12). Prior to his death, John had been imprisoned for an undefined length of time during which Jesus had been preaching in Galilee (Matt. 4:12, 17, 25; Mark 1:14, 39). His ministry must have commenced in early spring, for after the beginning of this period the record states that He was

---

[15] *Antiquities* xv. 11. 1-3.

passing through ripened grain fields (Mark 2:23), which were probably those that had been growing during the moist winter months. The imprisonment of John must have lasted for several weeks at the least. Herod kept him in prison and John sent his disciples to inquire of Jesus whether He was truly the promised Messiah or whether he should expect another. The question presupposes that John had been weighing the problem in his mind for some time and that he had finally decided to ask Jesus about it. Jesus' Galilean ministry, during which He rose to the height of the greatest popularity, must have occupied a year previous to the feeding of the five thousand, and probably embraced another Passover.

The Gospel of John states that before the Galilean ministry commenced Jesus was preaching in Judea concomitantly with John the Baptist (John 3:22), subsequent to another Passover (2:13). Since John had not been cast into prison, this preaching preceded the Galilean ministry featured in the Synoptics and probably occupied still another year during which Jesus may not have given all of His time to traveling and preaching. It is not improbable that both He and His disciples alternately worked and preached until John's incarceration left a clear field for Him. Realizing the need of continuing with the ministry of the kingdom, He began where John had been compelled to stop.

Prior to the initial Passover mentioned in John 2:13, He had already been recognized by the Baptist and had acquired a small following consisting chiefly of men who had been disciples of John (1:35-42; 2:2). The ministry of this period was not widely recognized, and the crowds seemingly did not follow Him until after the first Passover. The Johannine narrative does not purport to give a complete chronicle of Jesus' acts and by its selectivity implies that there was a wide ministry in Galilee — and possibly in other regions — which remained untold. While one cannot account for three or more years by a close sequence of events, it is difficult to compress the total span of Jesus' known activities into less time.

The general framework of the Synoptics begins with the preaching of John, who appeared in the wilderness of Judea, summoning men to repentance and baptizing those who responded to his call. He appealed to individuals rather than to the nation as a unit, and his objective was to prepare them for the Messiah whose coming was imminent. The call to repentance and baptism superseded the formal membership in Judaism insured by birth and circumcision, for it depended upon voluntary choice. He opened the door to a relationship with God which was based not on a racial birth, but on a new birth.

Klausner, writing from the standpoint of a Jewish scholar, says: "Baptism which had before been the symbol of purity of body now also became the symbol of purity of soul, of a new birth, in a certain sense."[16]   The same concept appears in Jesus' discourse with Nicodemus, which was definitely related to the ministry of John (John 3:5).

The length of John's ministry is uncertain. He must have commenced it at least some weeks prior to Jesus' baptism and have continued it simultaneously with Jesus' own preaching (vv. 22-24) until his imprisonment. A year may not be too long, since the interval included the Passover of Jesus' early preaching in Jerusalem (2:13, 23).   On the assumption that the Fourth Gospel maintains general chronological order, the baptism of Jesus, the temptation, the gathering of His first disciples, and the appearance in Cana of Galilee as a miracle-worker must have preceded the opening of His notable career as a prophet and healer. The first chapters of the Gospel of John indicate that after John baptized Jesus at the Jordan, he introduced many of his disciples to Jesus, and that they followed Him (1:29-51). When Jesus returned to Galilee, He took them with Him and at that time attended the wedding at Cana (2:1-11). Subsequently he spent an indefinite amount of time in Capernaum (v. 12). This early Galilean appearance preceded the visit to the Passover in Jerusalem at which He made His first contact with the Jewish priestly party through the cleansing of the Temple (vv. 13-22). John was still engaged in active preaching and baptizing (3:22-29; 4:1), though his popularity was diminishing by contrast with the following that Jesus and His disciples were acquiring. The writer of the Gospel states explicitly that John had not yet been imprisoned (3:24), so that the events recorded in connection with this period must have preceded those in the narrative of the Synoptics.

Jesus' independent ministry began after the imprisonment of John (Matt. 4:12; Mark 1:14; Luke 4:14-15). The fame of His early days in Cana and Capernaum, augmented by His immediate teaching and miracles, preceded Him, so that the multitudes began to follow at once. His inaugural speech was given in the synagogue at Nazareth, where His declaration that He was not appreciated by His fellow townsmen so aroused their anger that they threatened to kill Him (Luke 4:28-30). Leaving Nazareth, He toured the cities and villages of Galilee, teaching and preaching repentance in anticipation of the coming kingdom.

[16] Joseph Klausner, *Jesus of Nazareth: His Life, Times, and Teaching*, p. 246.

The exact sequence of this year in Jesus' life is uncertain. If the unnamed feast of John 5:1 is the Passover, it may well mark the beginning of the second year, as the Passover at the feeding of the five thousand (John 6:3) opened the third year. Mark gives the impression that at this time Jesus summoned men from their ordinary occupations to follow Him (Mark 1:16-20). They may have followed Him previously and have returned to their work, as He had to His own trade. If the preaching in Galilee began after the second Passover of His ministry, the main part of His teaching must have been given to the public before the third Passover which followed almost immediately after the feeding of the five thousand (Matt. 14:13-21; Mark 6:30-44; Luke 9:10-17; John 6:1-13). The second year of preaching brought immense popularity because of the authoritative and original character of the words and because of the numerous miracles of healing He performed. The feeding of the five thousand marked the peak of Jesus' popularity because of the size of the multitude, because of the spectacular character of the miracle itself, and because of the turning point which it marked in the faith of many of His disciples.

The last year of Jesus' life was shadowed by the specter of death. His refusal to accept the authority of the priesthood, His independent interpretation of the Old Testament Scriptures, and His popularity with the crowds made Him a marked man in the eyes of the Jewish hierarchy, who regarded His claims as blasphemy and who were jealous of His success. Herod Antipas, the ruler of Galilee, who had no particular religious interests or convictions, was alarmed to hear that a preacher and healer had captured the attention of the people. In superstitious fear, aggravated by a guilty conscience, he explained that John the Baptist had risen from the dead and was consequently able to perform supernatural works (Luke 9:7-9). The report of the Pharisees that Herod was seeking to kill Him (13:31) may have been exaggerated rumor or sheer propaganda intended to frighten Jesus, but in either case it substantiated Herod's potential hostility. According to Luke's judgment, Herod was probably more curious than inimical (9:9; 23:8).

The adulation of the populace had placed Jesus in a more dangerous position than that of John the Baptist. Whereas Herod had apprehended John because of a personal grudge, he would regard Jesus as a political menace and would be even more suspicious of Him if He allowed Himself to be hailed as a king. Neither Herod nor Rome would tolerate a rival, and Jesus knew it well.

Because of the converging trends of enmity, the certainty of a fatal outcome would have been evident to any person as astute as Jesus, apart from any assumption on His part of being destined for sacrifice. His prediction of death, however, was not simply the recognition of an unavoidable disaster but was the announcement of a purpose. Following the third Passover Jesus openly refused to become a revolutionary leader (John 6:15), and after the confession of Peter at Caesarea Philippi He informed His disciples that He "must go unto Jerusalem, and suffer many things of the elders and chief priests and scribes, and be killed, and the third day be raised up" (Matt. 16:21). While He did not stress His Messianic claims in speaking to the public, He acknowledged them when He was challenged, and He continually reminded His disciples that He would end His career with death and resurrection. During the last year the crowds dwindled and popular opinion concerning Him became increasingly confused and divided.

The refusal to conform to popular desire created an inevitable reaction. The multitude deserted Him, and even some of His own disciples "walked no more with him" (John 6:66). The defection of Judas may have begun at this point, for Jesus spoke of him in particular as He reviewed the situation and challenged the Twelve to stay with Him (vv. 67-71). He was caught between two hostilities: the suspicion of Herod (Luke 13:31), and the enmity of the Jews in Jerusalem, who hated Him because of His supposed infringement of the Sabbath law and His outward condemnation of the scribes and Pharisees (John 7:1; Mark 7:1-23). His movements in this period are uncertain, but He visited the territory of Tyre and Sidon (Mark 7:24), the Greek cities of the Decapolis (v. 31), Caesarea Philippi and its adjacent villages (8:27), and later Samaria (Luke 9:52). He traversed Galilee but did not want any man to know it (Mark 9:30). The Synoptics convey the impression that Jesus tried to stay out of Herod's territory; John indicates that He remained away from Jerusalem until the Feast of Tabernacles (John 7:2). One may conclude that the entire summer of the last year was a period of great uncertainty in which the popular opinion was fluctuating, favor was diminishing, and the shadow of the cross was deepening over Jesus' consciousness.

The turning point came at Caesarea Philippi, when Jesus questioned the disciples concerning their conceptions of Him. When Peter, spokesman for the Twelve, declared his belief that Jesus was the Messiah, the Son of the living God, He responded by commanding them not to divulge this fact. From that time His entire outlook changed, and He proceeded to teach them that He must be rejected officially by the nation, be killed, and rise on the third day (Matt. 16:21). Six days later came the Transfiguration, a preview of the glory of Christ vouchsafed to only three of His disciples, Peter, James, and John. Luke remarks that when the time

A Roman bridge and city gate from Caesarea Philippi, where Peter made his confession (Matt. 16:13). (Matson Photo Service.)

had come in which Jesus might be "received up" — the same term that he used in Acts to describe the Ascension (1:11) — He "stedfastly set his face to go to Jerusalem" (9:51). Although this section of the Gospel lacks continuity, the goal of Jerusalem appears at intervals (v. 51; 13:22, 34; 17:11; 18:31). The chronological sequence is not clear, and the content must be fitted to a scheme largely supplied by the other Gospels. It is quite likely that Luke had collected episodes and sayings of Jesus attributable to this period without possessing a consecutive arrangement of the order of events. John indicates that Jesus visited Jerusalem at the Feast of Tabernacles mentioned above (7:2, 37), and in December the Feast of Dedication (10:22), with visits to Perea before and after the latter feast (v. 40). The visit to Bethany to raise Lazarus from the dead must have taken place in the late winter.

The Last Week

The order of events in the last week of Jesus' life is fairly well defined. Six days before the Passover He came to Bethany, where He lodged with His friends Mary, Martha, and Lazarus. The fact that John mentions Lazarus' presence specifically may indicate that Lazarus had remained in seclusion since his miraculous restoration to life, and that he appeared at this same public occasion in Jesus' honor. John assigns the supper to His first evening in Bethany, possibly the evening of Saturday after the close of the Sabbath. Matthew and Mark record the meal among the last events of the Passover week, but a careful examination of their text (Matt. 26:6-13; Mark 14:3-9) shows that they do not place it definitely in the order of the events. It seems rather to have been introduced as a partial explanation of the treachery of Judas, whose underhanded negotiations with the high priest occurred at this time. Since John is more definite in his statement of time, preference should be given to his account rather than to a mere inference.

On the next day Jesus entered Jerusalem, attended by His disciples and a large following of supporters (John 12:12ff.). The Synoptic Gospels recount the preparation for the entry as well as its accomplishments; John's narrative is confined to the reaction of the multitudes. At least two groups were present: the pilgrims who had come to the feast from Galilee (v. 12), and the local residents of Bethany (v. 17). The general acclaim only aggravated the antagonism of the chief priests and scribes, who became increasingly desperate as they saw their influence waning and the opportunity for action decreasing as the Passover approached. They feared to precipitate an uprising among the people by the apprehension of Jesus, for the Passover crowds were volatile, and the vigilant Roman procurator would intervene ruthlessly at the sign of a growing disturbance. On the other hand, if they did not act decisively against Jesus, the crowds might spontaneously make Him the spearhead of a revolution that would unseat the ruling hierarchy and give the Romans an excuse to enslave them completely. Fear created the dilemma from which the priests could extricate themselves only by destroying Jesus.

On Monday morning Jesus and His disciples emerged from seclusion in Bethany and made their way to the city. As He walked along the gardens that line the roadway He saw a fig tree covered with leaves. Approaching it in hope of finding upon it a bit of fruit that might have remained from the previous season, He found none, and pronounced upon the tree a curse of barrenness. Proceeding on His way He entered the Temple, where He expelled the concessionaires who were doing a brisk business in sacrificial animals and in changing foreign money for the sacred shekel required for the Temple redemption fee. The priests were doubly exasperated, for His abrupt interruption of the commerce showed that He claimed authority where they supposedly ruled, and the expulsion of the merchants interfered with the Temple revenues on which they relied for financial support. They did not dare to challenge Him by force, knowing that He commanded a powerful following, and they could not ignore Him, lest their indifference be interpreted as assent.

On Tuesday He reappeared in the Temple (Mark 11:19, 20, 27; Matt. 21:23; Luke 20:1) and was promptly attacked by His adversaries who endeavored to discredit Him with the crowd. Each time they sought to embarrass Him, He turned the tables on them successfully. When they tried to force Him into a ridiculous claim to authority, He asked them an equally embarrassing question and followed it with a pointed thrust. For instance, when they demanded that He explain what right He had to exert authority over the Temple, He countered by asking them whether John's authority for baptism were divine or human. If they had answered that it was divine, He would logically have inquired why the priesthood had not believed John. If they had dismissed John's authority as human, they would have risked the opposition of the multitudes who revered him. When they refused to commit themselves, He informed them that He would not make any pronouncements. Jesus left them with the understanding that His authority was also divine, and that they were rebelling against God by refusing to acknowledge it (Mark 11:29-33).

The Pharisees and Herodians devised a second attempt to ensnare Him by asking whether it would be right to pay tribute to Caesar or not. The question was dangerous, for if Jesus agreed that the Roman census money should be paid, He would be rated unpatriotic by the crowds, whereas if He said that the tribute should not be paid, He could be reported to the government as a subversive agitator. By compelling His interrogators to produce a denarius with the face of the reigning Caesar (Tiberius) stamped on it, He forced them to acknowledge that they were using Caesar's coinage, and then told them to give to Caesar what was his, and to God what belonged to Him. Jesus adroitly avoided any political entanglement and made His enemies responsible for righteousness.

The third contest of wits involved the Sadducees, who proposed a conundrum from the Old Testament levirate law. According to the Jewish code, any woman whose husband died leaving her childless could claim that his brother should marry her in order to preserve the family line. In the hypothetical case which they proposed, seven brothers in turn married one woman who survived them all and died childless. The Sadducees then asked whose wife she would be in the resurrection. Jesus could not repudiate the Law, which was the decree of God, and He could not approve of the domestic confusion which would inevitably follow the woman's being the wife of seven men simultaneously. His simple answer that in the resurrected state there is no physical marriage was not what these men had expected. His penetrative insight into their devices and His authoritative pronouncement concerning the age to come entrenched Him more securely than ever in the admiration of the crowds. The ensuing discourse flayed the scribes and Pharisees for their hypocrisy and malice, leaving them baffled and exasperated (Matt. 22:23-33; Mark 12:18-27; Luke 20:27-40).

Most interpreters have treated Wednesday as a day of retirement, unnoticed in the Synoptic account because Jesus remained outside of Jerusalem. The Olivet discourse may have taken place late on Tuesday afternoon (Matt. 24, 25; Mark 13:1-37; Luke 21:5-36), or possibly on Wednesday. Matthew (26:1-5) and Mark (14:1, 2) state that the discourses of Jesus were finished two days before the Passover, which would indicate that He concluded His teaching on the afternoon of Tuesday if the Passover began on the evening of Thursday.

All the Gospels agree that the crucifixion occurred at Passover season (Matt. 26:2; Mark 14:1, 2; Luke 22:1, 2; John 13:1), and that it marks a definite point from which chronology may be calculated. The chief problem consists in settling whether the meal which Jesus ate with His disciples on the night before His trial was the regular Passover meal or whether He ate it a day early in anticipation of His death. The question is complicated by a number of subsidiary problems: the variation of Jewish practice between Judeans and Galileans; the possibility of irregular observance by Jesus and His disciples, since He foresaw His death; and the larger chronological uncertainty concerning the precise year in which the fourteenth of Nisan fell on Friday.

The Synoptic Gospels state that the meal occurred on the day when the Passover should be sacrificed, the first day of unleavened bread (Matt. 26:17; Mark 14:12; Luke 22:7). Early that morning the disciples inquired of Jesus where He wanted to celebrate the feast, and He appointed Peter and John as a committee on arrangements to prepare the meal. He instructed them to enter Jerusalem and to look for a man carrying a pitcher of water, whom they should follow into a house, and there to inquire of the owner where Jesus might eat the Passover with His disciples. There were several unusual features in this rendezvous: (1) it was exceptional for a man to carry a pitcher of water unless he was a professional water-carrier; (2) the disciples did not engage in conversation with him, but followed him into the house; (3) the owner of the house had apparently been informed in advance of the Lord's intention. The indirectness of approach implies that Jesus had already made some secret contacts so that He might be able to enjoy an undisturbed evening with His disciples, even though He was in the midst of enemies with a price on His head. The absence of servants, which necessitated the footwashing described in John 13, may be attributed to His precaution against betrayal by any person outside of the Twelve. Jesus was already aware of Judas' intentions and had anticipated them, as His action showed.

The Johannine account seemingly takes exception to the statement of the Synoptics. John states that Pilate pronounced his sentence against Jesus on "the preparation of the Passover" (John 19:14). If the Passover were still in process of preparation prior to the crucifixion, the meal of the previous evening must have been the regular Passover Feast. The key to the problem lies in the meaning of the word "preparation" (Greek *paraskeuē*), which may refer either to the technical preparation for the feast, or simply to the weekday which normally preceded the Sabbath, and might in this instance be called "Passover Friday." John further stipulates that the next day was "a high day" (v. 31), which indicates that the usual weekly Sabbath was specially observed because of its coincidence with the Passover season.

On one point, at least, all Gospels are unanimous: the crucifixion occurred on Friday, for the body of Jesus had to be removed from the cross on the approach of the Sabbath. The Jewish day was reckoned from sunset to sunset, while the Roman day was reckoned from midnight to midnight. The Jewish Passover Friday would thus extend from late Thursday afternoon until late Friday afternoon, when the Sabbath began. For this reason the bodies of Jesus and of the brigands were removed from the crosses immediately after death and hastily buried. Jewish law required that a body should not remain on a gibbet overnight, and the friends of Jesus did not wish to handle a dead body on the Sabbath (Deut. 21:22, 23).

If, then, Jesus was crucified on Friday, when did He eat the Passover? Several solutions for this question have been proposed. There seems to have been no doubt that He and His disciples must have observed the rite on the evening of Thursday, which by Jewish reckoning would be the same day as the crucifixion. On the other hand, the Jewish officials at His trial on the following morning refused to enter Pilate's judgment hall lest they be defiled and consequently disqualified to partake of the Passover (John 18:28).

One possible solution for the apparent conflict is the interpretation of "preparation" as simply the name for the sixth day of the week. The term evidently denoted the day preceding the Sabbath, and is so employed in modern Greek. If this interpretation be adopted, "Passover" in John 18:39 would be generally applied to the entire period of the Feast of Unleavened Bread (cf. Exod. 12: 18). The priests consequently refused to enter Pilate's palace because leaven had not been purged from its halls in accord with the requirements of the feast.

The objection to this solution lies in the fact that the term "Passover" is usually restricted to the memorial feast rather than being extended to the observance of the entire week. The meal that Jesus and His disciples shared on Thursday evening was consequently not the regular Passover.

A second solution has been suggested by Ethelbert Stauffer.[17] Because of Jesus' repeated infringement of Sabbath law as the Jewish scribes interpreted it, and because He asserted personal authority above the Law, He was ruled to be an apostate. His personal consciousness of being the Son of God in a unique sense, which was explicitly challenged and acknowledged at His trial (Luke 22:66-71), had already brought virtual excommunication from orthodox Judaism. John plainly indicates that He had been repudiated by His own nation and driven into exile before the final crisis occurred (John 10:39-42; 11:47, 48, 53, 54). As an apostate, He would not have been able to present a lamb at the Temple for ceremonial slaughtering, nor could He have appeared publicly within its precincts for fear of arrest. There is no allusion to a lamb in the accounts of the Last Supper, although the bitter herbs, the bread, and the wine are expressly mentioned.

Such observance was not unknown at the time, for Jews of the Diaspora who were unable to make an annual pilgrimage to Jerusalem would not be present at the Temple, nor would they be able

17 Ethelbert Stauffer, *Jesus and His Story,* pp. 113-118.

to conform to all the provisions of the traditional ritual. The impossibility of maintaining a full observance of sacrificial law was generally recognized.[18]

A somewhat different hypothesis has been suggested by Massey Shepherd, Jr.

> John, following a Palestinian tradition based upon a Palestinian reckoning of the day of the Passover, recorded the true date. In the year that Jesus died, the Passover coincided with the Sabbath; hence, Jesus died on the eve of the Passover. Mark, followed by Matthew and Luke, wrote from the vantage point of one who followed the calendar of Diaspora Judaism, whose tradition recalled that in the year Jesus died the Passover fell on Friday. In other words, in that particular year the Jews in Palestine observed Passover on Saturday, those in the Dispersion observed it on Friday.[19]

By this hypothesis, Jesus ate the Passover with His disciples on the evening of Thursday, whereas the Synoptics indicate that the Jews were anticipating eating the Passover on Friday afternoon after the crucifixion. While it may be that Jews and Hellenists celebrated the Passover one day apart, the theory still does not solve the real problem, for Jesus referred to the Last Supper as "eating the passover" (Luke 22:8).

Probably the most satisfactory solution is to conclude that Jesus and the disciples ate the last supper on the evening of Thursday, which would be the beginning of Friday on the Jewish calendar, and that others may have continued the feast on the following day, which would still be Friday until sunset.

The consensus of Biblical evidence places the crucifixion on Friday, Nisan 15, whether one considers the day to have been begun on Jewish time at 6 P.M. Thursday evening, or on Roman time at the following midnight. For the purpose of chronological reckoning, there remains the question of the year in which Nisan 15 fell on Friday. There are four options: (1) Friday, April 11, A.D. 27; (2) Friday, March 18, A.D. 29; (3) Friday, April 7, A.D. 30; (4) Friday, April 3, A.D. 33. A dating in A.D. 27, though in better accord with the reckoning of subsequent events, is probably too early, for Jesus' public ministry would only have begun at that time. If Tiberius' fifteenth year can be reckoned from A.D. 12, the date in A.D. 29 is a possibility, though it would probably confine Jesus' ministry to a period of two years. The year of A.D. 33 seems less probable, both because it would fall four years after the latest reckoning for

[18] Compare Justin Martyr, *Dialogue with Trypho* xlvi. 2.

[19] Massey H. Shepherd, Jr., "Are Both the Synoptics and John Correct about the Date of Jesus' Death?" *JBL,* LXXX (1961), 123-132.

A rolling stone serving as covering for a tomb. It was this type of stone that the women feared they would be unable to roll away (Mark 16:3-4). The example pictured here is located in Herod's family tomb in Jerusalem, Israel. (Courtesy Prof. B. Van Elderen.)

Tiberius' fifteenth year, and because it would complicate unnecessarily the subsequent chronology of the development of the church. The most acceptable date is A.D. 30, which would allow for a two-or-three-year ministry, depending upon one's assumptions concerning the commencement of Tiberius' *imperium*.

At best, all datings are somewhat tentative in the absence of a fixed calendar and of categorical contemporary statements. The testimony of the church fathers from Hippolytus (A.D. 220) to Eusebius (A.D. 315) is conflicting and is based on data which are not more extensive than the available Biblical references, or which cannot be easily verified from official sources.[20]

The sequence of the resurrection is somewhat less confusing than that of the Passion week. The hasty burial of Jesus was accomplished on the late afternoon of Friday between His death at the ninth hour (Mark 15:34-39), or three o'clock and the beginning of the

20 George Ogg, *The Chronology of the Public Ministry of Jesus*, pp. 62-95.

Sabbath at six.   After six o'clock on Saturday, "when the sabbath was past" (16:1), Mary Magdalene and the other women purchased spices and planned to complete the preparation of the body "very early" on the following morning, the first day of the week. When they visited the grave at dawn (Matt. 28:1; Mark 16:2; Luke 24:1; John 20:1) and discovered that the stone had been rolled back from the doorway, they were puzzled and alarmed. Mary Magdalene, assuming that the body had been removed, hastened away to notify the disciples, while the other women approached the tomb more closely.   Upon entering, they were accosted by an angel, who informed them that Jesus had risen and pointed out the place where He had been laid, evidently still marked by the graveclothes.   Frightened and unnerved by the surprising news, they returned to Jerusalem only to meet Jesus, who instructed them to tell His disciples to proceed into Galilee, where He would rejoin them (Matt. 28:9, 10).

Mary, in the meantime, informed Peter and an unnamed disciple who ran to the tomb to investigate.   The unnamed disciple, having observed the graveclothes, evidently concluded that although the tomb was open, the body was still inside.   Peter, following a few steps behind his companion, entered immediately and discovered that the body was missing.   Puzzled by the strange phenomenon, and convinced that some unusual event had taken place, the disciples returned to their own group.

8

The Church in Jerusalem

The Birth of the Church

T HE DEATH, BURIAL, AND RESURRECTION OF JESUS OF NAZARETH
as recorded by the four Gospels are biographical events which
closed His early history but did not end His influence. According to His own testimony, He contemplated the formation of the
church (Matt. 16:18), an institution which should perpetuate His
teaching and cause, though He did not specify what method He would
take for its establishment. Prior to His ascension He commissioned
His disciples to preach repentance and remission of sins in His name
unto all the nations (Gentiles) (Luke 24:47), and to make disciples
of them (Matt. 28:19) by teaching them to observe His commandments. He prepared the basis for a new fellowship, although He did
not specify detailed plans for any formal organization.

The number of His followers who constituted the original nucleus of the church may have exceeded five hundred, for Paul
says that Jesus appeared after His resurrection to more than
five hundred brethren at once, the majority of whom were still
alive in the middle of the first century (I Cor. 15:6). Since these
may not all have been residents of Jerusalem, it is understandable that
only one hundred and twenty were present in the initial group that
assembled on the day of Pentecost (Acts 1:15). Included in this

A rock-hewn tomb at the site of Akeldama, the Field of Blood purchased by the chief priests with the thirty pieces of silver returned to them by Judas Iscariot after the betrayal. The field, also called the potter's field, was used for the burial of strangers. (Matson Photo Service.)

number were the eleven disciples, the women who had been witnesses of the crucifixion, Mary Magdalene, Joanna the wife of Chuzas, Herod's steward, Susanna, Mary the mother of James, Salome (Mark 16:1; Luke 8:3; 24:10), Mary the mother of Jesus, the brothers of Jesus, formerly unbelieving (John 7:5), and possibly others (Acts 1:14). The inner circle may not have been more than

The Valley of Hinnom, which runs along the west and south sides of Jerusalem. Here were located Gehenna (Matt. 5:39) and Akeldama, the Field of Blood (Acts 1:19). (Matson Photo Service.)

two dozen persons, but it must have been augmented by a large number of unnamed disciples who had been apprised of Jesus' command to stay in Jerusalem until they experienced the descent of the promised Spirit (Luke 24:49; Acts 1:4). The imperative quality of the command was justified by the prediction of John the Baptist that Jesus would baptize His followers in the Holy Spirit and fire

(Matt. 3:11; Mark 1:8; Luke 3:16; John 1:33), a promise repeated by all four Gospels. The uniform emphasis on the event testified to the fact that the early church considered itself the fulfillment of John's prediction, and that it attributed its origin to the irruption of a new divine vitality rather than to an attempt to perpetuate the memory of a teacher.

The fate of Judas is reported somewhat differently by Matthew and Luke. According to Matthew, he was overcome by remorse for his treachery and returned to the chief priests, confessing, "I have sinned, in that I have betrayed innocent blood" (27:4). When the priests repudiated him, he hurled the money at their feet and, leaving the sanctuary, departed to hang himself. The priests took the money to buy the potter's field for the burial of strangers (vv. 3-8). Luke says that Judas acquired a field with the money; that he fell headlong from a height, and died of a ruptured abdomen (Acts 1:18). Both authors agree that "the field of blood" was purchased with the thirty pieces of silver, and that Judas died a violent death. The Latin tradition harmonizes the records by saying that Judas hanged himself, but that the rope broke, and he was dashed to pieces. F. F. Bruce notes that Luke's statement is an explanatory parenthesis of the author rather than a part of Peter's original speech, for the fate of Judas would be common knowledge to the believers in Jerusalem.[1]

Pentecost, or the Feast of Weeks, was celebrated seven weeks after the Passover to present formally at the Temple the first bread made from the new harvest of spring grain (Exod. 34:22; Lev. 23:15-21; Deut. 16:9-11). It was one of the major gatherings of the Jewish people which brought many of the Dispersion from foreign countries. Since it was a convocation of the devout worshipers of Jehovah, the feast was an ideal occasion for the initial proclamation of the message of Jesus and for the manifestation of His power. With the descent of the Spirit upon the hundred and twenty disciples and the conversion of three thousand auditors of Peter's sermon the church began as an organism rather than as an organization, for no officers were appointed, nor was any formal program adopted. The church was a movement, fraternal in character and spontaneous in growth. The members did not depend upon a separate clerical group to manage their affairs but witnessed individually (Acts 2:44-47). The apostles maintained a ministry of healing and preaching (2:43; 4:33) that rapidly extended their influence within and beyond Jerusalem.

The phenomena accompanying the descent of the Holy Spirit were unique to the day of Pentecost. The sound like wind and

---

[1] F. F. Bruce, *The Book of Acts,* p. 49.

the appearance as tongues of fire marked the inauguration of a new movement much as the flaming manifestation of God's presence on Mt. Sinai opened the dispensation of Law (Exod. 19:18-20). Speaking with other tongues is mentioned in other passages (Acts 10:44-46; 19:6). In both of these instances a new group was brought into the church: one, the first group of Gentiles, and the other, disciples of John the Baptist who had not realized that the Spirit had come. The manifestation of Pentecost enabled the apostles to speak in languages intelligible to the hearers so that all present heard the message in their own dialects, and Peter's description of the event at the house of Cornelius implies that the converted Gentiles of Caesarea were equally endowed with the same gift. Whether the believers mentioned in Acts 19:1-6 spoke in recognizable language or in mystic tongues is not specified. The later exercise of tongue-speaking at Corinth may have been of a different order, involving the use of some type of speech which Paul described as "the tongues of men and angels" (I Cor. 13:1), and which was unrelated to any ordinary language (14:2).

The Formation of the Church

The first converts were almost wholly Jewish, though they did not all originate in Palestine. They came from such divergent directions as Parthia, Media, Elam, and Mesopotamia to the East; from Cappadocia, Pontus, Asia, Phrygia, and Pamphylia to the northwest; from Egypt, Libya, and Cyrene along the north coast of Africa; from Arabia to the southeast, and even from Rome. Although they were agreed on the common faith of Israel, they were cosmopolitan in cultural backgrounds. The pilgrim from Elam and the visitor from Rome had spent a large part of their lives in widely different environments and had become conditioned to them. Their one common bond was the Law; their central interest, the Temple worship. By accepting the messiahship of Jesus and submitting to baptism they were fused into a new fellowship.

Belief in the message of the messiahship of Jesus based on the resurrection was the initial distinctive of their theology. There had not been time for the development of a new ritual nor for the formulation of an elaborate body of doctrine. After making allowance for the probable Hellenistic influence that may have affected many of the pilgrims of the Dispersion, there still remains the fact that they had come to Jerusalem for the feast because of their fundamental allegiance to the tenets of Judaism. They did not cease to worship at the Temple, nor did they abandon the observance of the Levitical law. Peter's definitive message had been, "This Jesus did God raise up, whereof we all are witnesses. . . . Let all the house of

Israel know assuredly, that God hath made him both Lord and Christ, this Jesus whom ye crucified" (Acts 2:32, 36).

When the people responded to Peter's message by asking what action they should take, he answered in terms reminiscent of John the Baptist: "Repent ye, and be baptized every one of you in the name of Jesus Christ unto the remission of your sins; and ye shall receive the gift of the Holy Spirit" (v. 38). Three thousand responded to his invitation, thereby confessing that they were allying themselves with the followers of Jesus. At that point they were still Jews, but they had added two concepts to their theology: (1) Jesus of Nazareth was the promised Messiah of their nation, and (2) through Him they could obtain forgiveness of sins. The full implications of these propositions were not apprehended immediately, but they were the beginning of a complete Christian theology.

The church at Jerusalem in its initial stages was therefore an enlightened Judaism, which did not immediately sever its connections with the parent faith, but which sought to interpret it afresh in the light of the new revelation. There were, however, from the beginning some trends toward separation.

The cohesiveness of the new group was established by constant instruction in the principles of the new faith and by a common worship. "They continued stedfastly in the apostles' teaching and fellowship, in the breaking of bread and the prayers" (v. 42). "The apostles' teaching" implies a formulated body of material relating specifically to Christ that would not be found directly in the Law. While the exact content of that teaching is not defined, the logical inference from the passage implies that it concerned the life and teachings of Jesus with such doctrinal inferences as would be immediately obvious, such as Jesus' survival of death and His messiahship. On these tenets the subsequent theology of the new movement was founded, and by developing their implications Christianity began its independent existence.

The social bonds of the church were strengthened by the necessity of communal support. Possibly the sudden addition of converts who had been foreign pilgrims on the day of Pentecost and who had remained in Jerusalem beyond the time of normal departure because of their attachment to the new movement may have produced economic hardship. If they were unable to obtain employment in the city, or if they were boycotted because of their convictions, they would be left without financial resources. The believers assumed responsibility for these needs and sold their goods, giving to the church the prerogative of apportioning the proceeds to the needy. Some of the Hellenistic Jews shared in the giving, for Barnabas, a Jew of Cyprus, co-operated in the procedure (4:36, 37).

The Mount of Olives and the Kidron Valley. In the middle foreground is the so-called Absalom's Pillar. The large church to the left center is the Church of All Nations, surrounded by the Garden of Gethsemane. (Matson Photo Service.)

The consequent loyalties which bound the members of the community to each other created a feeling of social solidarity that distinguished them from their fellow Jews and made them a unique group.

Persecution

Because they differed from the rest of Judaism in their concept of the Messiah and in their social character, they found themselves in conflict with the existing order. Their emphatic assertion that Jesus' claims had been vindicated by His resurrection placed their opponents in the position of having rejected the purpose of God by murdering their own Messiah. The Sadducean priesthood in particular resented this charge (Acts 4:2), both because they did not believe in physical resurrection and because they were jealous of the following which the apostolic preachers were gaining (vv. 1, 2). The apostles' defense before the Sanhedrin was so pointed and logical that it could not be refuted (v. 14), and the general acclaim of their preaching and works indicated their popular support. The first attempt to suppress the Christian movement by force failed completely.

The persistent growth and increasing power manifested by the church could not be ignored. They met publicly in Solomon's porch, the long east colonnade that flanked the side of the Temple overlooking the Kidron valley, and their members grew daily (Acts 5:12-14). Miracles of healing similar to those of Jesus recurred at their meetings and their reputation was constantly spreading. According to the writer of Acts the high priest made a second attempt to arrest the leaders, Peter and John, who were miraculously released from prison and resumed their preaching in the Temple (vv. 17-25). When re-arrested and questioned by the Sanhedrin, they defended themselves with such vehemence that the council was enraged and was about to order their execution. Their defense was undertaken by a Pharisee, Gamaliel, grandson of Hillel, and one of the most eminent rabbis of his generation. He was renowned for his generous attitude toward non-Jewish scholarship and for his more liberal interpretation of the Law than the members of the stricter school of Shammai. He relaxed the strict application of the Sabbath laws concerning travel and forbade men to annul divorce proceedings without their wives' knowledge. Gamaliel's followers considered him to be the epitome of righteous living; with him, they said, perished purity and abstinence from evil.[2]

The historical allusions of Gamaliel to the insurrections under Theudas and Judas of Galilee (vv. 36, 37) have evoked sharp criticism. A Theudas is mentioned by Josephus, who asserts that he gathered a large number of followers at the Jordan, promising them that like Moses he would lead them dryshod across the river to inherit the land. Cuspius Fadus, the Roman procurator, attacked and dispersed the group and executed Theudas. In the same context Josephus refers to Judas of Galilee who incited a revolt of the Jews against Rome in the time of the second census under Quirinius in A.D. 6/7.[3] Gamaliel's speech reported in Acts reverses the order, placing Theudas before Judas. Since Cuspius Fadus was procurator from A.D. 44 to 46, the Theudas whom Josephus mentions could not conceivably have antedated Judas of Galilee, nor could Gamaliel

---

[2] Mishna *Sota* ix. 15. Quoted by F. F. Bruce, *op. cit.*, p. 146.
[3] *Antiquities of the Jews* xx. 5. 1,2.

have referred to him, since he was presumably speaking to a council during the high-priesthood of Caiaphas, which terminated in A.D. 36.

The discrepancy has been frequently charged to a historical blunder on the part of the author of Acts, who allegedly misread Josephus and utilized the information concerning Theudas and Judas as filling for a speech attributed to Gamaliel. On the other hand, there is no necessity for assuming that the Theudas of Acts and the Theudas of Josephus were the same, for the name was common, and there were numerous attempted revolts in Palestine during the first century, as Josephus himself asserted.[4] Moreover, it is doubtful whether Luke ever saw Josephus' works, for Acts was probably written not long after A.D. 60, or thirty years before *Antiquities*. Luke could have had access to sources as reliable as those of Josephus, and should be worthy of equal credence. Luke's general reputation for accuracy is even better than that of Josephus.[5]

The attitude of Gamaliel toward Peter and John accords with his benevolent disposition. He recommended tolerance on the grounds that if the apostles were right, the nation would be fighting against God, and that if they were wrong, they would fail, as had all other pretenders. His counsel of moderation mitigated the severity of the Sadducees so that the apostles were released after a disciplinary beating and an injunction to refrain from preaching in the name of Jesus. The action of the council did not deter them from their activities, but rather spurred them to new zeal. The church continued to increase in numbers and in strength.

Organization

Prior to the day of Pentecost the leadership of Jesus' followers was vested in the twelve disciples who had been nearest to Him and who had been chosen as His intimate associates and messengers (Luke 6:12-18). The defection of Judas left a gap in their ranks which was filled by Matthias, who was chosen by lot (Acts 1:15-26). The exact function of the Twelve in the post-resurrection period is not defined explicitly, but their action indicates that they assumed responsibility for preaching (2:14), for the instruction of catechumens (v. 42), for administration of funds (4:35), for discipline (5:1-11), and for the initiation of business (6:2). The government of the church was uncomplicated and informal, resting in the hands of the original preachers who had received their commission from Christ.

4 *Ibid.*, xvii. 10. 4.
5 See F. F. Bruce, *The Acts of the Apostles*, p. 147.

The administration of supplies for the poor necessitated a change in the organizational system of the church. The detailed work of distribution of money and goods exacted too much time from the apostles' preaching, so that assistance was needed. Furthermore, dissension arose between the Hebraists and Hellenists concerning their widows, for the Hellenists charged that theirs were unfairly treated in the daily distribution of food. Since the Hellenists were mainly visitors in Jerusalem and were not quite so strict in their observance of the Law as the Hebraists, it is likely that the latter, who as regular residents would form the majority of the church, might discriminate against the Hellenists. Rather than involve themselves in a long controversy and in petty detail, the apostles proposed that a committee be appointed to care for this business (6:2, 3).

The qualifications of the committee members indicate that both spiritual and business excellence were required. The method of appointment was essentially democratic, for the election was referred to the discretion of the church as a whole. Seven men were selected: Stephen, Philip, Prochorus, Nicanor, Timon, Parmenas, and Nicolaus. If their names, being Greek, are any index of their background, they were all Hellenists; Nicolaus was not even a Jew by birth, but a proselyte from Antioch. Their election was confirmed by apostolic recognition (v. 6), and they assumed their office.

The record of Acts does not state how long they functioned as a relief committee, nor even how well they discharged their task. The interim between their appointment and the persecution led by Saul of Tarsus which dispersed the members of the church, particularly the Hellenists, was quite short.

If the scattering of the disciples from Jerusalem affected chiefly the Hellenists of foreign origin, the need for the relief committee may have declined, since it was organized chiefly for the purpose of adjusting the claims of Hellenistic widows. Insofar as the committee itself was affected, Stephen was removed by death, and Philip was transferred to a different type of work outside of Jerusalem. The same situation may have been true of the others as well.

The appointment of these men shows that the early church assumed responsibility for the economic welfare of its poorer members, but not on a compulsory basis. Gifts were voluntary and were distributed according to individual need. The judgment upon Ananias and Sapphira (Acts 5) was not retribution because they had not contributed the total proceeds from the sale of their land to the welfare funds, but because they had pretended to give all when in reality they had kept back part of the price. The early church may have practiced community of goods to a limited extent in a local emergency, but by no stretch of imagination could it be called communistic.

The primitive church consisted of a voluntary association of men and women, activated by a new concept that the prophesied Messiah of the Old Testament had come, that He had been put to death by the consent of the Jewish hierarchy and by the Roman governor, that He had risen from death and had been translated into the presence of God, and that He had empowered His followers by the Holy Spirit to bear witness concerning Him.

Transition

At least two of the seven men who were appointed administrators of relief became preachers in their own right. The primacy among these was accorded to Stephen, whose apologetic defense of the new faith in the foreign synagogues in Jerusalem had brought him into direct conflict with their Jewish leaders. Because they could not refute his arguments, they employed false witnesses who agitated for his arrest and succeeded in bringing him before the tribunal of the Sanhedrin. There they charged him with saying that Jesus of Nazareth would destroy the Temple and would change the customs that Moses had decreed in the Law (Acts 6:8-14).

The reply of Stephen marked a turning point in the history of the church. He declared a new philosophy of faith, based not only on progress of revelation but also upon the people's rejection of revelation. In his review of Israel's spiritual history he showed how the national life began with God's choice of Abraham at the beginning of the patriarchal period. The revelation to Abraham of the exile and enslavement of his descendants in Egypt was fulfilled, but when God sent a deliverer to the people, he was rejected. The second generation that followed Moses to the borders of the promised land again repudiated him, and turned back to the wilderness. At the foot of Mt. Sinai on the eve of the giving of the Law, the people rebelled, and forced Aaron to make a golden calf, to which they bowed down in idolatrous worship. Later, when the kingdom of Israel was finally established, Solomon built a Temple which became an end in itself.

The general tenor of this address marked an incipient departure from a thoroughgoing Judaism. The charge that the people of Jerusalem had murdered their own Messiah incensed the leaders, who had condemned Jesus as an impostor. Stephen put the entire nation on the defensive when he asserted that they "had received the law as it was ordained by angels, and kept it not" (7:53). In addition, he had asserted that God does not dwell in buildings constructed by human hands, which was tantamount to saying that the Temple possessed no special sanctity as a center of worship (v. 48). In effect, he was contending that the focus of faith should be the Christ whom they had rejected, and that through Him men could find God anywhere, within or without the system of Judaism as his audience knew it.

Although these germinal principles of Christian faith were not fully developed until a later time by Paul and others, Stephen's opponents were astute enough to see their implications. Following his line of reasoning would lead to the abandonment of the ritual of the Temple. Such a conclusion was intolerable to both Pharisees and Sadducees, who were committed to the Law and its observances as they had always known it, and who had rejected Jesus, His teachings, and His acts. Their fury knew no bounds when Stephen "looked up stedfastly into heaven . . . and said, Behold, I see the heavens opened, and the Son of man standing on the right hand of God" (vv. 55, 56). To acknowledge the reality of this vision would be tantamount to accepting the validity of the resurrection and the soundness of Jesus' claims. The Sanhedrin regarded this as sheer blasphemy and consequently by mob action meted out to Stephen the punishment of stoning.

The martyrdom of Stephen bears a close resemblance to the death of Christ. Both were tried before the national council (Luke 22:66; Acts 6:12); both were accused by false witnesses (Mark 14:56-58; Acts 6:13, 14); both were charged with blasphemy (Mark 14:63, 64; Acts 7:56, 57); and both were victims of mob violence (Luke 23:18-23; Acts 7:57-59). Jesus' death, however, was accomplished indirectly through popular pressure on the Roman governor; Stephen was stoned by the people. There must have been at least a semblance of legal action, since Luke's account states that the witnesses laid down their garments at the feet of Saul while they picked up the first stones to cast at the victim. Under Jewish law stoning was prescribed as the capital punishment for idolatry or blasphemy (Deut. 13:1-11), and the regulations stipulated that the witnesses should be the first to cast the stones (17:1-7). In the case of Jesus the council admitted that it had no authority to inflict capital punishment and sought the co-operation of the Roman governor in the execution of the man whom they had condemned; at Stephen's trial they seemed to take the law into their own hands.

It has been suggested that the stoning of Stephen took place in the interim between the departure of Pilate from Judea in A.D. 36 and the arrival of his successor. A date after A.D. 36 is unlikely, however, for it does not allow sufficient time for the conversion and early ministry of Paul. More probably Pilate was at Caesarea, and knew nothing of this sudden violence which subsided immediately and left no permanent political effects. Jesus had for three years been a prominent figure in Galilee and had been definitely charged with claiming to be the king of the Jews. Stephen was relatively obscure, and the controversy over him was a religious matter internal to the Jewish community. In a country where violence was frequent, the death of one more Jew would be unnoticed or dismissed by the governor as a *fait accompli*.

Though the death of Stephen may have been relatively inconsequential to the Roman government, it was a pivotal point in the history of the church. The persecution which followed it caused a dispersion of Christians that initiated or augmented expansion in several directions. Among the direct effects were the ministry of Peter northward along the coastal plain of Philistia and Sharon to Caesarea; the visit of Philip, one of Stephen's colleagues, to Samaria; the migration af the unnamed Hellenists from Cyprus and Cyrene who founded the church at Syrian Antioch; and, most far-reaching of all, the conversion of Saul of Tarsus.

The chronology of the period cannot easily be synchronized with the history of the empire, since Acts contains few fixed dates that can serve as landmarks. The twelfth chapter mentions the death of Herod Agrippa I, which occurred in A.D. 44. Presumably the events narrated in the preceding text occurred prior to that date, quite possibly in the end of Tiberius' reign between A.D. 33 and 37.

Samaria

The evangelization of Samaria by Philip presupposes that the Christian believers were less hostile to the Samaritans than were their Jewish compatriots. If, as Stephen's address indicated, they felt that the Temple in Jerusalem was not the only place where acceptable worship to God could be offered, one great point of contention with the Samaritans would have been removed. Their doctrine that Jesus was the Messiah would not be wholly distasteful, for the Samaritans expected the advent of a Messiah "who would declare . . . all things" (John 4:25). The open proclamation of His person, supported by the miraculous signs which Philip continually performed, convinced the Samaritans of the claims of Jesus and brought an enthusiastic response.

Opposition to the message arose from one Simon, a self-styled "great man," who professed to possess supernatural powers (Acts 8:9, 10). The class to which he belonged was quite widespread and influential in the first century. Astrology, necromancy, soothsaying, and fortunetelling flourished where religion offered no sure guidance for personal life. Simon knew the art of preying upon the fears and hopes of superstitious people, and he succeeded in making a good profit from his fraudulent practices. In the ministry of the apostles he witnessed a power stronger than his own and, realizing that his influence and livelihood were jeopardized by the Spirit who worked in Philip, Peter, and John, he offered to pay them if they would share their secret with him. The sharp refusal of Peter to sell the gift of the Holy Spirit revealed that his power was of a totally different quality from that which Simon had exercised. The enduement of divine grace could not be purchased in the market, nor was it bestowed upon any individual for his private exploitation.

In the sub-apostolic Fathers and in the early apocryphal literature Simon Magus attained an undeserved prominence. Justin Martyr (c. A.D. 150) preserved the legend that Simon, a native of the Samaritan village called Gitto, moved to Rome in the days of Claudius and was deified by the Romans, who created a statue in his honor, inscribed in Latin, "Simoni, Sancto Deo."[6]   Irenaeus (A.D. 180) identified Simon the Samaritan with the churches of Luke's account, and also assigned him to the reign of Claudius, who, he said, created a monument for Simon. Irenaeus credited Simon with originating a heretical Gnostic sect served by profligate priests who practiced magical rites, worshiping Simon as Jupiter and his consort Helen as Minerva.[7]

Hippolytus (A.D. 170-236), Irenaeus' disciple, perpetuated the same tradition, enlarging it with more detail concerning the nature of Simon's heretical views.[8] According to Hippolytus, Simon claimed that the originating principle of all things is fire, which is imparted to man through sexual generation. Such generation is a manifestation of the emanation of world-power, by which Mind fructifies Intelligence. Simon indulged in mystical interpretation both of the Old Testament and of the Homeric poems. He allegorized the story of Helen of Troy, maintaining that she was the lost sheep who was claimed by the powers of the world. When he visited Tyre he purchased a female slave named Helen, who, he said, was a reincarnation of Helen of Troy, and whom he had to reclaim. He concluded his career by avowing that if he were buried alive, he would rise on the third day. His disciples accordingly interred him, but he failed to rise. His cult vanished shortly afterwards, for Origen states that in his time (c. A.D. 225) it could be found nowhere in the world.[9]

---

[6] *Apology* I, 26. 56; *Apology* II, 15.
[7] *Against Heresies* i. 28. 1-4.
[8] *Refutation of All Heresies* vi. 2. 4-15.
[9] *Against Celsus* vi. 11.

Whether Simon's influence were really as great as the Fathers say is difficult to decide. His claims seem too utterly fantastic to be believable; yet in that age they were undoubtedly credited by many. He was a good example of a wandering magician who made his living by preying on the fears of an ignorant populace. His tenets were an indirect compliment to Christianity, for he sought to propagate falsehood by imitating the truth.

Peter penetrated Simon's motives instantly by challenging his sincerity. His desire for acquiring the power of the Holy Spirit was prompted solely by a passion for prestige, and his rejoinder to Peter's rebuke, "Pray ye for me to the Lord, that none of the things which ye have spoken come upon me," expresses fear for his personal safety rather than repentance for his sacrilege.

The episode in Samaria had two consequences: the manifestation of the supremacy of the power of the Holy Spirit over opposing forces, and a new outreach into a territory which the Judaism of Jerusalem had never penetrated. The apostolic ministry of Peter and John which affected "many villages of the Samaritans" (Acts 8:25) and marked the breakdown of Jewish prejudice was the first step toward a universal proclamation of the gospel. Although the Samaritan church may not have survived the calamities attendant upon the war with the Romans in A.D. 66-70, it served to illustrate the expansion of the movement beyond the narrow confines of Judaism.

Ethiopia

Philip's preaching to the Ethiopian eunuch is a sample of the spread of Christianity in a different direction. Ethiopia was an independent native kingdom south of Egypt, lying between the present towns of Aswan and Khartoum. Breaking away from Egyptian control about 1000 B.C., it maintained a capital in Napata, which was abandoned in the third century B.C. for another site in Meroë. The new capital and its kingdom endured until the fourth century when an expedition from Abyssinia captured it and terminated its independence.

From the time of Ptolemy II (308-246 B.C.) of Egypt, Greek influence prevailed in the Ethiopian court. Greek literature and language were used by the aristocracy. Quite probably Greek was the official court language, which may account for the eunuch's ability to read the scroll of Isaiah which he carried with him in his chariot.

The government of Ethiopia was a matriarchy. "Candace" was a title for the queen rather than a proper name, as "Caesar" was

The rocky area of Petra, where the Nabateans fortified their city. The cupola in the top of the picture is the top of the temple ed-Deir. (Courtesy Prof. B. Van Elderen.)

applied to almost all of the Roman emperors. Evidently the queen governed by a bureaucracy in which the eunuch held the important post of secretary of the treasury. Ethiopia, which lay outside of the Roman empire, did not wield a strong political influence in the Middle East during the first century. It was, however, a strategic link between the Roman rim of civilization that surrounded the Mediterranean basin and the relatively unknown interior of Africa. No recorded connection exists between the conversion of the eunuch and the establishment of the Christian church in Ethiopia. The first missionary was Frumentius, a Syrian, who was appointed by Athanasius in A.D. 340. There may have been individual believers in the country before the fourth century, but they have left no reliable historical traces. Perhaps the eunuch's conversion opened a path for Christianity by initiating a small group of believers who formed the persisting nucleus around which later evangelists built the church.

Nabatea

Another border kingdom related to the events of this transitional period was Nabatea, the Arabian state that extended from the Euphrates on the northeast to the Red Sea on the south, whose capital was Petra.   The domain of the Nabateans is first noted in connection with the Maccabean wars.   Judas Maccabaeus and his brother Jonathan assisted them in liberating some of their brethren who had been besieged in Bozrah (I Macc. 5:24-28). The Nabateans were generally friendly to the Jews and assisted them on several occasions.   John Hyrcanus found refuge among them during his conflict with Antipater, the father of Herod the Great.[10]   With Aretas' aid he endeavored to reconquer his domain in Judea but was defeated by the intervention of the Romans under Scaurus, Pompey's lieutenant.[11]

In the Middle East Augustus and Tiberius followed the policy of fostering independent buffer states to act as a cushion between them and the Parthian empire.   To these client kingdoms such as

10 Josephus *Antiquities* xiv. 1. 3, 4.
11 *Ibid.,* xiv. 7. 3.

The façade of the temple ed-Deir in Petra, carved out of the rose-red Nubian sandstone. The man-made caves of Petra, many of them elaborately ornamented, call to mind Obadiah's prophecy against the Edomites, who inhabited this area centuries earlier: "The pride of thy heart hath deceived thee, O thou that dwellest in the clefts of the rock" (Obad. 3). (Courtesy Prof B. Van Elderen.)

Man sitting underneath cupola at the top of ed-Deir shows its immense dimensions. (Courtesy Prof. B. Van Elderen.)

Armenia or Judea, Rome gave great liberty, asking only for loyal adherence in the event of war. Such seems to have been the relation with the Nabateans, for while Scaurus defeated Aretas, he did not depose him nor annex his kingdom.

Coins indicate that Aretas III had extended his sovereignty as far as Damascus, and the Nabatean control persisted until A.D. 40, when Aretas IV closed his reign. Aretas IV was the father-in-law of Herod Antipas, whose daughter Herod divorced to marry Herodias. His long reign from 9 B.C. to A.D. 40 overlapped the stormy period that followed the death of Herod the Great, and it is not at all unlikely that refugees from Jerusalem fled to his realm for safety. Perhaps that accounts for the presence of Christians in Damascus at the time of the persecution after Stephen's death.[12]

Just why Damascus should have been under the rule of Aretas' deputy (ethnarch, II Cor. 11:32) when the city lay within the Roman province of Syria is not clear. It may be that the local Arabian government persisted even under the suzerainty of the Caesars. In any case, Paul's escape must have taken place before A.D. 40, which means that his conversion three years before was not later than A.D. 37, and probably was before A.D. 35.

The reason for the ethnarch's hostility to Paul may have been political. Paul's statement in II Corinthians accuses the ethnarch of attempting to kill him; Luke's account in Acts places the blame on the Jews (Acts 9:23). If the Nabateans were as friendly to the Jews of Paul's day as their ancestors had been to the Maccabeans, they may have feared that Paul would create a disturbance incurring the disfavor of the Romans. He would, therefore, be regarded as a disturbing threat to a delicately balanced peace and consequently needing restraint.

The Conversion of Paul

The persecution that followed the death of Stephen drove many of the believers out of Jerusalem into surrounding districts of Judea and Samaria (Acts 8:1). Some of them must have migrated as far as Damascus, for Paul, who took an active part in the repressive measures against them, requested letters from the chief priests authorizing him to search the synagogues of Damascus for such persons that he might bring them in chains to Jerusalem. No clear reason is given why the priests should have any jurisdiction in Damascus, which lay in the Nabatean territory under an independent king. The implication of the text suggests that Paul's authority was wholly ecclesiastical. Within the Jewish community all loyal

12 *Ibid.,* xviii. 5. 1, 2.

The city of Damacus, Syria. The tubelike structure running down the middle is a covered portion of the "street called Straight" (Acts 9:11). Notice the Moslem minarets rising above the buildings of the city. (Matson Photo Service.)

sons of Israel would acknowledge the authority of the high priests and would accede to their demands.

According to the Dead Sea Scrolls there was a sizable Jewish community in Damascus, independent of Palestinian Jewry. Evidently they enjoyed a greater religious liberty there than they did in the cities of Palestine. If the Christians knew that they could

The traditional site in the wall of Damascus where Paul was lowered in a basket to escape persecution (Acts 9:23-25). Later masonry covers the original wall. (Matson Photo Service.)

live in greater freedom under the Nabatean Arabs than in the uncertain political climate of Judea, they would logically take refuge in the Jewish settlement in Damascus.

The commission given to Paul by the chief priests permitting him to arrest believers "if he found any . . ." (Acts 9:2) seemingly indicates that not many had migrated that far. On the other hand,

The modern city wall of Damascus. It was at this point in the ancient city wall, according to tradition, that Paul escaped from the city. (Courtesy Prof. B. Van Elderen.)

Ananias' prayer presupposes that a Christian group existed in Damascus, whether it was large or small, whether it was well established or of recent origin (vv. 13, 14). Paul's sudden reversal of purpose and his vigorous preaching of Jesus as the Son of God inflamed such a controversy in the Jewish quarter that the civil authorities endeavored to arrest him, and he escaped only by being lowered to safety over the city wall in a basket (vv. 23-25; II Cor. 11:33). The hostility of the ethnarch was prompted by a desire to favor the Jewish population and by a natural fear of unwelcome Roman intervention.

The conversion of Paul at Damascus is one of the pivotal crises of New Testament history, for it transformed the chief antagonist of Christianity into its leading missionary and theologian and made a bigoted Pharisee into the apostle to the Gentiles. The book of Acts contains three distinct accounts of the event, told from three different viewpoints. The first is Luke's own digest (9:1-19),

Modern Damascus, looking northeast from the minaret of the Ommayad Mosque. (Matson Photo Service.)

incorporated into the sequence of historical narrative, and cited apparently for the purpose of explaining the origin of the Pauline ministry. The second (22:3-20) is part of Paul's speech from the steps of the castle of Antonia, in which he was explaining to the frenzied throng beneath him the reason for his presence in the city. The third was a reasoned defense of his career before Herod Agrippa II (26:1-23) and the Roman governor, Festus, who had requested Agrippa's assistance in formulating a précis of the case that he might send to Rome with the prisoner.

Three aspects of the same episode may seem to be either a careless use of sources or else needless repetition, especially in view of the relative brevity of Acts, but the purpose of the author must be taken into consideration. In telling the story of the early growth of the missionary enterprise, the conversion of Paul was a necessary link between the dispersion of the Jerusalem church and the wider Gentile ministry. The other two accounts are speeches which explain both the meaning of the conversion in retrospect and in relation to the total career and theology of the speaker.

As might be expected of narratives written or spoken on different occasions and separated by time, there are some variants between them. Luke's initial report states that Paul's companions heard the voice, but saw no figure (9:7); Paul in his speech from the castle stairs said that they "heard not the voice" (21:7). The apparent discrepancy may indicate that they heard a sound but did not distinguish the spoken words. The first narrative (9:5) records only Paul's initial question, "Who art thou, Lord?" with the answer; the speech to the mob (22:10) adds a second, "What shall I do, Lord?" The counsel of Ananias was reported differently in the first two accounts (9:10-17; 22:12-16), and was not mentioned at all in Acts 26, where Paul quotes the commission of Christ as given to him directly rather than being mediated through Ananias. In the main essentials, however, there is close agreement. The letter from the high priest commissioning Paul, the place outside the city of Damascus, the time at midday, the accompaniment of the dazzling light, the mysterious voice, Paul's prostration upon the ground and his blindness, the revelation of the glorified Christ, and the impartation of a new commission appear in each. The variations or omissions are undoubtedly due to the change of circumstances under which these three narratives were spoken. The intervention of Ananias would have been irrelevant to the defense before Agrippa, whereas in the initial historical account or in the speech to the Jewish mob in Jerusalem it would have strengthened Paul's case for Jewish readers.

Historically the most important aspect of Paul's conversion was its effect. Paul himself told Agrippa that he "was not disobedient unto the heavenly vision: but declared both to them of Damascus first, and at Jerusalem, and throughout all the country of Judea, and also to the Gentiles, that they should repent and turn to God, doing works worthy of repentance" (26:19, 20). His experience on the road to Damascus was the beginning of the evangelistic ministry that carried him westward from Jerusalem and Antioch across the northern Mediterranean world to Rome, and possibly to Spain.

Luke classifies Paul's conversion with the other manifestations of divine power in his annals of the infant church. The sudden reversal of his attitude and his complete committal to the person of Christ whom he had formerly disdained and rejected is one of the most dramatic episodes of history. The supernatural quality cannot reasonably be doubted, for no other cause can adequately explain the results.

The Preaching of Peter

The military might of Rome is reflected in Peter's visit to the household of Cornelius in Caesarea (Acts 10:1, 2). Founded originally by the Phoenicians, Caesarea was given to Herod the Great after the Romans had taken over Palestine. Herod rebuilt the city in Roman style and named it in honor of Augustus. It became the chief seaport of Palestine and the seat of the Roman governors. Since there was no good natural harbor large enough for extensive shipping, Herod built breakwaters extending for five hundred feet from the shore. He constructed a temple to Rome and Augustus, a theater, a hippodrome, an amphitheater, and two large aqueducts bringing a water supply from distant springs.[13] Recent exploration of the ocean floor of the ancient harbor has recovered many interesting objects such as coins, jars, seals, nails, which corroborate the historians' statements that Caesarea was a populous and thriving city.

The question has been raised whether it is likely that a Roman cohort would have been stationed in Caesarea prior to the death of Herod Agrippa I (A.D. 44), since he was recognized as the ruler of Judea. Agrippa I, however, did not succeed to the throne of Judea until after the death of Tiberius in A.D. 37, while the visit of Peter to Caesarea may well have taken place before that date. If so, the presence of the Roman detachment can be easily explained, for the entire territory had been placed under a Roman procurator since the deposition of Archelaus in A.D. 6. From A.D. 26 to 36,

---

13 Josephus, *Antiquities* xv. 9. 6; *Wars of the Jews* i. 21. 5-8.

At Caesarea, Herod built a city and a harbor, the remains of which can still be seen along the Mediterranean. It was from here that Paul sailed for Rome after his trial before Festus and Agrippa (Acts 25-27). (Matson Photo Service.)

the year before Tiberius' death, Pontius Pilate was procurator. He had at his disposal a large number of Roman troops, some of which were certainly quartered in Caesarea. Cornelius may well have been one of the centurions in charge. They were responsible for keeping order, and in a country as turbulent as Palestine, they were constantly on call. Inscriptional evidence shows that the Second Italian Cohort of Roman citizens was on duty in Syria in A.D. 69 and it may have been there at an earlier time.[14]

In the reign of Tiberius the new movement became solidly established in Jerusalem and slowly spread to surrounding territory. Since its constituency was largely Jewish, the Romans paid little attention to it, for Jews enjoyed the free exercise of religious privileges, and the differentiation between Judaism and Christianity at

[14] H. Dessau, *Inscriptiones Latinae Selectae*, No. 9168.

this stage would have been indistinguishable to the average Roman. Not until the reigns of Caligula and Claudius did Christianity begin to attract the attention of the government.

The visit of Peter to Caesarea was probably brief. Upon his return to Jerusalem he reported to the church concerning his activities, and with some difficulty persuaded them that his entrance into a Gentile's house had been justified by the results. The descent of the Holy Spirit upon Cornelius' household paralleled that of the day of Pentecost in Jerusalem and demonstrated that both Gentiles and Jews were equally acceptable to God on a basis of faith (11:15-18).

Persecution by Herod Agrippa I

The crisis that shook the Jerusalem church when Stephen was martyred was followed by another a few years later. Toward the close of the reign of Herod Agrippa I a widespread famine affected Palestine adversely and necessitated aid for the church. Prophets went from Jerusalem to Antioch, predicting a universal dearth of food and asking for assistance. The Gentile church responded generously and sent Barnabas and Paul to carry gifts. In all likelihood Paul held his first conference with the apostolate or its representatives concerning the validity of the Gentile mission at this time and was received with approbation (Gal. 2:1-10). The agreement of the apostolic leaders with his policies confirmed the unity of the churches and secured the support of the Jewish party during the earlier stages of missionary expansion.

Herod Agrippa I, grandson of Herod the Great, had been brought up in exile at Rome. He had been allowed to return to Palestine in A.D. 23, where he lived with his uncle Antipas and his wife, Agrippa's sister, Herodias. In A.D. 36 he returned to Rome, where Tiberius arrested him and put him in prison. He had previously become friendly with Caligula who, when he succeeded to the throne in A.D. 37, endowed Herod Agrippa with territory in the northeast section of Palestine. After Antipas' banishment in A.D. 39, Agrippa assumed control of Galilee and Perea. Two years later in A.D. 41 Claudius bestowed on him Judea and Samaria.

The rise of the Jewish church had incited his hostility. Knowing that he had to overcome the stigma of being an Idumean, he stressed his descent from the Hasmoneans through Mariamne and cultivated friendly relationships with his Jewish subjects. In the rising antagonism between the church of Jerusalem and the Jewish priesthood, Herod Agrippa took the part of the priests and inaugurated an official persecution of the believers. James the son of Zebedee was executed; Peter was imprisoned, and would have been killed had he not been released from prison miraculously (Acts 12:6-11). Making his way to the home of Mary, the mother of John Mark, where some of his friends were assembled to pray for his release, he reported his escape. After requesting that they inform James, the Lord's brother, who succeeded to the leadership of the church, Peter departed for an undisclosed destination.

No specific information is provided by Acts concerning the sphere of Peter's ministry within the next five years. He reappeared at the Council of Jerusalem in A.D. 48/50 and defended Paul against the Judaizing party. In the interim he may have spent some time in Antioch, for Paul mentions his visit to that city at a time prior to the Council. The visit must have taken place in the early years of the Antioch church when Barnabas and Paul were working together and when the principles of the church were still in a formative stage. Peter at first fraternized with the Gentiles; but when certain members of the Jerusalem church appeared who professed to represent its leader James, he withdrew from the Gentiles and refused to eat with them (Gal. 2:11, 12). Apparently he felt that his fellowship with Gentiles endangered his position with the Jerusalem church, which was largely composed of Jews who still meticulously observed the Law. James himself adhered strictly to the Law, though later he repudiated publicly the agitators who had invaded Antioch (Acts 15:24).

Paul challenged Peter in the presence of the entire church and rebuked him for his inconsistency. If Peter was willing to eat with Gentiles, why should he compel the Gentiles to become Jews? The report of the controversy given in Galatians is incomplete, for it shades off into Paul's discussion of justification by faith in Christ. Enough is said, however, to indicate that Peter was undecided, and that the Judaizing tendency to insist on circumcision as a condition of salvation affected not only Peter but Barnabas as well (Gal. 2:11-21).

The dating of this episode is not stated exactly, but it could scarcely have preceded the first journey from Antioch, since it assumes that Paul and Barnabas were working together and that the Judaizing controversy had already become an important issue. Neither could this encounter have followed the Council, for Paul and Barnabas parted company shortly afterwards (Acts 15:1, 2, 36-40). It may best be placed at Antioch shortly before the Council of Jerusalem, when the Judaizers from Jerusalem were still endeavoring to persuade the Antiochene Christians that they should be circumcised. If Peter's vacillation occurred after the Council, it could hardly be explained on rational grounds. Peter himself made the introductory speech defending the position of Paul and Barnabas

(vv. 6-11), and accepted the Council's vote that the Gentiles should be exempted from all requirements of the Law except for those bearing on their immoral practices, or upon comity with the Jewish believers. Even after making allowance for the impulsive and uncertain character of the great apostle, it seems hardly credible that his conduct could have been so hesitant and inconsistent if the decision of the Council had already been declared. His speech echoes Paul's declaration of freedom from the Law expressed in Galatians 2:16-20, as if Paul's rebuke had been accepted and had become a part of Peter's theology.

Following the Council, Peter disappeared from the narrative of Acts. For approximately fifteen years or more almost no hints are given concerning his whereabouts, except for one or two casual allusions in I Corinthians (1:12; 9:5).

The death of Herod Agrippa probably followed shortly after Peter's departure from Jerusalem. Having investigated the circumstances concerning Peter's escape, he condemned the guards to death for negligence and withdrew to Caesarea. Luke and Josephus agree substantially about the manner of his death, though the latter added some fanciful embellishments. According to Josephus' narrative, Herod returned to Caesarea in order to hold a festival in honor of Caesar. On the second day he appeared at the public theater clad in silver armor, which flashed so brilliantly in the sun that his admirers shouted, "He is a god!" and worshiped him. As he looked upward, he saw an owl perched on a rope over his head. He interpreted it as an ill omen, since an old German legionary had told him that the appearance of an owl would presage his death. He was stricken with violent abdominal pains and was carried to the palace, where he died five days later at the age of fifty-four.[15]

Herod Agrippa II, son of the deceased king, was residing in Rome at the time of his father's demise. Since he was only seventeen years of age, Claudius' advisers counseled him to defer the appointment of Agrippa II as his father's successor, especially because the kingdom was threatened by disorder of unruly soldiery. Claudius appointed Cuspius Fadus as procurator of Judea and of the rest of the kingdom.

The famine prophesied by Agabus occurred not long afterward. Josephus states that when Queen Helen of Adiabene visited Jerusalem she found the population starving. She purchased wheat in Egypt and figs in Cyprus to provide food.[16] In a later note he explains that the occasion of her visit was during the procuratorship of Cuspius Fadus and his successor Tiberius Alexander, who held

[15] *Antiquities* xix. 8. 2.
[16] *Ibid.,* xx. 2. 5.

office from A.D. 44 to 48.[17] The "relief visit" of Barnabas and
Paul to Jerusalem, sponsored by the church of Antioch, probably
coincided with this period, since the relief would hardly be sent
until the need became apparent. Probably it can be dated between
A.D. 46 and 48, since the first missionary tour began shortly after
Paul and Barnabas returned to Antioch from Jerusalem[18] and since
the tour itself was completed not later than the Council in 48/50.

Aside from the question of which variant of Acts 12:25 is correct,
there is no doubt that Barnabas and Paul were both present in Jerusalem prior to the first missionary journey. The visit may be
identified with the trip mentioned in Galatians 2:1-10, which Paul
cites with a different purpose in view. He asserts that he "went
up by revelation" (v. 2) to discuss with the apostles the message
which he was preaching among the Gentiles, but says nothing of
carrying relief funds. Since he had not preached among Gentiles
until after his first post-conversion visit to Jerusalem (Acts 9:26-31),
and since the second visit (Gal. 2:1-10) evidently followed his
association with Barnabas in Antioch (vv. 1, 2) and closely preceded
the visit of Peter (v. 11), it is extremely unlikely that there were
two visits in close proximity to each other. Paul had not appeared
in Judea in the interim between the two, for he stated emphatically
that he was unknown by face in the churches of Judea (Gal.
1:20, 22).

The relief visit of Barnabas and Paul produced numerous effects.
The funds which they carried enabled the Jerusalem church to survive the famine, although its strength probably diminished both in
numbers and resources. The approval of the elders in Jerusalem
obviated any danger of schism between them and the leaders of
the Gentile work which had been commenced at Antioch. Barnabas
and Paul rose to a new height of prominence in the church because
they had taken the initiative in social and theological progress. The
action of the infant church at Antioch betokened a vigorous growth
and presaged a rising influence that would eclipse that of the
Jerusalem church.

---

[17] *Ibid.*, xx. 5. 2.

[18] There is some question whether Acts 12:25 should read "from Jerusalem"
or "to Jerusalem." The former reading is supported by A, 33, numerous
minuscule mss., and the Syriac versions; the latter, by B, Aleph, and the bulk
of the uncials. "From Jerusalem" seems to make somewhat better sense,
because it continues the work of Barnabas and Paul after completing (*plerō-
santes* — aorist participle) their mission in Jerusalem. On the other hand, the
other reading "to Jerusalem" continues the activity of Barnabas and Paul after
the digression concerning Herod's persecution, and links the "famine visit"
with the new missionary venture of the church at Antioch. See F. F. Bruce,
The Acts of the Apostles, pp. 251, 252.

9

The Church at Antioch
During the Reign of Claudius

THE DISPERSION OF CHRISTIANS FROM JERUSALEM BY THE
persecution that followed the death of Stephen inaugurated a
second stage in the progress of the early church. Not only did
it open contacts with the outer world but also it compelled the Christians to seek a new base of operations as their mission expanded.
Jerusalem had become a dangerous spot for those who were progressive in missionary action. If Stephen's statement that "the Most
High dwelleth not in houses made with hands" (Acts 7:48)
aroused the angry protest of his compatriots in Jerusalem, what
could be expected if others boldly announced a mission to the
Gentiles? Philip's efforts in Samaria, his private counsel with the
eunuch from Ethiopia, and Peter's visitation at the house of the
Gentile Cornelius would be even less tolerable to them. Expansion
was inevitable if only as a means of escape from persecution,
though the command of Christ, "Make disciples of all the nations
[Gentiles]" (Matt. 28:19) demanded that they should carry His
message outside of the confines of Judea.

The City of Antioch

Antioch was the first large city in which the disciples of Jesus
began a work among Gentiles. Originally a mere village on the
Orontes River in northern Syria a few miles from the coast, it had

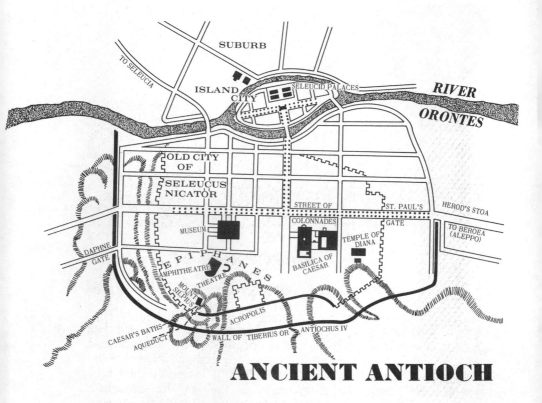

ANCIENT ANTIOCH

been taken by Seleucus I, successor of Alexander the Great and
founder of the Seleucid dynasty, to become the capital city. Seleucia,
the settlement at the mouth of the Orontes, was one of the best
harbors of the eastern Mediterranean Sea, and the river was navigable
through the coastal plain to the foot of the mountains. The river
valley which intersected the mountain range cut a pass for the
caravan route communicating with the cities of the Euphrates valley
and with the interior of the vast Asian continent. The main traveled roads from the Ionian cities and the hinterland of Asia Minor
in the northwest, from Egypt and Palestine on the south, and from
China, India and Arabia on the east converged at Antioch.

The strategic value of the location was developed by Seleucus I
who organized a thriving town from the Greek veterans of his
army, Jewish colonists, and a large number of native Syrians who
settled there because of the employment and commercial advantages
which the city afforded. From its inception the city prospered and

Antioch in Syria (modern Antakya, Turkey), looking across at Mt. Silpius and the Orontes River. It was at Antioch that the disciples were first called "Christians" (Acts 11:26), and that Paul began his missionary journeys (Acts 13:1-3). (Matson Photo Service.)

soon became, next to Alexandria, the greatest metropolis of the East. The silks of China, the ivory of India, the spices of Arabia, and countless other luxury items were brought to the West through Antioch, while manufactured goods and other commodities flowed in the opposite direction.

Unlike many ancient cities that grew out of unplanned and congested villages, Antioch was carefully designed by Seleucus, who employed a professional architect. It was built on the site of a former settlement between the slope of Mt. Silpius on the east and the Orontes River on the west in the level part of the valley, far enough from the mountain to avoid the landslides and deposits of silt washed down by the spring torrents. The streets were laid out in squares, oriented to the prevailing winds so that the westerly breezes of the summer would cool the buildings and colonnades. Temples, grain elevators, an aqueduct, and a sewage system were constructed. The original settlement probably comprised about one square mile, bordering westward on the river and extending eastward to the wall which later was replaced by the colonnaded street of the larger city.

Antioch grew and prospered during the period of the Seleucid dynasty. The Seleucids' use of mercenary troops introduced men of various nationalities into the community. Between 163 and 64 B.C. the Seleucid kings were engaged in interminable civil strife which weakened the country and wearied the people. The kingdom began to lapse into disorder and Antioch became a refuge for the Cilician pirates who infested the northeast corner of the Mediterranean. In 67 B.C. the proconsul of Cilicia, Quintus Marius Rex, visited the city and began preparations for building a palace and circus, perhaps in an attempt to gain political favor with the king. The chaotic conditions of the eastern Mediterranean induced the Roman Senate to pass the Gabinian Law, which gave Pompey control over all the waters and the land fifteen miles inland from the coastline. In a short but decisive campaign he swept the sea clear of pirates.

One year later Gaius Manilius, one of the tribunes, initiated a law which conferred upon Pompey authority over the provinces of Bithynia and Cilicia, and which gave him command of the war against Pontus and Armenia. Pompey annexed part of Pontus to Bithynia, parceled out the rest to allied states, and then annexed Syria and Judea. Antioch became a Roman city, the capital of the new province of Syria. The city maintained a semi-independent status, issuing its own coinage and enjoying a measure of self-government. Under the dictatorship of Julius Caesar, who visited Syria in 47 B.C., new public buildings were constructed and older structures were repaired. He built a theater on the slope of Mt. Silpius, an amphitheater, a public bath, and an aqueduct to bring a fresh supply of mountain water. Roman commercial interest in Syria increased.

The civil war between Caesar and Pompey, ending with the assassination of Caesar and the war between Antony and Octavian, introduced the Augustan age. The dominance of Augustus brought peace to Antioch as well as to the rest of the empire. Syria became an imperial province, directly under the supervision of the emperor, whose legate of consular or pretorian rank usually took precedence over all other officials in the East. The coins of this period show that immediately upon Augustus' succession the city was bereft of its independent titles, which may mean that it was treated as a subject state. Later, however, in A.D. 5/6, the older titles began to reappear in the coinage, as if Antioch were given better recognition as capital of the province.

Under Augustus and Tiberius the expansion and beautification of Antioch advanced notably. Some growth was inevitable after the Roman occupation in 63 B.C., for the military and diplomatic forces brought a new population and activity with them. The civil upheavals between the conquest by Pompey and the rise of Augustus prevented any solid growth and precluded any large building program because of the prevailing political uncertainty.

The emperor visited the city only twice, once after the battle of Actium (31-30 B.C.) and again ten years later. Having become well acquainted with its needs, he promoted public works. Agrippa, Augustus' son-in-law and coadjutor, sponsored extensive construction at Antioch, and Herod the Great of Judea, who was eager to ingratiate himself with Augustus, also contributed to the enlargement of the city.

The greatest achievement of the Augustan age was the construction of the central colonnaded street which bisected the city from north to south. It followed the line of the old wall erected by Seleucus Nicator on the east of the Orontes River. John Malalas, the early historian of Antioch, says that it was paved by Herod in honor of Augustus about 30 B.C., or perhaps a decade later.[1] The street was two miles in length, was roofed over to ensure shelter from sun and rain, and was lined with shops. It was the "miracle mile" of the ancient world. At the beginning of the second century the street was thirty feet wide, and the porticoes on either side were even a little wider. Probably the old wall along which it originally ran was demolished, allowing for expansion of the city toward Mt. Silpius.

The growth of population kept pace with the rising political and commercial importance of the metropolis. The advent of the Romans added a fourth element to the Greek, Jewish, and Syrian constituents. Each group occupied distinct quarters and seems

---

[1] John Malalas *Chronicle* 223. 17-19. For a full discussion of building operations in this period, see Glanville Downey, *A History of Antioch in Syria from Seleucus to the Arab Conquest,* pp. 171-189.

not to have mingled with any other except for commercial and political reasons.

The morals of Antioch have been bitterly criticized by ancient writers, but they may not have been worse than those of any other large center of the period. It is true that the intrigue, effeminacy, and idolatry of the Orient mingled there with the pleasure-seeking dissoluteness of the West, but that condition obtained in any frontier town. George Haddad, in a learned defense of the inhabitants, ascribes these accusations to the one-sided viewpoint of some chroniclers or to the puritanical diatribes of Chrysostom.[2] Even the pleasure-grove of Daphne, notorious among historians as a haunt of shameless debauchery, may have been only a general resort, neither better nor worse than the average one of the day. In any case, the Antiochenes, living as they did in a favorable climate, with wealth and leisure time at their disposal, were probably sophisticated and wanton, cosmopolitan in character, and luxurious in tastes.

Downey says that "the establishment of the Christian community at Antioch where the disciples were called Christians first" (Acts 11:26) took place in the last years of the reign of Tiberius or early in the reign of Caligula.[3] If the death of Stephen occurred about A.D. 35, it is unlikely that the church at Antioch began much earlier than A.D. 37, since some time would be required for the refugees to make their way northward and to begin the peaceful penetration of the city with the preaching of the Christian message. On the other hand, one of the seven colleagues of Stephen on the committee for the relief of widows was Nicolaus, "a proselyte of Antioch" (6:5). He must have been a Gentile who had first been attracted to Judaism by the purity of its ethical faith, and who was converted in Jerusalem at the beginning of the church. Perhaps he was one of those who went back to the Hellenistic world with the conviction that the salvation of Christ was intended for Gentiles as well as for Jews.

Jews in Antioch

In the third year of Caligula's reign there was an outburst of anti-Semitism. Malalas recounts the story that there was a riot in the circus between the factions of the Blues and the Greens, leading ultimately to disorders in which the populace initiated a pogrom against the Jews. Many were slaughtered and synagogues were burned. The emperor intervened by recalling his emissaries to

---

[2] George Haddad, *Aspects of Social Life in Antioch in the Hellenistic-Roman Period,* pp. 153-184.

[3] *Op. cit.,* p. 189.

Rome and by confiscating their property for allowing such a disturbance. He supplied funds for rebuilding parts of the city that had been destroyed in the rioting.

Just why the Jews were involved in this strife is not clear. There had been anti-Jewish tension in Alexandria in the summer of A.D. 38 when Herod Agrippa was publicly insulted by the Greek population during a visit to the city. Downey suggests that these outbursts may have been occasioned by dissension within the Jewish community, caused by Christian preaching.[4] The proclamation of Jesus as the Messiah provoked violent reaction on some occasions, creating such disturbances that the pagans feared insurrection and so undertook to suppress harshly the Jewish agitation. If this was so, the emperor would not understand the cause, much less try to account for it. Josephus says that when Titus visited the city in A.D. 70 the Jews were both numerous and unpopular.[5] At a later date Ignatius preached against the Jews.[6] Their alien customs and volatile temperament may have been irritating to the Gentile majority who resented their social aloofness and religious dissidence.

The Church in Antioch

When the refugees from Jerusalem began preaching to Jews in Phoenicia, Cyprus, and Antioch, they seem to have evoked only a moderate response; but the preaching to Greek Gentiles in Antioch was followed by a large number of conversions (Acts 11:21). The church at Jerusalem, which still remained the center of Christianity despite the scattering of many of its members, dispatched Barnabas to Antioch in order to organize and to guide the new group of believers. Evidently in their opinion the movement in Antioch was such a new venture that they were unsure what direction it would take.

Barnabas was thoroughly qualified for his task. A Levite Jew, presumably well trained in knowledge of the Scriptures and familiar with Jewish practices, he possessed broad sympathies and a kindly spirit. Born into a wealthy Jewish family of Cyprus (Acts 4:36, 37), he was accustomed to living among Gentiles and understood their manner of thinking. He was broad-minded enough to recognize true spiritual worth when he saw it, regardless of circumstances, for he sponsored Saul of Tarsus subsequent to his conversion when the church was justifiably fearful of him (9:26, 27). The result of Barnabas' preaching was beneficial, for "much people was added to the Lord" (11:24).

---

[4] *Ibid.*, pp. 192, 193.
[5] *Antiquities* xii. 3. 1; *Wars of the Jews* vii. 3. 3; 5. 2.
[6] *Magnesians* 10.

The length of Barnabas' ministry in Antioch prior to the "relief visit" to Jerusalem is not stated exactly. Calculating backwards from the death of Herod Agrippa I in the spring of A.D. 44, which, according to Acts, took place near the time of the "relief visit" and concurrently with the rising prominence of the church at Antioch, one may conclude that Paul and Barnabas had already been laboring together at Antioch for some time. The persecution of the church in Jerusalem preceded the death of Herod by a few days, or weeks at the most (12:20). Luke's phraseology is vague, for he says that the persecution under Herod took place "about that time" (v. 1), referring to the famine in the days of Claudius. If the famine occurred in the early spring of A.D. 44 because of a crop failure, the prediction of Agabus must have preceded it by an appreciable interval. Agabus' prophecy accompanied an influx of prophets from the Jerusalem church who may have been driven out by the pressure in Jerusalem that followed Stephen's death. The statement that the prediction was fulfilled "in the days of Claudius" gives the impression that it was first spoken before Claudius became emperor in A.D. 41. If it were announced in A.D. 39-40, and if Paul had already been associated with Barnabas in Antioch for a year previously (11:26), it seems probable that the church was founded not long after A.D. 37. That would allow four years for Paul's conversion, his stay in Damascus and Arabia (Gal. 1:17, 18), and sojourn in Syria and Cilicia (v. 21), and approximately three years between his conversion and the crucifixion. No one of these intervals can be determined exactly, but the conclusions given are probably as close as can be reckoned. Paul and Barnabas, therefore, must have collaborated in Antioch six or seven years before the time of Peter's arrival and the death of Herod.

The Antioch church must have been a haven of refuge for those whom Jewish opposition, terminating in the Herodian persecution, expelled from Judea. Undoubtedly they brought with them the oral teaching concerning Jesus that was largely embodied later in the Synoptic Gospels. John Mark may have composed the framework of his Gospel there, for the outline of Peter's address to the household of Cornelius bears a striking similarity to the structure of Mark (Acts 10:38-42), and the Gospel of Matthew is most frequently quoted by the Antiochian Fathers. It is even possible that Luke was a native of the city. If expulsion from Jerusalem forced some of the leaders to seek a freer environment, it is not surprising that under the protection of a Gentile government they resumed their preaching with greater vigor, and that the church rapidly expanded. Apparently the Hellenistic group constituted

A view of Antioch in Syria taken from Mt. Silpius. (Courtesy Prof. B. Van Elderen.)

the majority of those who had emigrated (11:19), and their number was increased later by the "prophets" of whom Agabus was one.

The Antioch church must have been composed of fairly well-to-do men if they were able to send a sizable relief offering to their brethren in Jerusalem, and the members were undoubtedly well known in the city, since they were publicly dubbed "Christians" by their compatriots (v. 26). In the five years or more that elapsed between the formation of a distinct body of believers and the emergence of a strong Gentile church there was a period of intense evangelism and teaching. It may have been at this time that the refugees from Herod's persecution reached Antioch and augmented the church.

A Missionary Center

The return of Barnabas and Paul from Jerusalem to Antioch after the "relief visit" indicated that their mission was completed and that they contemplated further labors. They brought back with them to Antioch John Mark, the young cousin of Barnabas, who had been residing in Jerusalem and had become interested in the ministry. These two apostles enlisted him for service, and probably took him to Antioch in order that he might acquire a broader vision. His experience in Jerusalem could have made him an eyewitness of the passion of Christ, which occurred about fifteen years previously, and would have afforded a personal knowledge of the growth of the Jerusalem church up to the time of his ministry. It may well be that he received the first impulse to write his Gospel while dealing with the Gentile converts who needed instruction.

Quite probably Barnabas and Paul did not set forth immediately on their first tour, though no long interval separated their return from the relief mission and the commission of the Spirit that sent them abroad on their new venture. There was a period of undetermined length, possibly a year, during which these two men in conjunction with others exercised their gifts of prophecy and teaching in the Antioch church. The names of the other men indicate that they must have been a cosmopolitan group. Barnabas was a native of Cyprus (Acts 4:36); Symeon may have been a Negro, since he was called Niger (the black one), or else a swarthy Arab; Lucius came from the African port of Cyrene, and Manaen (or Menahem) belonged to the Herodian aristocracy of Jerusalem (13:1). The divine choice selected Barnabas and Paul from these others to begin the formal missionary enterprise of the church.

Few movements have affected the world so profoundly as Christian missions. The messengers of the gospel have penetrated almost every land and tribe. Their message and their dedication have brought a new outlook and a new culture to millions of people and have become the greatest single civilizing agency in history. While the movement from Antioch was not the first of its kind, it was the first to affect the empire as a whole. The recognition of Christians as a distinct group in Antioch showed that they had begun to attract notice and to wield an influence separate from Judaism in which they had been cradled.

The Period of Claudius

During the period of the new expansion the imperial throne was occupied by Claudius (A.D. 41-54). When Caligula (A.D. 37-41) was assassinated, confusion reigned. Some of the older leaders of

Bust of the Roman emperor Claudius (A.D. *41-54*). (The Bettmann Archive.)

the Senate hoped fondly that the Republic might be reinstated, but the lapse of nearly three quarters of a century of imperial rule under the principate made such a consummation impossible. Some member of the ruling family, whether of the Claudian or of the Julian side, was destined to be Caligula's successor, for the military men and the populace at large desired continuity of government and the extension of the *Pax Romana* under one man rather than the chaotic rivalries which had emerged under the late Republic. The problem was quickly solved by the arbitrary action of the Pretorian Guard who took Caligula's uncle, Claudius, the weakling of the family whom they caught skulking behind a curtain, and whether in jest or in earnest nominated as Imperator. The Senate did not dare to withstand the Pretorians' pressure, and Claudius was duly appointed.

In early youth Claudius had suffered an attack of infantile paralysis which had left him with only partial control of his body, but which had not affected his brain. Although his slavering mouth, shaky limbs, and uncertain gait gave him the appearance of an imbecile, in reality he was quite the opposite. Because he seemed unfitted for public life he had devoted himself to studies, and by the time that he was elevated to his new position he had already acquired a good reputation as an antiquarian, historian, and essayist. He probably knew more about the history and policies of Rome than any of his predecessors, not excepting Augustus.

Salmon suggests that he may have escaped assassination in the bitter domestic conflicts of the Caesars because he was regarded as too harmless to be dangerous. More likely his interest in learning rather than politics removed him far enough from the arena so that he was overlooked.[7]

As soon as he succeeded to the rulership he executed the actual assassins of Caligula, and awarded a handsome largesse of 15,000 sesterces (about $750) to each of the Pretorians. He treated the Senate with respect and spared the senators who had been involved in the plot against Caligula. Taxes were reduced, gladiatorial shows were increased, and political exiles were recalled from banishment. There were numerous conspiracies against his life, but they were quickly suppressed, so that he achieved a state of settled peace early in his reign.

Claudius was eager for military conquest and embarked upon a project to annex new territory. He crushed a revolt in Mauretania and divided it into two imperial provinces, Mauretania Caesariensis on the east and Mauretania Tingitana on the west (A.D. 42). In

[7] Edward T. Salmon, *A History of the Roman World from 30 B.C. to A.D. 138,* pp. 157, 158.

the following year his generals invaded Britain and pushed the Roman frontier to the Thames. In A.D. 46 the vassal kingdom of Thrace was converted into a province at the death of its ruler. Judea also, after the death of Herod Agrippa I in A.D. 44, again became a Roman province.

Claudius had a definite interest in religion. Momigliano states that his religious policy was fundamental to his work as a ruler.[8] Perhaps his antiquarian tastes led him to take an interest in preserving and renewing the ancient religion of Rome. He expelled astrologers from Italy and endeavored to eliminate the Druids. On the other hand, he seems not to have been inimical to all foreign cults, for he introduced the Eleusinian mysteries into Rome.

His attitude to the Jews was enigmatic. At the beginning of his reign he lifted many oppressive restrictions which they had incurred by refusing to worship the emperor. He restored freedom of worship to the Jews of Alexandria and guaranteed identical privileges throughout the empire. Contrary to these generous policies, Dio Cassius says that Claudius forbade the right of assembly to Jews in Rome, and Suetonius reports that he expelled them from the city because of a disturbance created by one Chrestus.

It may be that whereas Claudius generally respected the religious rights of all people, including Jews, there was some particular reason for repressing the Jews in Rome. Suetonius' language may be a confusion of Chrestus, a common Greek name meaning "good," with Christus, the Greek word meaning "Messiah." Not only were the two words spelled almost alike, but the pronunciation in common Greek would be identical, so that the one could easily be mistaken for the other. Suetonius or his informant may therefore have assumed that Chrestus meant an individual, while the real issue was over the messiahship of Jesus. If the gospel had reached Rome during Claudius' reign and had produced the reaction among the Jewish inhabitants that it did elsewhere, there might well have been a riot in the Jewish quarter occasioned by the preaching of Christ in the synagogue. Suspicious of any commotion that smacked of insurrection, Claudius ordered all Jews to leave Rome. Among those exiled were Aquila and Priscilla, who took up residence in Corinth and with whom Paul worked when he visited that city (Acts 18:1-3).

A second possible link between the administration of Claudius and the growth of Christianity is the so-called Nazareth Decree, discovered originally in Nazareth. It became part of a collection

---

8 Arnoldo Momigliano, *Claudius: The Emperor and His Achievement,* p. 20.

of antiquities possessed by a scholar named Froehner, who noted that he received it in 1878. This plain marble slab is inscribed in rather irregular Greek script. After the death of Froehner it was deposited in the Louvre, where Michael Rostovtzeff found it in 1930. The inscription reads as follows:

> ORDINANCE OF CAESAR. IT IS MY PLEASURE THAT GRAVES AND TOMBS REMAIN UNDISTURBED IN PERPETUITY FOR THOSE WHO HAVE MADE THEM FOR THE CULT OF THEIR ANCESTORS, OR CHILDREN, OR MEMBERS OF THEIR HOUSE. IF, HOWEVER, ANY MAN LAY INFORMATION THAT ANOTHER HAS EITHER DEMOLISHED THEM, OR HAS IN ANY OTHER WAY EXTRACTED THE BURIED, OR HAS MALICIOUSLY TRANSFERRED THEM TO OTHER PLACES IN ORDER TO WRONG THEM, OR HAS DISPLACED THE SEALING OR OTHER STONES, AGAINST SUCH A ONE I ORDER THAT A TRIAL BE INSTITUTED, AS IN RESPECT OF THE GODS, SO IN REGARD TO THE CULT OF MORTALS. FOR IT SHALL BE MUCH MORE OBLIGATORY TO HONOR THE BURIED. LET IT BE ABSOLUTELY FORBIDDEN FOR ANYONE TO DISTURB THEM. IN THE CASE OF CONTRAVENTION I DESIRE THAT THE OFFENDER BE SENTENCED TO CAPITAL PUNISHMENT ON CHARGE OF VIOLATION OF SEPULTURE.[9]

To find a document of this sort in so obscure a place as Nazareth is unusual, and the content of the inscription material makes it more remarkable. Why should such an inscription have been posted publicly in Nazareth?

A few remarks on the character of the inscription will not be amiss. First of all, the Greek is probably a translation of a Latin document, rendered into Greek and carved in stone so that the Galileans could read it. Second, the inscription may not be a decree, but a rescript, or reply, sent by the emperor in answer to the written inquiry of some official concerning matters of policy. Third, the question of opening a tomb and stealing or removing a body must have been important enough to require an imperial punishment. Capital punishment such as the emperor prescribed was not generally exacted for trivial offenses.

The date of the stone has been placed at any time from the reign of Claudius to that of Hadrian. It cannot have been earlier than that of Claudius, since Galilee was not under Roman jurisdiction until that time; nor could it have been later than the time of Hadrian, when Galilee was devastated in the Second Revolt (A.D. 135). The epigraphical evidence indicates that the lettering and style belong to the earlier half of the first century, which points to the time of Claudius.

Claudius, as already indicated, had an interest in Jewish affairs. A rescript found among papyri in 1920 was written to the Alexandrian Jews in A.D. 41 and expressly forbade them to invite other Jews to come by sea from Syria. Claudius vowed that if they did

---

[9] For Greek text and comment, see E. M. Blaiklock, *Out of the Earth*, pp. 32-37.

not refrain from inviting such people, he would "proceed against them for fomenting a malady common to the world."[10]

Who were the Syrian Jews that he mentions? Judaism was not a new malady for there had been Jews in Rome before Claudius was emperor. Were these Christian Jews who embarked from Antioch of Syria to found a church in Alexandria? And was the Nazareth Decree a clumsy attempt to offset the teaching of the resurrection? Perhaps Claudius, alarmed by the dissension in the Jewish quarter of Rome and by the apprehensions of some Alexandrian Jews, endeavored to check the new faith at the beginning and to prohibit what he thought might be a new cult founded on an empty tomb and on a reputedly risen Christ.

Under Claudius the empire grew in population and in citizenship. The census of A.D. 47-48 showed nearly a million more than in the time of Augustus. Not only did the population increase by birth, but Claudius extended the franchise to the inhabitants of the provinces and granted seats in the Senate to many of their leaders. His mild administration kept the provinces in a state of contentment and promoted their prosperity.

During his regime the government became a bureaucracy through the creation of five new offices: the secretary *a rationibus,* who handled all public revenues; the secretary *ab epistulis,* who was charged with the royal correspondence; the secretary *a cognitionibus,* who planned judicial hearings; the secretary *a libellis,* who received petitions; and the secretary *a studiis,* who was the imperial librarian. The occupants of these offices were directly responsible to the emperor. Since they were not subordinate to the Senate, they were under no public restraint and frequently used their position to gain wealth for themselves. Though the burgeoning growth of the empire made such assistance necessary, it was the fatal beginning of a tendency to govern by deputies of the executive rather than by representatives of the people.

Although the New Testament says almost nothing about Roman politics, one can read between the lines the growing tension between the state and the church. Open persecution had not begun under Claudius, but the church was being watched and the political authorities of the day were endeavoring to assess its worth. Claudius was seeking to stabilize and to extend the empire, as the leaders of the church were attempting to enlarge the kingdom of Christ. The rescript of Claudius to the Alexandrians may reflect the zeal of the church at Antioch that sent not only Barnabas and Paul to Cyprus and Asia Minor, but that sent also others to Egypt.

10 Pap. Lond., 1912.

Paphos, Cyprus, where the proconsul Sergius Paulus was converted through the preaching of Paul and Barnabas and where the false prophet Bar-Jesus was blinded. (Acts 13:6-12). (Courtesy Embassy of Cyprus.)

The death of Herod Agrippa I marked a turning point in the history of Palestine. Grandson of Herod the Great, he had succeeded to the tetrarchy of his uncle Philip of Iturea. Having been brought up in Rome under the patronage of Tiberius' son Drusus, he was appointed to his kingdom in A.D. 37 by Caligula, with whom he had been friendly at the court. In addition, on the exile of Herod Antipas he was given the territories of Galilee and Perea. At the accession of Claudius, Judea was added to his realm. Probably the persecution of the church was a part of Herod's attempt to ingratiate himself with the Jews after taking over the territory of his grandfather. It must have occurred between A.D. 41, the date of Antipas' death, and A.D. 44, when he died. James, the brother of John, the son of Zebedee, was martyred, and Peter narrowly escaped with his life (Acts 12:1-19).

The First Mission from Antioch

The separation of Barnabas and Paul for a special ministry began the missionary record of the church. Probably they left Antioch in the spring of A.D. 46 as soon as the seaways were open, and sailed for Salamis, the seaport on the eastern end of Cyprus. It had been the capital of Cyprus but was supplanted by Paphos under Roman rule.

CYPRUS

The island of Cyprus had been a center of civilization from the earliest times. Trade with the mainland had flourished in the nineteenth century B.C. Copper and lumber were the chief exports. In the time of Alexander's successors it was ruled by the Ptolemies of Egypt. There were Jewish settlers in the island from the time of the Ptolemies. In the reign of Ptolemy Euergetes II (139-138 B.C.), Lucius, a Roman consul, sent a general letter urging that Jews should be kindly treated, and requesting that if any of them were of bad character, they should be sent to Simon, the high priest in Jerusalem. Cyprus is mentioned in the list of countries to whom the letter was sent (I Macc. 15:23). The Jewish population remained large, for there were synagogues throughout the island when Barnabas and Paul preached there.

The Romans annexed Cyprus to the empire in 55 B.C. In 22 B.C. it became a senatorial province under a proconsul, as Sergius Paulus, the official who listened to Barnabas and Paul, is entitled (Acts 13:7). Paphos, located on the western end of the island, became the capital. The Romans made it their chief seaport and naval station.

The proconsul himself, Sergius Paulus, was, like many of the Roman officials, an able and cultured man. He was interested in religion, for when Barnabas and Paul reached Paphos he was already toying with a Jewish magician, Bar-Jesus, who opposed the new preachers. Bar-Jesus belonged to a small but significant class of charlatans who used their knowledge of Scripture to create new

Salamis, once the capital of Cyprus, was the first stop made by Paul and Barnabas on their first missionary journey (Acts 13:5). (Courtesy Embassy of Cyprus.)

The ancient theater at Salamis, excavated by the Cyprus Department of Antiquities in 1960. The theater was destroyed in the fourth century A.D. *by an earthquake.* (Courtesy Embassy of Cyprus.)

charms and rites. He represented the type of antagonism which confronted Christianity in its spread across the world of that time. A little psychological trickery and scientific knowledge enabled him to pose as supernatural. Bar-Jesus met his match in Paul, for he could not duplicate the power of the Holy Spirit (Acts 13:4-12).

With the departure from Cyprus, probably in the late summer of A.D. 46, "Barnabas and Saul" became "Paul and his company." The change in order is significant, for hereafter in the book of Acts the order of the names is always the same. Luke does not explain the reason for the sudden change, but presumably Paul's vision and energy initiated the venture into the Gentile territory of Asia Minor so that he superseded Barnabas as the leader.

PAMPHYLIA

Perga, the first stop after Cyprus, was located eight miles from the coast and west of the river Cestrus, in the territory of Pamphylia. Little is known of the history of Perga in the Roman period. Two wide streets at right angles to each other divided the town into four sections. One ran from the acropolis to the south gate of the wall, the other extended east and west between two opposite gates. The streets were lined with colonnades filled with shops. A gymnasium, baths, theater, and stadium have been identified within the ruins.

From the low plain on which Perga was situated Paul and his associates made their way to the highlands of Pisidian Antioch at an elevation of approximately 3600 feet. Ramsay thinks that Paul suffered an acute attack of malarial fever in Perga and so changed his plans to strike inland in order to escape from further illness.[11]

PISIDIAN ANTIOCH

Antioch of Pisidia became a free city after the defeat of Antiochus III by the Romans in 188 B.C. In 36 B.C. Antony gave it to the Galatian king Amyntas; at his death it was included in the Roman province of Galatia. It became a colony for Roman veterans, and the city was officially named Colonia Caesarea, though the older name was not relinquished. Evidently it contained a large Jewish population besides the Roman colonists and the native Phrygians.

Pisidian Antioch was the first city in which Paul asserted himself as the new leader of the mission. The address given in the synagogue is preserved at some length, even though the existing text may be a condensation of the original sermon. In organization and style it illustrates the method and content of evangelistic preaching among the Jews. Paul's intent was not to repudiate the teachings of

[11] Sir William Ramsay, *St. Paul, the Traveller and the Roman Citizen*, pp. 91-97.

The remains of the Roman aqueduct which brought water from the foothills of the Sultan Dagh mountain range (background) to the city of Antioch in Pisidia, in central Asia Minor. (Courtesy Prof. B. Van Elderen.)

Ruins of a structure at Antioch in Pisidia, where Paul visited on his first missionary journey (Acts 13:14-50). (Courtesy Prof. B. Van Elderen.)

Judaism but rather to clarify them and to convince his hearers that the Old Testament predicted the Messiah who could only be Jesus of Nazareth.

The general technique involved three stages. Paul reviewed the history of the nation, emphasizing the critical acts of God that constituted the steps toward the fulfillment of His ultimate purpose of introducing a deliverer. He described the appearance of that deliverer in the person of Jesus, His rejection by the nation, and His vindication through the resurrection, and concluded with an appeal for personal faith in Him. The type of message, which closely paralleled Stephen's speech to the Sanhedrin, and which was repeated many times in the synagogues where Paul preached afterwards, was divisive. In almost every instance it was followed by dissension among the Jews and by hearty response from the Gentile proselytes, who found in Paul's theme of justification by faith (Acts 13:38, 39) a solution for their spiritual dilemma.

The ministry in Antioch of Pisidia ended abruptly when violent Jewish opposition coupled with political pressure drove Paul and

Barnabas from the city (v. 50). Taking the road which followed the caravan route to the east, they moved to Iconium.

ICONIUM

Iconium was located on the edge of a high plateau in a fertile plain. The settlement was ancient and was originally Phrygian, retaining the worship of a mother-goddess who was served by eunuch priests. Iconium was the chief city of Lycaonia and the center of a distinct national group which was gradually being absorbed by the Graeco-Roman civilization. The city grew under Roman rule and received the special attention of Claudius, who bestowed upon it the dignity of his own name by calling it Claudiconium. Acts indicates that there was a large Jewish settlement with a synagogue, which reacted to Paul's preaching as did the Jews of Pisidian Antioch (14:1-6).

LYSTRA

Leaving Iconium, Paul and Barnabas fled to Lystra (v. 6), a small town not far east of Iconium, located in a remote region of mountainous country. Because it was not on a major trade route, it never became a large city. Its populace, which included a large number of discharged soldiers, was engaged in agriculture. Inscriptions show that Latin was widely spoken in the immediate region.

Paul and Barnabas chose this region for its obscurity, because they desired to escape from the noisy and dangerous crowds of the larger cities who were easily incited against them. The healing of a lame man excited the wonder of the rustic multitude, who instantly prepared to worship Paul and Barnabas as deities that had suddenly appeared among men.

Precedent for their action may be explained by a legend that prevailed in this region. Ovid, a Roman poet of the Augustan period (43 B.C.-A.D. 17) narrated the story of Baucis and Philemon, an aged couple who lived in the hills of Phrygia.[12] Zeus, the father of gods and men, and Hermes, his messenger, had appeared in human form to visit the people of Phrygia and had been uniformly treated with coldness and discourtesy. Upon visiting the straw hut of the old couple, they were welcomed and afforded the best entertainment that they could give. Baucis and Philemon noted that though the guests drank freely of the wine which they had provided, the bowl never seemed to be drained. Eager to please their guests, they were

---

[12] *Metamorphoses* viii, 626ff. For translation, see Brookes Moore, *Ovid's Metamorphoses*, II, 374-383.

about to kill their only goose for meat, but the strangers demurred, telling them that though the rest of the population were about to be punished for their inhospitality, they would be rewarded. Taking them to the top of a mountain, they saw the fields surrounding their home sink into a swamp, in which the others perished. Their own rude hut was magically transformed into a gleaming temple. The gods then asked what they most desired, and they replied that they wished to become keepers of the new temple and then to depart life together so that neither might survive the other. The petition was granted, and when in extreme old age they were standing together before the shrine, they were simultaneously transformed into trees with a single trunk which, says Ovid, had been described to him by "old truthful men, who have no reason to deceive me."

The story is palpably mythological, but it illustrates the popular belief that the gods occasionally visited earth in the guise of mortal men. Sculptured images depict Zeus as a tall, dignified figure, wearing a full, curly beard. Hermes was slight, agile, and youthful. It is not surprising that the populace, after seeing the restoration of the cripple, and knowing the ancient legends, should have identified Barnabas and Paul with these two.

The mound of Lystra in Asia Minor, where Paul visited on his first missionary journey, as reported in Acts 14. At Lystra, Paul and Barnabas were mistakenly identified as Roman gods. (Courtesy Prof. B. Van Elderen.)

The site of Lystra (Acts 14:6) was established by the discovery of this three-and-a-half-foot stone altar inscribed in Latin. The fourth line of the inscription gives the Roman spelling of the name of the city — "LVSTRA." (Courtesy Prof. B. Van Elderen.)

The mound of Kerti Hüyük, an unexcavated site in central Turkey now identified with the site of ancient Derbe, according to evidence from inscriptions found there. Paul visited Derbe on his first missionary journey, as reported in Acts 14. (Courtesy Prof. B. Van Elderen.)

Under the direction of the priest of Zeus Propolis ("Zeus-before-the-city") they brought garlanded oxen in preparation for sacrifices. Because of the unfamiliar language, the apostles were unaware of the crowd's intentions until they were ready to offer the animals. The majority of the people were not Hellenistic Greeks, nor Latin-speaking colonists, but native Lycaonians who spoke their own dialect. Horrified to find themselves the objects of idolatrous worship, the apostles protested vigorously and were scarcely able to prevent the consummation of the sacrifice.

Luke's record of Paul's address on this occasion is an illuminating sample of accommodation to the psychology of a rural pagan audience. It contained no appeal to the Old Testament Scriptures, for the Lycaonian Gentiles would have possessed no knowledge of these writings. Paul appealed to their consciousness of "a living God, who made the heaven and the earth and the sea, and all that in them is . . . who did good and gave you from heaven rains and fruitful seasons, filling your hearts with food and gladness" (Acts 14: 15, 17). Since pagan belief credited rains and crops to the kindly

The First Derbe Inscription, discovered by M. Ballance in 1956.. The seventh line from the bottom reads, "the council and people of Derbe." The discovery of this stone was the first indication that Kerti Hüyük is to be identified with ancient Derbe. (Courtesy Prof. B. Van Elderen.)

This inscription, discovered at Kerti Hüyük in 1962, is one of the indications supporting that mound as the site of Derbe. The inscription mentions the "most-beloved-of-God Michael, bishop of Derbe," and dates from the late fourth century A.D. *(Courtesy Prof. B. Van Elderen.)*

intervention of the gods, Paul had a basis of understanding with his hearers and succeeded in deterring them from their idolatrous purpose. His ministry in Lystra might have been more successful had not the Jews of Pisidian Antioch and Iconium pursued him to this secluded place and incited the volatile crowd to stone him as an impostor, leaving him outside the city for dead.

The episode of Lystra illustrates two contrasting forces with which the Christian preachers had to contend throughout the first century. On one side was paganism, superstitious and often ignorant, which invented new gods or identified with old ones any manifestation of divine power, and which was more concerned with miracles than with morals. On the other hand was Jewish legalism, which had settled into a stereotyped ritual, and which was incapable of adjustment to the new revelation. Curiously enough, the two combined at Lystra in opposition to the gospel although they were essentially inimical to each other, for the local idolatry and Jewish monotheism would be mutually intolerant.

DERBE

Paul, having recovered from the stoning which so nearly proved fatal, set out for the town of Derbe,[13] located on the border of

---

[13] Little is known of the city of Derbe. The recent discovery by M. Ballance of an inscription at Kerti Hüyük, 13 miles from Karaman, in 1956, indicates that it was farther from Lystra than formerly supposed. See M. Ballance, "The Site of Derbe: A New Inscription," in *Anatolian Studies* VIII (1957), 147ff. The site would be northwest of Lystra, rather than southeast, as formerly supposed.

Galatia and Cilicia. There he and Barnabas were free from interference of enemies, and achieved some success, for Acts records
that they evangelized the city and made many disciples (Acts 14:
21).

Having reached the eastern boundary of Galatia, Paul and Barnabas retraced their steps along the same road by which they had come.
Presumably it would have been easier for them to have traveled
south to Tarsus by the main eastbound highway through the pass in
the Taurus Mountains called the Cilician Gates, and thence to
Antioch, but the return journey was necessitated by the condition
of the converts. They had been left in an unorganized state, and
the pressure which the Jewish community at Pisidian Antioch had
exerted could have crushed them. At the risk of their own safety
Paul and Barnabas chose the alternative of revisiting the believers
in order to organize churches among them.

The Appointment of Elders

The organization consisted chiefly in the appointment of "elders"
(*presbyteroi*) in each assembly (Acts 14:23). The language implies
that they were "handpicked" (*cheirotonesantes*), probably for their
spiritual maturity and stability. The term may mean either appointment by vote (II Cor. 8:19) or by individual designation (Acts
10:41). While the elevation of certain men to office may not have
been wholly arbitrary, Paul and Barnabas evidently assumed sufficient authority to take the initiative.

"Elder" or "presbyter" seems not to have become a full technical name for church office until a later time. Not the title, but the
position was important. The churches needed competent leadership
if they were to be effective as witnessing bodies. Paul followed generally the method of organizing churches under responsible pastors.
Toward the close of his career he enjoined Titus to do the same in
Crete (Tit. 1:5), and Timothy received a similar commission for
Ephesus (I Tim. 1:3).

The word *ecclesia* or church did not at this time carry all of the
connotations that appear in later writings. It meant simply "congregation" or "assembly," with no necessary religious implications.
In Acts 19:32, 39, 41 it describes the convocation of Ephesian
citizens who gathered in the theater to protest against Paul's presence
in the city. In Pauline usage, however, it was usually applied exclusively to the fellowship of believers, whether in a local setting
(I Cor. 1:2) or to the universal body of Christ (Eph. 1:22, 23).

The narrow pass of the Cilician Gates, leading south through the Taurus Mountains to the city of Tarsus, where Paul was born. It was this pass which opened trade routes from Tarsus to both the East and the West, making the city an important commercial center. (Courtesy Prof. B. Van Elderen.)

A flock of Angora goats being led through the Cilician Gates near the site of Tarsus, in modern Turkey. (Philip Gendreau.)

Paul and Barnabas were the self-conscious builders of a new culture founded on holiness, of a new society bound together by common loyalty to Christ, and of a new empire of which He was the invisible head. The first missionary journey confirmed their faith in Christ and strengthened their purpose in fulfilling His commission.

The mission was concluded by their return to Antioch, where they had been first appointed. The burden of their report was that "[God] had opened a door of faith unto the Gentiles" (Acts 14: 27). Paul and Barnabas had in their mission duplicated the experience of the first Christian evangelists at Antioch, who had seen proselytes and pagans turn to Christ through their preaching. Their

success had justified their contention that the new gospel could not
be restricted to the Jews, and that a wider field and greater responsibility awaited them in the numerous cities of the empire.

IO

The Judaizing Controversy

THE RAPID INFLUX OF GENTILE BELIEVERS INTO THE NEW church at Antioch and the successful mission of Paul and Barnabas in the predominantly Hellenistic cities of South Galatia posed a novel problem for the Christian movement. The trend away from a rigid application of the Old Testament Law had been evident from the ministry of Stephen, although ceremonial details had not been debated. Paul had deemed "the gospel which I preach among the Gentiles" sufficiently different to warrant discussing it with the elders in Jerusalem (Gal. 2:2), and although he obtained their approval, there were many in the Jewish church who looked upon him with suspicion. Strong opposition arose among the Jews of the Dispersion who resisted any modification of the legal tradition, and who were unready to accept Jesus of Nazareth as the risen Messiah. Not only did they reject Paul's message, but they also endeavored to impose the full observance of the ceremonial law, and especially the rite of circumcision, upon his Gentile converts. Many of these legalists professed to be believers in Christ, for Paul calls them "false brethren" — a term that he would not have applied to those outside the church.[1]

---

[1] In Romans 9:3 Paul applied "brethren" to the Jewish people, his "kinsmen according to the flesh." "False brethren," however, implies a contrast with the "true brethren" who shared his convictions, and who were consequently within the church.

The missionary phase of this problem is illustrated by Paul's correspondence with the Galatians and to a lesser extent in later letters. The crisis occurred about A.D. 48/50, almost exactly in the middle of the century. The eminent success of the Gentile church in Antioch and the enthusiastic reception given to Paul and Barnabas by the Gentile communities of Galatia evoked the jealousy of the synagogue adherents and the displeasure of the Jewish believers who had clung to the letter of the Mosaic Law. They resented the fact that Gentiles had received the blessings of the Messiah without submitting to the ceremonial restrictions which the Jews had so carefully observed.

The Galatian Problem

The genuineness of Paul's Epistle to the Galatians has never been challenged except by the most radical schools of Biblical criticism. Its historical background, however, contains a number of questions which have not yet been solved to the satisfaction of all scholars. To whom was it written? When was it written? How can the occasion which evoked it be related to the narrative of Acts?

Destination

The Roman province of Galatia derived its name from the Gauls who, early in the third century before Christ, invaded north central Asia Minor and established an independent kingdom. After Pompey's conquest of the Near East in 64 B.C., the territory was divided between Amyntas, who was appointed king of Pisidia and Phrygia, and Polemon, who was made king of Isauria and Lycaonia. Twenty-eight years later, under the administration of Mark Antony in 36 B.C., Amyntas was given Galatia and Lycaonia, and at Antony's death he took also Pamphylia, Cilicia, and Derbe.

Amyntas was killed in a war with tribesmen in 25 B.C. and the Romans annexed his kingdom. Pamphylia became a separate province, and part of Lycaonia including Derbe was given to Archelaus, ruler of Cappadocia. In A.D. 41, under Claudius, Derbe was restored to Galatia, and Pisidian Antioch and Lystra were made colonies. Thus the original territory of the Gauls and the southern territory which included much of Phrygia and Lycaonia became one province called Galatia. In A.D. 63 Nero added to the province the country called Pontus Polemoniacus, comprising the coast of the Black Sea on each side of Amisos in the province of Bithynia Pontus, the kingdom of Polemon II, and the Galatic territory of Pontus, called Pontus Galaticus.[2]

[2] Sir William Ramsay, *A Historical Commentary on St. Paul's Epistle to the Galatians,* p. 123. See also *Cambridge Ancient History,* X, 54, 261, 774.

In the reigns of Claudius (AD. 41-54) and of Nero (A.D. 54-68), when Paul and his companions were engaged in evangelizing the Galatian cities, the province included both the southern cities of Antioch of Pisidia, Iconium, Lystra, and Derbe, which are mentioned in Acts, and the northern districts, concerning which Acts records little or nothing. The problem concerns Paul's usage of "Galatia." Did he refer to ethnic Galatia, the northern territory where the Gauls had originally settled, or to the provincial name including the southern region where Acts places his ministry? (If Paul's language denotes northern Galatia, he must have regarded it as an ethnic division; if it includes the entire province, South Galatia could have been the scene of his early missionary activity.)

Paul's use of geographical terminology, however, indicates that he generally employed provincial rather than ethnic names. His epistles speak of the churches of Achaia (I Cor. 16:15; II Cor. 9:2), of Asia (I Cor. 16:19; II Tim. 1:15), of Macedonia (II Cor. 8:1), the regions of Syria and Cilicia (Gal. 1:21), Illyricum (Rom. 15: 19), and Dalmatia (II Tim. 4:10). Galatia, then, was the inclusive term which embraced not only the northern part of the province from which its name was derived, but also the southern section through which Paul and Barnabas passed on their first journey, and which they subsequently revisited.

On the other hand, J. B. Lightfoot argues on the basis of Acts 16:6 ("the region of Phrygia and Galatia") and of Acts 18:23 ("the region of Galatia and Phrygia") that Luke was speaking of divisions described primarily in ethnic rather than in provincial terms. He observes that since Phrygia is the name given to a division of land occupied by a national group, Galatia must equally refer to another, and consequently would be used exclusively of the Gallic north.[3]

The actual phraseology is "the Phrygio-Galatic region" (Acts 16:6). The words "Phrygia" and "Galatia" consequently describe a territory belonging both to Phrygia and Galatia, or that portion of Phrygia included in or bordering on Galatia. Leaving the cities of Derbe and Lystra, Paul and his company passed along the road that led to Iconium and on to Pisidia. Striking north from Pisidian Antioch, they moved along the Galatian border through the old Phrygian country until they came to the road leading to the northwestern coast, and then they proceeded toward Troas. The brief summary at the beginning of the third journey virtually repeats the same statement: "he . . . went through the region of Galatia, and Phrygia, in order, establishing all the disciples" (18:23).

3 J. B. Lightfoot, St. Paul's Epistle to the Galatians, pp. 19, 20.

From Antioch of Syria Paul retraced the steps of the second journey, but instead of traveling northwest to Troas after leaving the Galatian borders, he went due west to Ephesus.

Galatia, as designated by Paul, seems to mean the southern end of the province where he commenced his mission in Asia Minor. If so, then the Epistle to the Galatians was written to the churches of the southern, not of the northern districts of the province. The First Epistle of Peter, however, was written to the Christian Jews of the Dispersion who had settled in the north, for all the other provinces mentioned in the greeting are northern (I Pet. 1:1).

If this deduction is correct, the relation of Galatians to the account in Acts becomes more coherent and understandable. The Epistle fits better with the circumstances of the early controversy about circumcision than with the later procedure of the expanding church. The concession that circumcision was not necessary to salvation was the cause of the subsequent expansion in the sixth decade of the first century, rather than its result.

The presence of Judaizing agitators in the cities of South Galatia is more probable than in the cities of North Galatia. The emphasis in Acts concerns the persistent activity of those in Pisidian Antioch who pursued Paul to Iconium and Lystra and who tried to disrupt his work while he was still in Galatia. The establishment of a growing Gentile church would only aggravate their prejudices, and Paul's absence would afford an opportunity for them to interfere in its progress. The language of Galatians implies that Judaizers had definitely attempted to sway the sentiment of the churches toward legalism (Gal. 5:7, 9, 10, 12; 6:12, 13). Paul protested vehemently against their doctrine, telling the Gentile Christians that if they received circumcision they would be abandoning salvation by grace and would be alienated from Christ (5:2-4).

The Chronology of Galatians

The book of Galatians was written after a journey in which Paul had established the church and had left the area with the assurance that its foundations were secure. Because of the momentous crisis which it reflects and because of the chronological references which it contains, Galatians provides a valuable link in the sequence of early church history. The first two chapters which summarize Paul's early biography define certain pivotal events in his ministry that can be equated more or less satisfactorily with Luke's less definite dating.

Paul began the review of his biography by alluding to his persecution of the church and to his subsequent conversion which he connected with his call to the Gentiles. "When it was the good pleasure of God . . . who called me through his grace, to reveal his

Son in me, that I might preach him among the Gentiles . . . I went away into Arabia, and again I returned unto Damascus" (Gal. 1:15-17). The word "returned" implies that the call of God came to him at Damascus, and the episode coincides with the repeated accounts of his conversion in the book of Acts (Acts 9:3-8; 15; 22:6-11, 21; 26:12-20). The identification of these two accounts is indisputable and affords a fair beginning from which to reckon the chronology.

The first visit to Jerusalem after Paul's conversion occurred three years later, following a visit to Arabia and preaching in the synagogues of Damascus (Gal. 1:18). Paul states that the purpose of the trip was to interview Cephas, or Peter, with whom he spent fifteen days. Luke also speaks of his return to Jerusalem from Damascus, and implies that because of his controversy with the Hellenistic Jews his stay was brief (Acts 9:28-30), and that he soon left for Tarsus via Caesarea. These reports coincide fairly well, although Paul says that "other apostles saw I none, save James, the Lord's brother" (Gal. 1:19), while Luke states that "Barnabas took him and brought him to the apostles" (Acts 9:27). The discrepancy is not serious, for Luke may have used the term "apostles" a bit loosely to include leaders of the apostolic generation such as James, the Lord's brother, who was not classed among the original Twelve. In any case, Paul seems not to have exercised an extensive ministry outside Jerusalem, for he says that he was personally unknown to the Judean churches (Gal. 1:22). He quickly transferred his activities to Syria and Cilicia, the provinces north of Judea, in which Tarsus was located. There he was busily engaged in teaching and preaching when Barnabas left Antioch to find him (Acts 11:25).

The second visit to Jerusalem chronicled in Galatians (2:1-10) is more difficult to equate with the narrative of Acts. Paul says that it occurred "after the space of fourteen years," but the starting point for his reckoning is uncertain. If it were dated from his conversion, which probably occurred between A.D. 32 and 35, his trip to Jerusalem with Barnabas and Titus would fall somewhere between A.D. 46 and 49, and would coincide with the "relief visit," when he and Barnabas took to Jerusalem the funds from the Gentile church at Antioch (Acts 11:27-30). Again the Lukan and Pauline accounts differ. Luke mentions only the aspect of famine relief; Paul says, "I went up by revelation; and I laid before them the gospel which I preach among the Gentiles but privately before them who were of repute, lest by any means I should be running, or had run, in vain" (Gal. 2:2). Paul's visit may have been motivated both by the responsibility of delivering the relief money and by his personal desire to discuss his message with the leaders in Jerusalem. The difference in emphasis may depend upon the writer's purpose in citing the episode.

A more serious difficulty, however, is latent in the chronology. If the fourteen years preceding the second visit (2:1) are to be reckoned from the first visit (1:18), then a total of seventeen years elapsed between Paul's conversion and his trip to Jerusalem with Barnabas and Titus. On the assumption that his conversion took place in A.D. 32, the visit must be placed in A.D. 49, about the time of the Council of Jerusalem described in Acts 15:1-35. If this second visit be identified with the Jerusalem Council, the "relief visit" is ignored by the account in Galatians, notwithstanding Paul's protest that in giving a resumé of his ministry he adhered to absolute truth (Gal. 1:20). On the other hand, the identification of the second visit with the "relief" deputation seems chronologically irreconcilable.

Several solutions have been propounded for this dilemma. One attempts a reconciliation on the basis of the ancient method of reckoning time by which fractions of a year were counted as a full year. "Three years" might mean parts of two years with a full year between, and "fourteen years" would similarly comprise twelve calendar years, with a part of one year at the beginning and another at the end. By combining the fractions, the total interval might not amount to more than fifteen years, so that the date of the second visit could be placed in A.D. 47 rather than in A.D. 49, leaving room for the first journey of Paul before the Jerusalem Council.

John Knox contends that Paul's conversion cannot have preceded A.D. 34 or 35, that his visit to Jerusalem to interview Cephas (Peter) was not earlier than A.D. 37 or 38, and that the visit fourteen years later must have been between A.D. 50 and 53.[4] These dates do not conform to the schedule of Acts which places Paul's visit at Corinth during the proconsulship of Gallio in A.D. 51-52. The visits to Galatia preceded Paul's trip to Achaia, and he could not have completed the evangelization of South Galatia, have attended the Council of Jerusalem, have traversed South Galatia again, and have preached in Macedonia before A.D. 52, unless a longer span of time were allowed. Knox solves the conflict by declaring that the history of Acts is unreliable. Admittedly there are problems in the Pauline chronology that are still unsolved, but discarding the existing sources of information is not likely to aid discovery of the answers.

Luke does not profess to supply a complete table of intervals by which the annals of Paul's life may be reconstructed. His allusions to time are sometimes general to the point of vagueness. On

4 John Knox, *Chapters in a Life of Paul,* pp. 76-78.

the other hand, one cannot safely assume that his data are faulty simply because they are difficult to correlate with other historical sources. Since there are few fixed points by which the sequence of events can be calculated, it is wiser to defer a final verdict until fuller information becomes available.

The traditional view identifying the visit of Paul and Barnabas to Jerusalem, as recorded in Galatians 2:1-10, with the Jerusalem Council of Acts 15 requires a later date for the writing of Galatians. Such a dating relieves the difficulty of fitting the seventeen years between the first and third visits into a period before A.D. 46, but it creates other problems. If Paul knew the decrees of the Council at the time that he wrote Galatians, he would have needed only to reproduce them in order to refute the position of those who insisted on circumcision for the Gentiles. It seems incongruous that he should not have quoted the decision made in Jerusalem if it had already been rendered. The debate at Antioch had arisen just after Paul had returned from the evangelization of South Galatia, and the controversy grew out of his preaching to the Gentiles. It is much more plausible that the writing of Galatians should have preceded the Council than that it should have followed.

Furthermore, the interview of Paul with the apostles recorded in Galatians 2:1ff. varies in numerous respects from that of the Council in Acts 15. The two have many differing features which make identification difficult, if not impossible. The meeting recorded in Galatians was a private conference (Gal. 2:2); the one recorded in Acts was a public convocation in which the church of Jerusalem participated (Acts 15:1). In Galatians Titus was cited as an example of the Gentile converts; in Acts 15 he is not mentioned. The visit described in Galatians was intended to prevent misunderstanding concerning Paul's relation to the Law (Gal. 2:2); the conference reported in Acts was intended to correct misunderstanding. Galatians lays the blame for friction at the door of the "false brethren" (2:4); the Council of Jerusalem was prompted by a general controversy arising from the legalistic teaching of members of the Jerusalem church who claimed James' authority, but whom he later disavowed (Acts 15:24). Finally, the Council resulted in a decision which was publicized throughout the Gentile churches, whereas the interview of Galatians 2 ended in a personal agreement among the apostles (Gal. 2:7-9). Although the argument from silence does not constitute final proof, it seems strange that Paul would not have quoted to the Galatian churches the letter of the Council if it had been promulgated prior to the writing of the Epistle to the Galatians.

The vacillation of Peter between eating with the Gentiles at Antioch and withdrawal from their company when Jewish Christians appeared (Gal. 2:10ff.) seems much more likely to have occurred before the Council than afterwards. Had the relation of Christian Gentiles been already settled, he could scarcely have been so uncertain of his own position. It is much more likely that Peter had joined Paul and Barnabas in their fellowship but had recoiled when he was criticized for eating in the company of Gentiles. Later, having recovered himself after Paul's rebuke, he championed the Gentile cause at the Council (Acts 15:7-11).

In the light of the foregoing considerations a more acceptable chronology identifies Paul's second appearance in Jerusalem with the "relief visit," and assigns the fifteen or seventeen years to the preceding interval that dates from his conversion. The book of Galatians fits better into the atmosphere of the Jewish controversy than it does into the era that followed the Council.

The Significance of the Controversy

Whatever chronological scheme be adopted, the focal point of the controversy was the same. Must pagans become Jews in order to be perfected Christians? Paul registered a vigorous "No" to this question, and wrote accordingly. When the problem became central in the church of Antioch he spared no effort in an attempt to answer it.

The debate was not to be taken lightly; it was fraught with serious implications. To what extent were Gentiles to be bound by the ceremonial laws of the Old Testament? Would believers in the person of Christ as proclaimed by the apostolic preachers be free to form their own judgments and standards? If the growing church were repudiated by the Jews, should it seek to maintain the Jewish heritage, or should it launch out independently? Unless these questions were settled, the relation between Christianity and Judaism would remain unstable, and Christianity would either be abandoned by Judaism, or else two schismatic bodies would be created. One would be the Judaistic church, differing from Judaism only by acknowledging Jesus of Nazareth to be the true Messiah, and the other would be the free Gentile church that would repudiate all the Judaic heritage and become rootless by discarding all previous revelation.

On the assumption that the identification of the events in Acts 11:29-30 and Galatians 2:1-10 is correct, one may deduce that the Jewish-Gentile tension over circumcision had been growing for some time. Perhaps the dispersion of Jerusalem Christians, which began between A.D. 32 and 35 at the death of Stephen and was aggravated by the persecution of Herod in A.D. 44, had left in Jerusalem a majority of the stricter party of Jewish believers, who reacted against the more tolerant attitude of the Hellenistic Jews toward the Gentile brethren.

Quite possibly the news of Paul's missionary success had aroused the protest of the Judaistic members of the church in Jerusalem, while at the same time the Judaizers in Galatia had involved the church there. Galatians 2:11-13 shows that the Judaizers in Antioch had succeeded in influencing temporarily both Peter and Barnabas, and that Paul had rebuked Peter sharply for his inconsistent conduct. The episode in Antioch must have preceded the Council at Jerusalem, since at the latter Peter staunchly defended Paul's position, and characterized the Law as "a yoke . . . which neither we nor our fathers were able to bear" (Acts 15:10). It is hardly conceivable that Peter would have abandoned a publicly avowed position soon after he had taken it, though he could have vacillated in practice after a private agreement.

The argument in Antioch between the Judaizers from Jerusalem and the champions of Gentile freedom brought into sharper focus the trouble into which the churches of Galatia had been plunged by a similar controversy. Since Paul and Barnabas were embroiled in a dispute which involved the fate of the entire church, the Christians of Antioch appointed them with others as delegates to represent them in an assembly at Jerusalem where the questions might be settled to the satisfaction of all. On the way through Phoenicia and Samaria, non-Jewish territories, they cheered the churches by announcing the conversion of the Gentiles. Evidently the Gentiles had misgivings as to whether they could be saved unless they conformed wholly to the requirements of the Law. They were reassured of the reality of their salvation when they heard of the experience of others.

Upon arriving at Jerusalem the delegation from Antioch was cordially received by the church as a whole and by its leaders (15:4). The opposing faction proved to be Pharisees who had carried over into the Christian faith some of the legal rigidity characteristic of their sect. They had the first opportunity to state their case, and they argued that Gentiles must be circumcised and be taught to keep the Law of Moses (v. 5).

The defense was threefold, being presented by three men with different approaches. Peter made the initial speech, in which he declared that he had been divinely selected to introduce the gospel to the Gentiles. He countered any possible charge of subjectivism by reminding the church that the Holy Spirit had been given to the Gentiles as a seal of God's favor and the proof of salvation. If the Gentiles were thus acknowledged by God apart from circumcision, why should the church impose further conditions upon them?

Peter's testimony was doubly effective because he had originally been unwilling to preach to the Gentiles, and had consented to do so only when urged by a divine command (10:9-16). The Jerusalem church had received a full report of his visit to the house of Cornelius (11:1-18), and had accepted his explanation as adequate. The church could not consistently repudiate it, for Peter's honesty was unquestionable, and its commitment was already settled. Peter then enunciated the principle for which Paul was contending, saying, "But we believe that we shall be saved through the grace of the Lord Jesus, in like manner as they" (15:11). He maintained the conviction which had come to him through his new experience, and stood by the agreement which had been concluded with Paul when he visited Jerusalem (Gal. 2:9).

Following Peter's address, Paul and Barnabas narrated their experience among the Gentiles, including the "signs and wonders" by which God had manifested His approval of their enterprise. Luke implies that if God had not favored the Gentile mission, it would not have been attended with such success. Significantly both Peter's speech and the report of Paul and Barnabas appealed to the same two criteria that appear in Paul's question, "He that supplieth to you the Spirit, and worketh miracles among you, doeth he it by the works of the law or by the hearing of faith?" (Gal. 3:5). A comparison of the content of Galatians 2:11-20 and 3:14 with Acts 15:6-21 reveals the numerous similarities of argument which convey the impression that the speeches at Jerusalem were only summaries of the debate which began at Antioch. The presentations of both Peter and Paul stress the attestation of Gentile salvation by the enduement of the Holy Spirit and by the performance of miracles (Acts 15:8, 12; Gal. 3:2,5); both speak of the Law as a "yoke" (Acts 15:10; Gal. 5:1); and both emphasize the "grace" of Christ (Acts 15:11; Gal. 5:4).

The last address quoted by Luke is that of James (Acts 15:14-21). As the leader of the church in Jerusalem he could not be accused of partiality to Gentiles, nor had his contacts with Paul been so frequent that he would have been swayed by Paul's influence. His decisive words were marked by soberness and fairness. Quoting Amos 9:11, 12 from the Greek Septuagint, which differs from the traditional Hebrew text, he asserted that the restoration of David's tabernacle would induce other men to seek God, even the Gentiles, who had become His worshipers. By his use of this text he declared that he anticipated the salvation of the Gentiles, whose conversion had been predicted by the prophets. In the light of this prophecy he recommended that no unnecessary restrictions be imposed upon the Gentile converts, and that they be required to observe four rules of comity: to abstain from the defilement of idolatry, from sexual promiscuity, from eating the flesh of strangled animals, and from blood.

These four requirements dealt with the practices most repulsive to the Jewish believers. Idolatry was a direct contravention of the first commandment, "Thou shalt have no other gods before me" (Exod. 20:3). Even if the Gentiles placed no importance on eating meat sacrificed to idols, since the images were impotent, they should refrain from any indulgence that would offend their Jewish brethren (cf. I Cor. 10:25-31). Fornication was a common Gentile sin that violated the Jewish standards of chastity and that often accompanied the ecstatic rites of heathen worship. "Blood" and "things strangled" referred to the dietary laws which were ceremonial rather than moral in essence, but which were so ingrained in the Jewish mode of life that to disregard them would cause needless offense. The first two mentioned were both discussed in Paul's writings to the churches and were a part of the ethical code for Christian and Jew alike; the second pair were ceremonial regulations which the church members were asked to observe for the sake of maintaining peace. Nowhere in the New Testament are these two latter stipulations emphasized. They seem to have been forgotten as the separation between Christianity and Judaism became wider.

James reminded the churches that those who wished to follow the Mosaic Law completely could resort to the synagogues where the content of the Torah was expounded every Sabbath. Reiterating the ordinances of the Law would be superfluous; the church existed to proclaim Jesus as the Messiah.

The pronouncement of James was acceptable to all concerned, and on agreement of the apostles, the elders, and the entire assembly it was inscribed in letters for transmission to the Gentile churches in Antioch, Syria, and Cilicia. The Council disavowed any connection with Judaizers and delegated Barnabas and Paul, together with Judas and Silas, to publicize the verdict of the assembly (Acts 15:25-29). The announcement of the decision relieved the tension. Judas and Silas did not remain long in Antioch; Paul and Barnabas continued their teaching and preaching for a longer interval (vv. 33-35), but ultimately resumed their broader mission.

The historical effects of the decision were far-reaching. Quite probably the controversy did not cease instantly; there may have been echoes of it in distant cities and churches for many years. The letter to the Philippians which Paul wrote during his imprisonment ten years or more afterward instructed his followers to "beware of the concision, for we are of the circumcision, who worship by the Spirit of God, and glory in Christ Jesus, and have no confidence in the flesh . . ." (Phil. 3:2, 3). Nevertheless the main objective of liberty for the Gentiles had been attained so that they were no longer under bondage to the Law and its ceremonies. With the growing separation of synagogue and church, the question became less important and ultimately ceased to be a major issue.

II

The Missionary Expansion

THE DECISION OF THE COUNCIL OF JERUSALEM OPENED A NEW era in the expansion of the church. The barrier between the circumcised Jew and the uncircumcised Gentile had been broken by the concession that Gentiles need not keep the Law to obtain salvation. The emissaries of the Gentile church at Antioch no longer felt under constraint and were able to preach freely anywhere the doctrine of salvation by faith in Christ.

The Galatian Ministry

The contention within the churches had left an aftermath of uneasiness and uncertainty, although there seems to have been no permanent schism. Wondering whether his letter had proved beneficial to the young Christian communities, Paul proposed to Barnabas that they should revisit the cities where they had preached in order to consolidate the results. Barnabas was quite ready to accompany him but requested that they should take with them John Mark, the young disciple from Jerusalem who had set out with them on the previous journey and had then disappointed them by quitting just when they began the pioneering stage of the mission (Acts 13: 13; 15:37, 38). Paul demurred, for he was unwilling to accept as a co-worker one who had been tested and had failed. The ensuing dispute divided the former partners. Paul took Silas, one of the delegates sent by the Council of Jerusalem to Antioch, and returned to Cilicia and Syria, where he had begun his ministry shortly after his conversion (Gal. 1:21). Barnabas, accompanied by his young relative John Mark, sailed for Cyprus.

Except for a casual reference in I Corinthians 9:6, written five years later from Ephesus, Barnabas disappeared from the stage of New Testament history. Paul refers to him later in such a way as to imply that he was known in the European and Asian churches (I Cor. 9:6; Col. 4:10). One might infer from the allusion that no lasting enmity existed between them, although at the time of separation the altercation was sharp (Acts 15:39). Barnabas already had completed the mission in Cyprus, his home territory, and had moved to other fields, while Paul had been steadily progressing westward in Asia Minor.

Although the dissension between Paul and Barnabas was lamentable, the situation that produced it reflects the conscientious attitude of the men. To Paul, the work was too important to be endangered by the carelessness or cowardice of a man who shrank from difficulties and who proved unreliable in a crisis. To Barnabas, the man who failed deserved another chance to make good. Barnabas gave him the opportunity to recover himself by serving as an assistant evangelist. Mark's later association with Paul in Rome (Col. 4:10) shows that he regained his usefulness in the missionary enterprise, and that Barnabas' decision was amply vindicated.

Luke summarizes Paul's Galatian campaign in one short paragraph, illustrating its effects rather than narrating them (Acts 16:1-6). Paul entered the Galatian country from the east rather than from the west, traveling by the ancient road that led from Tarsus northward through the Cilician Gates, and then westward to the hinterland of Asia Minor and the Ionian coast. The populous cities along the route afforded a promising field for the new message, and the success of the gospel in Southern Galatia encouraged Paul and his associates to extend their mission even farther.

The road led him back to the cities of Derbe, Lystra, Iconium, and Antioch of Pisidia, where he had ministered on the first journey. At Lystra his party was augmented by Timothy, who was probably a convert of his earlier visit. Timothy's ancestry illustrated the problem which had plagued the Galatian churches, for his mother was a devout Jewess but his father was a Greek. Intermarriage between pagans and Jews was not uncommon, for the Dispersion had carried the Jews far afield and had tended to break down the isolation in which they had lived while clustered in Palestine or in small settlements of their own.

With the Graeco-Roman tolerance of religious preferences, Timothy's father was probably nondescript in conviction; his mother and grandmother were students of the Old Testament and had reared Timothy carefully in their ancestral faith (II Tim. 1:5; 3:15). His conversion and entrance upon the mission posed a dilemma for Paul. Timothy, contrary to Jewish custom, had not been circumcised as an infant and had been brought up as a Gentile. If Paul insisted on circumcision, he would seemingly violate the principle for which he had contended so vehemently both in his epistles to the churches and in debate in Jerusalem. If he refused to circumcise Timothy, he would alienate the Jewish brethren who undoubtedly regarded Timothy as a Jew, since he was born of a Jewish mother and had been educated in the Law. At the risk of being called inconsistent, Paul had him circumcised to avert the very charge that was later leveled at him, namely, that he had taught "all the Jews who are among the Gentiles to forsake Moses, telling them not to circumcise their children neither to walk after the customs [of the Law]" (Acts 21:21). Since he was about to launch an evangelistic campaign in the cities of Asia, he could not afford to leave any loophole for false accusations.

The circumcision of Timothy may also have had another value. Since he was the offspring of a mixed marriage, the Jewish population may have looked upon him as illegitimate because he did not belong to Judaism. Racially, he would be counted with his mother's people, but only if he identified himself with them religiously.[1]

The action was not a compromise of principle, for Paul did not object to circumcision of Jews who observed the rite for the sake of the Law and not as a means of attaining salvation. He did refuse to impose it upon Gentiles. Titus, his young associate at Antioch, had not been compelled to submit (Gal. 2:3), and Paul had told the Galatians emphatically that if they received circumcision as an acceptance of justification by the Law, Christ would mean nothing to them. Certainly if the circumcision of Timothy were contrary to principle, Paul could not have simultaneously publicized the decrees of the Council of Jerusalem, as indeed he did (Acts 16:4). He desired to end Timothy's anomalous status so that he could be classed definitely as a Jewish Christian.

The visitation of the Galatian churches probably occupied the larger part of the summer. As fall approached he began to move

---

[1] See F. F. Bruce, *The Acts of the Apostles,* pp. 308 and 86, n. Bruce quotes the Mishna *Bikkurim* i. 4, which stipulates that a proselyte who is the son of a Jewish mother can claim Jewish descent, whereas the son of a Gentile mother cannot.

westward in order to reach the cities of Asia before the cold winter
began.

Luke's phrase, "the region of Phrygia and Galatia," or more
literally, "the Phrygio-Galatic region" (16:6), is ambiguous to
modern students, though it may not have been to the original readers.
It may apply to the territory inhabited by the Phrygians who were
subject to the provincial government of Galatia, or it may mean
the border where the two nationalities intermingled. The difference
of interpretation depends on the usage of the term "Phrygia," which
is properly a noun. If used as a noun, "Phrygia and the Galatian
region" would involve both Galatian Phrygia and the Gallic settlements; if understood as an adjective, the single article means that
the same region was both Phrygian and Galatian. In any case, the
border country which Paul evangelized must have been adjacent to
the road which he traversed in his journey toward the province of
Asia, his next objective.

The Journey Westward

For some undefined reason Paul never entered Asia. Luke observes that he was "forbidden of the Holy Spirit to speak the word
in Asia" (Acts 16:6), giving the ultimate reason of God's provi-
dence but not the proximate reason of the immediate circumstance.
He may have traveled west from Pisidian Antioch until near the
provincial border, and then, being deterred from proceeding directly
down the valley of the Meander River to Ephesus, he may have
turned northward on the road that skirted the border of Galatia and
approached Dorylaeum and Nicea in Bithynia. Again his progress
was checked, for "the Spirit of Jesus suffered them not" (v. 7).
Turning westward again, he crossed Mysia and finally reached Troas.

Asia was a rich and populous province, with highlands in the
interior suitable for lumbering and grazing, and with a low coastline
admirably suited to commerce and shipping. From the tenth mil-
lennium B.C. Greek colonists had settled there and had maintained
their foothold against the older tribes of the interior. Greek enterprise and Greek liberty characterized its temper, and under Roman
rule it had prospered. The last native sovereign, Attalus III, had
bequeathed his kingdom to the Romans, who organized it into a
province.

Bithynia was a senatorial province northeast of Asia, of less
strategic importance, which also Rome acquired by bequest. Nico-
medes III, king of Bithynia, had left it to Rome at his death in
75 B.C., but Mithradates, king of Pontus, disputed Rome's claim.
In the war that followed, Mithradates experienced initial success

but was finally defeated. By the middle of the first century Bithynia was a stable and peaceful province.

Troas, the city where Paul stopped, was located on the western coast by the Aegean Sea. It was not the ancient Troy, though it lay in the same general region. Under Augustus' rule it was constituted a Roman colony and became the outstanding seaport of northwest Asia, through which passed the shipping to the ports of Macedonia and Achaia. Paul's vision of the man from Macedonia may have been prompted by seeing strangers near the docks and markets of Troas, clothed with the wide-brimmed Macedonian hat, flowing cloak, and boots. Realizing that the country to the east was closed to him, and having received the summons to Macedonia, Paul crossed the Aegean Sea and entered Europe.

The Evangelization of Macedonia

The province of Macedonia had been organized in 148 B.C., after the Roman conquest in 168 B.C. The people were mountaineers, hardy and impassive. Under Alexander the Great they had composed the core of the Greek army that carried his banners from the Aegean Sea to the Indus River, and that had Hellenized the Middle East. They were less volatile than the Greeks who lived to the south and consequently maintained a more even quality of Christian profession.

PHILIPPI

From Neapolis, the modern Kavalla, Paul and his associates journeyed along the *Via Egnatia*, which provided the main military and commercial highway across Macedonia. The first city of importance was Philippi, about ten miles west. Originally a small mining town, founded to exploit the adjacent gold fields, it had survived the failure of the lodes because of its commercial importance. Philip of Macedon had fortified the city and had named it for himself.

In 42 B.C., during the civil wars, the armies of Mark Antony and of Octavian clashed in rivalry for command of the empire. Octavian was victorious and proceeded immediately to restore peace. He rewarded many of the soldiers who had fought for him by giving them lands near Philippi. The city was made into a Roman colony, which accorded to its inhabitants the full rights of Roman citizens, and was consequently named Colonia Julia Augusta Philippensis.

The population of Philippi consisted largely of Roman military personnel, either retired legionaries and officers who made it their permanent home or those who were stationed there on duty. Descendants of the original colonists helped to preserve the Roman

The theater at Philippi, located in front of the acropolis of the city. The theater probably dates from the fourth century B.C., *and was rebuilt in the second century* A.D. (Courtesy Prof. B. Van Elderen.)

atmosphere. They guarded their privileges jealously and resented any activity that might evoke official disapproval. The Jewish community in Philippi was too small to support a synagogue but held a weekly prayer meeting outside the city on the river bank. Lydia, a business woman who entertained Paul, was herself a proselyte rather than a Jewess, and was not a native of the city (Acts 16:14). Coming from Thyatira, one of the textile centers of Asia, she had set up business in Philippi and resided there for the commercial advantages which the city afforded. The Roman population would probably possess more wealth than did the native Greeks and would be better prospects for her dyed luxury goods.

Paul's ministry in Philippi was profoundly affected by the outward conditions which he encountered. His experience with the fortune-telling slave girl reflected the superstitious preoccupation with occultism that gripped the lower classes. Their desire for a knowledge of the future made her utterances valuable, and her owners exploited her to their advantage. When Paul commanded the demon to leave her, she lost the power of divination and so became an economic loss to her masters. She was, however, only one of many who made a living in this fashion in the cities of the empire.

The arrest and incarceration of Paul that followed the exorcism of the demon resulted from fanatical resentment of any anti-Roman propaganda. The charge, "These men, being Jews, do exceedingly trouble our city, and set forth customs which it is not lawful for us to receive, or to observe, being Romans" (vv. 20, 21), was obviously false, but was shrewdly calculated to rouse the masses against Paul and his companions. Without any inquiry concerning his status, he was instantly mobbed, beaten, and consigned to the local jail. When the occurrence of the earthquake frightened the magistrates of the city into releasing Paul and Silas, he was able to demand that they make public amends for their act because he possessed Roman citizenship. The city officials appeared personally at the jail and with abject apologies discharged Paul and Silas from their imprisonment.

The Roman background of Philippi's government appears in the names given to the officials. "Rulers" (*archontas*, v. 19) was a general term for the chief authorities of any city. "Magistrates" (*strategoi*, v. 35) is the equivalent of the Latin *praetors*, a title which the rulers of colonies usually preferred. "Serjeants" (*rhab-*

Remains of the Via Egnatia at Philippi. The Via Egnatia was the chief overland route from Asia to Rome, and Paul no doubt passed over this road on his way from Neapolis (the seaport of Philippi, Acts 16:11) to Philippi. (Courtesy Prof. B. Van Elderen.)

One of the remaining Christian churches of the Byzantine period to be found at Philippi. (Courtesy Prof. B. Van Elderen.)

douchous, v. 35), or literally "rod-bearers," were the Roman *lictors*, who executed the sentence pronounced by the praetors in any civil or criminal case. Philippi was organized on the Roman pattern for colonial municipalities. Paul's experience with the local administration may have been the first official contact with the Roman colonial system in the course of his ministry. Antioch, and most of the cities where he had preached previously, were Greek rather than Roman. Antioch of Pisidia and Lystra were colonies also, but Paul seems not to have dealt with the civil authorities in these places.

The language of Acts hints strongly that the evangelistic party divided at Philippi, leaving Luke to shepherd the young church there, while Paul and Silas moved farther inland. The "we" section ends abruptly (vv. 11-17) with Paul's arrest, and does not reappear until Paul's return to Philippi on the third journey several years later (20:5-8). Although the author maintains complete silence concerning his activities during this period, one may fairly deduce that he was in charge of the work, and that the loyalty and growth of the Philippian church were traceable to his ministry.

THESSALONICA

Leaving Philippi after release from prison, Paul and Silas resumed their journey along the Egnatian Way. Thirty miles southeast of Philippi they passed through Amphipolis, the "surrounded" city, so named because it was located in a loop of the Strymon River that bordered three sides. Amphipolis was the capital of the district, but in Luke's estimation less important than Philippi (Acts 16:12). Apollonia, the next stop, was another thirty miles west of Amphipolis on the same road. Since thirty miles made approximately a day's journey, it may well be that Paul merely stopped overnight on his way to Thessalonica, which lay thirty-eight miles west of Apollonia. If he did preach in these intervening cities, Luke has supplied no record of his activities.

Thessalonica was the largest and most important city of Macedonia. Located on the main highway from east to west, and possessing a commodious harbor, it was a noted center for trade. It was founded in 316 B.C., shortly after the death of Alexander the Great, by Cassander, one of his generals, and was named for Cassander's wife who was Alexander's sister. It became the capital of the second district of the Roman province and also of the province as a whole.

A riverside near Philippi, no doubt much like the one where Paul preached to Lydia and the other women (Acts 16:13), since there was no synagogue in Philippi. (Courtesy Prof. B. Van Elderen.)

The Jewish population of Thessalonica was more numerous and aggressive than that of Philippi, perhaps because of the difference in the cities. Thessalonica was cosmopolitan and commercial; Philippi was a Roman colony, with a larger admixture of military men and retired legionaries. Jews would be less likely to live among the Romans who disliked them than in a Greek city where commerce predominated and where they could establish their own neighborhood. The existence of a synagogue and the ability of the Jews to make a protest that created a stir among the populace indicate that they had considerable numbers and influence. Their accusation that Paul and Silas "act contrary to the decrees of Caesar, saying that there is another king, one Jesus" (Acts 17:7) shows that they professed complete loyalty to Rome rather than any allegiance to the Temple at Jerusalem or to the homeland of Judea. They were more concerned for their immediate security under the imperial rule than for an idealistic restoration of the independent commonwealth of Israel.

The reference to "the decrees of Caesar" arouses one's curiosity. At this time the reigning Caesar was Claudius, who had expelled the Jews from Rome (18:2). Suetonius states that he had ordered them to leave the city because of an insurrection begun by one Chrestus.[2] The exact reason for this revolt is not specified, but Claudius' action reflects his suspicion concerning any possible uprising that might challenge his rule. The Jewish leaders knew how to play upon the prejudices of their Roman neighbors by suggesting that Paul and Silas were subversive persons who were advocating the rule of another king. Fearful that Roman vengeance would fall upon their city if they tolerated even the suggestion of rebellion, they quickly compelled Jason, a new convert, and the other believers to give bail for the good behavior of the apostles. The latter, realizing that their presence in the city was an embarrassment to the church, left immediately for Berea.

The language reflects the Roman legal background. "King" (*basilea*) was the term generally applied to the emperor in the lands east of Rome, so that the concept of a rival ruler actually appears in the text. The phrase "taking security" (*labontes to hikanon*) is a literal rendering of the Latin *satis accipere,* which refers to giving or taking bail.[3] Whether there were additional specific "decrees" of Claudius that defined treason, issued because he feared for his life, cannot be established because historical evidence is lacking.

On the other hand, Claudius' experience with attempted sedition helps to explain his attitude. In A.D. 48 Claudius' third wife,

[2] *Claudius* 25. 4.
[3] F. F. Bruce, *op. cit.,* p. 327.

Messalina, formed an attachment for a young nobleman named Gaius Silius and was apparently plotting against the emperor's life. The situation became known to the freedmen of the palace, who feared for their own safety. They disclosed the entire affair to Claudius and demanded that Messalina be put to death. The execution of the guilty couple was promptly ordered. Claudius' last wife, Agrippina, was her niece. She had already been married twice, and by her first husband, Cnaeus Domitius Ahenobarbus, she had a son, Lucius. Claudius married her for political reasons, since by the marriage he might effect a union of the two imperial lines, the Julian and the Claudian. Her son, Lucius Domitius Ahenobarbus, better known as Nero, was married to Claudius' daughter, Octavia, and Claudius adopted him as heir presumptive to the imperial throne. Claudius' own son, Britannicus, was set aside in favor of his stepson.[4]

The uncertainty concerning succession and the treachery of Messalina and her paramour may well have made Claudius apprehensive of further plots, so that the rumor of an uprising in any city would have brought down upon it the full force of imperial reprisal. Conspiracy within the Senate was a perennial threat, for the senators resented the imperial encroachments upon their political powers. It is said that Claudius tried in private court and executed thirty-five senators and two hundred knights during his reign of thirteen years. Though the episode in Thessalonica was not large enough to create any general public alarm, contemporary conditions in the empire and the neurotic disposition of Claudius afforded ample cause for insecurity in Thessalonica.

With his usual accuracy Luke designated the city officials *politarchs,* translated in the ARV as "rulers of the city" (Acts 17:8). The translated term sounds like a general description, while as a matter of fact it was a technical title. Although it does not exist in any piece of contemporary literature, it appears in inscriptions found in Thessalonica, one of which was carved on the arch of the city gate. When the gate was demolished to make room for widening the modern street, the inscription was deposited at the British Museum.[5] The names that appear in it, Sosipater, Lucius, Pontius, Secundus, Sabinus, Demetrius, Parmenion, Meniskos, are mixed Latin and Greek, but at least two of them, Sosipater and Secundus, appear in the list of Macedonians mentioned in Acts 20:4, 5. While it is extremely improbable that any of the politarchs mentioned in the inscription can be identified with personages in Acts, the

---

4 Edward T. Salmon, *op. cit.,* pp. 170-174.
5 J. A. Thompson, *The Bible and Archaeology,* pp. 386, 387.

coincidence of names does show that these were common in the Greek cities. The "atmosphere" of Thessalonica has been correctly preserved in the written record.

BEREA

The successive expulsions from Philippi and Thessalonica may have caused Paul to seek a place where he could obtain some respite from tension. Berea was located sixty miles from Thessalonica, about twice the ordinary unit of travel to which he had been accustomed, and was not situated directly on the Egnatian Way. Cicero called it "a town difficult of access" (*oppidum devium*).[6] Perhaps the Thessalonian believers thought that Paul's enemies would not pursue him to so obscure a place, but that he would find an opportunity to preach in the local synagogue. To a degree their expectation was justified, for the Berean Jews proved to be more unprejudiced; but the Thessalonians had underestimated the zeal of Paul's opponents. The Thessalonian Jews, learning that the Bereans had received him favorably and that Gentiles were accepting his message (Acts 17:12), descended upon Berea and proceeded to agitate the crowds against him. Leaving Silas and Timothy to consolidate the work, Paul's friends conducted him to the seaboard, and thence to Athens.

The evangelization of Macedonia was conducted against persistent opposition, but it seems to have been effective. Both the Philippian and Thessalonian churches prospered and maintained their loyalty to Paul and his message. From the beginning of his Macedonian campaign the Philippians had supported him (Phil. 4:15) and the Thessalonians had co-operated with him in the labors both in Macedonia and in Achaia (I Thess. 1:6-10).

The Evangelization of Achaia

The sudden interruption of Paul's plan for an extended campaign in Macedonia compelled him to seek refuge outside of the province. Assured that he was beyond the reach of his antagonists, his Macedonian friends returned to their homes, bearing his instructions for his companions, Silas and Timothy, to rejoin him as soon as possible (Acts 17:15). He seems to have been uncertain of what the next stage of his work should be, and he was waiting for them to arrive before formulating new plans.

Achaia, and particularly the city of Athens, presented a new challenge to Christianity. According to the record of Acts, Paul's preaching hitherto had been mostly in the synagogues which were

6 *In Pisonem* xxxvi. 89.

scattered through the towns and cities of Asia Minor and Macedonia. His Gentile converts had come largely from the ring of proselytes which surrounded the Jewish core of the synagogue, so that the paganism of these Gentiles had already been partially relinquished when Paul met them. There were some exceptions. At Lystra he preached to the townsmen who were worshipers of Jupiter-before-the-city (14:11-18), and at Thessalonica many "turned unto God from idols to serve a living and true God" (I Thess. 1:10). Lystra, however, was a relatively small city, and the initial approach at Thessalonica was to the adherents of the synagogue. At Athens and at Corinth the preponderance of his contacts was with the pagan population, although he still maintained his usual procedure of "the Jew first" (Rom. 1:16).

ATHENS

Athens, though partially decadent, was still the intellectual capital of the Mediterranean world. The aura of the Periclean age, in which the city rose to the height of its political, commercial, and cultural ascendancy, had not completely vanished, although the rise of the Macedonian empire eclipsed completely the independence of Athens. In science and in literary scholarship it was superseded by Alexandria, but in philosophy it retained its supremacy. Under the Roman conquest Athens was looted but not destroyed and was treated with more respect than many conquered territories because of its heritage. It retained the status of a free city and in the second century A.D. supported a flourishing university. Its political and commercial pre-eminence had passed to Corinth, but the protection of Rome afforded security from invasion, and its inhabitants enjoyed the serene leisure that fosters academic pursuits. Luke's comment that the Athenians spent all their time in hearing or repeating the latest novelty (Acts 17:21) was accurate characterization.

If Paul terminated his voyage from Macedonia at the docks of the Piraeus, the seaport of Athens, he walked the five miles northeastward along a road paralleling the ruins of the long walls built five centuries before to connect Athens with its naval base. Approaching from the west side, he would pass the Dipylon cemetery where were buried many of the famous citizens of Athens. The tombs, some of which were still standing, were ornately sculptured. Entering through the Dipylon Gate on the west, he would proceed eastward past the Hephaestion, a temple dedicated to Hephaistos or Vulcan, patron of the metalworkers whose quarter was adjacent to it. Known now as the Theseum, the Hephaestion is still standing, and is one of the best preserved temples of Greece. At the end of

The Theseum in the Athenian agora, the best preserved Greek temple in the world. The temple was built in the middle of the fifth century B.C., *and was identified with Theseus in the middle ages, although it is quite certain that it was originally dedicated to Hephaestus (Vulcan).* (Philip Gendreau.)

the avenue was the agora or public square, surrounded by the important buildings of the city and dominated by the Acropolis, a rocky hill five hundred feet high, which was crowned by the Parthenon and the Erechtheum. Flanking the Agora were the Stoa of Zeus, containing the offices of the chief archon, head of the state religion, the temple of Apollos Patroös, the Bouleuterion, meeting place of the Athenian Council of Five Hundred, the temple of Ares, god of war, and the Odeon, or Music Hall, a public auditorium where musical and oratorical contests were held. On the eastern side of the square was the Stoa of Attalos, which housed numerous offices and shops, and which has been recently restored.

The Acropolis lay farther to the east, approached by ascending steps and stairways. Probably Paul climbed to the top and surveyed the temples which then were still intact. Images and altars abounded on every side, among which was the altar dedicated To

AN UNKNOWN GOD, from which he took his topic for the famous Areopagus address.[7]

The Areopagus, or Mars' Hill, lay directly to the east of the Acropolis. A rough stairway cut in the rock still ascends the hill from the southeast. On this eminence the court of Athens originally convened. Whether the "Areopagus" of Acts 17 referred to the hill or to the court which in Paul's day met in one of the colonnades near the Agora cannot be determined exactly. The court held jurisdiction over moral and religious cases and seems also to have functioned as a licensing board for public teachers. Ramsay contends that the language refers to the assembly rather than to the location, since Paul "stood in the midst of them" (vv. 22, 23).[8] Paul's appearance was

[7] The description of Athens in Paul's day is given succinctly and vividly by William A. McDonald in "Archaeology and St. Paul's Journeys in Greek Lands; Part II, Athens," in *The Biblical Archaeologist*, IV (1941), 1-10.

[8] Sir William Ramsay, *St. Paul, the Traveler and the Roman Citizen*, pp. 243-247.

The Bacchus temple at Baalbek, Lebanon. This temple was dedicated to the Greek gods Zeus (Jupiter), Aphrodite (Venus), and Hermes (Mercury). (Courtesy KLM — Royal Dutch Airlines.)

not a trial in the formal sense of the term but rather a hearing to determine the nature of his message and his qualifications for teaching.

The address which Paul delivered on this occasion reflects his reaction to the intellectual climate of Athens. Standing before the university court in the midst of pantheistic Stoics and deistic Epicureans, and the curious crowd of idlers who usually spent their time disputing in the market place, he formulated an apologetic unexcelled for brevity and directness. Taking his cue from an altar inscribed To an Unknown God, such as was seen by Pausanias, a traveler of the second century, he skillfully presented the God of the Old Testament who had created the world and all of the races of men who inhabit it. He quoted the Greek poets Aratus[9] and Epimenides,[10] who had said that mankind is the offspring of Zeus. Arguing from the assent of their own poets to the transcendence of God, Paul reminded his audience that they could not logically picture Him as

[9] *Phaenomena 5.*
[10] *De Oraculis.*

The rocky outcropping of the Areopagus, or Mars' Hill, near the Acropolis in Athens. Paul preached here at the invitation of the Athenians and foreigners who "spent their time in nothing else, but either to tell or to hear some new thing" (Acts 17:21). (Courtesy Prof. B. Van Elderen.)

The Acropolis at Athens, dominated by the ruins of the Parthenon. Most of the temples on the Acropolis were built during the Golden Age of Pericles in the fifth century B.C. *(Ewing Galloway.)*

an image of metal or stone. Since His offspring are persons, not idols, the supreme deity must be a person.

The atmosphere of the sophisticated and blasé Athenians is preserved in the Lukan narrative. The epithet "seedpicker" which they applied to Paul (v. 18) was a slang term, originally referring to a bird that picked up stray crumbs and seeds from the street, and later denoted a man who posed as an expert, though he possessed only scraps of knowledge. The crowd listened to his message until he mentioned the resurrection, at which some openly ridiculed him, while others dismissed him with polite indifference (v. 32). At least one member of the Areopagus, Dionysius, and a woman called Damaris, perhaps one of the educated *hetairai* or courtesans who played a prominent part in Athenian society, responded to his message.

The Erechtheum on the Acropolis. This beautiful temple was used by the Turkish commandant in Athens as a harem during the fifteenth century. (Courtesy National Tourist Organization of Greece.)

Paul's ministry in Athens seems to have created no great impression. He aroused neither enthusiasm nor anger. The Athenians considered him to be an academic freak rather than a dangerous agitator and disregarded him.

CORINTH

The atmosphere of Corinth was quite different from that of Athens. Located on the isthmus between the northern part of the Greek mainland and the Peloponnesus on the south, it commanded three harbors and the short road that carried the trade flowing between

The ruins of the temple of Nike, the goddess of victory, on the Acropolis in Athens. (Courtesy National Tourist Organization of Greece.)

east and west. The Acrocorinthus, a rocky hill eighteen hundred feet high, could easily be defended against attack, and springs affording a copious supply of water made it a natural site for a trading post. The Phoenicians established the original settlement but were displaced by Greek invaders. Corinth built a maritime empire that survived until the Macedonian conquest (335-197 B.C.), but because of a revolt against Rome it was razed to the ground in 146 B.C., and lay deserted for a century.

Julius Caesar rebuilt the city in 46 B.C., colonizing it with Greek settlers from the surrounding region and with retired legionaries.

The canal at Corinth, connecting the Ionian Sea with the Aegean. In A.D.
*67, the emperor Nero made the first attempt to build a canal here; prior to
that, ships were dragged across the four-mile isthmus. The present canal, begun in 1881, shortens the distance from the Aegean Sea to Athens by 202
miles for those ships able to navigate its 69-foot width and 26-foot depth.*
(Courtesy Prof. B. Van Elderen.)

Ruins of Corinth. In the background is the slope of the Acrocorinthus, which rises 1500 feet above the city. (Courtesy Prof. B. Van Elderen.)

Corinth became the capital of Achaia, and its harbors, Cenchrea and Schoenus on the east and Lechaeum on the west, did a thriving business. Rather than take the stormy and hazardous route around Cape Malea at the south of Greece, larger ships transferred their cargoes from one harbor to another through Corinth, while smaller craft were transported on rollers across the land bridge from the Aegean Sea to the western Gulf of Lechaeum, or vice versa. A canal across the Isthmus of Corinth was begun by Nero, but it was not completed until recent times.

The commercial prosperity of Corinth attracted visitors and settlers from every quarter of the Mediterranean world. Roman officials and military men, Greek farmers from the adjacent countryside, Syrian merchants with their exotic wares, and sailors from the Ionian coast mingled in its streets and shops.

The moral status of Corinth was the logical outcome of its religious and social history. The cult of Astarte, the oriental goddess of fertility, probably had been introduced by the Phoenician traders, and had been perpetuated in the worship of the corresponding Greek goddess Aphrodite. Her shrine was served by one thousand sacred prostitutes who ministered in the temple on the Acropolis. Although the destruction of the city in 146 B.C. had interrupted the temple ritual, Corinth had retained its reputation for being a dissolute city. Its sudden rise to wealth, its transient population, and the unlimited license which it afforded to all visitors made it a favorite resort for those who abandoned all restraint in their pleasures. The relative newness of the city gave it an air of modernity, and the constant flow of trade built the wealth of its merchant princes.

The life of Corinth in Paul's time is well attested by the ruins of the agora that the traveler sees today. Entering along the Lechaeum road from the north, one passes first between the fish market and the baths. The fish market originally was surmounted by a large tank in which live fish could be kept until they were purchased. The baths and public latrines were just across the road, where they could utilize the overflow of water from the open pool fed by the spring of Peirene farther up the southern slope. North of the fish market was the Basilica, which was the Roman center for business and legal offices. The sanctuary of Apollo next to the

The Lechaeum Road, which ran from Lechaeum, the harbor city on the western shore of the Corinthian isthmus, to the agora at Corinth. On this road an inscription was found reading "Synagogue of the Hebrews," possibly indicating the site where Paul preached (Acts 18:4). (Courtesy Prof. B. Van Elderen.)

The ruins of the ancient Corinthian agora, or market place, seen from the Acrocorinthus. In the center of the picture the seven remaining pillars of the temple of Apollo can be seen. (Courtesy Prof. B. Van Elderen.)

baths probably occupied the site of the meat market in Paul's day, where the surplus offerings of the temple were placed on sale.

At the public square the road ended in a formal gate, the Propylea, east of which was the spring of Peirene. Although the pools are no longer full, one can still see the remnants of the ornate paintings on its walls and hear the gurgle of subterranean streams under its empty chambers.

On the west side of the Propylea was the open square, flanked on north and south by rows of shops with arched roofs, opening into a long colonnade. In almost every shop on the south side was a circular opening in the floor, somewhat resembling a manhole. These apertures, now sealed, were wells that gave access to a flowing underground stream that fed the pools of Peirene, into which pots of perishable foods and amphorae of wine could be lowered for cooling — the Corinthian method of refrigeration. Since almost every shop was equipped with a well, one may conclude that the Corinthians must have consumed a great deal of wine. Paul's statement that drunkards do not inherit the kingdom of heaven (I Cor. 6:10) would be uniquely appropriate for Corinth.

In the center of the Agora or market place was a stone platform about six or seven feet high, faced with marble, which was probably the governor's judgment seat or *bema* on which Gallio sat to hear complaints and to try the cases brought before him. Without doubt it was the site of Paul's trial before the proconsul when he was charged with propagating illegal worship. Gallio vindicated him by dismissing the case (Acts 18:12-17).

Across the west end of the Agora was another line of shops, in front of which passed the road to Sicyon on the north and to the Acrocorinthus on the south. Almost parallel to it, but farther east, a road led out of the Agora southward to Cenchrea, Corinth's port on the Aegean Sea.

The statuary, pottery, and inscriptions of Corinth give mute witness to the city's prosperity and art in the time of Paul. The most tantalizing inscription is a block of marble found on a pavement near the city theater. Originally filled with bronze letters, the empty sockets still read

ERASTUS   PRO.   AED.
S.   P.   STRAVIT

The seven remaining Doric columns of the temple of Apollo in Corinth, probably built in the sixth century before Christ. (Courtesy Prof. B. Van Elderen.)

or, in full, *Erastus pro aedilitate sua pecunia stravit* — "Erastus, for the office of aedile, laid [the pavement] at his own expense." It may well be that this Erastus was identical with Paul's friend whom he calls "the treasurer of the city," when writing from Corinth to the Roman church (Rom. 16:23). The *aedile* was originally an officer appointed to superintend the buildings of a city but later was charged with other duties, including treasurer's functions. *Oikonomos,* the word for "treasurer" in Romans, would be an approximate equivalent for *aedile.* It is not unlikely that the man whose name is memorialized in the pavement was the convert and friend of Paul.

No traces of Christian influence have been found in the first-century ruins of the city, but the Christian church did not erect buildings until the fourth century, when the Edict of Constantine freed it from persecution and gave it good standing in the community. The discoveries in Corinth,[11] however, have corroborated the testimony of antiquity to its history and character, and have given new vividness to the implications of Paul's visits and correspondence.

The initial evangelization of Corinth began as usual in the Jewish community. A synagogue had been established in the city, the existence of which has been confirmed by the discovery of a broken lintel bearing the inscription [ΣYN] ΑΓΩΓHΕΒΡ [ΑΙΩΝ] (synagogue of Hebrews). Unfortunately the building to which the lintel belonged has disappeared so that its original location cannot be determined. The colony of Jews had been recently augmented by refugees from Rome, expelled under the edict of Claudius. Paul's friends, Aquila and Priscilla, had shared the exile of their fellows and had moved to Corinth to engage in business. They may have been aided by friends, for the Jews of the Diaspora maintained connections which constituted a fraternal network extending across the empire from the Euphrates to Spain. Any member of their race could find hospitality and employment among people of his own kind wherever he traveled.

The reference to Gallio in the narrative of Acts provides another chronological connection between the progress of early Christianity and the known events of secular history. Lucius Junius Novatus was the son of Marcus Annaeus Seneca and the brother of Seneca,[12] the famous Stoic philosopher and tutor of Nero. He was adopted by a wealthy friend, from whom he took his name, Lucius Junius Gallio. An inscription found in Delphi mentions that he was a

---

[11] See William A. Macdonald, "Archaeology and St. Paul's Journeys in Greek Lands: Part III, Corinth" in *The Biblical Archaeologist* V (1942), 36-48.

[12] *De Vita Beata* 1. Dio Cassius lxi. 35.

friend of Caesar and that he was proconsul of Achaia after the twenty-sixth acclamation of Claudius as *imperator*. The emperor names himself "Tiberius Claudius Caesar Augustus Germanicus, Pontifex Maximus, of tribunician authority for the twelfth time, imperator for the twenty-sixth time, father of his country, consul for the fifth time. . . ." The dating of the twelfth tribunician year and the twenty-sixth acclamation places the inscription between January and August of the year A.D. 52. Since Gallio must have been holding office long enough to have made a report to Claudius and to have received the emperor's commendation, he probably took office about July 1 of A.D. 51. Paul had presumably arrived in Corinth before Gallio, perhaps as early as A.D. 50, if he left Jerusalem in the summer of A.D. 48, shortly after the Council of Jerusalem.

The action of Gallio at Corinth accords with what is known of his training and character. As a typical Roman politician he was suave, courteous, self-restrained, and dignified. Seneca, his brother, described him as a lovable and upright person. Because of his mild disposition, the Jews may have assumed that he would lend a ready ear to their accusations against Paul, especially since he might wish to gain the favor of all parties when beginning his term of office. Gallio, however, was disgusted with their petty squabbles and refused to take sides in the quarrel. Roman law was tolerant of all religious differences and never interfered in the worship of its subjects as long as they maintained their allegiance to the empire. The statement that "Gallio cared for none of these things" reflects his unwillingness to intervene in a dispute which had no standing in a Roman court. He was appointed to administer the law, not to be a referee in a religious controversy. The Jews were a turbulent group, and only a short time before, Claudius had expelled them from Rome. When they turned against each other, Gallio felt no obligation to interfere.

Ill health cut short Gallio's stay in Corinth, forcing his resignation.[13] Some years afterward, when his brother Seneca was compelled by Nero to commit suicide, he escaped by pleading for his life before the Senate,[14] but was later put to death on suspicion of treason.[15]

The planting of the church in Corinth seemed to bring more rapid response and greater growth than in Athens, although the problems were numerous and severe. Because of the volatile nature of the population, the acceptance of Paul's message was enthusiastic, but the church members were far more extreme and mercurial than

[13] Seneca, *Epistulae Morales* civ. 1.
[14] Tacitus, *Annals* xv. 73.
[15] Dio Cassius, lxii. 25.

those in Macedonia. The Corinthian correspondence indicates how narrowly the church escaped dissolution because of its schismatic tendencies, immoral conduct, emotional extravagances, and downright unbelief. Despite these weaknesses the church righted itself, and in the later years of the first century it still maintained an active testimony.[16]

The Evangelization of Asia

Leaving Corinth at the end of eighteen months, probably early in the summer of A.D. 53,[17] Paul returned to Caesarea and Antioch (Acts 18:22). The duration of his visit is indeterminate. Luke says only that "he spent some time there" (v. 23). Since he traveled from Antioch northward overland, he may have left in the summer or early fall and have traveled westward on the road which crossed the Taurus Mountains through the Cilician Gates. Having traversed again the Galatian region and the Phrygian mountain plateau, Paul finally reached Ephesus where he spent the longest amount of consecutive time that he ever devoted to ministry in one place.

Ephesus was the gateway to Asia. Situated at the mouth of the Cayster River, it was the entrance for shipping from the West, and the point of departure for the caravans between the Ionian coast and the East. The highway led from Ephesus across central Asia Minor through the Cilician Gates to Antioch, and thence across Syria to the Euphrates valley, Persia, and India. The harbor of Ephesus was capacious, though it was already beginning to fill with silt which the Cayster brought down from the mountains. In Paul's day it was still accessible to ships of moderate size, although the large Alexandrian merchantmen had begun to avoid it.

Ephesus had been founded by colonists from Athens in the eleventh century B.C., who displaced the original inhabitants and who began a Greek civilization on the Ionian coast. The strategic location of the city favored its growth and it became a military prize both for the naval states of Greece and for the successive kingdoms that dominated Asia Minor, including those of the Lydians and the Persians. Alexander the Great received the homage of the Ephesian rulers in 334 B.C. In 188 B.C. the Romans wrested it from Antiochus the Great, and then gave it to Eumenes, the king of Pergamum. When his son and successor, Attalus, died in 133 B.C., he assigned

---

16 See I Clement I.
17 See David Smith, *Life and Letters of St. Paul*, pp. 651-653. Smith thinks that Paul left Corinth in February, A.D. 53, reached Jerusalem by early May, and then proceeded to Antioch. He was settled in Ephesus before winter.

The "Marble Way," in Ephesus, which runs from the Bouleterion past the Prion Hill (right), into which the amphitheater was cut during the time of the emperor Claudius. Behind the well-preserved wall on the left was the agora, or marketplace of the city. (Courtesy Prof. B. VanElderen.)

This marsh in Ephesus now covers the site of the magnificent temple of Artemis, or Diana, of the Ephesians. (Courtesy Prof. B. Van Elderen.)

it to the Romans who incorporated it into the province of Asia. Ephesus became the chief city of the new province, though the capital was later moved to Pergamum.

The great temple, one of the seven wonders of the world, had been rebuilt after its destruction by fire in 356 B.C. Its immense size, 360 feet in length and 180 feet in breadth exclusive of its platform, its ornate carvings and its varied paintings, as well as the image of Artemis which supposedly fell from heaven, made it the religious center of all Asia.

From the temple a street led westward to the city gate, near which was a stadium built into the side of the adjacent mountain. An inscription shows that it was constructed during the reign of Nero (A.D. 54-68), which would coincide with the time of Paul's visit (A.D. 53-56). South of the stadium was the theater, set in the side of the mountain, accommodating about twenty-five thousand people. It served as the public auditorium for the city and was the scene of the riot protesting Paul's supposed attack upon the

worship of Artemis (Acts 19:23-34). Directly from the theater
a wide street lined with shops and colonnades led down to the docks
in the harbor.

The temple cult was not Greek by origin but was rather the worship
of the native fertility goddess, whom the early colonists had identified
with Artemis, goddess of the woods and hunt. Enshrined in the
temple was an image which reputedly had fallen from heaven, representing the figure of a crowned woman, with many breasts to
signify fertility. In addition to the worship of the traditional deity,
Ephesus was renowned for its patronage of occult arts. "Ephesian
letters," or formulations of magical charms, were famous.[18]

The friendliness of the "Asiarchs" toward Paul at the time of the
disturbance in Ephesus is surprising. According to Strabo,[19] they
were elected from the aristocracy of the province, who, because of
their wealth and public interest, were elevated to public office.

[18] J. Finegan, "Ephesus," in *The Interpreter's Dictionary of the Bible,* II,
114-118.
[19] *Geography* xiv. 1. 42.

*The great theater at Ephesus. Although these remains date from a recon-
struction of the theater after the time of Paul's visit to the city, the plan of the
building is probably the same to a large extent.* (Courtesy Prof. B. Van
Elderen.)

The arch of the gate to the temple of Hadrian in Ephesus. This temple was constructed around A.D. *130.* (Courtesy Turkish Information Office.)

They were entrusted with the supervision of religious festivals and were influential in the provincial assembly. Their warning to Paul not to risk his safety in the disorderly assemblage in the theater indicates that at least some of them were sympathetic with him and felt no religious hostility (Acts 19:31). Perhaps their attitude was determined more by an aversion to the Jews who had agitated the mob than by a direct interest in Paul's message.

Asia proved a fruitful field for evangelism. In three years the entire territory had heard the Christian message, and Christian churches had been founded in almost every large town or city.

Pergamum, Sardis, Thyatira, Laodicea, Philadelphia, Smyrna, Colosse, Hierapolis, Magnesia, Tralles, and many other cities became
centers where Christian preaching and teaching were disseminated
among the people.

The conflict between Paul and the silversmiths at Ephesus gave
a new dimension to the inherent antagonism between paganism and
Christianity. In Athens the opposition was intellectual, for the
hearers of Paul's message dismissed it as foolish and philosophically
untenable. The same attitude appeared at Corinth, where the
Gentiles rejected it as "foolishness" (I Cor. 1:23). In Ephesus
Paul's critics attacked his message from the economic standpoint,
because his success had caused a marked diminution of demand for
the souvenir shrines which the metallurgists manufactured (Acts
19:23-27). Their trade and pocketbooks were consequently
endangered, so that they agitated vigorously against the new faith.
Although no court action was taken against the Christian leaders,
the episode foreshadowed the rise of the church into public notice
and the persecutions which the empire later initiated.

The reign of Claudius ended while Paul was preaching at Ephesus.
Poisoned by his fourth wife Agrippina, Nero's mother, who wished
to insure the succession for her son while he was still young enough
to be molded to her will, he was replaced by Nero.

*A statue of Artemis, the patron god-
dess of the Ephesians. The idea of this
goddess was developed from a Lydian
fertility goddess, and she was later
identified with Diana of the Roman
pantheon. The ovals on the statue
represent either eggs or breasts, both
signs of fertility.* (Courtesy Prof. B.
Van Elderen.)

12

The Consolidation of the Churches: The Reign of Nero

N ERO WAS ONLY SEVENTEEN YEARS OLD WHEN HE WAS PRE-
sented by the Pretorian Guard for imperial office, in the same
manner as his predecessor Claudius had been presented.[1]
The Senate confirmed the decision with the usual pomp and ceremony. At the outset Nero declared that he would abolish the
private courts of Claudius which had condemned to death many of
the aristocracy, that he would curb the use of freedmen as public
officials, and that he would restore to the Senate many of the
prerogatives which Claudius had gradually transferred to himself
or to his bureaucracy. Nero's initial attitude seemed auspicious,
and Rome breathed more freely.

For the first eight years of his reign the government remained
stable and its administration was satisfactory. Nero's advisers, Seneca, the philosopher, and Burrus, prefect of the Pretorian Guard,
were the controlling powers. Burrus supervised the governmental
and military administration; Seneca composed Nero's official
speeches and supplied advice on public relations. Nero was more interested in amusing himself with licentious pleasures and dilettante art
than in becoming involved with the serious affairs of state. The
governmental machinery which had been created by Claudius still
functioned efficiently, and to a large degree the state was self-

[1] *Vide supra*, p. 220.

A bronze sestertium, a Roman coin equal to ¼ denarius, depicting Nero, the emperor from 54-68. Nero was generally feared and despised after his first eight years in office. His extravagant building projects included a palace extending from the Palatine to the Esquiline Hills, near where the Colosseum now stands. This palace was destroyed by the fire in A.D. *64, and was replaced by the magnificent* Domus Aurea, *or golden house. He also constructed the Thermae of Nero, of which the writer Martial said: "What was worse than Nero? What is better than Nero's warm baths?"* (The Bettmann Archive.)

sustaining. Even when tensions developed at Rome, the provinces were not immediately affected so that the period from A.D. 54 to 59, known as "the golden quinquennium," was comparatively peaceful and prosperous.

Within the first three years after Nero's accession Paul had completed his ministry at Ephesus and then had turned westward to revisit the European provinces. New problems had begun to emerge, reflecting the pressures of the times. The narrative of Acts devotes only a few verses to a cryptic summary of the visit:

And after the uproar ceased, Paul having sent for the disciples and exhorted them, took leave of them, and departed to go into Macedonia. And when he had gone through those parts, and had given them much exhortation, he came into Greece [Achaia]. And when he had spent three months there, and a plot was laid against him by the Jews as he was about to set sail for Syria, he determined to return through Macedonia. . . . And we sailed away from Philippi after the days of unleavened bread, and came unto them to Troas in five days; where we tarried seven days (Acts 20:1-3, 6).

The time spent in Macedonia and Achaia may have occupied most of the winter of A.D. 56/57, since the return trip to Jerusalem was terminated by Pentecost (v. 16). The stay in Greece had a dual objective: (1) to collect the funds which the churches of Macedonia and Achaia had been gathering for the relief of the impoverished Jewish church in Jerusalem, and (2) to consolidate the work which had been begun four years earlier. The churches of Macedonia had remained loyal to Paul and had contributed generously to the relief project which he was promoting. With fewer resources than the wealthier commercial cities of Achaia, they had given beyond all normal expectations and had manifested a spiritual vitality that surprised even Paul (II Cor. 8:1-5). They had supported him generously in the past when he was engaged in the evangelization of Achaia (11.9) and had responded willingly to his appeal for the needs of his countrymen.

The Corinthians were of less stable character than the Macedonians. Paul's visit to them was preceded by many misgivings and heartaches, for he had been troubled by their past divisiveness and immorality and was uncertain of the reception that they might accord to him in the future. He realized that a visit was imperative to confirm the work that had been begun in Corinth, but he dreaded the encounter because he anticipated opposition from the dissident element in the church. He feared that drastic discipline might disrupt the church and discredit it in the eyes of the world. His original intention called for sailing directly to Corinth before visiting Mace-

The Roman Forum with the Colosseum and Arch of Titus visible in the background. (Courtesy KLM — Royal Dutch Airlines.)

donia, but the condition of the church had altered his plans. Instead he sent Titus as his emissary to prepare the way while he proceeded to Macedonia (1:15-18, 23; 2:12, 13). Feeling that the Corinthians held a personal antagonism toward him, he deputed Titus to take the collection gathered for the poor in Jerusalem and to reunite the divided church (8:16-23). Since Paul received no report at Troas from the mission, he moved into Macedonia, where he awaited Titus. Titus' arrival with news of the Corinthians' repentance brought relief from his anxiety concerning the church (7:5-7). Immediately he traveled southward to Achaia, where he spent three months completing the work that Titus had begun and gathering together the last of the funds pledged for Jerusalem (Acts 20:3; II Cor. 9).

Although the New Testament is not very specific concerning the results of this ministry, it seems reasonably certain that the visit of Paul to Macedonia and Achaia stabilized the church, leaving it strong and self-sustaining. The disciplining of erring members, the

A view of the Roman Forum as seen through the Arch of Septimius Severus.
(Courtesy Ente Provinciale per il Turismo di Roma.)

firm establishment of a group with a definite theology, ordered worship, consistent giving, missionary zeal, and social cohesion created the nucleus for a new society, a state within a state. When the first signs of imperial disintegration appeared in Nero's reign, the church began to develop a culture of its own. Against the background of official corruption and of declining public morals the Christian churches created a new and purer society that contrasted sharply with the decadent paganism.

Paul's arrest in Jerusalem and consequent imprisonment coincided approximately with the change in Nero's attitude. Within the palace circles there was bitter strife. Agrippina, Nero's mother, was actuated by an inordinate ambition to become the controlling regent of the empire. Her image appeared with Nero's on the coins of the realm; she shared the throne when he received foreign envoys; and she assumed the royal title of *Augusta*. The attempt to dominate her son alienated her advisers, who, to preserve their own position, sought to counteract her influence. As Nero grew to maturity he dissociated himself to a greater extent from her and also from the advisers Seneca and Burrus. Agrippina, realizing that Nero paid little heed to her, endeavored to exert pressure on him by championing the cause of his cousin, Britannicus. Nero retaliated by poisoning Britannicus at a public banquet and by forcing his mother into

The Roman Colosseum, which was begun during the reign of Vespasian and completed in A.D. *80 under Titus. To the left of the Colosseum stands the Arch of Constantine.* (Courtesy BOAC — British Overseas Airways Corporation.)

exile. He plotted her death by placing her on a ship so constructed that it would sink easily, but she escaped. In A.D. 59 he secured her assassination on the pretense that she had conspired against him. Three years later he rid himself of Seneca and Burrus and launched on the course of combined frivolity and tyranny that has made his name a synonym for evil.

Prior to assuming the reins of government, Nero had spent his time competing in chariot races and musical contests. He appeared on the stage, singing, or playing the lyre, or dancing. Although his performances were mediocre and his delight in them childish, his indulgence would probably have harmed him little, aside from his own loss of dignity. Under the influence of Poppea, his mistress, and Tigellinus, the coarse and brutal successor of Burrus as prefect of the Pretorian Guard, Nero engaged in all manner of extravagances and capricious cruelty. Having exhausted the imperial treasury by his heedless expenditures, he looked for some method of replenishing it. Heavy taxation of the estates of childless couples, false accusations followed by confiscation of wealth, and outright murder of the aristocracy or else invitation to suicide made life unbearable. Wealthy men lived in dread of the emperor's displeasure, and so great was the terror that the senatorial class endured unimaginable insults and mistreatment as the price of staying alive. Men betrayed their best friends, perjured themselves, and stooped to any infamy to avert the emperor's hatred or cupidity. The Senate was reduced to abject servility. It applauded all of Nero's deeds, confirmed his decisions, and originated nothing. He or his henchmen dictated the policies of state.

Rome experienced in A.D. 64 one of the most disastrous conflagrations of its history. Beginning among the cluttered shops near the Circus Maximus, it raged through the city for more than a week and, after seeming to be checked, broke out a second time with redoubled violence. Three of the fourteen wards of the city were devastated and seven others were seriously damaged. Many of the oldest buildings were destroyed completely. Suetonius did not hesitate to charge Nero with deliberately setting the fire in order to gain more space for his private palace and with gloating over the burning city as he stood on a nearby tower, singing "The Sack of Troy." Suetonius may have been merely repeating a rumor, or he may have been venting his personal hatred of Nero, but he was depicting the emperor as many of his contemporaries saw him.[2]

The charge of incendiarism was probably unjustified. According to Tacitus, who was not friendly to him, Nero did his utmost to

2 *Nero* vi. 38, 39.

The Arch of Septimius Severus in the Roman Forum. The arch was constructed in A.D. 203. (Courtesy ENIT — Italian State Tourist Office.)

extinguish the flames and to aid the homeless and injured. He levied a tax for relief and lowered the price of grain to allow cheaper food for the poor. There was a kindly side to Nero which endeared him to the populace.[3]

After the fire Nero engaged in a campaign of slum clearance. The streets were widened; new parks were introduced; and the new construction contained more fireproof materials, such as stone and brick. On the Caelian and Esquiline hills, at the lower end of the Forum, Nero built a "Golden House," an enormous palace encircled by a colonnade three miles in length, embracing lakes, lanes, and woods. In its anteroom stood a colossal statue of himself which was 120 feet high.

[3] *Annals* xv. 39.

In order to divert suspicion from himself, Nero instituted persecution of the Christians, who had just come into public notice. Tacitus, in writing of his reign, says:

> But by no human contrivance, whether lavish distributions of money or of offerings to appease the gods, could Nero rid himself of the ugly rumor that the fire was due to his orders. So, to dispel the report, he substituted as the guilty persons and inflicted unheard-of punishments on those who, detested for their abominable crimes, were vulgarly called Christians. The source of that name was Christus, who in the principate of Tiberius had been put to death by the procurator Pontius Pilate. Checked for a moment, the pernicious superstition broke out again not only through Judea, the home of the pest, but also through Rome, to which from all quarters everything outrageous and shameful finds its way and becomes the vogue.
>
> So those who first confessed were hurried to the trial, and then, on their showing, an immense number were involved in the same fate, not so much on the charge of incendiaries as from hatred of the human race. And their death was aggravated with mocker-

The remains of the arena of the Roman Colosseum. Through the years the original flooring has deteriorated, offering a view of the underground chambers where the wild beasts and human victims were kept prior to performances. (Courtesy KLM — Royal Dutch Airlines.)

ies, insomuch that, wrapped in the hides of wild beasts, they were torn to pieces by dogs, or fastened to crosses to be set on fire, that when the darkness fell they might be burned to illuminate the night. Nero had offered his own gardens for the spectacle, and exhibited a circus show, mingling with the crowd, himself dressed as a charioteer or riding in a chariot. Whence it came about that, though the victims were guilty and deserved the most exemplary punishment, a sense of pity was aroused by the feeling that they were sacrificed not on the altar of public interest, but to satisfy the cruelty of one man.[4]

Dire as it was, the persecution under Nero was not universal nor did it last long. The provinces were probably unaffected. Tacitus does not say that extermination of Christians became a settled and studied policy. Persecution seems to have been sudden, temporary, and local, and incited by the emperor's whim rather than by political or religious principle.

Tacitus, however, confirms the fact that Christians had in his day become separated from the Jews and that they were recognized as a distinct and influential body. They were disliked by the Romans not so much because they were suspected of immoral conduct as because they were "haters of mankind." No explanation is given of this curious accusation. Certainly the Christians were neither subversive nor anti-social. Perhaps their more rigid ethical code kept them from participating in many of the pagan indulgences and debaucheries so that they gained the reputation of aloofness and snobbishness. The Romans regarded Christianity as merely one more foreign cult that had been imported from the East and that was not acceptable to the best Roman culture.

The rebuilding of Rome after the fire and the extravagant luxury of Nero's Golden House laid a heavy burden on the treasury, which demanded new confiscations of private property. Any man of wealth expected momentarily that he would be accused of some fanciful crime and condemned to death in order that the emperor might appropriate his possessions. The senatorial class became increasingly insecure and sought relief in a plot to assassinate Nero and to place one of its more popular members, C. Calpurnius Piso, on the throne. Unfortunately for them the plot was discovered. Forty-one persons were implicated directly or indirectly, twenty were adjudged guilty, and sixteen were executed. Seneca and his nephew Lucan the poet were both involved and suffered the penalty with the others. Although he was by no means free from the vices of his time, Seneca had been a wise and humane administrator and advo-

---

[4] *Ibid.*, xv. 44.

cated moral principles far above those held by most of his contemporaries.

The discovery of the plot frightened Nero, for it revealed the powerful undercurrent of hostility to his rule that moved beneath the superficial outward semblance of popularity. The moral tone of the empire dropped rapidly. The Senate became the rubber stamp for his desires, and any individual who was even suspected of independence was marked for death. Corbulo, his most able general, was driven to suicide. Instead of paying serious attention to the business of the empire, Nero began a tour of Greece as a singer, dancer, and charioteer in public contests. Irrespective of the merit of the performances, he was uniformly awarded first prize and returned to Rome to claim a triumph.

Nero had commenced the building of a canal across the Isthmus of Corinth and had planned new military conquests, but the growing stories of unrest cut short his project. C. Julius Vindex, legate of the province of Gallia Lugdunensis, raised an army of Gauls and revolted. Galba, the governor of Spain, and other imperial legates lent him their support. The rebellion was crushed by Virginius Rufus, governor of Upper Germany, but the tide of hostility had risen too high to be checked. In the meantime, Galba was still in command of Spain, and the prefect of the Pretorian Guard, Sabinus, had defected. Rebellion had broken out in Judea, and the shifting fortunes of the Jewish War added to the problems confronting the emperor. Had Nero been capable of acting calmly and courageously, he might have been able to salvage the situation; but when he learned of the treachery of the Pretorians, his personal bodyguard, he fled. Hearing that the Senate had condemned him, he died by his own hand, exclaiming, "What an artist is perishing!" He was buried in the family vault of the Domitian clan by Acte, a freedwoman who had been his loyal consort, and a few servants.

In this turbulent and evil period Paul came to the capital city. His appeal to Nero, the reigning Caesar, had ensured his destination, for as a Roman citizen he could not be denied access to the emperor's judgment seat. Under the custody of a centurion who was charged with the safe conduct of a number of prisoners he made the tedious voyage from Caesarea to Myra, on the southern coast of Asia Minor, and there transshipped for Rome in an Alexandrian freighter (Acts 27:1-6). Proceeding to Crete, they were delayed until early October when shipping became dangerous due to the likelihood of storms. In an attempt to move from one Cretan harbor to another, the ship was caught in a violent northeaster that drove the dismasted vessel for two weeks through pounding seas and finally wrecked it on the island of Malta. There they spent the

The Appian Way, the famous Roman road on which Paul traveled the last 150 miles of his journey to Rome. After reaching Puteoli (Acts 28:19), Paul no doubt went to Capua, where the original Appian Way, built three and a half centuries earlier, led to Rome. (Ewing Galloway.)

winter and in the spring sailed for Rome in another ship that had wintered in the island harbor (28:11).

Paul's arrival in Rome cannot have been earlier than A.D. 58, and more likely must be dated between A.D. 60 and 62. He was kept under house arrest for two years, with freedom to entertain guests and to preach openly to all those who visited him. At this point the Lukan narrative ends, leaving the reader in suspense concerning Paul's fate. No statement relative to the outcome of the trial is available; there is no certainty as far as Acts is concerned whether Paul was released or executed.

Of the possible alternatives release seems probable. Although the Christian movement must have been gaining headway in Rome, the great fire had not yet occurred, and there was no reason for charging Paul with any illegal action. Festus, the procurator of

Judea, had been unable to formulate any charges against him, and Herod Agrippa II, who had been enlisted by Festus as an expert in Jewish affairs, openly declared that Paul was innocent of any crime. It may well be that he was discharged at the end of the two years by default of the witnesses, who did not appear against him. The journey to Rome would have been long and costly, and it is extremely doubtful whether the Jewish authorities in Jerusalem would have deemed it worthwhile to send a delegation to Rome to testify against Paul, especially if the case were not sure to be presented within two years.

Since the Pastoral Epistles indicate travels near the end of Paul's career which cannot be fitted into his itineraries prior to the voyage to Rome, it seems likely that they presuppose a release at the first hearing and an interval of a few years before his final arrest, imprisonment, and death. Paul refers to a "first defense," when his companions forsook him, but which ended in "deliverance out of

The Ponte Milvio, *outside of Rome, reconstructed on the site of the Milvian Bridge, where the emperor Constantine, inspired by a vision telling him to battle under the sign of the cross, defeated the pretender Maxentius in* A.D. *312. By winning this battle, Constantine established himself as emperor, and Christianity as the state religion.* (Burton Holmes, from Ewing Galloway.)

Marcus Aurelius, Roman emperor from 161-180. This Stoic philosopher led one of the major persecutions of Christians. (Courtesy Ente Provinciale per il Turismo di Roma.)

the mouth of the lion" (II Tim. 4:16, 17). The consequence of the release was an expansion of his preaching among the Gentiles (v. 17). Perhaps he was able to carry on an unrestricted ministry for a few years, but was arrested as a dangerous leader of the Christians when they became suspect after the fire of A.D. 64.

The Consolidation of the Churches

Perilous and uncertain as this period may have been for Paul, it seems to have brought new strength to the church. The intensive teaching of the message of Christ began to shape a new ethic which contrasted sharply with the prevalent standards of paganism. The collections of the sayings of Christ that appeared in the unwritten and written Gospel tradition embodied principles of conduct that were the direct antithesis of ordinary practice. By way of example, the Beatitudes, as recorded by Matthew, undoubtedly reproduce the teaching of Jesus as proclaimed by His disciples, but their very existence in written form shows that they were accepted and cherished by the churches that preserved them. Each represented a concept foreign to the spirit of the times, and while the Christian community may not have observed these precepts perfectly, they constitute a standard which changed the attitude and culture of the believers.

Jesus said, "Blessed are the poor in spirit: for theirs is the kingdom of heaven." Paganism said, "Possessions belong to those who take them." Jesus said, "Blessed are they that mourn, for they shall be comforted." Paganism said, "Enjoy yourself; tomorrow will be too late." Jesus said, "Blessed are they that hunger and thirst after righteousness, for they shall be filled." Paganism said, "Do what seems best in your own sight, and be content." Jesus said, "Blessed are the merciful, for they shall obtain mercy." Paganism said, "Crush the other man before he crushes you." Jesus said, "Blessed are the pure in heart, for they shall see God." Paganism said, "Let yourself go." Jesus said, "Blessed are the peacemakers, for they shall be called the sons of God." Paganism said, "Life is a struggle, and every man is a potential enemy." The Christian and the pagan ideals were diametrically opposed to each other.

There were numerous philosophers like Seneca and, later, Marcus Aurelius, who advocated high moral sentiments and lofty ideals, but they represented the minority rather than the majority of their contemporaries. Sexual license, the debasing influence of the theater, the bloody spectacles of the arena, and the gluttonous feasts of exotic luxuries prevailed in high society and set the model for the lower classes, who fortunately did not always pursue these evils to identical extremes. The ideals of the philosophers, however, were more often discussed than practiced, and they lacked the dynamic to arrest the slow decline of the national morale.

The Christian ethic as set forth in the Gospels and in the Epistles was a healthy antidote to the looseness of paganism. The practical sections of the Prison Epistles of Paul draw a sharp distinction between the conduct of a Christian and of an idolater.

This I say therefore, and testify in the Lord, that ye no longer walk as the Gentiles also walk, in the vanity of their mind, being darkened in their understanding, alienated from the life of God, because of the ignorance that is in them, because of the hardening of their heart; who being past feeling gave themselves up to lasciviousness, to work all uncleanness with greediness (Eph. 4:17-19).

Following this statement of the requirement placed upon the Christian, Paul inveighed against lying, anger, theft, corrupt speech, fornication, obscenity, idolatry, and drunkenness. In positive fashion he set new standards for the relation of husbands and wives, parents and children, masters and slaves (5:22-6:9). A similar set of injunctions appears in the Epistle to the Colossians (Col. 3:5-4:1). Both describe the standards of the new faith which had begun to penetrate the Roman world and to provide a moral dynamic that the philosophers could not create.

Although the church was by no means flawless, as the reproofs of Paul show, the acceptance of Jesus' moral standards and the effort of the community to maintain them distinguished the Christians from all their contemporaries. A norm of conduct was set for the church which permanently fixed its character. However much it may have departed from the norm at one time or another, the ideal was recognized, and even the surrounding world acknowledged that it was different. The name "Christian" may have carried with it social opprobrium and may have connoted to the pagan society an anti-social attitude and even criminality (I Pet. 4:15), but the conduct of Christians soon made the name a synonym for upright living and patient endurance. Both by visitation and by correspondence Paul succeeded in establishing a new pattern of behavior for the churches.

The Establishment of Doctrinal Stability

The converts to Christ came from many different backgrounds and would naturally begin their new life with widely varied presuppositions. An attempt to formulate a new faith in terms of pagan concepts would only distort or pervert the revelation of God. Dissension and disruption would be the inevitable result of such procedure. The church needed positive teaching of revealed truth, organized coherently and applicable to practical situations. Again the Prison Epistles show indications that Paul's closing years were devoted to the consolidation of the theology that he had preached. Colossians contains a Christology calculated to counteract the Gnostic theosophy of Asia which would have sublimated the gospel into nebulous mysticism or superstitious bondage. Paul asserted that in Christ the divine fullness (Greek *pleroma*) dwelt bodily, not simply apparently (Col. 2:9). He is the true image of the invisible God, in contrast to the sculptured statues that filled the Roman cities (1:15).

The saviourhood of Christ is stated clearly in these epistles. Paul says that "in him we have redemption through his blood" (Eph.

1:7; that those who "once were far off are made nigh in the blood of Christ" (2:13), and that He reconciles Jew and Gentile together unto God through the cross (v. 16). Redemption, or deliverance from the power and guilt of evil, and reconciliation, or restoration to the favor of God, are the keys to a serene and progressive life because they constitute the proper basis for a new relationship with God. Without these, the church could have no message of value for the harassed and despairing populace.

The doctrine of the church gave a new self-respect to the association of believers. Ephesians, the epistle of the church, characterizes it in three ways: the body, the bride, and the building of Christ. As the body of Christ it is energized by the central life and held together as an organism. Nowhere in Ephesians is the church called the bride of Christ, but the analogy is plain from the words, "Husbands, love your wives, as Christ also loved the church, and gave himself up for it" (5:25). The concept of the building appears in the metaphor of the temple, of which Christ is the chief cornerstone and the believers are individual stones, taken from various sources, but built into a unified structure to become a shrine for the Spirit of God. No such concept of a society had been previously promulgated. Israel had been a chosen people, created by God's purpose, rescued from national slavery, and finally established in its own land. Through long generations of alternating apostasy and repentance the nation had been preserved until its independent existence was ended by defeat and dispersion. Notwithstanding its failure, it remained the repository of God's revelation and the instrument of His purpose, but never does the Old Testament refer to it as His "body" in the sense that the church is the "body" of Christ. The church is the organic manifestation of Christ's character and purpose on earth as the human body expresses the personality of its owner.

This stress on the nature of the church in Ephesians is part of the instruction which the new society received as it emerged from obscurity into an influential position in the empire. It needed to realize its spiritual character and obligations lest it would become merely one more association like the trade guilds which abounded. The consciousness of identity and mission depended upon a clear and coherent theology which defined the main themes of revelation, and which related them to the ordinary aspect of daily life. Paul saw the necessity for such instruction and supplied it both through letters calculated for local emergencies, such as Colossians, and through more general treatises, such as Ephesians. In his later correspondence he urged his understudies, Timothy and Titus, to avoid useless controversy and to adhere to positive teaching which would produce a high ethic (I Tim. 1:3ff.). A definite doctrinal standard was set (6:3), to which the church was obligated to subscribe, centering in the person of the risen Christ (II Tim. 2:8). Condensed summaries of doctrine appear in Titus 2:11-14 and 3:4-7.

The stress on doctrinal truth in the Pauline Epistles indicates that the need for definition and instruction was particularly great in the transitional period between the time of the apostles and the generation that followed them. No vague or amorphous set of beliefs would have been able to withstand the numerous religious and philosophical influences that confronted the church as it grew to prominence. As long as its units were isolated and obscure, they could maintain their faith by withdrawal, but if they intended to fulfill their commission for evangelization, and if they expected to achieve any semblance of unity, the common core of faith must be expanded into a defensible system. The process of development was begun by positive teaching; the expansion of the scriptural principles underlying this theology has continued to the present day. However numerous doctrinal errors may have been, the theological basis for preaching has always been necessary, for errors cannot be corrected unless there is an abiding standard by which they can be judged. Paul understood this principle well when he admonished Timothy not to quibble over trivialities, but to adhere unswervingly to "the sound doctrine, according to the gospel of the glory of the blessed God, which was committed to my trust" (I Tim. 1:10-11).

The fact that the church of the late first century survived the pressure of paganism and Gnosticism and that it emerged into the second century with a core of fixed beliefs shows that someone had laid a firm foundation for its convictions. Apparently the persistent indoctrination by the apostles and their immediate understudies had been effective. The distinctive character of Christianity, though only imperfectly understood by observers, had been shaped and was fairly well defined by the end of Nero's reign.

The Acceptance of Financial Responsibility

The inauguration of any new institution or society requires finances, either for the expansion of the organization itself or for the needs of its members. Christianity required both, for the evangelization of the Roman world demanded the support of the evangelists, and the character of the church called for relief of the poor.

The creation of a sense of financial responsibility in the churches was one of Paul's last great undertakings. The Macedonian churches had to some degree voluntarily underwritten his expenses shortly after their inception, so that he received aid from them almost as soon as he left for Achaia (Phil. 4:16). He accepted their gift, but set an example of self-support for the churches by working with his own hands (II Thess. 3:7-12). In Corinth Paul labored at tent-making to pay his expenses and those of his associates (Acts 18:1-3; II Cor. 11:7), rather than to demand funds from those to whom he was preaching. He encouraged the churches to be generous (II Cor. 11:8, 9), and urged them to make their giving systematic and proportionate to their income (I Cor. 16:1, 2).

Paul endeavored to inculcate in the Gentile churches a sense of responsibility for their less fortunate Jewish brethren. The church at Jerusalem existed in a more hostile environment than did the other churches because it deviated from the religious norm of Judaism, and because the rising nationalism that led to the Jewish revolt of A.D. 66 would regard it as a traitorous element. To cement the friendship between the Gentile and Jewish churches Paul raised a fund from the churches of Galatia, Macedonia, and Achaia for the needy in Jerusalem (Rom. 15:25-28). The unity of the body of Christ which he expounded in Ephesians became practical in the mutual sharing of material and spiritual blessings. The underlying motive for Paul's concern was not only charitable but also educational, for he told the Philippians that he was seeking not merely gifts as an end in themselves, but fruit that should abound to their account (4:17). This mutual sharing he called a "fellowship" (v. 15) and evidently regarded it as an important element in uniting the individual churches into one body.

The Growth of a Community Consciousness

Because communications were difficult, the churches of the first century were not so closely knit in outward organization as churches in the twentieth century are. Travel was slower; literary activity was circumscribed because written materials had to be copied by hand; and under a government that was jealous of any organized movement, conventions were impossible. United organizational activity as it is conducted today was practically unknown until the fourth century, when the church emerged from the catacombs into imperial favor.

The concept of unity, however, was not entirely lacking. As observed above, the New Testament speaks both of "the churches," or local assemblies (Gal. 1:2), and of "the church" as the undivided body of Christ (Eph. 1:22, 23). The latter concept received special emphasis in the closing years of Paul's ministry, for he endeavored to foster unity within and between the churches. The revealed purpose of God in redemption (vv. 11-14) and the outward manifestation of that purpose in a community of believers (2:10) comprising both Jew and Gentile in one new body (3:4-

The steps leading up to the cathedral in Jerash, Jordan. In A.D. 375, Epiphanius, bishop of Salamis, referred to a fountain in this church which reputedly flowed with wine every year on the anniversary of the miracle at the wedding in Cana (John 2). The church probably dates to A.D. 365. (Courtesy KLM — Royal Dutch Airlines.)

11) is the acme of the revealed mystery of God. In the Pastoral Epistles, which belong to the period between A.D. 62 and 68, there is a reference to "the church of the living God, the pillar and ground of the truth" (I Tim. 3:15). The words imply that the church has set the standard for individual behavior and that it possesses a recognized set of ethical and spiritual standards for believers.

The Recognition of the Church

Because the church began as a movement within Judaism, it was at first largely ignored. Although its initial expansion must have been rapid, its divergence from Jewish ceremonials and its acceptance of Jesus as the Messiah did not distinguish it sufficiently in the eyes of the public to arouse much antagonism. Judaism was a *religio licita,* and the Christians, as a sect of Judaism, enjoyed the privilege of protection.

As the hostility between Christian believers and the synagogue increased, the church assumed a more distinctive character. Expulsion from the synagogue compelled it to develop its own worship and its own society. At first the small groups of believers met in isolated homes, but as their numbers grew, they could conceal neither their numbers nor their principles. Since they were openly separated from Judaism, they became a *religio illicita*, with no official standing, nor even the right to exist. No definite action was taken against them, but they were liable to prosecution if the magistrates found a plausible excuse for harassing them, and they could claim no immunity or redress.

Until the time of Paul's appeal to Caesar he had been treated as a Jew. He had appeared before the Sanhedrin, and the Roman procurators, Felix and Festus, had worked in conjunction with the Jewish authorities in Jerusalem. Because of their influence, he had been left in prison by Felix, and to escape a repetition of the same fate under Festus he had appealed to Caesar. On whatever charge he appeared before the imperial court in Rome, his status as a Christian would be discussed, and the existence of the new sect would be patent to the court.

The great fire at Rome marked the point at which this new sect was publicly identified as a new superstition, distinct from Judaism. There is not sufficient evidence in the records to show that this new concept was connected with Paul's appearance before Nero. Whether he made his defense before the emperor himself or before some lesser official, he would have made plain the meaning of his teaching and would unquestionably have contended that he had a gospel for

Gentiles as well as for Jews. The hearing may well have been in A.D. 62; the fire destroyed the greater part of Rome in A.D. 64. Perhaps the emperor or some of his advisers remembered Paul's defense. If Paul had alluded to judgment in the same way in which he wrote of it in II Thessalonians, "in flaming fire rendering vengeance to them that know not God" (1:7), his language would have aroused the suspicion that the Christians were responsible for the conflagration and would have furnished a plausible basis for their arrest and punishment. In any case, the action of Nero brought them into prominence and set the Christian church over against the state. The antagonism of the two aroused the empire to take cognizance of the church and forced the church to organize for the struggle with the empire.

13

The Growth of the Institutional Church
Under the Flavians

T HE INEVITABLE CONSEQUENCE OF NERO'S PERFIDIOUS AND
irresponsible conduct was revolt. Public misfortunes and de-
feats in Britain which devastated two important towns, and in
Armenia, where the Roman legions were captured and the entire
province of Syria was endangered, aroused popular resentment. Rival
generals in various provinces sought to seize the empire to gratify
their lust for power and produced almost complete chaos.

The Year of Anarchy

Suetonius opens his account of the interregnum of the three
emperors by saying that "the race of the Caesars perished with
Nero."[1] He recognized that the first age of the Principate had closed
and that a new one had begun. Nero was succeeded by Galba, who
had begun his military career as the governor of Upper Germany,
where he put the legions under strict training. After the accession
of Claudius he was made proconsul of Africa, where he subdued an
insurrection and reorganized the administration of the province.

Galba remained in retirement during the first part of Nero's
reign but about A.D. 60 he was appointed to the governorship of
Spain. At the outset he ruled in strict and vigorous fashion, but

---

[1] *Lives of the Caesars. Galba* vii. 1.

gradually he relaxed his activity in order that Nero, so he said, might not become jealous of his efficiency. Suetonius added that when Vindex appealed to him to join the Gallic revolt, he did so because he had intercepted dispatches sent by Nero ordering his death.[2] He was hailed as emperor and, after a narrow escape from assassination, assumed the title of Caesar and made his way to Rome.

Unfortunately Galba made enemies faster than friends. He became notorious for his cruelty to those who opposed him and for his penuriousness. His underlings sold offices and favors with reckless indifference to justice. He alienated the armies by refusing to bestow the usual gifts dispensed by a new emperor. The legions of Upper Germany refused to renew their allegiance to him, supporting their general, Aulus Vitellius. Galba adopted as his son L. Calpurnius Piso, but he was not accepted by the Pretorians, who supported Salvius Otho. Otho assassinated Galba and took the throne for himself.

Otho was quickly opposed by the legions of Vitellius which were stationed in Germany and reinforced by other troops from Gaul and Britain. They invaded Italy and defeated Otho's forces decisively near Cremona. Otho committed suicide, and Vitellius' generals seized Rome. When Vitellius arrived, the city was already his. He refrained from outward tyranny and desisted from the extortions practiced by Nero. He was, however, lazy and improvident. His troops plundered the capital and his vicegerents squandered the public funds.

The armies of the East, which were largely engaged in the Jewish war, refused to accept the choice of the German legions and acclaimed Titus Flavius Vespasianus as emperor. Vespasian did not come from royal blood but had made for himself a creditable reputation in military affairs and had been delegated by Nero to crush the Jewish uprising in Syria.

Vespasian left the campaign in charge of his older son Titus and hastened to Alexandria, where he was proclaimed emperor. By cutting off the grain supply for Rome he crippled the remaining forces of Otho. The legions stationed along the Danube joined his campaign and marched against Rome. In another battle at Cremona they slaughtered the armies of Vitellius, who was killed in the sack of the city. Rome was ravaged by the soldiery of the Eastern generals, who could not control them. Vespasian's general Mummius finally reached Rome in January of A.D. 70 and restored order to the city. He dismissed the riotous legions and kept peace until the arrival of Vespasian in midsummer.

2 *Ibid.,* vii. 9.

The year of the four emperors disclosed a fatal weakness in the empire: there was no adequate machinery for the orderly succession of rule from one emperor to another. Heredity was unsatisfactory, for it might produce such rulers as the sour Tiberius, the mad Caligula, the handicapped Claudius, or the irresponsible Nero. While Tiberius and Claudius were fairly good administrators, Caligula and Nero were wholly unfit to be heads of state. Since there was a provision for free election, the throne was the prey of the strongest. The general who could command the largest army and arrive at Rome first could be placed in the seat of power. From the days of Claudius, who was made emperor by the Pretorian Guard, down to the close of the empire, military control became the key to sovereignty. Although there were emperors who, like Marcus Aurelius, ruled benevolently and justly, there was no way of averting the possibility of tyranny if an unworthy candidate were influential enough to seize power.

The Flavian Dynasty

Vespasian inherited a number of problems from the civil war that preceded his reign, chief of which were national revolts in Germany, Gaul, and Judea, and an insolvent treasury. Julius Civilis, the leader of the native German troops, had supported Vitellius and had ostensibly capitulated to Vespasian after Vitellius' death. Julius, however, had openly forsworn Rome and had sought to unite the Gauls and free Germans north of the Rhine in a movement for independence. Several Roman garrisons were expelled from the border camps, and he was soon possessor of a large section of the Rhine frontier. Two of the Gallic tribes, the Treveri and Lingones, supported him and endeavored to bring with them the rest of the Gauls, but gained little response. The Gauls had become too thoroughly Romanized and enjoyed their civil and commercial privileges too much to forfeit them in a war which could end only to their disadvantage.

Vespasian soon appeared in Germany with an army and the rebellion was dissipated. The insurgent legions renewed their allegiance to Rome, the Gallic tribes laid down arms, and the dissident Germans retreated across the Rhine. Vespasian did not indulge in harsh reprisals, but he reorganized the army and discharged the disgruntled legions.

The Jewish revolt was brought to an end under Titus, as already indicated. With the conquest and destruction of Jerusalem the Jewish commonwealth and Temple worship ended. Judaism persisted as a religion, but disassociated from any political organization or state.

*A first-century "manhole," a movable stone block in the street at Hercula-
neum, revealing the sewer systems used by the citizens there until the destruction of the city along with Pompeii in* A.D. *79.* (Courtesy Prof. B. Van
Elderen.)

Vespasian proved to be a strong and efficient ruler. He was impervious to flattery, economical in finances, relatively simple in tastes, and respected by the army. He succeeded in restoring the credit of the public treasury, though he had to raise the taxes to do so, and at the same time he carried on a large program of public construction. He rebuilt the Capitoline Temple, which had been burned in the civil war, and by the use of Jewish slaves erected the Colosseum on part of the site of Nero's Golden House. He subsidized public education and improved the provincial government. In Britain and Germany he annexed new territory to protect the Roman frontiers, constructed two new forts on the Danube, and in Asia Minor and Africa he reorganized the government in the interest of greater efficiency. By the time of his death in A.D. 79 he had restored peace throughout the empire and had increased its strength and security.

Titus

The reign of Titus was brief (A.D. 79-81) but successful. In many respects he was a contrast to his father Vespasian. In public

Aerial view of Pompeii, one of the cities destroyed by the eruption of Mt. Vesuvius in A.D. 79. The large rectangular area in the center across from the open forum is the cloth-exchange of Eumachia. (Courtesy Istituto Italiano di Cultura, New York.)

Pillars remaining from the civil forum in Pompeii. In the background is Mt. Vesuvius, whose eruption destroyed the city, preserving many of its remains for posterity. (Courtesy ENIT — Italian State Tourist office.)

appearance he was as handsome as his father had been homely and was much more suave and urbane. Genial and friendly, he was greatly beloved by the populace. His chief fault was his excessive generosity. While he was not so prodigal personally as Nero, he spent so much for public buildings, welfare funds, and games in the arena that the treasury was rapidly depleted.

His short reign was shadowed by two major national disasters. The eruption of Vesuvius in A.D. 79 overwhelmed the cities of Pompeii, Stabiae, and Herculaneum under a rain of volcanic ash and a torrent of lava and mud. In the following year Rome suffered a conflagration that destroyed the newly built temple of Jupiter Capitolinus and ruined the heart of the city. Titus organized relief for the homeless and sold many of his personal possessions that he might grant aid to the stricken community. He died of fever in September, A.D. 81, and was genuinely mourned by all of his subjects.

Domitian

Titus was succeeded by his brother Domitian, who was his complete opposite. Left in Rome by his father and brother who were campaigning in Judea, he narrowly escaped death at the hands of Vitellius' followers. By disposition he was aloof, humorless, avaricious, and cruel. Suetonius charges him with constant plotting against his brother Titus and with degrading his memory after death.[3]

Domitian continued the rebuilding of Rome after the fire and increased the games and doles for the populace. He waged war along the northern frontier against the Sarmatians, the Chatti, and the Dacians, and suppressed a revolt in Upper Germany. In the early years of his life he maintained a reputation for fairness and justice. To keep a proper balance in agriculture he ordered that half of the vineyards in the provinces be turned into wheat land. He raised the pay of the army and restricted the amount of money

[3] *Ibid., Domitian* viii. 2.

Roman houses along the Via dell'Abbondanza (Street of Abundance) in Pompeii. (Courtesy Istituto Italiano di Cultura, New York.)

that soldiers might keep in deposit at headquarters in order that
revolutions might not be easily financed. Public officials were
placed under strict surveillance to prevent graft and bribery. Theaters
were censored, and moral offences were severely punished.

Unfortunately, like Nero, he did not continue in the same way in
which he began his career. One historian suggests that he had been
embittered in his youth by frustrated ambition.[4] Neither his father
Vespasian nor his brother Titus gave him the opportunity to assert
himself, and while at first he seemed to be a worthy successor,
the inner twist of his nature was soon manifested.

Because of his hostility to the Senate, Domitian inaugurated a
reign of terror that kept Rome in a state of constant apprehension.
Financial pressure compelled him to seek new money for the treasury and, like Nero, he proceeded to extort it from the wealthy men
within the city. He assumed the right of voting first in the Senate,
so that anyone who voted differently would be a marked man. By
assuming the title of perpetual censor he obtained full control of
the membership of the Senate. He was the first of the emperors
to demand that he be saluted as *Dominus et Deus,* "Lord and God,"
though many of his predecessors had been deified at death, and a
few, like Augustus, had been worshiped during their lifetime.

Domitian's tendency to autocracy was strengthened by the revolt
of Germany in the winter of A.D. 88/89. Though the rebellion was
quelled, he became intensely fearful of all rivalry and listened to
every word of idle gossip that hinted disloyalty. Anyone suspected
of anti-imperial tendencies was promptly removed. The last eleven
years of his reign from A.D. 85 to 96, beginning with his assumption
of the perpetual censorship, were marked by a growing oppressive-
ness and tension.

The nervous fear within the Senate and even within the imperial
household rapidly became unbearable. Domitian's wife's steward
Stephanus, who had been accused of embezzlement, offered his aid
to a group of conspirators who were determined to free themselves
from the menace. He bandaged his arm on the pretense that he
had injured it, but concealed a dagger in the folds. Under the guise
of disclosing a conspiracy he gained a private audience with Domitian and stabbed him while the emperor was reading a paper which
he had handed to him. In the ensuing struggle Stephanus was
joined by others who completed the murder. The body was cremated
by his nurse at her suburban home and the ashes were deposited
in the temple of the Flavian family. With Domitian the Flavian
dynasty ended.

---

[4] Albert E. Trever, *History of Ancient Civilization.* Volume II: *The
Roman World,* p. 487.

An artisan carving cameos at the site of the temple of the god Apollo in Pompeii. (Courtesy ENIT — Italian State Tourist Office.)

In spite of the chaotic year of the four emperors (A.D. 68/69), the last third of the first century was a period of comparative prosperity for Rome. The Flavian emperors were better rulers than Nero and succeeded in strengthening the military and financial structure of the empire. Public works such as aqueducts, temples, libraries, and schools were promoted. The provincial governors were carefully

selected and held to a strict account for their discharge of office.
Despite his personal digressions, Domitian enforced with severity
the ancient Roman laws against vice and actually buried alive one
of the Vestal Virgins for unchastity. Had he been able to preserve
as good relations with the Senate as his father had, he might have
been numbered among Rome's best rulers.

The Organization of the Church

Between the years from A.D. 62 to 96 the church entered upon a
new stage of development. The eyewitnesses of the life of Jesus
were rapidly diminishing, and the initial spontaneous movement of
adherents was crystallizing into an organization comparable to that
of the Jewish synagogue, on which it was partially modeled. From
the inception of the missionary expansion the leaders had recognized
the necessity of some form of government which should be responsible
for the propagation of the faith. The need became more imperative
as the movement spread from Palestine to other lands and from
within the synagogue to other cultures.

The Pastoral Epistles of Paul, the anonymous Epistle to the Hebrews, and the Johannine writings including Revelation may generally
be attributed to this period and may be assumed to reflect its
changes. The Pastoral Epistles deal chiefly with the internal government of the church and with the offices which were created to care
for the needs of its members. The other Epistles supply some information concerning the relation of the church to the external world,
especially as it encountered social and religious conflict.

The Offices of the Church

The earliest officials of the church were the apostles, who held a
position of primacy because they were its pioneers and founders
rather than because of election by the congregations. The primitive
group in Jerusalem elected seven "deacons" to assist in relief work
(Acts 6:1-6), and their function seems to have been perpetuated
in the Gentile congregations. In his letter to Philippi, Paul mentions
them as a distinct class, though he does not define their duties
(Phil. 1:1). If the word "deacon" (Greek, *diakonos*) describes their
position, they were engaged in the material ministry of the church,
feeding the poor and aiding the helpless. Undoubtedly they did
not confine their efforts to this work but engaged in evangelistic
endeavors as Stephen also had done.

The terms "bishop" and "elder" were probably interchangeable, for
Acts 20:17 and 28 apply them to the leaders of the Ephesian church
whom Paul met at Miletus. "Bishop" or "overseer" describes the
activity of the person; "elder," his position of seniority. They apply

to the same office, differing only in the aspect emphasized. The elders were teachers, pastors, and preachers who were responsible for the instruction and guidance of the church (Acts 11:30; I Pet. 5:1-4). Although the duties of these persons seem to be clearly marked and recognized, there is nevertheless no hint of the breach between clergy and laity that appeared in later centuries.

The position of the elder exposed him to danger both from the external world and from the inner community. As the leader of the Christian group he would be a marked man and would be singled out by the state in time of persecution, while within the church he could easily become a target for misunderstanding and slander. Paul forbade Timothy to allow a charge against any elder unless it were adequately substantiated by witnesses (I Tim. 5:19).

The disciplinary functions of the elder are illustrated by the smaller Johannine Epistles, which probably can be dated in the later Flavian period (c. A.D. 85). The anonymous "elder" expressed gratification over those who were "walking in truth" (II John 4; III John 3). He assumed authority to rebuke recalcitrant individuals within the church, such as Diotrephes who had arrogated to himself the right to exclude from worship visiting Christians (III John 9, 10). The elder promised that upon his arrival he would deal severely with Diotrephes. He also expressed disapprobation of unauthorized preachers who "confess not that Jesus Christ cometh in the flesh" (II John 7). He forbade the congregation to extend hospitality to such persons (vv. 10, 11).

Evidently the eldership had acquired considerable governing power by the time these epistles were written. A populace accustomed to autocratic rule would not have resented such authority, but would rather welcome it. As pioneer preachers gathered disciples who were dependent on their word for the knowledge of truth, they wielded increasing influence and were accorded greater power.

From the very earliest days the church had assumed responsibility for the relief of widows (Acts 6:1-3). As the community expanded, such relief became more necessary. Independent support for single women was almost impossible in the Roman world; they were nearly always dependent upon the nearest male relative. The church undertook to aid them but required them to be officially enrolled after passing certain stipulated character tests (I Tim. 5:5-16). The provision applied only to the elderly and incompetent, for those who had family connections were assigned to the care of their relatives and the younger widows were urged to marry rather than to become wandering gossips and busybodies.

The Johannine Epistles indicate that the church had developed an itinerant ministry, independent of any supervising council and supported by the group to whom they ministered. Describing heretical teachers, the elder says:

If anyone cometh unto you, and bringeth not this teaching [of Christ], *receive him not into your house, and give him no greeting* (II John 10).

The warning would have been unnecessary had it not been customary for traveling preachers to move from city to city, relying upon the hospitality of local churches for food and shelter. The legitimacy of this procedure is recognized in the Third Epistle, where the elder commends the church for receiving such persons:

Beloved, thou doest a faithful work in whatsoever thou doest to them that are brethren and strangers withal; who bare witness to thy love before the church: whom thou wilt do well to set forward on their journey worthily of God: because that for the sake of the Name they went forth, taking nothing of the Gentiles (III John 5-8).

These itinerants were evangelists who usually preached to Gentiles, but who were supported by the believers at the scene of their preaching. The strictures of the elder were not directed against the general procedure of such men, but against the pretensions of those who misused the method to peddle falsehood.

The system of itinerant preaching was probably a continuation of the initial method employed by the apostles. If Christian believers were not fully organized into churches comparable in structure to those of the twentieth century, there were doubtless many small communities dependent upon occasional visits for their spiritual stimulus rather than upon a regular pastor. Local pressures and the imperial distrust of any new organizations may have made a fixed ministry difficult, if not impossible.

The discussion of the requirements for the ministry in the Pastoral Epistles indicates that the church was endeavoring to cope with opposition and opportunities that demanded strong and intelligent leadership. Careful selection of officials was imperative if the church was to be trained for its task. There was not, however, any complicated ecclesiastical system but a simple and rather informal arrangement of duties that facilitated flexible and efficient operation.

The Discipline of the Church

The unrestrained license of the pagan world affected the church as new converts joined its ranks. Many of them had no concept of ethical standards and needed to be taught the rudiments of moral conduct. Others, coming from Judaism, were well versed in the Old Testament Law, which provided a stringent code of morality.

The church could neither adopt the loose morals of paganism nor could it enforce all the minute provisions of the Mosaic Law upon Gentile converts. It was consequently compelled to work out principles of its own, based upon the essence of the Law, upon the teachings of Jesus which revitalized it, and upon the new Christian consciousness of right and wrong created by the Holy Spirit.

Discipline began with doctrine, for conduct is shaped by belief. Paul's first mandate to Timothy, who had been assigned to the task of correcting the errors of the Ephesian church, was "to charge certain men not to teach a different doctrine" (I Tim. 1:3-11). Evidently they had become involved in debating trivial and useless questions rather than in instructing their people in major ethical precepts. In a civilization filled with "the lawless and unruly, the ungodly and sinners, the unholy and profane, with murderers of fathers and murderers of mothers [Nero?], with abusers of themselves with men, menstealers, liars, false swearers," the church had a greater task than debating theories. The moral needs mentioned echo the reports of the historians and satirists of this period; in fact, the Roman chroniclers and *littérateurs*, hardened as they were to evil, are no less condemnatory of the abuses of the time than were the apostolic writers.

Worship was regulated by discipline. Prayer was prescribed. The behavior of women was discussed extensively. In the upper strata of Roman society a woman had attained a considerable degree of independence, for she could control her own property and had complete social freedom. If her husband were wealthy, she had slaves to fulfill her slightest wish. Much of her time was spent in adornment with fashionable coiffures and dress. Juvenal satirized women who caroused at night with men and engaged in learned literary conversations at the dinner table. The Oriental cults were attractive to them; their mysterious and frequently immoral rites ensnared many who had investigated them purely out of curiosity.[5] With these dangers in mind, Paul enjoined Timothy to teach women to adorn themselves with modest clothing; not to indulge in elaborate hair arrangements and in jewelry, nor to be overbearing (I Tim. 2:9-15). In contrast to the bold and ostentatious women of fashionable paganism, the Christians were enjoined to exhibit the attractiveness of modesty and sobriety.

The injunction to "charge them that are rich in this present world, that they be not highminded, nor have their hope set on the uncertainty of riches, but on God" (6:17), must have had singular significance in the days of Nero, when the danger of confiscation made wealth a liability rather than an asset. There were

5 Juvenal, *Satire* VI; 415-456; 511-545.

wealthy men among the Christians in the province of Asia who could easily have been targets of the emperor's avarice. Instead of hoarding property they were urged to invest it where it could not be seized by any earthly power.

The Extension of the Church

At the time of Paul's first imprisonment he had completed the evangelization of southern Galatia, Asia, Macedonia, Achaia, and up to the borders of Illyricum (Rom. 15:19). During that same time Christian groups had been established in Pontus, northern Galatia, Cappadocia, and Bithynia (I Pet. 1:1). Since the latter provinces are mentioned by Peter, it is likely that he was the first preacher to carry the message thither. The New Testament tells nothing of the expansion of Christianity to Egypt and North Africa, to the Euphrates valley, the highlands of the Caucasus, or to Spain and Gaul. Nevertheless it is probable that these regions were visited by the end of the first century, and certainly before the middle of the second. There were enough Christians in Rome by A.D. 64 to attract the attention of Nero and to create fear of their influence. No exact calculation of their numbers is possible since there is no adequate basis for an estimate, but by the middle of the first century there must have been a substantial Christian population scattered through the eastern provinces. Their identity was well known, for Peter alludes to the word "Christian" as the popular nickname for the followers of Jesus (I Pet. 4:16).

The letters to the churches of Asia in Revelation 2 and 3 confirm the conclusion that Asia had become the center for westward expansion. Although there were other churches than those mentioned in Revelation, these seemed to be the best known and the most prosperous. All of them were maintaining a precarious resistance to the opposition of the state or of local pagan cults and were threatened with declension and corruption. Their survival is attested by the later letters of Ignatius, a deacon of Antioch, who wrote to many of these same groups, commending them for their faithfulness and urging them to keep their faith. His genuine letters, comprising those to the Ephesians, Magnesians, Trallians, Romans, Philadelphians, and Smyrnaeans, show that these churches were active in the early years of the second century, and that they were well known outside of Asia. Ignatius stated that the Ephesian church was "renowned throughout the world,"[6] and implies in the letter to the Smyrnaeans that they were acquainted with the church at Antioch by correspondence.[7] Although in Ignatius' time each

[6] *Ephesians* viii.
[7] *Smyrnaeans* xi.

church seems to have maintained an independent existence under the leadership of its own bishop and presbyters, there was a comity among them that bound them together in spiritual solidarity.

The Theology of the Church

In contrast to the intellectual and religious confusion that prevailed in the early empire, the Christian community gained steadily in clarity of thought and in definiteness of creedal confession. The Epistles written prior to A.D. 62 contain fewer allusions to formulated theology than do those which originate in the following period. Creedal expression begins to appear more clearly in the Pastoral Epistles of Paul. The repeated phrase, "Faithful is the saying . . ." usually introduces a theological statement or epigram relating to some positive aspect of the Christian life, particularly within the realm of soteriology. For example:

> *Faithful is the saying that —*
> 1. *Christ Jesus came into the world to save sinners; of whom I am chief* (I Tim. 1:15).
> 2. *We have our hope set on the living God, who is the Saviour of all men, specially of them that believe* (I Tim. 4:10).
> 3. *If we died with him, we shall also live with him: if we endure, we shall also reign with him: if we shall deny him, he also will deny us: if we are faithless, he abideth faithful; for he cannot deny himself* (II Tim. 2:11-13).

The Epistle to Titus, belonging to the same group, contains two capsule statements of theology (2:11-14; 3:4-7) which comprise allusions to the doctrines of grace, love, salvation apart from works, regeneration, the inward working of the Holy Spirit, the saviourhood of Christ, justification by grace, heirship of the believer, the return of Christ, and eternal life. The allusions show that the terminology in which they are couched is familiar to the church, and they imply a breadth of doctrinal knowledge that would exceed that of the present day.

A different theological development appears in the overtones of the Johannine Gospel and Epistles, which reflect the philosophical and mystical influences of the Orient. The person of Christ had been reduced to a vague spirit or ideal which had not been independently incarnate but which pervaded the spiritual atmosphere of the church. In an effort to escape from the trammels of materialism, the opposite extreme had been reached in denying the objective reality of Jesus.

Against this teaching John raised a vigorous protest. He introduced his Epistle by the claim that he had seen, heard, and handled the living Christ (I John 1:1), and asserted that *every spirit that confesseth that Jesus Christ is come in the flesh is of God: and every spirit that confesseth not Jesus is not of God: and this is the spirit of the antichrist, whereof ye have heard that it cometh; and now it is in the world already* (4:2,3). The tendency to dissipate historical reality into a cloud of idealistic fancy was sternly checked, and the danger of the absorption of Christianity into a broad cult of ritualism was averted.

Both the Gospel and the Epistles emphasize the material reality of Jesus' person. He "became flesh" (John 1:14), was "weary" (4:6), "groaned in spirit and was troubled" (11:33), suffered thirst (19:28), and died (19:30). He was involved in every kind of human relationships: weddings, funerals, dinners, meetings, conflicts with enemies, and conferences with friends. The human contacts were all normal, yet His person transcended the ordinary limitations of human nature so that even His enemies said, "Never man [Greek, *anthrōpos*] so spake" (7:46), and John himself called Him the Son of God (I John 5:5). While the metaphysical implications of this title were not fully discussed in the theology of the first century, the essential deity of Christ is plainly declared and was maintained in the succeeding literature of the sub-apostolic age. Polycarp spoke of "Jesus Christ Himself, who is the Son of God and our everlasting High Priest,"[8] and Ignatius said, "There is one Physician who is possessed both of flesh and spirit: both made and not made: God existing in flesh; true life in death; both of Mary and of God; first passible [subject to suffering] and then impassible [incapable of suffering], even Jesus Christ our Lord."[9]

While the full conflict with Gnosticism did not open until the last third of the second century, the trends toward dualism and mysticism were clearly manifest in the religious world, and the church was being compelled to face the issues. The Johannine writings reflect the beginnings of the conflict which reached its climax in the time of Irenaeus (c. A.D. 180).

The documents discovered in 1945 at Nag Hammadi, upper Egypt, have shown that Gnostic teaching had penetrated a village church in Egypt by the middle of the second century, and that it had absorbed or distorted many of the sayings of Jesus that appear in the canonical Gospels.[10] R. M. Grant observes that there seemed to be two waves of Gnostic thinking, one after the fall of Jerusalem

[8] *Philippians* XII.
[9] *Ephesians* VII.
[10] See *The Gospel According to Thomas.* Coptic text established and translated by H. Guillamont, H. Pueck, G. Quispel, W. Till, and Yesaiah 'abd Al Masih.

in A.D. 70, and the second after the ill-fated revolt of Bar Kochba in A.D. 135. Gnosticism may have been a reaction from the failure of Jewish and Jewish-Christian anticipation of the early establishment of the Messianic kingdom.[11] The calamitous outcome of these revolts may have caused a turn from material hopes to the concept of a purely spiritual triumph, based on an allegorical exegesis.

Perhaps the Johannine writings belonged in the interval immediately after A.D. 70, when the Gnostic influence was strengthening in Asia and in Palestine. The later use of these works by Gnostics such as Valentinus shows familiarity with them, and implies that the Gnostics found in them material they could use, although the Gospel of John was originally written to combat the results of an earlier trend of similar character.

The Relation of the Church and the Empire

With the destruction of the Jewish state, and the consequent changing status of the Jewish people from a nation to a religious group, the Christians were compelled to decide whether they would continue to be a branch of Judaism or whether they would create their own society. Perhaps because of the preponderance of Gentile adherents they chose to abandon the Law and to steer a separate course. The consequent transition from Judaic Christianity to a freer and more independent expression of faith is illustrated by the Epistle to the Hebrews.

Hebrews was written for second-generation Christians (Heb. 2:3), possibly at Rome, who had already suffered the plundering of their personal property (10:34) and who might be required to resist to the point of bloodshed (12:4). They were being compelled to choose whether they would stay within the bounds of Judaism or whether they would assert their independence. To declare themselves boldly to be Christians would subject them to public ridicule and they would forfeit all the political and social privileges they could enjoy in Judaism. In the light of Nero's savage though brief persecution they would naturally hesitate to declare themselves. Since the siege of Jerusalem was progressing under Vespasian and Titus, and while Rome itself was at the mercy of rapacious soldiery, the Christian congregation at Rome would naturally feel that their status was dangerously uncertain and that the old regime was "ready to pass away" (8:15). Irrespective of whether the epistle was written to a Jewish or Gentile group — though the former

11 Robert M. Grant, "Gnosticism," in *Interpreter's Dictionary of the Bible,* II, 406.

alternative is more probable — it reflects hesitancy on the part of believers.

The writer, however, did not share the current doubt and pessimism. The vanishing of the old order was for him merely the introduction of a new covenant which was superior to the old. He assured his readers that Christ had taken away fear of death (2:14) and that the removal of the Levitical priesthood merely cleared the way for the enduring priesthood of Christ (7:23-25). He reminded them that the blood of Christ is a better sacrifice than that of bulls and goats (9:13-15) and that the hope of believers is not in the present city, but in the abiding city to come (13:14). The entire tone of the epistle is hopeful, acknowledging the dangers and pressures of the present but cherishing faith in the purpose of God for the future.

The Petrine Epistles are products of the same period, though they differ from each other in tone. I Peter bespeaks an atmosphere of apprehension. A "fiery trial" threatens the churches, though it has not fallen upon them as yet (4:12). They will be "reproached for the name of Christ" (v. 14) and will be classed with criminals. Peter commanded them to conduct themselves so scrupulously and graciously that their accusers would be disarmed (2:11, 12), and he urged them especially to be law-abiding, observing carefully every ordinance and holding in honor the emperor (king) and his legates (governors) (vv. 13, 14, 17). Their relation with the government may have been growing increasingly precarious so that forcible repression seemed inevitable.

II Peter is concerned much less with the political scene than with ecclesiastical irregularities. The rise of an apostate group of people within the church who were theologically perverse and morally corrupt evoked the strictures of the second chapter. The allusion to Paul and his writings conveys the impression that this document belongs to the days immediately after Paul's death and shortly before that of the author's, though no precise time can be fixed. The unsettled condition of the church, the brazenness of the pseudo-teachers, and the rapid disappearance of the apostolic generation produced a pessimism from which the church had to rally. The use of prophecy, the appeal to the Scriptures (3:15ff.), and the expectation of the return of Christ (vv. 10ff.) were important elements in building a strong Christian consciousness and courage.

By the year A.D. 85 the church was launched on an independent course. Having survived its first conflict with Roman authority in the person of Nero, it sought to confirm its position theologically and politically. Doctrinal standards were defined, and the relation of church and state consequently became more antagonistic. The struggle for survival was commencing.

14

The End of the First Century

Christianity Under the Flavians

A LTHOUGH THE FLAVIAN EMPERORS RETRIEVED THE DIGNITY OF the imperial purple from the weakness and contempt into which Nero had plunged it, there was no mistaking the fact that they established a more autocratic government than any of their predecessors. Vespasian held the consulship in every year of his reign except two; Titus was his associate at least twice. He assumed the censorship in order to purge the Senate of unworthy members, and by the exercise of this official control he insured the obedience of that body rather than its co-operation. He did, however, treat the Senate with respect and abstained from using force or from imposing his will upon the empire without the Senate's assent.

Titus did not survive long enough to develop any permanent governmental policies, although he retained the consulate during his brief rule. His brother Domitian went further than his predecessors by holding the consulate for the first eight years of his reign in succession, and for seventeen terms in all. Whereas Vespasian relinquished the censorship, Domitian had himself made *censor perpetuus,* or censor for life. He demanded the first vote in the Senate, which gave him the opportunity of declaring his preference on every legislative question and consequently of swaying the policies of state. He tended to pay less attention to the Senate as time went on and to insist on the finality of his own decisions. In addition,

323

he was the first emperor to demand directly that he be worshiped as deity. Domitian was serious in his claims and with boundless egotism assumed the prerogatives of a god. He desired to be hailed as Jupiter's son and heir, the earthly vicegerent and representative of the king of the universe.

Domitian's personal ambition coupled with the worship of the Roman state created a new politico-religious atmosphere inimical to the growing church. The renewed emphasis on the importance of national religion, which involved polytheism, the establishment of emperor worship, and the suppression of any group that resisted state policies or that was even suspected of being hostile to the existing order placed the Christians in a disadvantageous position. They had only recently been brought into prominence by the fall of the Jewish state, and the distinction had become more apparent when Jews were separated from all others by the *fiscus Judaicus* or tax which Vespasian had imposed on them. The Christians' habits of private worship and their consistent devotion to an invisible deity laid them open to charges of conspiracy and atheism. There is no specific record in the Roman historians of a wholesale concerted persecution of Christians in this period, but there can be little doubt that the social and religious atmosphere of the empire was becoming increasingly unfavorable and that in some localities Christians were brought to trial and martyred for their faith.

A few vague hints of such persecuting activity have survived. Suetonius records that Domitian "put to death his own cousin, suddenly and on a very slight suspicion, almost before the end of his consulship; and yet Flavius was a man of most contemptible laziness and Domitian had besides openly named his sons, who were then young, as his successors. . . ."[1] Dio Cassius, as reported by Xiphilin, a monk of the eleventh century, states that Flavius Clemens, consul in A.D. 95 and a cousin of the emperor, was tried with his wife Domatilla on a charge of atheism. Clemens was executed; his wife was banished. Dio adds that Acilius Glabrio, consul in A.D. 91, had also been exiled, and that a number of persons had "gone astray after the manner of the Jews."[2]

Ramsay admits that Dio as reported by Xiphilin "is not very high authority," but he argues that Clemens, Domatilla, and Acilius Glabrio were prosecuted under the same general charge, and that "atheism" and "going astray after the manner of the Jews" must reflect Christianity.[3] The charge that Clemens was "lazy" may

[1] *Lives of the Caesars, Domitian* vii. 15. 1.
[2] *Roman History. Epitome* lxvii. 14. 1-3.
[3] Sir William Ramsay, *The Church in the Roman Empire Before A.D. 170,* pp. 262ff.

simply mean that he refrained from active participation in public
life either because he did not wish to incur the personal jealousy
of Domitian or because he was not in accord with the ethics and
practices of the pagan court. Failure to participate in the social
and political life would be considered as laziness by the average
Roman for whom such activity constituted the highest achievement.
If Clemens were a Christian, he might naturally shrink from involvement in the corruption incident to the court life. It is possible
that he may have been a Christian at heart but that he did not dare
to declare his faith openly.

There is better evidence for the Christian connections of Domatilla. The earliest Christian catacomb on the Ardentine Way in
Rome was named for her, and the ground in which it was built
originally belonged to her family. Eusebius stated that she was the
niece of Flavius Clemens and that she was banished in the fifteenth
year of Domitian.[4] The early believers could scarcely have established a burial ground on her property without the consent of the
family, nor is it likely that the family would have given consent
unless they had been Christians.

Dio Cassius remarks that Acilius Glabrio, who had been associated with Trajan in the office of consul, was executed approximately
at the same time, "having been accused of the same crimes as most
of the others."[5] Whether or not Glabrio was a Christian is not
explicitly stated. Ramsay suggests that fragmentary inscriptions
found by De Reese near a group of catacombs in the Via Salaria
near Rome seem to indicate that the burial plot belonged to the
family of the Acilii Glabriones.[6] He admits that the case is not
conclusive but holds that probability is strong.

As far as Acilius Glabrio is concerned, the casual remark of Dio
Cassius is insufficient to make a case for Christian martyrdom.
Whether or not Titus Flavius Clemens and his wife were Christians
may be disputed, but if they were, their punishment was attributed
to political and personal reasons rather than to religious causes.
Undoubtedly Domitian was jealous of his throne and seized any
pretext to remove possible rivals. He may have regarded Christians
as dangerously seditious, but although popular distrust of them
was growing, Domitian did not initiate a wholesale persecution of
them — at least, none is recorded in extant historical sources. On
the other hand, he seems to have inaugurated a policy which persisted until the reign of Hadrian. The rank and file of Christians

4 *Historia Ecclesiae* iii. 18.
5 *Loc. cit.*
6 *Op. cit.*, p. 262.

were left undisturbed as long as they created no breach of the public peace. Occasionally their leaders were arrested, interrogated, and executed or banished. Neither Suetonius nor Dio Cassius intimates that there was a long and vacillating struggle between Domitian and the Christians, and that they finally won. There is greater probability that he was motivated chiefly by political reasons, and that the martyrs — if any — suffered more because they were reputedly dangerous to the state than because of their theological convictions.[7]

The close of the century found the Christians in an ambiguous position. They could no longer claim immunities by virtue of being classified with the Jews, for the political independence of the latter had been destroyed. Though their privileges of free worship as holding a *religio licita* were not revoked, they were out of favor with the government and were subjected to heavier taxation. When the Christians disavowed connection with the Jews, they lost the standing that Judaism could give them. If they asserted their own claims and maintained an independent existence, their doctrines were subject to misunderstanding and their cohesive fellowship was misrepresented as political sedition. The very word "Christian" became a contemptuous nickname, if not indeed a criminal charge.

The Reign of Nerva

Nerva, an aged senator, succeeded Domitian. He was as mild as Domitian had been tyrannical. He released all those who had been imprisoned on suspicion of disloyalty and recalled the exiles. Confiscated property was restored to its rightful owners. Public expenditures were reduced in order to rebuild the treasury. The Senate once again was freed from oppressive fear. Dio Cassius, in summarizing Nerva's accomplishments during his brief reign of two years, adds one significant sentence: "No persons were permitted to accuse any one of *majestas* [disrespect for the emperor] or of adopting the Jewish way of life."[8]

"The Jewish way of life" seems to refer to becoming a proselyte to Jewish faith, but it could be a Roman pagan's way of describing the act of becoming a Christian. The prohibition of proselyting may have been extended to Christians. If their active evangelism provoked the fear and anger of Domitian, he may well have exercised repressive measures which Nerva relaxed.

---

[7] See Elmer T. Merrill, *Essays in Early Christian History,* pp. 148-173. Merrill probably makes too sweeping a case against Domitian's alleged persecution, while Ramsay overworks the evidence for it.

[8] *Op. cit.,* lxviii. i. 2.

Bust of Trajan, Roman emperor from A.D. *98-117.* (The Bettmann Archive)

If "adopting the Jewish way of life" does refer to Christian conversion, the church must have been vigorous and active in the last
third of the century. Since it was not a political movement, and
since it probably operated quietly on an individual basis rather than
by mass appeal, it escaped the notice of contemporary historians.
Its effects, however, became perceptible as larger numbers turned
from the pagan worship and social practices to a way of life that
accorded more closely with that of the Jews than with that of any
other known group.

The Administration of Trajan

The mild and humane attitude of Nerva brought relief to the tension that Domitian's autocratic rule had engendered. The release from fear produced a reaction against the misdeeds of the past, and in the new regime men became bold enough to accuse wrongdoers whom they had not previously dared to challenge. Nerva, because of his age and ill health, was unable to control firmly the warring factions. Numerous conspiracies were hatched, and on several occasions his life was in danger, though he averted assassination by his courage and honesty. Fronto, the consul, repeatedly commented that it was bad to have an emperor under whom nobody could do anything, but worse to have one under whom anybody could do anything. The permanent peace of the empire required a stronger hand than Nerva's, though he had afforded a welcome respite from Domitian's cruelties.

An incipient revolt of the Pretorian Guard warned Nerva that he must declare who his successor would be. He announced that his choice would be Marcus Ulpius Nerva Trajanus, the governor of Germany, whom he adopted publicly as his son. Trajan had just completed a successful military campaign and was popular with his troops. He was a courageous soldier, a competent administrator, and maintained a strict self-discipline. He adhered to justice in his dealings with his subjects and was free from the capricious excesses of Nero and the rapacity of Domitian. According to the chroniclers of his reign, he was devoid of arrogance and conceit.

Under Trajan the empire rose to the zenith of its power. He extended his conquests northward across the Danube River and the province of Dacia, and southward to the line of the desert in North Africa, which increased the agricultural lands available for settlement. He attempted an advance eastward against the Parthians, who had deposed the king of the buffer state of Armenia and had placed on the throne a member of the Parthian royalty. Trajan ordered the governor of Syria to annex the kingdom of the Nabatean Arabs on the eastern border of Syria and Palestine and then invaded Armenia. He deposed the Parthian ruler and made Armenia a Roman province. Moving eastward into northern Mesopotamia, he took direct control of the small independent states on the Parthian border. In the spring of A.D. 116 Trajan resumed his attack by invading Adiabene, a state on the east of the Tigris River which had retained its allegiance to Parthia. He moved his troops down the Tigris to Babylon, only to learn that the territory north of him had revolted and that the Parthians were ready to attack Assyria and Armenia. Trajan realized that he did not have sufficient resources to hold the eastern territory and after suppressing the revolt he voluntarily withdrew his lines to the west.   Rome never succeeded in establishing sovereignty over Mesopotamia.

The attempted conquest of the East was hindered by a Jewish revolt which began in Cyrenaica in A.D. 115 and affected settlements in Cyprus, Egypt, Palestine, and even Mesopotamia.   According to Dio Cassius,[9] the Jews massacred their Gentile neighbors with the utmost brutality.   Trajan succeeded in suppressing the strife except in Egypt, where the conflict was finally settled by Hadrian.   The Jewish unrest, however, smoldered until the Second Revolt in A.D. 135.

Trajan's health broke in the summer of A.D. 117.   He left Antioch to return to Rome, but his condition rapidly grew worse and he died in Cilicia in August.

Of all the emperors up to his time, Trajan was the strongest and best.   He refrained from extortion and from proscription of his enemies.   He gave the provinces a sound government and stabilized the borders. The Parthian danger was checked, though he was unable to subjugate the kingdoms of the Middle East.   His fairness and justice were generally acknowledged.

Trajan and Christianity

Under the clement rule of Trajan there was no wholesale persecution of the church, though there may have been occasional flurries of persecution in the provinces when Christians became strongly self-assertive or when governors decided that they were subversive. The classic example of the Roman attitude in this period is preserved in the letters of Pliny the Younger, whom Trajan had appointed to the governorship of Bithynia.   Pliny was a novice in the affairs of state who wrote frequent and persistent despatches to his chief concerning all kinds of problems, great and small.   In one of his last communications he presented the problem of the Christians in his province.   His letter is quoted here in its entirety, along with Trajan's reply:

Pliny to the Emperor Trajan
Letter XCVII

It is my invariable rule, Sir, to refer to you in all matters where I feel doubtful; for who is more capable of removing my scruples, or informing my ignorance?   Having never been present at any trials concerning those who profess Christianity, I am unacquainted not only with the nature of their crimes, or the measure of their punishment, but how far it is proper to enter into an

9 *Ibid.*

examination concerning them. Whether, therefore, any difference is usually made with respect to ages, or no distinction is to be observed between the young and the adult; whether repentance entitles them to a pardon; or if a man has been once a Christian, it avails nothing to desist from his error; whether the very profession of Christianity, unattended with any criminal act, or only the crimes themselves inherent in the profession are punishable; on all these points I have great doubt. In the meanwhile, the methods I have observed toward those who have been brought before me as Christians is this: I asked them whether they were Christians; if they admitted it, I repeated the question twice, and threatened them with punishment; if they persisted, I ordered them to be at once punished: for I was persuaded, whatever the nature of their opinions might be, a contumacious and inflexible obstinacy certainly deserved correction. There were others also brought before me possessed with the same infatuation, but being Roman citizens, I directed them to be sent to Rome. But this crime spreading (as is usually the case) while it was actually under prosecution, several instances of the same nature occurred. An anonymous information was laid before me, containing a charge against several persons, who upon examination denied they were Christians or had ever been so. They repeated after me an invocation to the gods, and offered religious rites with wine and incense before your statue (which for that purpose I had ordered to be brought, together with those of the gods), and even reviled the name of Christ: whereas there is no forcing, it is said, those who are Christians into any of these compliances: I thought it proper, therefore, to discharge them. Some among those who were accused by a witness in person at first confessed themselves Christians, but immediately after denied it; the rest owned indeed that they had been of that number formerly, but had now (some above three, others more, and a few above twenty years ago) renounced that error. They all worshiped your statue and the images of the gods, uttering imprecations at the same time against the name of Christ. They affirmed the whole of their guilt, or their error, was that they met on a stated day before it was light, and addressed a form of prayer to Christ, as to a divinity, binding themselves by a solemn oath, not for the purposes of any wicked design, but never to commit any fraud, theft, or adultery, never to falsify their word, nor deny a trust when they should be called upon to deliver it up; after which it was their custom to separate, and then reassemble, to eat in common a harmless meal. From this custom, however, they desisted after the publication of my edict, by which, according to your commands, I forbade the meeting of any assemblies. After receiving this account, I judged it so much the more necessary to endeavor to extort the real truth, by putting two female slaves to the torture, who were said to officiate in their religious rites: but all I could discover was evidence of an absurd and extravagant superstition. I deemed it expedient, therefore, to adjourn all further proceedings, in order to consult you. For it appears to be a matter highly deserving your consideration, more especially as great numbers must be involved in the danger of these prosecutions, which have already extended, and are still likely to extend, to persons of all ranks and ages, and even of both sexes. In fact, this contagious superstition is not confined to the cities only, but has spread its infection among the neighboring villages and country. Nevertheless, it still seems possible to restrain its progress. The temples, at least, which were once almost deserted, begin now to be frequented; and the sacred rites, after a long intermission, are again revived; while there is a general demand for the victims, which till lately found very few purchasers. From all this it is easy to conjecture what numbers might be reclaimed if a general pardon were granted to those who shall repent of their error.

Reply: Trajan to Pliny
Letter XCVIII

You have adopted the right course, my dearest Secundus, in investigating the charges against the Christians who were brought before you. It is not possible to lay down any general rule for all such cases. Do not go out of your way to look for them. If indeed they should be brought before you, and the crime is proved, they must be punished; with the restriction, however, that where the party denies he is a Christian, and shall make it evident that he is not, by invoking our gods, let him (notwithstanding any former suspicion) be pardoned upon his repentance. Anonymous informations ought not to be received in any sort of prosecution. It is introducing a very dangerous precedent, and is quite foreign to the spirit of our age.[10]

The inquiry of Pliny reveals that he was a member of the Roman aristocracy, was only slightly acquainted with Christians, and was not at all aware of the true nature of Christianity. Evidently those who were arrested and brought to trial were not charged with specific offenses; the fact that they were Christians was sufficient presumption of guilt. Such a presumption implies a previously established ruling that would outlaw Christianity in general, dating either from the early reign of Trajan or from some imperial decree under the Flavians or Nero.

A clue is provided by Pliny's statement that his edict against them was prompted by Trajan's commands that forbade the meeting of any assemblies. The issue was not primarily religious or theological, for the Romans were generally tolerant of national or alien religions, but rather that any independent association, particularly in the provinces, was regarded by the emperor as potentially subver-

---

[10] *Letters of Pliny the Younger.*

sive. The worship of the emperor's image was a means of fostering
political unity and was demanded in order that the provincials,
whatever their local religion might be, should be united with the
rest of the empire in a common loyalty to its head. Pliny admitted
that he was in doubt whether the profession of Christianity should
in itself be considered a crime, or whether the offense lay in the acts
connected with the profession.

The tests which he applied, demanding an invocation to the gods,
the ceremonial offering of wine and incense before the emperor's
statue, and cursing the name of Christ, prove that he or his predecessors had accurate comprehension of the Christians' monotheism. No
Christian believer could conscientiously ascribe deity to a man, nor
make offerings to an image. What the Romans regarded as a political gesture, or a worship that could be given to any god of
one's choice, the Christians considered to be idolatry and blasphemy.

The reply of Trajan shows that neither he nor the stated policy
of the empire called for a general pogrom of Christians. As long
as they maintained their worship privately and did not interefere
with the affairs of state, they might be allowed to practice their own
religion. Prohibition of unlicensed assemblies had long been a
policy of Rome; and Trajan even restricted the formation of an
association of firemen because he felt that it would have political
repercussions. Furthermore, if the growth of Christianity endangered the state religion, the state itself might be undermined. Both
Pliny and Trajan were motivated by a desire to preserve the government rather than by any particular religious antipathy.

Pliny's report of the evidence concerning the movement secured
under torture affords one of the earliest insights into its nature.
The believers met regularly early in the morning to worship Christ
"as a divinity." They insisted on a strict code of ethics: to abstain
from fraud, theft, and adultery, never to lie, nor to default on an
obligation. At the end of the assembly they ate a common meal
and then adjourned. Pliny did not specify what he had learned
concerning their teaching; he called it "an absurd and extravagant
superstition." To a materially minded Roman the essential teachings of Christianity would seem ridiculous; as Paul said, "the word
of the cross is to them that perish foolishness" (I Cor. 1:18).

The advance of Christianity in Bithynia must have been rapid, for
Pliny stated that the temples had been almost deserted and that
the sacred rites had fallen into disuse. Not only were the cities
affected but the rural villages also had felt the influence of the new
faith.

Pliny was hopeful that the "contagious superstition" would decline.
He noted that the temples were once more attended by worshipers,

and that the market for sacrificial animals had revived. He was quite sure that if pardon were extended to those who would recant, a large number might be reclaimed.

The relative mildness of Trajan's attitude appears in his confirmation of the policy outlined above. He refused to countenance irresponsible charges. Punishment should be administered only to those who were proven guilty, and any who publicly denied or renounced the Christian faith should be pardoned. His comment that acting on "anonymous information . . . is a very dangerous precedent, and is quite foreign to the spirit of our age" has a modern ring. Trajan's attitude was much more irenic than that of Domitian and indicates that, according to his lights, he endeavored to be tolerant and just.

In spite of occasional local persecutions the church did not fare too badly under Trajan. There must have been a tremendous wave of evangelism under Domitian and his successor to have created the recession of paganism of which Pliny spoke. Nevertheless, the irreconcilable difference between the pagan and Christian viewpoints made persecution a constant threat. The Romans were jealous of any mass movement that might undermine the solidarity of the state, particularly because the empire contained so many nationally minded blocs that could easily become self-assertive. To a great extent Christianity was an underground movement devoid of public meetings or open organization, though its existence was well known.

The Reaction of the Church

Of all the Christian documents assignable to the last third of the first century, the Apocalypse is the most eloquent of the tension between church and empire. Written as a report of prophetic visions bestowed to John the Seer, who was exiled to Patmos in the last years of Domitian's reign,[11] it reflects the conditions of its time and is couched in the language of an oppressed people. Although its symbolism speaks of a world yet to come, much of its imagery is drawn from the civilization in which the Seer and his contemporaries lived.

Persecution and martyrdom are reflected in the letters to the seven churches. The church of Smyrna was warned that it was about to suffer and that it would have tribulation for ten days (Rev. 3:9, 10). Pergamum, where the first temple to Rome and Augustus had been erected, was called "Satan's throne" (2:13). Laodicea, which had prospered under the commerce that passed from the hinterland of Asia down the Lycus valley to the coast, was

11 Irenaeus, *Against Heresies* v. 30. 3.

The Monastery of St. John on Patmos, the Greek island in the Aegean Sea off the coast of Turkey, where John was imprisoned (Rev. 1:9) during the reign of Domitian. The monastery was built in the late eleventh century by St. Christodulus. (Courtesy National Tourist Organization of Greece.)

condemned for its complacent indifference. Five of the seven churches showed signs of declension similar to that which encouraged Pliny to anticipate a wholesale reversion to paganism. The promise given to the one who overcomes at the end of each letter suggests that some exhortation was needed to prevent apostasy and a return to the old way of life.

The wealth and prodigality of Rome were symbolized in the figure of the great harlot who rode the seven-headed beast. Glittering with jewels, robed splendidly in scarlet and purple, and drunk with the blood of saints and martyrs (17:4-6) she is "the great city which reigneth over the kings of the earth" (v. 18). A center for commerce and for pleasure and the dominating power of the world, her doom foreshadowed the ultimate collapse of the last godless civilization of earth.

The picture of the woman arrayed with the sun and with the moon under her feet, crowned with twelve stars and giving birth to a child which was caught up to the throne of God, may be a conscious parallel to the claims of Domitian for his young son who died in A.D. 83. The emperor proclaimed him to be a god and issued a new series of coins in honor of his memory. The coin depicts the

Ruins of the Roman forum in Smyrna (modern Izmir), one of the seven churches of Asia Minor (Rev. 2:8-11). (Courtesy Prof. B. Van Elderen.)

Remains of statues representing Poseidon (Neptune) and Demeter (Ceres) in the Roman forum at Smyrna. Because of splendor such as this, Smyrna claimed to be "first of Asia in beauty." (Courtesy Turkish Information Office.)

child's mother as the mother of the gods, with the inscription, "Mother of the Divine Caesar." A gold coin of A.D. 83, inscribed with the legend *Divus Caesar Imp[erator] Domitiani F[ilius]*, "the deified Caesar, son of the Emperor Domitian," it represented the dead child seated in heaven, surrounded by seven stars. It meant that he had been translated to the celestial sphere, from which vantage-point he ruled the world.[12]

---

[12] Ethelbert Stauffer, *Christ and the Caesars,* pp. 151-152.

Whereas the coin of Domitian glorified the human princeling as a divine ruler, the Apocalypse presented Jesus Christ, the Lord of heaven and earth, who will rule all the nations with a rod of iron. It may be that the Revelation had no direct reference to Domitian's claim, but the parallel imagery seems almost too similar to be accidental. The Apocalypse indicates also that the dragon, Satan, attempted to swallow the child but was cheated of his prey when it was taken up to heaven. Christ, snatched from the jaws of death, has become the founder of a new age, while the child of Domitian was impotent to accomplish the salvation which his supposed translation promised.

The totalitarianism of Rome may be the model for the figure of "the beast out of the sea" in Revelation 13. He is invincible in war, arrogant and blasphemous in his claims, hostile to the saints, and possesses authority "over every tribe and people and tongue and nation." The second beast, representing religious authority, could compel the worship of the first beast and enforce economic sanctions so that "no man should be able to buy or to sell, save he that hath the mark, even the name of the beast or the number of his name"

Remains of the Roman amphitheater at Pergamum, one of the seven churches of Asia Minor (Rev. 2:12-17). (Courtesy Turkish Information Office.)

A reconstructed Roman amphitheater and the temple of Aesculapius (Greek Asklepios), the god of healing, in Pergamum. (Courtesy Turkish Information Office.)

(v. 17). Although there is no clear evidence that Domitian enforced the regulation of sales to this extreme, the use of the concept in predictive prophecy shows that it was a potential threat which could easily become actual. Imperial control of the grain trade with Egypt placed the food supply of Rome in the hands of one man and gave him almost unlimited power over the populace.

The First Epistle of Clement to the Corinthians was contemporaneous with Revelation and reflects the external social conditions of the same period. Because it is a letter of fraternal counsel, it has much less to say concerning the political and social background than the Apocalypse. It does, however, express the attitude of the church at Rome at the end of the century and affords some hints of its status.

The introduction to the Epistle of Clement alludes to "the sudden and successive calamitous events which have happened to ourselves,"

Columns remaining from the temple of Artemis or Diana at Sardis, one of the seven churches of Asia Minor (Rev. 3:1-6). The city was noted for its luxury and licentiousness. (Courtesy Prof. B. Van Elderen.)

Detail of one of the capitals from the Artemis temple at Sardis, showing its immense size. (Courtesy Prof. B. Van Elderen.)

and which had delayed the communication which the church at Rome had intended to send to the sister church at Corinth.[13] The allusion is vague, perhaps designedly so; and one cannot easily ascertain whether it refers to some attack from without or to some heresy within. It may be a reference to persecution, for Clement adds in a subsequent paragraph:

> Through envy and jealousy, the greatest and most righteous pillars of the Church have been persecuted and put to death. Let us set before our eyes the illustrious apostles. Peter, through unrighteous envy, endured not one or two, but numerous labors; and when he had at length suffered martyrdom, departed to the place of glory due to him . . . . Paul also obtained the reward of patient endurance. . . . After preaching both in the east and the west, he gained the illustrious reputation due to his faith, having taught righteousness to the whole world and come to the extreme limit of the west, and suffered martyrdom under the prefect.

[13] I Clement i.

> To these men . . . there is to be added a great company of the elect, who, having through envy endured many indignities and tortures, furnished us with a most excellent example.[14]

If these martyrdoms can be connected with Clement's first reference to "the sudden and successive calamities," there must have been an outburst of persecution in Rome not long previous to the penning of this letter, for Clement says that it occurred "in our generation." By the time that he wrote, the persecution had ceased, for his references apply to past time, not to the present.

The applicability of I Clement to the last of Domitian's reign has been challenged by E. T. Merrill who contends that it was written about the end of the first third of the second century.[15] He is extremely skeptical of an earlier date for the following reasons:

1. The quarrelsome factions had died out in the Corinthian church.
2. The age of the apostles was definitely past.
3. The phrase "our own generation," which has been frequently interpreted as connecting the author with the hearers of the apostles, may mean only the contrast of recent times with the past, and does not necessitate dating the work in the first century.
4. The reference to the death of the apostles is vague, as if the details of their lives were not fresh in the memory of the church.

Merrill's arguments are not wholly convincing. The factions of the Corinthian church would not necessarily have ceased with the acceptance of the Pauline rebuke. There was revival in the church before Paul's last visit that changed the atmosphere completely and that brought the chief offender to penitence (II Cor. 7:5-13), but new schisms could have arisen later. The apostolic generation would have largely died out by the middle sixties, and I Clement, according to the best external testimony available, was not written until thirty years later. The general allusion to the death of the apostles may only reflect the prevalent imprecise method of narrating history, for the church was more concerned with survival than with discussing the minutiae of past events. While not all the legends concerning the identity of Clement, such as his being the companion of Paul mentioned in Philippians 4:3 or the bishop of Rome, are necessarily true, there seems to be little room for doubt that he was an important presbyter of the church, and that the book belongs to the first century. This epistle assuredly alludes to painful persecution which took place in the generation preceding, but which had ceased. It seems most likely that the epistle was completed either in the last year of Domitian or in the early reign of Trajan.

---

[14] *Ibid.,* v, vi.
[15] *Op. cit.,* pp. 235-241.

A second body of literature bearing on this period are the seven letters of Ignatius, who died in A.D. 107, during the reign of Trajan. Of fifteen epistles ascribed to him, seven are absolutely genuine and only in a short recension. The longer form of the seven letters contains numerous interpolations which cannot be credited to the sub-apostolic age.

Little is known of the actual life of Ignatius. When Trajan visited Antioch in A.D. 107, Ignatius boldly confessed himself as a Christian and was sentenced to be sent to the wild beasts in the arena at Rome. Under guard of ten soldiers whose ferocity caused him to call them "leopards,"[16] while en route to his death, he wrote these farewell letters to the churches whom he had served. The churches themselves seem not to have been in serious peril, even though he, their leader, was condemned to death. The difference between him and them illustrates the principle embodied in the correspondence of Trajan and Pliny, that the Christians should not be prosecuted unless they confessed openly that they were Christians and refused to recant. Ignatius had publicly declared his faith and was the acknowledged champion of the believers in Syria. Trajan, recognizing that Ignatius defied his authority, and that he was prominent among the Christians, pronounced the death penalty.

Although the church under Trajan may have been insecure, it was evidently not subjected to constant persecution. The fact that Ignatius could write to independent groups and teach them in person shows that the rank and file were left unharmed. Ignatius might have been exempt had he not insisted on presenting himself to the emperor for martyrdom. He exhibited a new spirit of seeking martyrdom for its own sake that he might be held in heavenly honor by Christ. His devotion and heroism were typical of many leaders in his time.

16 *Epistle to the Romans* v.

15

The Church and the New Era

U NDER THE ORDERLY AND AGGRESSIVE RULERSHIP OF TRAJAN
the Roman empire reached its widest expansion. From
Britain to the Sahara and from the pillars of Hercules to the
Euphrates River the legions held the barbarians at bay while commerce and culture flourished. Trajan's firmness and restraint had
merited the respect of his subjects and had laid a good foundation
for peace and sobriety. The excesses of a Caligula or of a Nero
and the tyranny of a Domitian were forgotten in the relatively serene
period of the "good emperors," of whom Trajan was the first.

The last campaign against the Parthians had proved too strenuous
for Trajan's failing health. He had been afflicted with dropsy for
two or three years, and on his way back to Rome from the East
he suffered a paralytic stroke that immobilized him. He died at
Selinous on the southern coast of Asia Minor on August 9, A.D. 117.

The Accession of Hadrian

Trajan appointed as his successor Hadrian, his cousin, who was
commander of the army in the East. Probably Plotina, Trajan's
wife, influenced him strongly in this choice. For a number of years
she had mothered Hadrian in lieu of children of her own, and because Trajan was incapable of writing, she had signed the final
documents. Whether the decision were Trajan's or hers, it was

343

Sculpture of the emperor Hadrian, now in the British Museum. On the site of Jerusalem, which had been destroyed by Vespasian and Titus fifty years earlier, Hadrian founded the pagan city Aelia Capitolina. (The Bettmann Archive.)

fortunate, for Hadrian was familiar with Trajan's procedures and possessed the energy and the knowledge to complement them. He proved to be one of the most learned, industrious, and proficient of the long succession of emperors.

The Early Career of Hadrian

Hadrian was born at Italica, a town in southern Spain, on January 24, A.D. 76. His full name was Publius Aelius Hadrianus, or Publius, of the Aelian family, who came from Hadria in northern Italy. Italica, his birthplace, was one of the largest and finest colonial settlements in the Roman provinces. Its cultural level was superior to that of most provincial towns. The surrounding open country provided ample scope for an outdoor life, so that Hadrian developed a penchant for athletics and hunting.

When Hadrian was ten years old his father died, and he was committed by his mother to the guardianship of his cousin Trajan and of a Roman knight named Acilius Attianus. Trajan was transferred to the Rhine country for military service, and consequently the responsibility for Hadrian devolved upon Attianus, who took him to Rome, where he spent the next five years.

Hadrian did not enjoy his life in Rome. There was no opportunity for indulging his favorite sports, nor did he seem to develop any attachment for the court society. He did acquire a fondness for Greek literature which persisted the rest of his life. Attianus sent him back to Spain in order to remove him from the unhealthy atmosphere of the capital. His brother-in-law, who was much older than he, looked askance upon his passion for hunting and reported unfavorably concerning him to Trajan. Trajan promptly removed him to Rome, where he entered government service. He was appointed a petty officer in the Second Legion Auxiliary and was despatched to Budapest on the northern boundary. There he learned what the frontier meant and the value of holding it unbroken against the restless hordes of nomads who filled the Hungarian plain.

In the following year he was transferred to the Fifth Legion Macedonian, which was stationed just south of the Danube near the Black Sea. Upon Trajan's accession in A.D. 98, Hadrian was again transferred to the Twenty-second Legion in Upper Germany. His long military experience on the borders gave him an acute awareness of their importance and of the necessity of adequate defense — a lesson that he turned to good account in later years.

Trajan took a definite interest in Hadrian from the beginning of his career in the army. In his initial visit to the Danubian frontier he took Hadrian with him, and upon returning to Rome, Plotina selected a wife for Hadrian, Sabina, the grand-niece of

Trajan. Unfortunately the match was unhappy, and though Hadrian never discarded her, she proved to be no asset to his reign.

During the nineteen years of Trajan's rule from A.D. 98 to 117 Hadrian was closely associated with him in military operations. He participated in the wars in Dacia, in Transjordan, and in Parthia. Little detail is available concerning these, but Hadrian had ample opportunity to gain extensive military experience. Between the wars he engaged in public affairs and served for one term as governor of Hungary. He left this post to become Trajan's private secretary and speech writer.

When Trajan undertook his last campaign against the Parthians, Hadrian accompanied him to the East. Trajan appointed him governor of Syria, where he held the supply lines while the emperor himself led his troops deep into the Parthian territory. The strain of this campaign and its ultimate failure, despite the immediate progress of conquest, accelerated the decline of Trajan's health. On his deathbed Trajan declared the formal adoption of Hadrian, and the news of his final elevation to the imperial office reached him at Antioch the day after Trajan died.

The long schooling in military and political life had prepared Hadrian well for the task that Trajan bequeathed to him. Although the empire had reached the height of its power and was prosperous, its problems were multiplying. The tribes along the northern Danube were pressing hard on the borders, the eastern frontiers were still uncertain since the Parthians were unsubdued, and the Jews were in a state of incipient revolt. Trajan's extensive military campaigns had reduced the treasury and drastic action was necessary to replenish it. At least two plots against Hadrian's life were uncovered. Fortunately they were quashed before they were consummated. For all of these emergencies Hadrian proved adequate.

Hadrian as Emperor

In his reorganization of the state he made himself the benevolent autocrat, whose image is that of a father rather than that of a god. In order to revive the ancient cult of Rome, he assumed the prerogatives of the *pontifex maximus,* the high priest of the empire. Curiously enough, Hadrian could not be called a religious man, for he seemed to have few personal convictions, if any. In this respect he was probably not greatly different from the majority of Romans, who regarded their gods as fallible beings of a higher class than themselves, endowed with greater powers. To him good terms with the gods were advisable, and to worship them provided a strong bond of social coherence, but there was no such concept of holiness or of personal relationship as obtained in Judaism or in Christianity. For a sense of individual relationship or of personal immortality the populace turned to the Eastern cults, the mystery religions, that had been infiltrating Rome since the time of Claudius and even earlier.

Hadrian came to realize that while the ancestral traditions might suffice for the western half of the empire, the Greek and Oriental East demanded a personal deity. In keeping with his general procedure of putting himself on the level of his subjects wherever he happened to be, he was initiated into the Eleusinian mysteries while visiting Greece.[1] In Rome he promoted the erection of the temple of Romulus and Remus, and at Athens he completed the Olympeion, in which his statue was placed. The Athenians hailed him as a new divine manifestation of Zeus. Wherever he went he promoted a cult that would appeal to the local population and at the same time unite their worship with that of the state.

Both Jews and Christians rebelled against this procedure. Hadrian's visit to the barren site of the devastated Temple in Jerusalem convinced him that the Jews should be brought under the aegis of Rome. On the hill where the Temple of Jehovah had stood he built another to Jupiter and changed the name of the city to *Aelia Capitolina*. Not only did he in Jewish eyes desecrate the sacred spot by building a heathen shrine where their center of worship had stood, but he actually changed the name of the city to wipe out all memory of their past. Furthermore, he forbade the rite of circumcision on pain of death. Since Hadrian was a Hellenist by culture, he revolted from any mutilation of the human body. Furthermore, in his desire to make all citizens of the empire equal, he wished to avoid all distinguishing marks. To the Jews, however, circumcision was obedience to a divine command which they could disobey only at the risk of being severed from their heritage. Every child was thus marked from infancy as a loyal follower of the Law and as a member of the people of God. To forego the rite or to retract it would be tantamount to repudiating their faith and to renouncing their salvation.

Because Hadrian's acceptance of divine titles and his contemptuous treatment of their city and customs seemed to be sheer blasphemy, the Jews revolted once again. In Alexandria they assaulted and massacred many Gentiles and laid waste a large part of the city. After Hadrian's general, Turbo, had intervened and repressed the uprising, Hadrian expelled the Jews and rebuilt the city. The crisis must have been drastic, for Alexandria had a large Jewish population that inhabited its own quarter and had virtually an independent government. Expulsion of the Jews would deprive the city of

---

[1] Dio Cassius, lxix. 2. 1.

Professor Yigael Yadin of the Hebrew University of Jerusalem examining fragments of the Bar Kochba letters found at Wadi Muraba'at near the Dead Sea. Simon Bar Kochba was the leader of the second Jewish revolt against the Romans, following Hadrian's rebuilding of Jerusalem in the second century. (Courtesy Israel Information Services.)

many inhabitants and of some of the best and most cultured of its citizens.

The more serious revolt began in Judea in A.D. 132. Simon Bar Kochba (Son of a Star), a self-pronounced messiah, declared the independence of Judea. He seized Jerusalem, issued coins, and attempted to restore the Temple ritual. At the outset his revolt succeeded, and by maintaining guerrilla warfare he fought the Romans to a standstill. He reorganized Judaism by insisting on circumcision and by persecuting the Christians who had separated from the nation. By his open hostility the final breach between Christians and Jews was fixed.

The struggle for Jerusalem was soon begun, for the Romans attacked in force. Bar Kochba constructed a fortified wall on the north side of the city, the only point from which it could be attacked. Hadrian sent Sextus Julius Severus, the governor of Britain, to command the imperial forces. No fewer than six legions with numerous auxiliary troops were engaged in the conflict which covered the entire countryside, but which focused on Jerusalem. Casualties were heavy on both sides. The Twenty-second Legion was annihilated, and the losses of others were so heavy that when Hadrian made his final report to the Senate he omitted the conventional formula, "If you and your children are well, all is well; I and the army are in good

A scene on the Via Dolorosa, the traditional Way of the Cross which Jesus followed from Pilate's judgment hall to Calvary. (Courtesy KLM — Royal Dutch Airlines.)

health." In the end the Romans were victorious, for they were better trained and better equipped than Bar Kochba's guerrillas. By the use of small raiding parties Sextus Severus stripped the land of supplies and chased Bar Kochba's followers into the desert. As recently as 1959 some of his letters were recovered from the caves near the Dead Sea, which indicate that Roman troops had reconquered Galilee and that supplies from the farms were becoming scarce.[2] Driven from Jerusalem, the Jews made a last stand near Bettir, a rocky eminence southwest of the city, where they were starved into submission by the Roman siege. Dio Cassius reported that fifty fortified posts and nine hundred eighty-five villages were demolished, and that 580,000 men were killed in battle, in addition to a much larger number who died of famine, disease, and fire.[3] The devastation of Judea was complete. The leading rabbis were executed by torture, and Jewish slaves were sold on the open market for the price of a horse.[4] The site of the Temple was plowed and sowed to salt, and the rubble of the ruins filled the hollows of the Tyropean valley which intersected the city from north to south. Only the massive retaining wall of the Temple area erected by Herod the Great still remained, known today as the Wailing Wall, where the Jews used to congregate to lament the fall of their nation.

In order to stamp out the memory of the nation Hadrian rebuilt the city as a garrison town. The Tenth Legion was stationed in a camp near the remains of Herod's palace, and on the leveled surface of the site he constructed a typical Roman commune. Two intersecting streets, one running north and south and the other east and west, are still traceable in the layout of modern Jerusalem. The entrance to Hadrian's Forum is visible in an ancient portal beneath the Russian Convent, and one of the decorative gates is preserved in the Arch of the *Ecce Homo* which is located on the modern street known as the *Via Dolorosa*. The northern gate was located where the Damascus Gate now stands. In the Forum stood the temples of Jupiter Capitolinus, Juno, and Venus-Aphrodite, traditionally over the mount of Golgotha, where the crucifixion took place. A theater, circus, and baths were situated near the Pool of Siloam at the south end of the town.

Jerusalem ceased to be Jewish and became increasingly Gentile. A small Greek-speaking church remained there, though the larger Christian population was concentrated in the capital, Caesarea. Hadrian seems to have been favorable to Christians, for though

---

[2] Yigael Yadin, "New Discoveries in The Judean Desert," *Biblical Archaeologist* (1961), pp. 34-50.

[3] *Op. cit.*, lxix.14.

[4] Michel Join-Lambert, *Jerusalem,* pp. 100-105.

there were sporadic local persecutions during his reign, he did not wage a campaign of extermination against them. His attitude was like that of Trajan, who was willing to ignore their presence if they did not become a danger to the state. In a letter to a governor of Asia Hadrian confirmed Trajan's policy and sternly ordered that no attention should be paid to informants who endeavored to blackmail Christians without proper legal charges.

Hadrian's action insured the separation of Christianity from Judaism. As long as a Jewish church existed in Jerusalem and Judea, it formed a link between Judaism and Christianity. With the dispersion of the Christians from Jerusalem the link was permanently broken. The Christian church became the rival of the Roman state, and when the struggle ended with the capitulation of the emperor Constantine to Christianity, the spiritual scepter passed from the gods of Rome to the church of Christ.

Undoubtedly Hadrian was unconscious of his contribution to the growth of the movement. He was ignorant of its significance, and the work of Quadratus, the earliest apologist, seems to have left no particular impression on him. Salmon comments that "nowhere does he seem to have been interested in religion for spiritual reasons; he simply was not interested in moral or metaphysical speculation."[5]

Of all the Roman emperors, Hadrian traveled the most widely. From A.D. 120 to 133 he was absent from Rome almost continuously. He visited personally the frontiers in Gaul, Spain, Syria, Cappadocia, Bithynia, Greece, where he stayed six months in Athens, Africa, and Judea. He was deeply interested in the welfare of the provinces and sought to make them an integral part of the empire rather than subject colonies. Wherever he went he introduced stricter training and discipline for the legions who were defending the frontiers, and he inaugurated a vast program of public works for their benefit. For Corinth and Athens he built aqueducts; Ephesus and Trapezus were granted new harbors; extensive road and bridge building projects were undertaken in Spain and in the Danubian provinces. He fostered the growth of the urban centers and founded a large number of new cities, several of which carried his name, as Adrianople in Greece does to the present day.

The last years of Hadrian's reign were filled with gloom. He was afflicted with dropsy and tuberculosis. Ill health preyed upon his mind and he became morose, vindictive, and unpredictable. His wife Sabina had refused him children so that he had no heir of his own. Antinous, a Bithynian youth who became his constant companion,

---

[5] Edward T. Salmon, *A History of the Roman World from 30 B.C. to A.D. 138*, p. 306.

The so-called Street of Columns in Jerash (Gerasa), Transjordan, one of the cities of the Decapolis. Among the extensive ruins in this site is an arch welcoming the widely-traveled emperor Hadrian to the city in A.D. 130. (Courtesy KLM — Royal Dutch Airlines.)

and whom he may have cherished as a son, was unaccountably drowned in the Nile during their visit to Egypt. Two years before his death Hadrian had executed his brother-in-law, Servianus, and the grandson of the latter, Fuscus. He had selected as his heir Lucius Ceionius Commodus, an indolent young aristocrat, who slept on a bed covered with a net filled with rose petals under a coverlet of lilies. Just why a practical man like Hadrian ever chose him is a mystery; perhaps Hadrian liked his aesthetic qualities. He appointed Lucius a consul and sent him to the Danubian frontier. After one year of service he died of tuberculosis on the first day of January, A.D. 138.

Hadrian was greatly depressed by his death and did not recover from the shock. He gradually declined in strength and realized that a successor must be chosen. He selected Titus Aurelius Antoninus, a senator fifty-one years old, of unimpeachable character and an administrator of reliable, though not brilliant, quality. In turn he required Antoninus to adopt Marcus Aurelius Varus, a nephew, and also the younger Lucius Annius. The arrangement proved salutary, for Antoninus succeeded in preserving the peace

The forum at Gerasa surrounded by colonnades, leading out into the Street of Columns. (Courtesy KLM — Royal Dutch Airlines.)

which Hadrian had established, and Marcus Aurelius Varus, who followed him, became the renowned philosopher-emperor whose "Meditations" are still a classic.

Hadrian lived only six months after their appointment. The pain of his disease was maddening, and on several occasions he either attempted suicide or endeavored to persuade one of his servants to kill him. In the last summer of his life he went to Baiae, a resort on the northern side of the Bay of Naples, where he penned his farewell to his own soul:

> *Charming, wandering little sprite,*
> *Body's guest and company,*
> *Whither now you take your flight,*
> *Cold and comfortless and white,*
> *Leaving all your jollity?*

Hadrian was the most versatile and conscientious of all the Roman emperors. He was by turns an aesthete, an athlete, an architect, a traveler, an organizer, a military expert, a judge, and a sportsman. He possessed the great advantage of having an apprenticeship for office under his predecessor, Trajan. Through his successive appointments to posts on the frontier he gained a practical understanding of the current military problems and an insight into the needs of the army. Constant traveling on state business acquainted him with the varied cultures of the peoples under his rule. Assiduous study of these cultures fostered cosmopolitan interests that were reflected in his later life. Promotion of building projects sprang from his interest in architecture; constant contact with the public acquainted him with popular desires and needs, so that on numerous occasions he exhibited unusual discretion as a judge. He tried to act in the best interests of the empire.

Hadrian did not continue Trajan's policy of imperialistic expansion. He realized that the conquest of Parthia would cost more in manpower and in funds than the empire could afford; in fact, Trajan had already seriously imperilled the solvency of the treasury. Instead, Hadrian assumed a policy of defense by abandoning all territories east of the Euphrates and the Syrian desert and by fortifying the northern boundaries along the Rhine and the Danube. In Britain he constructed a wall eighty Roman miles in length from the Solway to the Tyne to check the incursions of the Picts and the Scots into the southern settlements. Though the defensive policy was ultimately fatal to the welfare of the empire, the immediate effect was beneficial. For a period of sixty years Rome was at peace and enjoyed some of the most prosperous years that it had ever known.[6]

---

[6] Cf. Salmon's discussion, *op. cit.,* pp. 302-304.

The remains of a statue of Hadrian, located in the Athenian agora, the market place where Paul spoke. (Courtesy Prof. B. Van Elderen.)

Hadrian treated the provinces more as sister nations than as subjects of the state and endeavored to draw them into closer contact with the central government. Public works and buildings were provided where needed; new cities were founded to care for the urban population; laws were revised and codified; distressed areas were aided by imperial funds. In some respects, however, his solicitude was harmful. The grants of funds weakened the sense of community responsibility for improvement, and the supervisors whom he assigned were often so efficient that the local government shirked its rightful tasks.

Hadrian's greatest weakness was in public relations. Because of his protracted absence from Rome, he was not well known to the Roman aristocracy or to the people. At times he was tactless, and the execution of four adversaries of senatorial rank who had plotted against him at his accession was never forgiven by their colleagues. Although he denied emphatically and probably truthfully that he was responsible, since the executions had taken place before he reached Rome, his enemies retained their suspicion. The moods of ill temper in his later life, exacerbated by his physical pain, deepened their dislike. His bluntness also alienated many, so that according to Dio Cassius' report he died "hated by the people."[7] The Senate refused to vote him the usual honors and reversed its position only on the plea of Antoninus, who declined to assume the throne if the Senate repudiated Hadrian's acts.

The Church

Between the close of the first century and the latter part of the second century the church enjoyed a period of relative peace and of prosperous growth. Lactantius, a western Latin father of the late third and early fourth century, wrote:

> In the times that followed Domitian, while many well-deserving princes guided the helm of the Roman empire, the church suffered no violent assault from her enemies, and she extended her hands into the east and into the west insomuch that there was not the most distant corner of the earth to which the divine religion had not penetrated or any nation of manners so barbarous that did not, by being converted to the worship of God, become mild and gentle.[8]

This period Lactantius defined as beginning with the death of Domitian and ending with the persecution of Decius about A.D. 250. The procedure for this tolerance had already been set down by Trajan and was continued by Hadrian.

[7] *Op. cit.,* lxix. 23. 2; lxx.1. 1-3.
[8] *Of the Manner in Which Persecutors Died* iii.

The Arch of Constantine in Rome, located along the Via Triumphalis directly west of the Colosseum. The emperor Constantine established Christianity as the state religion of Rome in A.D. 313 with the Edict of Milan, two years after his predecessor Galerius had decreed an end to persecution of Christians with the Edict of Toleration. (Courtesy Unesco/A. Vorontzoff.)

The general imperial policy is well defined by the rescript of Hadrian to Minucius Fundanus, proconsul of Asia, appended to Justin Martyr's *Apology*[9] to the emperor Antoninus Pius (A.D. 138-161), Hadrian's successor, and reproduced by Eusebius:

> To Minucius Fundanus. I have received an epistle, written to me by the most illustrious Serenius Granianus, whom you have succeeded. I do not wish, therefore, that the matter should be passed by without examination, lest innocent persons be harassed, and occasion be given to the informers for malicious proceedings. Accordingly, if the inhabitants of your province will so far sustain this petition of theirs as to accuse the Christians in some court of law, I do not prohibit them from doing so, but I will not allow them to make use of mere entreaties and outcries. For it is far more just, if anyone desires to make an accusation, that you give judgment upon it. If therefore anyone makes the accusation and furnishes proof that the said men do anything contrary to the laws, you shall adjudge punishments in proportion to the offense. And

this, by Hercules, you shall give special heed to, that if anyone shall, through mere calumny, bring an accusation against any of these persons, you shall award him more severe punishments in proportion to his wickedness.[10]

The genuineness of the foregoing rescript, though challenged by a number of scholars, has been defended by men of such diverse viewpoints as Renan, Lightfoot, Harnack, and Ramsay, and is generally admitted.   Merrill[11] agrees that a forger would hardly have known who the predecessor of Minucius Fundanus was nor could Justin Martyr have sent to a living emperor a spurious rescript of his predecessor.

No official by the name of Serenius Granianus can be located in contemporary Roman history.   There was a suffect consul Granianus in A.D. 106, and Minucius Fundanus in the next year, but the inscriptions that mention these names do not say that either was governor of Asia.   The full name of the former was Quintus Licinius Silvanus Granianus Quadratus Proculus.   It is possible that Serenius was a copyist's error for Silvanus.[12]   Between Justin Martyr's copy of the letter and Eusebius' reproduction more than one hundred and fifty years intervened, and small changes may have occurred during that time, especially in a period of warfare.

The content of the rescript shows that Christians had not ceased to be an administrative problem since the days of Pliny.   The exact date of Granianus cannot be fixed, but probably it was about A.D. 125. The proconsuls had been urged by some citizens hostile to Christians to take immediate action against the propagandists of the new faith.   Hadrian instructed the proconsul to adhere to the regular process of the law and not to punish innocent citizens who might be accused solely because of prejudice.   If the informers were willing to make a formal accusation in a court, the case should be tried, and if adequate proof of crime could be adduced, proper penalties should be exacted.   If, however, the accusations were false, the informers themselves should be punished.

It is quite possible that if the Christians in Asia were numerous and powerful, there were among them some who could have been victims of blackmail.   By charging them with being Christians, the accusers could harass them, and then agree to drop the case

---

[9] *First Apology* lxviii.

[10] *Historia Ecclesiae* iv. 9.   The quoted text is a combination of Justin Martyr and Eusebius.

[11] *Op. cit.,* pp. 203, 206, 207.

[12] Probably Serenius is a variant of the more common Roman *cognomen* Serenus.

out of court for a substantial payment of money or goods. Such a situation seems to have been implied in the language of the rescript.

From this letter one may conclude that under Hadrian's rule there was no general persecution of Christians. There may have been a few scattered martyrdoms of believers who were haled before local magistrates, but the church was not under threat of wholesale extermination. Nevertheless, the essential conflict between cynicism and faith, between idolatry and spiritual worship, between immorality and ethical purity, between the sovereignty of the emperor and the lordship of Christ continued unabated. Inevitably there must come a crisis when one or the other would prevail. After Hadrian's death the shaky spiritual foundations of the empire became more apparent, and through the anarchy and disasters of the third century the fate of Christianity hung in the balance. With the victory of Constantine at the Milvian Bridge in A.D. 312 Rome gained a Christian emperor, and the political struggle was ended.

Beginning with the revival of Judaism under the Maccabees in 168 B.C. and continuing to the end of Hadrian's reign in A.D. 138, the antecedents and consequents of the advent of Christ made history. The collapse of the Second Jewish Commonwealth and the slow spiritual decay of the Western world left a vacuum which only the creation of a regenerate church could fill. Ceremonialism and political formalism were not satisfying to the spirit; a new life was demanded. On the foundation of the Old Testament revelation the Christian message was built, and its appeal to the Gentiles offered them personal faith in a living Sovereign greater and more permanent than the Caesars. As Rome declined, Christianity increased, until it was able to provide the light for dark ages and the stabilizing force in a world made chaotic by Rome's fall.

Appendixes

EVENTS IN THE BIBLICAL WORLD FROM 312 - 4 B.C.

Date (B.C.)	Egypt	Judea	Syria
312	Ptolemy I invades Palestine.		Demetrius repulses Ptolemy. Accession of Seleucus I Nicator.
300			Founds Antioch.
285	Ptolemy I abdicates; succeeded by Ptolemy II Philadelphus, who builds library at Alexandria.	Under Egyptian rule.	
280			Antiochus I Soter surrenders Macedonia and Thrace to Ptolemy II.
278			Checks invasion of Gauls into Asia Minor.
262			Killed in war with Pergamum.
261			Antiochus II succeeds to throne; at war with Ptolemy II.
250			Peace declared; Antiochus marries Ptolemy's daughter.
246	Ptolemy III Euergetes captures Syria.		Seleucus II Callinicus becomes king.
227			Seleucus III Soter succeeds his father; assassinated after four years.
223			Antiochus III the Great succeeds his brother.
221	Ptolemy IV Philopator becomes king of Egypt.		
217	Defeats Antiochus III at battle of Raphia, conquers Lebanon.		
204	Ptolemy V Epiphanes succeeds to throne.	Palestine under Seleucid rule.	
198			Antiochus reconquers Palestine from Egypt.
192			Invades Greece; defeated by Rome.
188			Driven out of Asia by the Romans.
187			Dies; succeeded by Seleucus IV Philopator.
181	Ptolemy V dies; succeeded by Ptolemy VI Philometor.		
175			Seleucus IV assassinated by Heliodorus; succeeded by his younger brother Antiochus IV Epiphanes.
175-170		Attempt by Seleucids to Hellenize Jews and Samaritans; Temple at Jerusalem desecrated.	

Date	Egypt	Judea	Syria
170			*Antiochus* invades Egypt, captures *Ptolemy VI;* expelled by Romans.
168	*Ptolemy VII Physcon* placed on throne after capture of *Ptolemy VI.* Strife between brothers, who were co-kings.	Maccabean revolt; Syrians withdraw from Palestine.	
165		Restoration of Temple worship; defeat of Maccabees in battle; withdrawal of Syrians.	
163			*Antiochus IV* dies in Persia; Successor *Antiochus V Eupator* assassinated.
162		Conflict between Maccabees and Hellenizers over priesthood; expulsion of Hellenizers. Treaty with Romans.	Accession of *Demetrius I.* Roman intervention.
160		Judas Maccabaeus succeeded by brother Jonathan.	
157		Conflict between Jonathan and Hellenizers.	
152	*Ptolemy VI* supports *Alexander Balas.*	Jonathan accepts high-priesthood from *Balas;* offers support.	*Alexander Balas,* pretender to throne, lands in Syria. Supported by Romans.
150			*Demetrius I* defeated, killed by *Balas.*
146	*Ptolemy VI* transfers allegiance to *Demetrius II;* killed in battle.		
145	*Ptolemy VII Euergetes II* seizes throne.		*Antiochus VI Dionysius* placed on throne by Trypho as regent.
143		Jonathan captured by *Trypho.* Brother Simon takes command; beginning of Hasmonean line.	*Trypho* usurps throne; *Demetrius II* driven from Antioch.
142		Treaty with Syria concluded, grants freedom to Judea.	
141		Simon takes Gazara; expels Seleucid garrison from Jerusalem.	
140		Simon governor, commander of army, high priest.	
139			*Demetrius II* imprisoned by Parthians for 10 years; Trypho executes *Antiochus VI,* seizes throne. Trypho defeated in battle, succeeded by *Antiochus VII Sidetes,* Demetrius' brother.

Date	Egypt	Judea	Syria
135		Simon, wife, two sons killed; succeeded by John Hyrcanus.	
129			*Antiochus VII* killed in Parthian campaign; *Demetrius II* returns, occupies throne. Rivalry of heirs; decline of Seleucid empire.
126			Accession of *Seleucus V*; followed by *Antiochus VIII Grypus*.
116	Accession of *Ptolemy VIII Soter II* (Lathyrus).		
108	Retires to Cyprus; succeeded by *Ptolemy IX Alexander*.		
105		Aristobulus succeeds to the throne, imprisons Antigonus and Alexander. Dies, succeeded by his widow Alexandra.	
104		Alexander Jannaeus becomes king, marries Alexandra. War with Ptolemy Lathyrus; alliance with Cleopatra; nation revolts.	
96			Accession of *Seleucus VI Epiphanes Nicator*.
95		Alexander defeated by Demetrius; recovers troops, expels Syrians.	Accession of *Antiochus XI Epiphanes Philadelphus*. Accession of *Philip I*. *Demetrius Eucerus III* invades Judea, withdraws.
88	*Ptolemy IX* killed in sea battle; *Ptolemy VIII* returns.		
86			Accession of *Antiochus XII Dionysius Epiphanes*.
80	Death of *Ptolemy VIII; Ptolemy X* assassinates stepmother; displaced by *Ptolemy XI Philopator Philadelphus*, illegitimate son of *Ptolemy VIII*. Exiled 58-55; restored by Romans.		
78		Death of Alexander; succeeded by his widow Alexandra. Hyrcanus becomes high priest; deposed by brother Aristobulus. Antipater of Idumea sides with Hyrcanus.	
66			End of Seleucid dominion; Syria, Palestine conquered by Romans under Pompey.

Date	Egypt	Judea	Syria
64		Pompey arbitrates high priest dispute for Hyrcanus. Takes Jerusalem. Aristobulus and sons exiled in Rome; Judea a Roman province.	
57-55	Intervention in Egypt by Aulus Gabinius, proconsul of Syria.	Revolts by Aristobulus and sons suppressed.	
54		Temple plundered by Crassus.	
51	Death of *Ptolemy XI;* succeeded by son *Ptolemy XII* and daughter Cleopatra.		
47	Conquest of Egypt by Julius Caesar; end of Ptolemaic dynasty.		
46		Antipater becomes procurator of Judea; Herod prefect of Galilee.	
43		Death of Antipater.	
40-37		Antigonus governs Judea with Parthian support; Herod escapes to Rome; recognized as king of the Jews.	
39			Expulsion of Parthians from Syria by Ventidius Bassus
31	Battle of Actium: defeat of Antony and Cleopatra by Octavian. Rome annexes Egypt, which is no longer independent power.		
19		Reconstruction of Temple begun by Herod the Great.	
4		Death of Herod.	

Date	Judea	Christianity	Rome
B.C.			
27			Accession of Augustus to principate.
7/5		Birth of Jesus, Bethlehem.	First census under Quirinius.
4	Death of Herod the Great. Archelaus appointed ethnarch of Judea; Antipas tetrarch of Galilee, Perea; Philip tetrarch of Iturea, Trachonitis.		
A.D.			
6	Deposition and exile of Archelaus.		
14			Death of Augustus; accession of Tiberius.
18	Caiaphas succeeds Annas as high priest.		
26	Pontius Pilate appointed governor of Judea.	(?) Opening of Jesus' ministry.	Retirement of Tiberius to Capri.
30		Crucifixion of Jesus; rise of Christian church.	
32/33		Death of Stephen; conversion of Paul.	
34	Death of Herod Philip.		
36	Removal of Pontius Pilate.		
37			Death of Tiberius; accession of Caligula.
41		(?) Founding of church at Antioch.	Death of Caligula; accession of Claudius.
43/44		Martyrdom of James; Peter imprisoned.	
44	Death of Herod Agrippa I.		
46	Famine; procuratorships of Cuspius Fadus, Tiberius Alexander.	(?) "Famine visit" of Paul and Barnabas to Jerusalem.	
46/48		First missionary journey of Paul, Barnabas.	
48/50		Council of Jerusalem.	
48/49		Second missionary journey of Paul.	
49			Expulsion of Jews from Rome.
51			Accession of Gallio as proconsu of Achaia.
52	Felix appointed procurator of Judea.		
53		Third missionary journey of Paul; Ephesian ministry.	

Date	Judea	Christianity	Rome
54			Death of Claudius; accession of Nero.
56/58		Imprisonment of Paul in Caesarea.	
59	Porcius Festus succeeds Felix as procurator.		
59/60		Paul before Festus, Agrippa; appeal to Caesar.	
61	Interim between Festus and Albinus.	Death of James, the Lord's brother, in Jerusalem.	
64			Great fire in Rome; persecution of Christians.
65/67		Threat of persecution in the provinces.	
66	Opening of First Revolt; war with Rome.		
68/69			Death of Nero. Year of four emperors: Galba, Otho, Vitellius, Vespasian.
70	Capture and destruction of Jerusalem by Titus.		
79			Accession of Titus; destruction of Pompeii by Vesuvius.
81			Accession of Domitian.
95		Persecution under Domitian.	
96			Death of Domitian; accession of Nerva.
98			Retirement, death of Nerva; accession of Trajan.
107		Martyrdom of Ignatius.	
115	Jewish revolt in Cyrene, Egypt, Palestine, Mesopotamia.		
117			Death of Trajan; accession of Hadrian. Consolidation of Roman empire.
132-135	Second Revolt under Simon Bar-Kochba. Complete destruction of Jerusalem; city rebuilt by Hadrian as Aelia Capitolina.		
138			Death of Hadrian.

GENEALOGICAL CHART OF THE HASMONEAN FAMILY

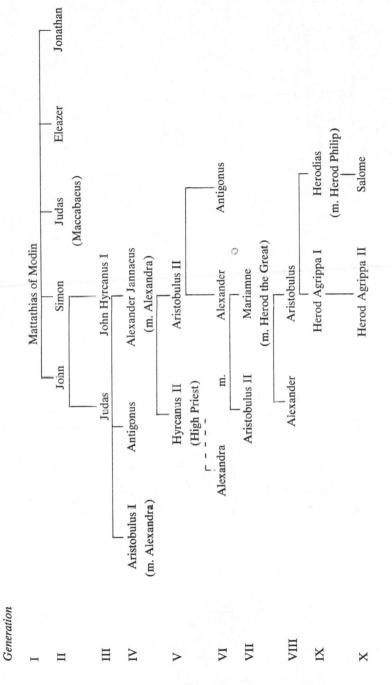

THE HERODIAN FAMILY

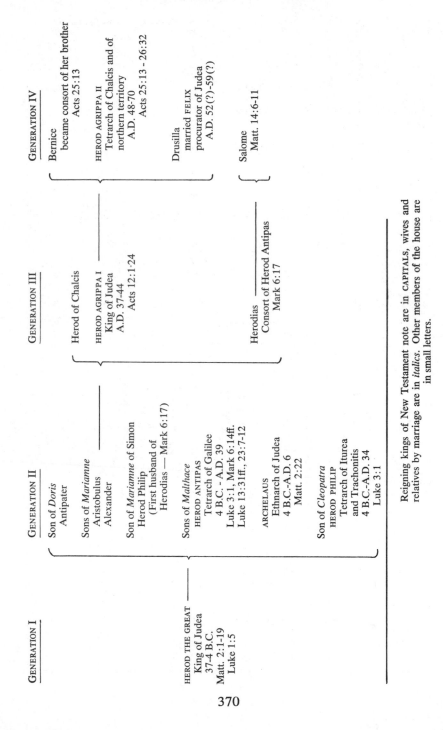

GENERATION I

HEROD THE GREAT
King of Judea
37-4 B.C.
Matt. 2:1-19
Luke 1:5

GENERATION II

Son of *Doris*
Antipater

Sons of *Mariamne*
Aristobulus
Alexander

Son of *Mariamne* of Simon
Herod Philip
(First husband of
Herodias — Mark 6:17)

Sons of *Malthace*
HEROD ANTIPAS
Tetrarch of Galilee
4 B.C. - A.D. 39
Luke 3:1, Mark 6:14ff.
Luke 13:31ff., 23:7-12

ARCHELAUS
Ethnarch of Judea
4 B.C.-A.D. 6
Matt. 2:22

Son of *Cleopatra*
HEROD PHILIP
Tetrarch of Iturea
and Trachonitis
4 B.C.-A.D. 34
Luke 3:1

GENERATION III

Herod of Chalcis

HEROD AGRIPPA I
King of Judea
A.D. 37-44
Acts 12:1-24

Herodias
Consort of Herod Antipas
Mark 6:17

GENERATION IV

Bernice
became consort of her brother
Acts 25:13

HEROD AGRIPPA II
Tetrarch of Chalcis and of
northern territory
A.D. 48-70
Acts 25:13 - 26:32

Drusilla
married FELIX
procurator of Judea
A.D. 52(?)-59(?)

Salome
Matt. 14:6-11

Reigning kings of New Testament note are in CAPITALS, wives and relatives by marriage are in *italics*. Other members of the house are in small letters.

370

THE ROMAN PROCURATORS OF JUDEA

Date	Procurator	Relation to New Testament
5		
A.D. 6		
	Coponius	
10 A.D. 10		
	M. Ambivius	
A.D. 13		
15 A.D. 15	Annius Rufus	
20	Valerius Gratus	
25		
A.D. 26		
30	*Pontius Pilate*	Crucifixion of Jesus
35		
A.D. 36		
A.D. 38	Marcellus	
40		
	Maryllus	
A.D. 44		
45	Cuspius Fadus	
A.D. 46		
A.D. 48	Tiberius Alexander	
50	Ventidius Cumanus	
A.D. 52		
55	*M. Antonius Felix*	Trial of Paul: Acts 23, 24
A.D. 59		
60	*Porcius Festus*	Trial of Paul: Acts 25, 26
A.D. 61		
	Albinus	
65 A.D. 65		
	Gessius Florus	
70	*Siege of Jersualem*	
	Vettulenus Cerialis	
	Lucilius Bassus	
75		
80	M. Salvienus	
	Flavius Silva	
85		
A.D. 86	Pompeius Longinus	
90		

THE ROMAN EMPERORS FROM AUGUSTUS TO HADRIAN

Date	Name	Event	Reference
30 B.C.- A.D. 14	Augustus	Birth of Christ	Luke 2:1
A.D. 14-37	Tiberius	Ministry and death of Jesus Christ	Luke 3:1
A.D. 37-41	Caligula		
A.D. 41-54	Claudius	Famine Expulsion of Jews from Rome	Acts 11:28 Acts 18:2
A.D. 54-68	Nero	Trial of Paul Persecution at Rome	Acts 25:10-12 Acts 27:24 II Tim. 4:16, 17
A.D. 68	Galba		
A.D. 69	Otho		
A.D. 69	Vitellius		
A.D. 69-79	Vespasian	Destruction of Jerusalem	
A.D. 79-81	Titus		
A.D. 81-96	Domitian	Persecution (?)	
A.D. 96-98	Nerva		
A.D. 98-117	Trajan		
A.D.117-138	Hadrian		

Bibliography

The following bibliography does not attempt to include all titles pertinent to the subject of New Testament times, for such a collection would constitute a book in itself. It does represent the major modern authorities in which source materials may be found and the varied viewpoints they offer on the period under discussion. Foreign titles have been generally omitted, since they are not easily available to the average student. The subjoined list will supplement the main ideas of the text and will enable the reader to indulge in excursions of his own into the fascinating bypaths of Biblical history and archaeology. For a more extensive bibliography of works on individual books of the New Testament the reader is directed to the author's *New Testament Survey*.

GENERAL WORKS

Angus, Samuel. *The Environment of Early Christianity*. New York: Scribner, 1920.
———— *The Mystery Religions and Christianity*. New York: Scribner, [1928].
Ante-Nicene Fathers, The. The Writings of the Fathers down to A.D. 325. Translated by Alexander Roberts and James Donaldson. American Reprint of Edinburgh Edition, edited by A. Cleveland Coxe. 10 vols. Grand Rapids: Eerdmans, 1951.
Apostolic Fathers, The. Translation by Kirsopp Lake. 2 vols. Loeb Classical Library. London: Heinemann; New York: Putnam, 1919.
Apuleius. *The Golden Ass*. Translated by W. Adlington (1566), revised by S. Gaselee. Loeb Classical Library. London: Heinemann; New York: Putnam, 1935.
Audet, Père J. P. *La Didache*. Paris: Études Bibliques, 1958.

Bailey, Cyril. *Phases in the Religion of Ancient Rome*. Berkeley: University of California Press, 1932.
Barrett, C. K. *The New Testament Background. Selected Documents, Edited with Introductions*. London: S. P. C. K., 1958.

Battenhouse, Henry Martin. *New Testament History and Literature*. New York: Nelson, 1937.

Blaiklock, E. M. *The Century of the New Testament*. London: Inter-Varsity Fellowship, 1962.

——————— *Out of the Earth*. Revised and Enlarged Edition. Grand Rapids: Eerdmans, 1957.

——————— *Rome in the New Testament*. London: Inter-Varsity Fellowship, 1959.

Boak, A. E. R. *A History of Rome to 565 A.D.* Fourth Edition. New York: Macmillan, 1953.

Botsford, George Willis. *Hellenic History*. New York: Macmillan, 1923.

Brandon, S. G. F. *The Fall of Jerusalem and the Christian Church*. London: S. P. C. K., 1957.

Bruce, F. F. *The Acts of the Apostles*. Second Edition. Grand Rapids: Eerdmans, 1953.

——————— *The Book of Acts* in "The New International Commentary on the New Testament." Grand Rapids: Eerdmans, 1956.

——————— *Second Thoughts on the Dead Sea Scrolls*. Grand Rapids: Eerdmans, 1961.

——————— *The Spreading Flame*. Grand Rapids: Eerdmans, 1953.

Buchan, John. *Augustus*. Boston: Houghton, 1937.

Burr, A. G. *The Apostle Paul and the Roman Law*. Privately printed at Bismarck, North Dakota, 1928.

Burrows, Millar. *The Dead Sea Scrolls*. New York: Viking, 1955.

——————— *More Light on the Dead Sea Scrolls*, with translations of important recent discoveries. New York: Viking, 1958.

Busch, Fritz-Otto. *The Five Herods*. Translated from the German by E. W. Dickes. London: Robert Hale, 1958.

Cadbury, Henry J. *The Book of Acts in History*. London: A. and C. Black, 1955.

Cambridge Ancient History. Eds. S. A. Cook, F. E. Adcock, M. P. Charlesworth. Vol. VII: *The Hellenistic Monarchies and the Rise of Rome*. Vol. VIII: *Rome and the Mediterranean, 218-133 B.C.* Vol. X: *The Augustan Empire, 44 B.C. - A.D. 70*. Vol. XI: *The Imperial Peace, A.D. 70-192*, New York: Macmillan, 1930.

Carcopino, Jerome. *Daily Life in Ancient Rome: The People and the City at the Height of the Empire*. Edited with Bibliography and Notes by Henry T. Rowell. Translated from the French by E. O. Lorimer. New Haven: Yale University Press, 1940.

Carrington, Philip. *The Early Church*. Vol. I: *The First Christian Century*. Cambridge: University Press, 1957.

Cary, M. *A History of Rome Down to the Reign of Constantine*. Second Edition. London: Macmillan, 1957.

Charles, R. H. *The Revelation of St. John*. New York: Scribner, 1920.

Charlesworth, M. P. *Documents Illustrating the Reigns of Claudius and Nero*. Cambridge: University Press, 1951.

Cicero, Marcus Tullius. *The Orations of Marcus Tullius Cicero*. Yonge's Translation. Vol. II. London: G. Bell, 1894.

Cornfeld, Gaalyahu, Ed. *Daniel to Paul: Jews in Conflict with Graeco-Roman Civilization*. Historical and Religious Background to the Hasmoneans, Dead Sea Scrolls, The New Testament World, Early Christianity, and the Bar-Kochba War. New York: Macmillan, 1962.

Corpus Inscriptionum Graecarum, edited by Augustus Boeckhius. Berlin: Reimerus, 1828-1879.

Craig, Clarence Tucker. *The Beginning of Christianity.* New York & Nashville: Abingdon, 1943.

Cross, Frank L. *The Early Christian Fathers.* London: Duckworth, 1960.

Cross, Frank Moore. *The Ancient Library of Qumran and Modern Biblical Studies. The Haskell Lectures,* 1955-57. Garden City, N.Y.: Doubleday, 1958.

Cumont, Franz. *Astrology and Religion Among the Greeks and Romans.* American Lectures on the History of Religions: Series of 1911-12. New York & London: Putnam, 1912.

Davies, Wm. D. *Christian Origins and Judaism.* Philadelphia: Westminster, 1962.

Deissmann, Adolf. *Bible Studies.* Edinburgh: T. & T. Clark, 1901.

——————— *Light from the Ancient East.* Translated by Lionel R. M. Strachan. Second Edition. London: Hodder, 1911.

Dill, Samuel. *Roman Society from Nero to Marcus Aurelius.* London: Macmillan, 1905.

Dio Cassius. *Roman History,* with English Translation by Earnest Cary, in Loeb Classical Library. Vols. VII, VIII. New York: Putnam, 1925.

Downey, Glanville. *Antioch in the Days of Theodosius the Great.* Norman, Okla.: University of Oklahoma Press, 1962.

——————— *A History of Antioch in Syria from Seleucus to the Arab Conquest.* Princeton, N.J.: University Press, 1961.

Eusebius Pamphilus. *Ecclesiastical History.* Translated from the original by Rev. C. F. Cruse, and Historical View of the Council of Nice with a translation of documents by the Rev. Isaac Boyd. Philadelphia: Davis & Bros., 1840.

——————— *Die Chronik des Hieronymus,* volume 7. Berlin: Akademie Verlag, 1956.

Fairweather, William. *The Background of the Epistles.* Edinburgh: T. & T. Clark, 1935.

——————— *The Background of the Gospels.* Twentieth Series of the Cunningham Lectures. Third Edition. Edinburgh: T. & T. Clark, 1920.

——————— *From the Exile to the Advent.* Edinburgh: T. & T. Clark, 1894, 1952.

——————— *Jesus and the Greeks.* Edinburgh: T. & T. Clark, 1924.

Festugière, A. J. *Antioche Paienne et Chrétienne.* Libanius, Chrysostome, et les moines de Syrie. Paris. Éditions de E. de Borcard, 1959.

Finkelstein, Louis. *The Pharisees.* 2 vols. Philadelphia: Jewish Publication Society of America, 1938.

Foakes-Jackson, F. J. and Kirsopp Lake. *The Beginnings of Christianity.* Part I: *The Acts of the Apostles.* 5 vols. London: Macmillan, 1920.

Friedländer, Ludwig. *Roman Life and Manners Under the Early Empire.* Authorized Translation of the Seventh Enlarged and Revised Edition of the *Sittensgeschichte Roms* by Leonard A. Magnus. Second Edition. 4 vols. London: Routledge; New York: Dutton, n.d.

Franzmann, Martin H. *The Word of the Lord Grows.* St. Louis, Mo.: Concordia, 1961.

Gaster, Theodore H., Ed. *The Dead Sea Scriptures in English Translation.* Garden City, N. Y.: Doubleday, [1956].

Geldenhuys, Norval, *The Gospel of Luke* in "New International Commentary on the New Testament," Grand Rapids: Eerdmans, 1956.

Gospel According to Thomas, The. Coptic Text established and translated by H. Guillamont, H. Pueck, G. Quispel, W. Till, and Yesaiah 'Abd Al Masih. New York: Harper, 1952.

Gough, Michael. *The Early Christians.* London: Thames and Hudson, 1961.

Grant, Frederick C. *An Introduction to New Testament Thought.* New York & Nashville: Abingdon, 1950.

———— *Roman Hellenism and the New Testament.* Edinburgh & London: Oliver & Boyd, 1962.

Grant, Michael. *The World of Rome.* New York: The New American Library, 1961.

Guignebert, Charles. *The Jewish World in the Time of Jesus.* Translated by S. H. Hooke. New York: K. Paul, Trench, Trubner & Co., 1939.

Guthrie, Donald. *New Testament Introduction: The Pauline Epistles.* Chicago: Inter-Varsity Press, 1961.

Haddad, George. *Aspects of Social Life in Antioch in the Hellenistic-Roman Period.* New York: Hafner, 1949.

Haines, C. R. *Heathen Contact with Christianity During Its First Century and a Half.* Cambridge: Deighton, Bell & Co., 1923.

Harding, G. Lankester. *The Antiquities of Jordan.* New York: Crowell, 1959.

Hardy, E. G. *Christianity and the Roman Government.* London: G. Allen; New York: Macmillan, 1925.

Harrison, P. N. *Polycarp's Two Epistles to the Philippians.* Cambridge: University Press, 1936.

Head, Eldred Douglas. *New Testament Life and Literature As Reflected in the Papyri.* Nashville: Broadman, 1952.

Heichelheim, F. M. "Roman Syria" in *An Economic Survey of Ancient Rome.* Vol. IV. Edited by Tenney Frank. Paterson, N. J.: Pageant Books, 1959.

Heichelheim, F. M. and Cedric Yeo. *A History of the Roman People.* Englewood Cliffs, N. J.: Prentice-Hall, 1962.

Henshaw, T. *New Testament Literature.* London: Allen & Unwin, 1952.

Howlett, Duncan. *The Essenes and Christianity,* New York: Harper, 1957.

Hyde, Walter Woodburn. *Paganism to Christianity in the Roman Empire.* Philadelphia: University Press, 1946.

Join-Lambert, Michel. *Jerusalem.* Translated by Charlotte Haldane. London: Elek Books; New York: Putnam, 1958.

Josephus. *The Jewish War,* Books I-III, with an English Translation by H. St. John Thackeray, Loeb Classical Library. London: Heinemann; New York: Putnam, 1927.

———— *The Life; Against Apion,* with an English Translation by H. St. John Thackeray. 8 vols. Vol. I. Loeb Classical Library. London: Heinemann; New York: Putnam, 1926.

———— *The Works of Flavius Josephus,* translated by William Whiston. 2 vols. London: Chatto, 1889.

Juvenal and Persius. *Satires,* with an English Translation by G. G. Ramsay. Loeb Classical Library. London: Heinemann; New York: Putnam, 1928.

Klausner, Joseph. *Jesus of Nazareth: His Life, Times, and Teaching.* Translated from the original Hebrew by Herbert Danby. New York: Macmillan, 1944.

Knox, John. *Chapters in a Life of Paul.* New York, Nashville: Abingdon, 1950.

Lactantius. *Of the Manner in Which Persecutors Died.* See *Ante-Nicene Fathers,* VIII, 301-322.

LaSor, William Sanford. *The Amazing Dead Sea Scrolls and the Christian Faith.* Chicago: Moody, 1958.

Legge, Francis. *Forerunners and Rivals of Christianity.* New York: Peter Smith, 1915.

Lewin, Thomas. *Fasti Sacri.* London: Longmans, 1865.

Lightfoot, J. B. *The Apostolic Fathers,* Part I. Edited and Completed by J. R. Harmer. London: Macmillan, 1891.

————— *The Apostolic Fathers,* Part II, Vols. I, II. London: Macmillan, 1885.

————— *St. Paul's Epistle to the Galatians,* 10th Ed. London: Macmillan, 1890.

Loewe, H. (ed.). *Judaism and Christianity.* Vol. II: *The Contact of Pharisaism with Other Cultures.* London: Sheldon Press, 1937.

Maccabees, The First Book of. Tedesche, Sidney and Solomon Zeitlin, Editors. The English Translation by Sidney Tedesche; Introduction and Commentary by Solomon Zeitlin. New York: Harper, 1950.

Macgregor, G. H. C. and A. C. Purdy. *Jew and Greek: Tutors Unto Christ.* New York: Scribner, 1936.

Maclear, G. F. *A Class Book of New Testament History.* Grand Rapids: Eerdmans, 1956. First printed in 1866.

Magie, David. *Roman Rule in Asia Minor to the End of the Third Century After Christ.* Vol. I: Text; Vol. II: Notes. Princeton, N. J.: University Press, 1950.

Mahaffy, John Pentland. *A History of Egypt Under the Ptolemaic Dynasty.* New York: Scribner, 1899.

Marcus, Ralph. *A Selected Bibliography (1920-1945) of the Jews in the Hellenistic World.* Reprinted from the *Proceedings of the American Academy for Jewish Research,* XVI (1947). New York, 1947.

Marsh, Frank Burr. *The Reign of Tiberius.* Oxford: University Press. London: Humphrey Milford, 1931.

Mattingly, Harold. *Roman Imperial Civilization.* London: E. Arnold, 1957.

Merrill, Elmer T. *Essays in Early Christian History.* London: Macmillan, 1924.

Metzger, Henri. *St. Paul's Journeys in the Greek Orient.* Translated by S. H. Hooke. *Studies in Biblical Archaeology No. 4.* London: S. C. M. Press, 1955.

Momigliano, Arnolde. *Claudius: The Emperor and His Achievement.* Translated by W. D. Hogarth, with a New Bibliography (1942-59). New York: Barnes & Noble, 1961.

Montefiore, Hugh. *Josephus and the New Testament.* London: A. M. Mowbray & Co., 1962.

Moore, Brookes (ed.). *Ovid's Metamorphoses.* Vol. II. Boston: Marshall Jones, 1911.

Moore, Frank G. *The Roman's World.* New York: Columbia University Press, 1936.

Mould, Elmer W. K. *Essentials of Bible History.* 2 vols. New York: Nelson, 1939.

Moulton, James Hope, and George Milligan. *The Vocabulary of the Greek New Testament.* Grand Rapids: Eerdmans, 1949.

Murphy, Roland E. *The Dead Sea Scrolls and the Bible.* Westminster, Maryland: Newman Press, 1956.

Mylonas, George E. *Eleusis and the Eleusinian Mysteries*. Princeton, N. J.: University Press, 1961.

Oesterley, W. O. E. and T. H. Robinson. *Hebrew Religion: Its Origin and Development*. Second, Revised and Enlarged Edition. New York: Macmillan, 1937.
——— *History of Israel*. 2 vols. Oxford: Clarendon, 1932.
——— *Jews and Judaism During the Greek Period*. London, S. P. C. K., 1941.

Ogg, George. *The Chronology of the Public Ministry of Jesus*. Cambridge: University Press, 1940.

Parkes, James. *The Foundations of Judaism and Christianity*. Chicago: Quadrangle Books, 1960.

Pausanias. *Description of Greece*, with an English Translation by W. H. S. Jones. 6 vols. Books I & II, Vol. I. Loeb Classical Library. London: Heinemann; New York: Putnam, 1918.

Perowne, Stewart. *Hadrian*. New York: Norton, 1961.
——— *The Later Herods*. London: Hodder, 1958.
——— *The Life and Times of Herod the Great*. London: Hodder, 1956.

Pfeiffer, Charles F. *Between the Testaments*. Grand Rapids: Baker, 1959.

Pfeiffer, Robert H. *History of New Testament Times with an Introduction to Apocrypha*. New York: Harper, 1949.

Pliny. *The Letters of Pliny the Younger* in *Handy Literal Translations*. Melmoth's Translation, Revised by Bosanquet. Vol. II; Books VI-X. New York: Hinds, n.d.

Ramsay, Sir William M. *The Bearing of Recent Discovery on the Trustworthiness of the New Testament*. New York: Doran, 1920.
——— *The Church in the Roman Empire Before A.D. 170*. New York: Putnam, 1893.
——— *The Cities of St. Paul*. London: Hodder, n.d.
——— *A Historical Commentary on St. Paul's Epistle to the Galatians*. New York: Putnam, 1900.
——— *St. Paul, the Traveller and the Roman Citizen*. New York: Putnam, 1909.
——— *Was Christ Born at Bethlehem?* New York: Putnam; London: Hodder, 1898.

Res Gestae Divi Augusti Monumentum Ancyranum. Translated by Shipley. New York: Putnam, 1924.

Rostovtzeff, M. *A History of the Ancient World*. Vol. II: *Rome*. Translated from the Russian by J. R. Duff. Oxford: Clarendon, 1938.
——— *The Social and Economic History of the Hellenistic World*. 2 vols. Oxford: Clarendon, 1941.

Salmon, Edward T. *A History of the Roman World from 30 B.C. to A.D. 138*. New York: Macmillan, 1944.

Schürer, Emil. *A History of the Jewish People in the Time of Jesus Christ*. Translated by John Macpherson. Second and Revised Edition. 5 vols. New York: Scribner, 1891.

Scramuzza, Vincent M. *The Emperor Claudius*. Cambridge, Mass.: Harvard University Press; London: Humphrey Milford, 1940.

Seneca. *Moral Essays* with an English Translation by John W. Basore. 3 vols. London: Heinemann; Cambridge, Mass.: Harvard University Press, 1951.

Sherwin-White, A. N. *Roman Society and Roman Law in the New Testament.* The Sarum Lectures, 1960-61. Oxford: Clarendon, 1963.

Smith, David. *The Life and Letters of St. Paul.* New York: Doran, n.d.

Starr, Chester G. *Civilization and the Caesars: The Intellectual Revolution in the Roman Empire.* Ithaca, N. Y.: Cornell University Press, 1954.

Stauffer, Ethelbert. *Christ and the Caesars.* Translated from the German by K. & R. Gregor Smith. London: SCM Press, 1955.

————— *Jesus and His Story.* Translated from the German by Richard and Clara Winston. New York: Knopf, 1960.

Strabo. *The Geography of Strabo* with an English Translation by Horace L. Jones. 8 vols. Loeb Classical Library. London: Heinemann; New York: Putnam, 1929.

Suetonius. *Lives of the Twelve Caesars.* Translated by J. C. Rolfe. 2 vols. Loeb Classical Library. New York: Putnam, 1930.

Tacitus. *The Complete Works of Tacitus.* Translated from the Latin by Alfred John Church and William Jackson Brodribb. Edited by Moses Hadas. New York: The Modern Library (Random House), 1942.

Thompson, J. A. *The Bible and Archaeology.* Grand Rapids: Eerdmans, 1962.

Toynbee, Arnold J. *Hellenism.* New York & London: Oxford University Press, 1959.

Trever, Albert E. *History of Ancient Civilization.* Vol. II. New York: Harcourt, 1939.

Velleius Paterculus. *Compendium of Roman History: Res Gestae Divi Augusti.* English Translation by F. W. Shipley. Loeb Classical Library. London: Heinemann; New York: Putnam, 1924.

Waddy, Lawrence. *Pax Romana and World Peace.* New York: Norton, n.d.

Wade, G. W. *New Testament History.* London: Methuen, 1922.

Walker, Williston. *A History of the Christian Church.* Revised by Cyril C. Richardson, Wilhelm Pauck, Robert T. Handy. New York: Scribner, 1959.

Weiss, Johannes. *Earliest Christianity: A History of the Period A.D. 30-150.* Vol. I. English Translation edited with a new introduction and bibliography by Frederick C. Grant. New York: Harper, 1959.

Wiseman, D. A. *Illustrations from Biblical Archaeology.* Grand Rapids: Eerdmans, 1958.

PERIODICAL ARTICLES

Ballance, M. "The Site of Derbe: A New Inscription," *Anatolian Studies,* VIII (1957), 147ff.

Broneer, Oscar. "Athens," *Biblical Archaeologist,* XXI (1958), 1, pp. 2-28.

Cadoux, C. J. "A Tentative Synthetic Chronology of the Apostolic Age," *Journal of Biblical Literature,* LVI (1937), 177.

Fritsch, Charles T. and Immanuel Ben-Dor. "The Link Expedition to Israel, 1960," *Biblical Archaeologist,* XXIV (1961) 2, pp. 50-59.

Gapp, K. S. "The Universal Famine Under Claudius," *Harvard Theological Review,* 28 (1935), 258-265.

Knox, D. B. "The Date of the Epistle to the Galatians," *Evangelical Quarterly,* XII (1941), 262-268.

Martin, Ralph P. "A Footnote to Pliny's Account of Christian Worship," *Vox Evangelica,* III (1964), 51-57.

McDonald, Wm. A. "Archaeology and St. Paul's Journeys in Greek Lands. Part II: Athens," *The Biblical Archaeologist,* IV (1941), 1-10.

Oakley, H. Carey. "The Greek and Roman Background of the New Testament," *Vox Evangelica* I (1962), 7-23.

Oliver, J. H. "A Roman Interdict from Palestine," *Classical Philology,* 49 (1954), 150-182.

Ramsay, Sir William. "Pauline Chronology," *Expositor,* Fifth Series, V (1887), 208, 209.

Shepherd, Massey H., Jr., "Are Both the Synoptics and John Correct About the Date of Jesus' Death?" *Journal of Biblical Literature,* LXXX (1961), 123-132.

Sherwin-White, A.N. "The Early Persecutions and Roman Law Again," *Journal of Theological Studies,* New Series, III (1952), 199 - 213.

Vardaman, Jerry. "A New Inscription Which Mentions Pilate as 'Prefect,'" *Journal of Biblical Literature,* LXXXI (1962), 70, 71.

Yadin, Yigael. "New Discoveries in the Judean Desert," *Biblical Archaeologist,* XXIV (1961), 34-50.

ENCYCLOPEDIA ARTICLES AND ESSAYS

Bevan, E. R. "The Jews in the Hellenistic Period" in *Cambridge Ancient History,* IX (1932), 387-434.

————— "The Ptolemies" in *Encyclopedia Britannica* (revision of 1962), XVIII, 731b-733b.

Bruce, F. F. "Israel" in *New Bible Dictionary.* Ed. J. D. Douglas. Grand Rapids: Eerdmans, 1962. Pp. 582, 583.

Cullmann, Oscar. "Beginnings of Christianity" in *The Scrolls and the New Testament,* ed. Krister Stendahl. New York: Harper, 1958.

Finegan, Jack. "Ephesus" in *The Interpreter's Dictionary of the Bible.* New York: Abingdon, 1962. II, 114-118.

Grant, Robert M. "Gnosticism" in *The Interpreter's Dictionary of the Bible.* New York: Abingdon, 1962. II, 404-406.

Taylor, Lily Ross. "The Asiarchs" in *The Beginnings of Christianity.* Ed. F. J. Foakes Jackson and Kirsopp Lake. London: Macmillan, 1933. V, 256-262.

Turner, C. H. "Chronology of the New Testament" in *Dictionary of the Bible.* Ed. James Hastings. 5 vols. New York: Scribner, 1911. I, 403-425.

Index of Subjects

381

Index of Persons

Acte, 293
Agabus, 207, 216
Agathokleia, 30
Agrippa, Marcus Vipsanius, 136
Agrippina, 282, 288
Alcimus, 39-41
Alexander I Balas, 41-43
Alexander II Zabinas, 44
Alexander Jannaeus, 45, 46, 103
Alexander (son of Aristobulus), 48
Alexander (son of Herod the Great), 62-64
Alexander the Great, 25, 28, 71, 73, 88, 117 255, 277
Alexandra, 46, 51
Amyntas, 227, 240
Ananias (of Damascus), 201, 202
Ananias (of Jerusalem), 188
Annas, 129, 158, 159
Antigonus, 25, 30, 55-57
Antinous, 351
Antiochus I Soter, 30
Antiochus II Theos, 31
Antiochus III the Great, 30-32, 277
Antiochus IV Epiphanes, 6, 10, 32-34, 36, 38, 46, 48, 87, 95
Antiochus V Eupator, 39
Antiochus VI Dionysius, 43
Antiochus VII Sidetes, 44, 45
Antipas, 65, 129, 140, 143, 157, 165-169, 197, 205
Antipater, 25, 47, 48, 51, 52, 62-64, 195
Antoninus Pius (Titus Aurelius Antoninus), 353, 357

Antonius, Marcus; Mark Antony, 49, 50, 52, 54, 56, 57, 59, 212, 227, 255
Apollonius, 34, 42
Aquila, 221, 275
Aratus, 266
Archelaus, 15, 65, 143
Aretas, 47, 51, 159, 195, 197
Aristobulus, 45, 48, 51, 62, 64
Asinius, Gaius, 134
Athanasius, 194
Attalus, 254, 277
Attianus, Acilius, 345
Augustine, 126
Augustus, Caesar (Octavian), 49, 50, 54, 56-59, 61, 62, 65, 73, 108, 112-114, 118, 123, 129-132, 134, 135, 137, 142, 143, 149, 150, 157, 161, 165, 195, 212, 213, 220, 223, 255
Aurelius, see Marcus Aurelius

Bacchides, 39-41
Bogoas, see Bigvai
Bar-Jesus, 224-226
Bar-Kochba, Simon, 348, 350
Barnabas, 184, 206, 208, 215, 216, 218, 224-226, 229, 230, 235, 237-241, 243, 244, 246-249, 251, 252
Berenice, 8
Bigvai (Bogoas), 84
Britannicus, 288
Brutus, 50, 54
Burrus, 283, 288, 289

Caiaphas, 95, 129, 130, 158, 159, 187,

384

Index of Places

389

Index of Texts